GATEKEEPERS

The Clarendon Lectures in Management Studies are jointly organized by Oxford University Press and the Saïd Business School. Every year a leading international academic is invited to give a series of lectures on a topic related to management education and research, broadly defined. The lectures form the basis of a book subsequently published by Oxford University Press.

Gatekeepers:

The Professions and Corporate Governance

John C. Coffee Jr.

Adolf A. Berle Professor of Law at Columbia University
Law School
and
Director of its Center on Corporate Governance

UNIVERSITY PRESS

OXFORD

UNIVERSITY PRESS

Great Clarendon Street, Oxford OX2 6DP

Oxford University Press is a department of the University of Oxford.

It furthers the University's objective of excellence in research, scholarship,
and education by publishing worldwide in
Oxford New York

Auckland Cape Town Dar es Salaam Hong Kong Karachi
Kuala Lumpur Madrid Melbourne Mexico City Nairobi
New Delhi Shanghai Taipei Toronto

With offices in

Argentina Austria Brazil Chile Czech Republic France Greece
Guatemala Hungary Italy Japan Poland Portugal Singapore
South Korea Switzerland Thailand Turkey Ukraine Vietnam

Oxford is a registerd trade mark of Oxford University Press
in the UK and in certain other countries

Published in the United States
by Oxford University Press Inc., New York

British Library Cataloguing in Publication Data

Data available

Library of Congress Cataloging in Publication Data

Data available

Typeset by SPI Publishers Services, Pondicherry, India
Printed in Great Britain
on acid-free paper by Biddles Ltd., King's Lynn

ISBN 0-19-928809-7 978-0-19-928809-0

1 3 5 7 9 10 8 6 4 2

Contents

List of Figures

List of Tables

1

Introduction

Academics tend to plough and re-plough the same furrow over and over. Nowhere is this truer than in the case of the scholars of corporate governance, who have studied the board of directors and shareholders endlessly. Useful and necessary as this research is, it leaves a blind spot. It ignores the professional agents of the board and the shareholders, who inform and advise them: auditors, attorneys, securities analysts, credit-rating agencies and investment bankers. The recent performance of these agents has been the subject of much debate and criticism, but little in-depth study. This volume intends to explore this blind spot more thoroughly than it has been examined before. It will ask: How have these professions evolved, performed, and changed in their behavior over the last century?

This assessment is undertaken in part because of a thesis that needs to be boldly stated at the outset: all boards of directors are prisoners of their gatekeepers. No board of directors—no matter how able and well-intentioned its members—can outperform its professional advisors. Only if the board's agents properly advise and warn it, can the board function efficiently.

This book will explore the institutional history of each of the principal professions that serve investors in the corporate governance context, advance hypotheses as to why gatekeepers have recently failed investors, and suggest models for reform. But first, this chapter will seek in a more limited fashion to clarify the concept of what is meant by the term 'gatekeeper' and to explain why they play a critical role in corporate governance.

What Are Gatekeepers? The term 'gatekeeper' has been used in many different settings across the social sciences, usually in ways that are more metaphorical than precise.[1] Typically, the term connotes some form of outside or independent watchdog or monitor—someone who screens out flaws or defects or who verifies compliance with standards or procedures.

Within the corporate context, the prior academic commentary has usually used the term 'gatekeeper' to mean an independent professional who plays one of two distinct roles, which tend to overlap in practice. First, the gatekeeper may be a professional who is positioned so as to be able to prevent wrongdoing by withholding necessary cooperation or consent.[2] For example, an investment banking firm can refuse to underwrite the issuer's securities if it finds that the issuer's disclosures are materially deficient; similarly, an auditor or an attorney who discovers a serious problem with a corporate client's financial statements or disclosures can prevent a merger from closing by declining to deliver an opinion that is a necessary precondition for that transaction. In this first sense, the gatekeeper is a private policeman who has been structured into the process to prevent wrongdoing. By withholding its approval, it closes the gate, typically denying the issuer access to the capital markets. So defined, even the board of directors can be seen as a gatekeeper, and the Securities and Exchange Commission certainly is a public gatekeeper.[3]

However, defining gatekeepers simply in terms of their capacity to veto or withhold consent misses what is most distinctive about the professionals who serve investors in the corporate context. Inherently, they are repeat players who provide certification or verification services to investors, vouching for someone else who has a greater incentive than they to deceive. Thus, a second and superior definition of the gatekeeper is an agent who acts as a reputational intermediary to assure investors as to the quality of the 'signal' sent by the corporate issuer. The reputational intermediary does so by lending or 'pledging' its reputational capital to the corporation, thus enabling investors or the market to rely on the corporation's own disclosures or assurances where they otherwise might not. The gatekeeper has such reputational capital because it is a repeat player who has served many clients over many years. Examples of gatekeepers providing such certification or verification services to investors are obvious: the auditor certifies that the corporation's financial statements comply with generally accepted accounting principles; the investment banker delivers a fairness opinion in a cash-out merger that assures the minority shareholders of the company that they have received a 'fair' price; and the credit-rating agency assigns a rating to the corporation's debt securities. The securities analyst best illustrates the difference in these two definitions, as it has no power to block or veto any transaction, but its positive evaluation may lend credibility to the subject company's own disclosures or predictions. Under this second definition, however, the board of directors typically does not qualify as a gatekeeper because its members typically serve too few corporations to have developed reputational capital as monitors.[4]

Central to this model is the concept of reputational capital and the subsidiary idea that it can be pledged or placed at risk by the gatekeeper's vouching for its client's assertions or projections. As always, there is a gap between theory and reality, and in the real world, events do not play out in quite this frictionless fashion. For example, that reputational capital is important also explains why entry into the market for gatekeeping services is often restricted. Put simply, one cannot be a credible gatekeeper without significant reputational capital. Because new entrants typically lack such capital, they thus face a high barrier to entry. This, in turn, implies a tendency for such markets to be concentrated and even oligopolistic in character. As will be seen, in such a concentrated market, gatekeepers can collude, or at least engage in consciously parallel behavior, that subordinates the protection of reputational capital to other goals. Rather than compete to enhance their reputations, they may quietly permit their reputations to become noisy and indistinct, so long as entry to new firms into the market is restricted.

Although the principal gatekeeping professions—for example, the auditor, the attorney, and the securities analyst—are well known even to laymen, the professional role of the gatekeeper serving investors is not that old. As will be seen, the modern auditor developed with the appearance of dispersed stock ownership in the United Kingdom in the mid-19th century; the securities attorney dates essentially from the passage of securities legislation in the early 20th century, and the securities analyst has even less history. New gatekeeping professions continue to appear: most recently and notably, the proxy advisor (such as Institutional Shareholder Services (or 'ISS'), the largest and oldest of these firms),[5] upon whom institutional investors rely heavily in determining how to vote their massive share portfolios. But no sooner does a new gatekeeper appear, then new conflicts of interest also arise to potentially compromise its independence and objectivity.[6]

Although many problems surround the performance of gatekeepers, one problem overshadows all others: typically, the party paying the gatekeeper will be the party that the gatekeeper is expected to monitor. Auditors, attorneys and investment bankers—all are typically paid by the corporation that hires them. Although the gatekeeper is hired to assure investors, its actual principal is the corporation, and its instructions typically come from the corporate managers running the corporation. This difficulty has not stopped the U.S. Supreme Court from broadly postulating duties owed directly by the gatekeeper to investors. Thus, in *United States* v. *Arthur Young* & *Co.*,[7] a unanimous Court found that:

By certifying the public reports that collectively depict a corporation's financial status, the independent auditor assumes a *public* responsibility transcending any employment relationship with the client. The independent public accountant performing this special function owes ultimate allegiance to the corporation's creditors and stockholders, as well as to the investing public. This 'public watchdog' function demands that the accountant maintain total independence from the client at all times and requires complete fidelity to the public trust.[8]

As a normative proposition, this is fine, heady, aspirational stuff, but as an empirical description, it fails to recognize the control that the employing corporation has over the gatekeeper. Put simply, the real question is whether one can trust a watchdog hired and paid by the party to be watched?

Given these pervasive conflicts, why do investors trust gatekeepers? The most logical answer takes us back to why the second or 'reputational intermediary' model of gatekeepers outperforms the first or 'private policeman' model. The gatekeeper is trusted to the extent that it is a repeat player who possesses significant reputational capital that would be lost or depreciated if it were found to have condoned wrongdoing. In theory, so long as the gatekeeper has reputational capital at risk whose value exceeds the expected profit that it will receive from the client, it logically should be faithful to investors and not provide a false or reckless certification. Once, this answer went unchallenged. Indeed, one well-known and highly intelligent federal judge justified the dismissal of a securities class action against a major auditing firm by explaining that it would simply be 'irrational' for auditors to acquiesce in fraud.[9] Today, such an unqualified position seems overstated. Nonetheless, the sudden collapse of Arthur Andersen following its involvement in the Enron scandal actually illustrates how profoundly illogical acquiescence in fraud can be for a well-established gatekeeper. Andersen closed its doors less because of its criminal conviction than because it had come to have 'negative' reputational capital. Its clients shed it to avoid that taint, and even the subsequent reversal of its conviction could not restore its once illustrious brand name.

This point that reputational intermediaries face losses that exceed the likely one-time gain from acquiescence in fraud fits a more general pattern. In a seminal article, Oliver Williamson, a leading institutional economist, has explained that, even in the absence of legal remedies, a long-term or 'relational' contract can be made self-enforcing through the use of bonding mechanisms that function as if the party making the representation had given a hostage as security for the accuracy of its promise or representation.[10] The reputational intermediary's reputational capital represents the functional equivalent of such a bond or hostage. This may explain the universality of gatekeepers, even in nations in which investors lack effective litigation remedies.

In this light, as a law enforcement strategy, the deliberate use of gatekeepers makes sense on either of two alternative rationales. First, if the gatekeeper has significant reputational capital at risk, then, even in the absence of effective litigation remedies, the gatekeeper will have reason to resist the client's demands that it acquiesce in fraud or illegality, because it faces potential losses far exceeding any one-time payments from its client for its cooperation in the fraud. Second, if the gatekeeper is subject to effective litigation remedies, then, even in the absence of significant reputational capital, the gatekeeper will face losses exceeding the expected gains from involvement in fraud. Because the gatekeeper is inherently an agent of its principal, its expected fee or commission is likely to be far less than the gain that the principal itself expects to make from the transaction. As a result, because the gatekeeper/agent expects less profit than its principal does, it can be more easily deterred than its principal. Thus, whether because of the risk of litigation or fear of a devalued reputation, gatekeepers should be less willing than their principals to violate the law. Hence, by focusing on the gatekeeper, law enforcement wisely focuses on the weakest link in the chain and may be able to interdict misconduct, even when it cannot effectively deter the principal.

Why Do Gatekeepers Fail?   Consider the relationship of Enron and Arthur Andersen & Co., its auditor. Both for Enron and its senior management, a policy of inflating its financial results made at least short-term sense, because it enabled them to make acquisitions, avoid bankruptcy, and exploit stock options worth billions of dollars. For Arthur Andersen, however, the trade-off was very different. Enron was a valuable client that it saw as potentially worth as much as $100 million a year in revenues.[11] Yet, in its final year before the Enron scandal forced its dissolution, Andersen made revenues of over $9 billion.[12] Thus, to the extent that the Enron scandal destroyed it, Andersen is an example of (i) a gatekeeper that faced (and suffered) a loss of reputational capital far exceeding its expected gain from the client, and (ii) an agent that should logically have been more easily deterred than its principal.

But Andersen was not deterred—and it was destroyed. Thus, the Enron/Andersen example is instructive both to the extent that it shows the obvious logic of a law enforcement strategy focused on gatekeepers and the limits of that logic. Similarly, this book is premised on the belief that focusing enforcement on gatekeepers could work—but has not worked adequately to date. To understand why gatekeepers can and do fail is a necessary precondition to any sensible discussion of gatekeeper reform. This book will identify a number of reasons that can explain gatekeeper failure, including:

(1) agency cost problems that make acquiescence in misconduct rational for the agents and employees of the gatekeeper, even though it is irrational for the gatekeeper, itself;

(2) imperfectly competitive markets for gatekeeper services that allow rival firms to collude or pursue consciously parallel practices;

(3) a possible decline in value of the gatekeeper's reputational capital, with the result that the gatekeeper no longer protects it as zealously; and

(4) reduced exposure to litigation.

All these explanations are briefly surveyed in Chapter 3. Still, the intent of this book is not to debunk or abandon the concept of gate-keepers as a law enforcement mechanism in the face of these problems, but rather to rehabilitate and redesign it.

Why Are Gatekeepers Important?   An epidemic of corporate and financial irregularity crested in the United States in 2002 and convinced most commentators that corporate governance in the United States needed to be strengthened. Almost reflexively, most commentators focused on the board of directors and suggested ways in which it should be upgraded.[13] Others have stressed the need for higher ethical standards,[14] and a smaller number has suggested enhancing the power of shareholders.[15] This book takes no sides in this debate, but it does insist that no reform is likely to achieve its goal unless the corporation's gatekeepers function in an objective and unbiased fashion. In this light, several points need to be made and underlined at the outset:

1   *Gatekeepers enable a corporation to credibly signal above average quality and thereby achieve a lower cost of capital.* All public corporations face what is known as the 'market for lemons' problem.[16] Unless they can distinguish themselves from their peers, investors will price their stock in terms of the average quality of all corporations. This means that they may discount

their earnings or prospects by a common factor—even though some corporations are above average in quality and some below average. But gatekeepers, if they are trusted, can render the corporation's statements and signals more credible and thus lower their cost of capital (and increase their stock price).

2 *No board can outperform its gatekeepers.* The board of directors in the United States is today composed of directors who are essentially part-time performers with other demanding responsibilities. So structured, the board is blind, except to the extent that the corporation's managers or its independent gatekeepers advise it of impending problems. In the absence of independent professionals—auditors, attorneys and analysts—boards will predictably receive a stream of selectively edited information from corporate managers that presents the incumbent management in the most favorable light possible.

3 *Over recent decades, the board of directors has already been extensively reformed and is now an independent, harder-working and more proactive body.* This is not to claim that no further improvements are possible or that various boards did not make egregious mistakes. But some factual comparisons show the extent of the transformation of the board. As of 1997, 80 percent of U.S. public corporations had a majority independent board, 90 percent had no interlocking directorships. By 2003, average board size had decreased to 9.5 directors, consistent with the consensus view that a smaller board can monitor management better.[17] Today, in the largest public corporations, there may be only one director (the CEO) who is an employee, and typically no more than one or two other insiders will serve on the board.[18] Directors are also spending much more time on the task of being a director, averaging 183 hours annually at Fortune 1000 companies in 2002—up from 156 hours in 2001.[19] In the wake of recent scandals, both the New York Stock Exchange and Nasdaq today require listed corporations to have a majority of independent directors, to mandate that certain critical board committees be entirely composed of independent directors, and to tighten their definitions of independence. Eighty percent of U.S. public corporations now have adopted the 'lead director' concept, up from only 32 percent in 2002.[20] No doubt further improvements are possible, but it is increasingly questionable whether any further movement in the direction of increased independence can improve firm performance.[21] In short, most of what can conceivably be done to make the board more active and more independent has already been

done. Yet, independent boards proved unable to detect or prevent the wave of financial irregularities that surfaced in 2000 to 2002. Again, this suggests that even strong and well-motivated boards are the informational prisoners of their gatekeepers.

4 *Logically, one cannot explain the sudden outburst of financial irregularity that surfaced in 2001 to 2003 by attributing it to the failure of the board of directors. Rather, because boards have only improved over the interval from 1980 to 2000, one needs to explain this increase in financial irregularity by identifying other actors whose performance deteriorated.* While boards may not have risen to the challenge in many cases, they were not the direct cause of Enron, WorldCom and other corporate fiascos. Because boards became stronger and more independent over the interval of 1980 to 2000, their shortcomings cannot explain the sharp and sudden increase in financial irregularity that surfaced in 2001. To explain such a change, one must point to actors whose performance declined, rather than improved. This book will argue that the behavior of both corporate managers and gatekeepers changed in the 1990s, and that the latter in particular came under increased pressure to acquiesce in fraud. Such an explanation can account for the timing of this sudden outburst in financial irregularity, while the simple explanation that the board failed cannot.

In making these points it is necessary that the significance of context and culture be recognized and that any claim of universality be abandoned. As will be spelled out in Chapter 4, gatekeepers probably play a larger and more critical role within the dispersed ownership structure that characterizes Anglo-American corporate governance than they do in Europe or elsewhere, where concentrated ownership remains the norm. Once ownership and control are separated (as they have long been in the United States),[22] both shareholders and the board must depend on gatekeepers for an unbiased flow of information. In these dispersed ownership governance systems, individual shareholders own small stakes in percentage terms and face significant collective action costs in seeking to hold corporate managements accountable. Ultimately, it is not necessary to argue that gatekeeper reform is more important than board reform or enhanced power for shareholders. All that need be concluded is that dispersed shareholders and part-time directors depend on gatekeepers. Effective corporate governance requires a chain of actors: directors, managers, and gatekeepers. No chain is stronger than its weakest link. Much evidence will be advanced to suggest that during the 1990s gatekeepers became the weakest link.

The Strategic Options   At the beginning of this introduction, it was explained that gatekeepers typically provide certification and verification services to investors and that they are typically hired and paid by the corporate managers that they are to watch. But two further points need to be added to this description. first, this pattern under which corporate managers hire their own gatekeepers did not always prevail. Once, shareholders retained or at least paid their agents (the security analyst, for example, was compensated out of the brokerage commissions of investors). This suggests that the principal–agent relationship surrounding gatekeepers can be reconsidered and restructured, and Chapter 10 will attempt to do this. Secondly, the role of the gatekeeper needs to be viewed in a more abstract and theoretical light. Investors face significant information asymmetries—meaning that they know much less about corporate affairs and proposed transactions than do the managers who run the corporation. To reduce these asymmetries, investors have two basic strategies that they can follow: First, they can employ an essentially legal strategy and rely on litigation in order to hold their corporate managers and agents accountable and redress any breach of fiduciary duty or contract right.

Second, the major alternative to such a law-centered system is to rely on gatekeepers—that is, on professional agents who will monitor management and alert shareholders as to opportunistic behavior by their managers. This latter system works less based on litigation or even private contracting, and more based on bonding and reputational capital. The first strategy works *ex post*, while the second operates *ex ante*, seeking to detect and prevent problems before they become crises. The aim of both strategies, however, is to reduce informational asymmetries (and thereby produce a more transparent market).

In reality, the United States uses both strategies (i.e. both legal remedies and reputational intermediaries), and neither has been wholly successful. In response to the epidemic of corporate financial scandals that broke out in the United States between 2000 and 2003, Congress enacted the Sarbanes-Oxley Act of 2002, which principally focused on the role and responsibilities of gatekeepers. Yet, even if that Act has tamed some of the more egregious problems (and here considerable controversy exists), the interests of gatekeepers and investors remain less than fully aligned. Equally important, in other countries, the ability to use litigation to enforce corporate accountability is simply less available. Institutions well known in the United States—such as the class action and the contingent fee—are simply unavailable or are considered ethically unacceptable. Arguably, more reliance may have to be placed in these countries on a gatekeeper strategy.

Above all, reform requires a theory. Many contemporary reforms, including some of those in the Sarbanes-Oxley Act, lack any serious theory of why gatekeepers fail and how they can be rehabilitated. What led the professions of accounting, law, and securities analysis to perform poorly during this last epidemic of financial irregularity? Will the next stock market bubble simply repeat this process? To this end, this book will examine in depth the institutional background of each of the principal professions that serve investors in the corporate governance and capital markets context. Its goal is to explain why gatekeepers failed and how they can be best reformed. The standard explanations—conflicts of interest, and the declining threat of enforcement—are relevant to this explanation, but not decisive. To get to the core of the problem, one needs to understand when reputational intermediaries work and when they fail.

Endnotes

1. For example, peer review is a mechanism used by academic and scientific journals to screen out flawed research, and thus such panels function as 'gatekeepers.' (See E. Rae Harcum & Ellen F. Rosen, The Gatekeepers of Psychology: Evaluation of Peer Review (1993). Political scientists regard congressional committees as the gatekeepers of the legislative process. See Arthur T. Denzau & Robert McKay, *Gatekeeping and Monopoly Power of Committees: An Analysis of Sincere and Sophisticated Behavior*, 27 Am. J. Pol. Sci. 740 (1983)). Economic analysis frequently views financial intermediaries, particularly banks, as gatekeepers. See Ronald J. Mann, *Regulating Internet Payment Intermediaries*, 81 Tex. L. Rev. 681, 708 (2004) (viewing banks as the 'gatekeeper' who will monitor internet intermediaries and 'exclude those that cannot be induced to behave appropriately'). The point here is only that an endless list of examples of 'gatekeepers' across all fields of social science can be compiled, but the common defining characteristic is a monitoring role with some power to screen out or at least to grade or rate the persons or entities scrutinized by the 'gatekeeper.'

2. This is the definition of 'gatekeeper' originally given by Reinier Kraakman in probably the first serious attempt to examine the role of gatekeepers in corporate law. See Reinier H. Kraakman, *Gatekeepers: The Anatomy of a Third-Party Enforcement Strategy*, 2 J. L. Econ. & Org. 53, 53–56, 61–66 (1986); see also Assaf Hamdani, *Gatekeeper Liability*, 77 S. Calif. L. Rev. 53 (2003).

3. An obvious distinction can be drawn between public and private gatekeepers. See Kraakman, n 2 above, at 75 n 67. Because, under the Securities Act of 1933, an issuer may not sell securities to the public in the United States until the SEC declares its registration statement to be effective,

the SEC is an obvious gatekeeper whose withheld consent denies the issuer access to the capital markets.

4. To be sure, some directors do have well-known reputations (e.g. Warren Buffett), and the directors of a failed corporation do suffer some reputational injury. But their reputations typically derive from their business or other careers (that is, the typical director may be a CEO of another firm), and not from being a professional monitor.

5. Now 20 years old, ISS has some 130 analysts and tracks some 28,000 companies worldwide. Its chief rival is Glass Lewis & Co., which has some 70 analysts and follows about 8,000 companies. See Michael Liedtke, 'Shareholder Watchdogs fight for Turf,' *Newsday*, May 15, 2005, 2005 WLNR 7848542.

6. ISS is principally paid by its institutional investor clients, but it has been criticized for also accepting fees from corporations for advising them on how to increase their corporate governance ratings from ISS. Ibid. Critics claim that those corporations that hire ISS as a consultant receive higher ratings and typically win the support of ISS in contested elections.

7. 465 U.S. 805 (1984).

8. Ibid. at 817–818.

9. In *DiLeo v. Ernst & Young*, 901 F.2d 624, 629 (7th Cir. 1990), Judge Frank Easterbrook wrote for the Seventh Circuit that:

> An accountant's greatest asset is its reputation for honesty, followed closely by its reputation for careful work. Fees for two years' audits could not approach the losses [that the auditor] would suffer from a perception that it would muffle a client's fraud ... [The audit firm's] partners shared none of the gain from any fraud and were exposed to a large fraction of the loss. It would have been irrational for any of them to have joined cause with [the client].

> See also *Melder v. Morris*, 27 F. 3d 1097, 1103 (5th Cir. 1994) (expressing similar views).

10. See Oliver E. Williamson, *Credible Commitments: Using Hostages to Support Exchanges*, 73 Am. Econ. Rev. 519 (1983). By 'hostage,' Williamson essentially means transaction-specific assets that are pledged.

11. Andersen actually received $52 million ($27 million in consulting fees and $25 million in audit fees) from Enron in its final year, but its partners discussed the prospect of Enron becoming a $100 million annual client. See Robert Prentice, *Enron: A Brief Behavioral Autopsy*, 40 Am. Bus. L. J. 417, 432 n 79 (2003).

12. Arthur Andersen's total revenues for its final year ending August 31, 2001 were $9.3 billion. See Melissa Klein, 'Guilty Verdict Draws Mixed Reactions: Profession Mulls Post-Andersen Future,' Acct. Today, July 8, 2002 at 1.

13. See, e.g. Jeffrey N. Gordon, *What Enron Means for the Management and Control of the Modern Business Corporation: Some Initial Reflections*, 69

U. Chi. L. Rev. 1233 (2002); Symposium, *The Changing Role of Directors in Corporate Governance*, 38 Wake Forest L. Rev. C. 839 (2003).

14. See, e.g. Roger C. Cramton, *Enron and the Corporate Lawyer: A Primer on Legal and Ethical Issues*, 58 Bus. Law. 143 (2002).

15. See, e.g. Lucian A. Bebchuk, *The Case for Increasing Shareholder Power*, 118 Harv. L. Rev. 833 (2005).

16. See George A. Akerlot, *The Market for Lemons: Qualitative Uncertainty and the Market Mechanism*, 84 Q. J. Econ. 488 (1970). Gatekeepers are, of course, not the only means by which corporations can credibly signal; other bonding devices are certainly possible, including executive compensation.

17. See Vidhi Chhaochharia and Yaniv Grinstein, *The Transformation of U.S. Corporate Boards: 1997–2003*, (May 2004) (http://ssrn.com/abstract=556270). This is the most recent empirical study of board independence, and it finds significant improvement over the 1997 to 2003 period. In 1992, the typical public board had 15 members, so real change seems observable here, as the current level has been reduced to 9.5.

18. As of 2004, the typical board of a publicly held corporation had ten members, of which only two were inside directors. See Korn/Ferry International, 31st Annual Board of Directors Study (2004) Table A at p 10.

19. See Korn/Ferry International, 29th Annual Board of Directors Study (2002) at p 3.

20. See Korn/Ferry International, 31st Annual Board of Directors Survey (2004) at p 6. Under this concept, the independent lead director chairs periodic board meetings to review the performance of the chief executive officer (in the latter's absence). It is a substitute, possibly imperfect, for the non-executive chairman, which is common in the U.K., but atypical in the U.S.

21. Some believe that further movement in the direction of increased director independence may even adversely affect firm performance. See Sanjai Bhagat and Bernard Black, *The Uncertain Relationship Between Board Composition and Firm Performance*, 54 Bus. Law. 921 (1999); Sanjai Bhagat and Bernard Black, *The Non-Correlation Between Board Independence and Long-Term Performance*, 27 Journal of Corporation Law 231 (2002).

22. See Adolf A. Berle, Jr. and Gardiner C. Means, The Modern Corporation And Private Property (1932) (describing the separation of ownership and control that had by then arisen in U.S. publicly-held firms).

Part I

What Happened?

2

The Failure of the Gatekeepers

A wave of corporate scandals crested in the United States between late 2001 and the end of 2002. Hundreds of public corporations restated their financial statements, scores were sued by the Securities and Exchange Commission (SEC), and some executives were criminally prosecuted. But only two scandals became iconic in character: Enron and World-Com. Because they were larger in scale (resulting in the two largest bankruptcies in U.S. history),[1] and because their failures revealed a stunningly complete breakdown in all systems of internal control and external monitoring, their joint collapse within a few months of each other destabilized the capital markets, undercut the credibility of U.S. financial reporting, and provoked swift and punitive political reform.

Unlike other contemporaneous and more traditional corporate scandals—for example, Tyco, HealthSouth or Adelphia—Enron and WorldCom were not simple stories about insiders looting their corporation. Rather, Enron and WorldCom were complex financial frauds in which the primary goal was to maximize the company's stock price. Self-dealing was present, but it was not the underlying motive for misconduct. Instead, driving the principal actors in these two scandals was a fervent desire to maximize the corporation's stock price by any means necessary—sometimes by fabricating earnings, sometimes by deferring expenses, sometimes by hiding liabilities or engaging in bizarre off-balance sheet transactions. Success in this effort depended, however, upon the assistance, or at least the acquiescence, of the corporation's auditors and its other professional watchdogs. Thus, the key mystery becomes: *Why did the watchdogs not bark?*

Because they did not bark, the United States' much-vaunted system of corporate governance was suddenly compromised. Red flags had not simply been missed; rather, the sentries upon whom investors relied appeared to have willfully shut their eyes. Particularly in the case of Enron, it was as if the lookouts on the Titanic had seen the iceberg—and then collectively pretended it was not there. To be sure, this collective failure involved not only the professional monitors—boards of directors, auditors, securities analysts, and credit-rating agencies—but also the most sophisticated institutional investors, who had remained heavily invested in Enron and WorldCom until within weeks of their respective bankruptcies. Much like the adults in the Hans Christian Andersen fairy tale, The Emperor's New Clothes, a tacit conspiracy seems to have arisen not to see the Emperor's nakedness, and this collective blindness continued well after the first skeptics had publicly observed that Enron was a suspect company with impenetrably complex financial statements.

That gatekeepers failed is not by itself surprising. The history of financial frauds reveals many similar failures over the last century. That gatekeepers failed en masse is probably more surprising. But truly startling is the fact that this major outburst of financial fraud in the U.S. was not paralleled by a similar epidemic in Europe over the same 2000 to 2002 period. As will be seen, there were major frauds in Europe (such as Parmalat), but they neither had the same motivation nor peaked over this period. Perplexing as this contrast may seem, it underscores a key point: there are different characteristic types of failure by gatekeepers. Fraud against shareholders has taken a characteristically different form in Europe and other industrial economies than it has in the United States or the United Kingdom. Indeed, financial statement restatements are uncommon in Europe. If Enron is the iconic U.S. scandal, Parmalat presents the paradigmatic case for Europe, and they are very different—except for the fact that gatekeepers failed in both cases. These differences will be contrasted in Chapter 3, but, for the present, the point is that gatekeepers play different roles in different corporate governance systems.

In the wake of the Enron and WorldCom scandals, Congress rewrote the federal securities laws, invading an area traditionally reserved for state regulation in order to pass the Sarbanes-Oxley Act in 2002. The principal intent of that legislation was to protect the integrity of financial reporting by redesigning the network of institutions and intermediaries who served investors in order that the capital markets would not be systematically deceived again. Pursuant to Sarbanes-Oxley, audit committees were strengthened, auditors were subjected to a new system of quasi-public self-regulation, attorneys were commanded to report crimes or fraud up-the-ladder promptly, analysts were separated by a new Chinese Wall from underwriters in order to reduce the latter's influence over them, and senior corporate managers were required to certify personally the accuracy of their corporation's financial results on a quarterly basis. Whether Congress got it right or wrong, whether it went too far or not far enough, remains subject to heated debate.

But this debate cannot go far until one first resolves what caused Enron, WorldCom, and a host of similar scandals. While almost everyone has a theory, the focus has generally tended to be on the board of directors. After all, the boards of Enron and WorldCom did strange and reckless things: the Enron board waived its conflict of interest policy so that Andrew Fastow, its chief financial officer, could run special purpose entities that traded extensively with Enron, reaping secret profits running into millions of dollars in the process, and the WorldCom board extended loans and guarantees to its financially strained chief executive totaling $250 million. Reform proposals therefore have tended to concentrate on upgrading the board's independence and processes.

Yet, while board performance can no doubt be upgraded, the board of directors may be the institution least responsible for the eruption of the corporate financial irregularity that broke into the open in 2001 to 2002. Why? Boards of directors have only improved over the last 40 years, becoming gradually more proactive and independent. Although the corporate scandals of 2001–2002 represent a major discontinuity, one cannot explain a discontinuity by attributing it to an actor (i.e. the board of directors) whose performance over the same period actually improved. Rather, a truly causal account must relate a sudden failure in corporate governance to actors whose performance deteriorated over the same period. While boards did not decline in performance during the 1990s, a good case can be made that the performance of gatekeepers over this period did deteriorate.

This initial chapter will recover familiar territory. Others have dissected the collapse of Enron and WorldCom in far more lurid and colorful terms, emphasizing what was bizarre and tawdry in the failure of each. This account will disdain any attempt at a journalistic exposé and instead focus on the role of the gatekeepers. Why was it that in each case the board did not understand what was happening—until it was too late? This approach does not seek to exculpate either board, but does suggest that the failure of gatekeepers, along with the active misconduct of the management in each company, better explains these two monumental failures and also similar irregularities at a host of other public U.S. companies over this period. Such a demonstration is intended to set the stage for an analysis of how gatekeepers can best be rehabilitated. The premise here should be made explicit: corporate governance does not work, nor can management be held accountable, in the absence of a system that makes gatekeepers reasonably faithful to the interests of investors.

The Enron House of Cards

Enron in Overview

Enron filed for bankruptcy on December 2, 2001 in what was then the largest bankruptcy in U.S. history. At the time of its December 2001 collapse, Enron ranked as the seventh largest company in the U.S. with over $100 billion in gross revenues and 20,000 employees worldwide.[2] Indeed, as of early 2001, Enron was by almost any measure the most successful U.S. corporation of the prior decade. On December 31, 2000, Enron's stock was at $83.13—a figure seventy times its earnings and six times its book value.[3] Even when the dot.com bubble burst in 2000, Enron's stock price continued to escalate, seemingly immune from market volatility and unaffected by the decline of other high-tech stocks. In 1999, Enron's stock price had appreciated 56 percent, but in 2000, it again rose an astounding 87 percent, while the market index as a whole declined 10 percent for that year.[4] Contemporaneously, Enron was winning every conceivable award. For six years in a row, it was voted the 'Most Innovative' corporation in America on Fortune's annual list of 'Most Admired' corporations, and in February 2001, Fortune also ranked Enron second in 'quality of management' among all U.S. corporations.[5]

By the end of 2001, however, Enron had been disgraced, bankrupted and effectively shut down. Surprisingly, no exogenously caused crisis overtook Enron during 2001—no business reversal, no regional economic downturn or panic, no huge tort liability crisis or criminal proceeding, not even any revelation that affected the public's perception of the quality of Enron's goods or services. Instead, the market simply learned that Enron incurred more liabilities and earned less profits than it had believed. These revelations placed Enron in default of its loan and debt covenants, in part because Enron was required to preserve an 'investment grade' credit rating. Once it became clear that Enron could not hope to preserve that 'investment grade' rating and would be in default without it, Enron's only hope lay in a hastily arranged merger with Dynergy, a much smaller competitor in its field. Although Dynergy did enter into a merger agreement with Enron on November 9, 2001, it retained the right to conduct a 'due diligence' investigation of Enron. During the course of that investigation, it quickly learned enough to call off the deal on November 28, 2001. Immediately, on the same day, the major credit rating agencies responded by downgrading Enron's debt to below investment grade (or 'junk bond') status. Days later, Enron filed for bankruptcy on December 2, 2001. Somehow, the credit rating agencies could not discover (or at least reveal) what Dynergy quickly found: that Enron was a house of cards.

Ultimately, Enron's gatekeepers did hold the critical power over its access to the capital markets, because Enron was able to borrow money only so long as it maintained an 'investment grade' rating. But the gatekeepers who should have discovered Enron's fatal flaws never acknowledged any awareness of Enron's problems until after Enron was forced to restate its financial statements in October 2002. Even then, they responded only equivocally. Yet, on a fairly brief inspection, Dynergy was able to detect serious financial problems and a debt to equity ratio much higher than had been publicly disclosed, which discovery caused it to back out of the merger.[6] The difference was that Dynergy was motivated by its own self-interest to look for fraud, while Enron's gatekeepers were motivated by their own self-interest not to question too skeptically. As will be seen, this pattern persists across a host of examples.

Viewed historically, Enron's ability to exploit and manipulate accounting conventions was to a considerable degree a product of deregulation and the rapid pace of change within its industry. Founded in 1985 as the product of a merger of two natural gas pipeline companies—Houston Natural Gas and Internorth—Enron owned from its outset the largest interstate network of pipelines. As late as 1990, it remained primarily in the pipeline business. But deregulation profoundly changed that business. Deregulation of gas prices led to increased use of spot market transactions[7] and naturally produced greater volatility in gas prices. Based on the advice of Jeff Skilling, then a McKinsey consultant and later Enron's chief operating officer and briefly in 2001 its chief executive officer, Enron decided that it could exploit this volatility because of its superior knowledge of market conditions gained as the owner of the nation's largest gas pipeline. Skilling's advice was that Enron should create a natural gas 'bank' that would intermediate between suppliers and buyers of natural gas. Based on his vision of Enron as an online energy trading company, Enron began to offer utilities and other major customers long-term fixed price contracts for natural gas; it then protected itself by using financial derivatives—chiefly, swaps contracts—to hedge this risk.

This aspect of Enron's business model largely worked. It could profit from trading in the natural gas market where it had superior information. By 1992, Enron had become the largest seller of natural gas in North America, and its trading activities were the second largest contributor to its overall income.[8] Then, extending his original proposal that Enron become a trading company, Skilling proposed in the late 1990s that Enron should transform itself further by adopting what he termed an 'asset light' policy. Because it received too little return on the ownership of 'heavy assets'—such as pipelines or production facilities—Skilling recommended that Enron dispose of them, except to the extent that they generated useful information that informed its trading activities. His basic premise, spelled out in an October 2000 presentation to the Enron Finance Committee, was that Enron had '[l]imited cash flow to service additional debt' and '[l]imited earnings to cover dilution of additional equity.'[9] Therefore, it needed to shed high-cost, low-return fixed assets in order to give Enron a less leveraged balance sheet and thereby enable it to borrow more money to pursue its online energy trading business activities.

But there was one problem in this strategy. To shed its fixed assets, Enron had to find buyers, and many of Enron's larger fixed assets were either overvalued or otherwise unattractive to strategic buyers. Enron's solution to this problem was ultimately the cause of its downfall. If third parties could not be found to buy its assets, Enron perfected the alternative of selling those assets to itself—or, more accurately, to controlled affiliates in non-transparent transactions. As a result of an obscure accounting convention, Enron found that it could transfer its 'heavy assets' off its own balance sheet by selling them to 'unconsolidated affiliates,' at least so long as independent financial buyers held a minimum stake (equal to at 3 percent of the affiliate's total debt and equity) in the 'unconsolidated affiliate.' As a practical matter, this meant that Enron only had to find someone to take 3 percent (with Enron still holding the remaining 97 percent) in order to camouflage its ownership. By late 2000, Enron owned and controlled for all practical purposes a total of $60 billion in assets, of which $27 billion (or 45%) were held in Enron's 'unconsolidated affiliates.'[10] Thus, Enron had become 'asset lite,' but its loss of 'weight' was illusory, because it remained liable on the debt incurred to finance these 'heavy assets,' which debt had also been transferred (at least nominally) to the books of the 'unconsolidated affiliate.'

By the late 1990s, Enron had come to believe—recklessly, as it turned out—that it could profit by trading in a variety of volatile markets: energy, electricity, broadband communications, et cetera. Although Enron had expertise in natural gas, it proved clueless about the technical complexities of broadband where its grandiose plans could never truly be implemented (the 'last mile' between the network and the consumer frustrated it and most other entrepreneurs). Thus, whatever the information advantages that Enron had with respect to energy prices, Enron appears to have known no more than other sophisticated traders in these other volatile markets. Fundamentally, its business model was flawed, and its management collectively suffered from hubris in believing that it could generalize its success in energy trading, broadly extending it to unrelated markets. Nonetheless, Enron disguised its lack of success in these other markets and postponed disaster by exploiting accounting rules and conventions, particularly in two areas where accounting rules were in transition and had never been authoritatively resolved. By using extremely aggressive interpretations of these rules, Enron was able to present only an opaque picture of its operations that hid much and revealed little.

The first of these two areas involved the accounting for long-term contracts, which contracts were the staple of Enron's trading businesses. At its simplest, Enron would enter into a long-term contract to supply a large customer with energy at a fixed price and would receive at the outset a sizable cash 'prepay' or down payment. To determine Enron's profit, accounting rules required Enron to 'present value' such long-term contracts—or, more specifically, to use 'mark-to-market' accounting. This approach required management to forecast often speculative variables—such as energy prices or interest rates—far into the future.

Enron took to this task like a duck to water. It enthusiastically valued 20-year contracts, always estimating their net future cash flows to produce a large profit for Enron. Probably the most extreme example was a 20-year contract, entered into in July 2000, with Blockbuster Video to develop a system of entertainment-on-demand services across a range of U.S. cities by year-end. Enron's role was to store and broadcast the entertainment on its still undeveloped broadband network. Based on only a few pilot projects in three cities, Enron recognized profits of $110 million from the Blockbuster deal, even though it had not yet solved such technical problems as delivering broadband over the 'last mile' to the consumer or gauging the level of market demand. Similarly, Enron marked to market a 15-year contract to supply electricity to Eli Lilly's Indianapolis plant, valuing the contract at over $500 million. Yet, because Enron had to estimate the present value of the costs of servicing this contract in order to book a profit and because Indiana had not yet deregulated electricity, this forced Enron to predict when, over the 15-year period, Indiana would deregulate electricity prices and what the impact would be on the costs of servicing the contract. At this point, once predictions as speculative as this can determine a company's current earnings, anything goes, and those inclined toward wishful thinking can report higher income than those inclined towards more conservative financial reporting.

Although the use of 'mark-to-market' accounting inflated Enron's results, this practice was not the one that most misled investors or that was most responsible for Enron's downfall. That honor falls to Enron's extraordinarily aggressive use of 'special purpose entities' (or SPEs) to hide liabilities that it had incurred. SPEs are shell firms to which a parent corporation may transfer both assets and associated liabilities in order to avoid showing them on its own balance sheet. In 'structured financings,' SPEs are legitimately used because some of the parent's assets can be contributed to the SPE so that they are isolated from the parent's liabilities. This gives the SPE a superior credit to that of its parent and thus makes the SPE the better obligor, because, based on its superior creditworthiness, it would pay a lower interest rate. But the key attraction of SPEs to Enron had little to do with economizing on interest costs. Instead, Enron's fascination with SPEs derived from their utility in permitting Enron to inflate its financial reporting. Because accounting rules permitted (or at least were read by Enron and its accountants to permit) a parent corporation to treat the SPE as an 'unconsolidated affiliate' so long as some minimum equity investment was made by unaffiliated investors and the unaffiliated investors controlled the SPE's operations, Enron found that it could use SPEs to implement Skilling's 'asset light' strategy, even though Enron could not shed its heavy assets by selling them in arm's length transactions to independent third parties.

By transferring a pipeline or a production facility to an SPE, Enron took an expensive asset off its balance sheet, along with the equally (or more) expensive debt that had financed its acquisition. Fundamentally, this enabled Enron to preserve its 'investment grade' credit rating. Moreover, if the asset transfer was only to a shell firm (i.e. an SPE) that was nominally independent but still was effectively controlled by Enron, then Enron got the best of both worlds: a slimmed down balance sheet, which enabled it to borrow new funds and at a potentially lower interest rate, and the informational advantages about the trading conditions in the relevant market that came from its de facto control of the asset. Additionally, if the asset had deteriorated in value (as some of Enron's disastrous foreign investments had certainly done), such a transfer to an SPE was attractive for still another reason: the liabilities so transferred to the SPE exceeded the current value of the asset. To be sure, Enron remained contingently liable on these debts, because the creditors had not released Enron, but the primary obligor became the SPE.

All these transfers would have meant little if Enron had been required to consolidate its SPEs with its own financial results. In fact, neither the SEC, nor the Financial Accounting Standards Board ('FASB'), the two primary bodies that promulgate accounting rules in the United States, had ever definitively ruled what the minimum stakes were that the outside investors must hold in an SPE in order to justify its nonconsolidation on the parent corporation's consolidated financial statements. Instead, an advisory arm of the FASB, known as the Emerging Issues Task Force, which was largely controlled by the major accounting firms, had indicated that an investment equal to at least 3 percent of the SPE's total debt and equity should normally be sufficient to justify nonconsolidation. Accounting firms and the corporate bar eagerly seized on this advice and read it as a firm '3 percent rule.'

Enron stretched these rules regarding SPEs to their limit—and beyond. Overall, it had created hundreds of SPEs by 2000, and the aggregate capital invested in these off-balance sheet SPEs appears to have been between $15 and $20 billion.[11] Extraordinarily favorable as the '3 percent rule' was, Enron did not even comply with it, but instead violated it in a variety of ways. Even under the most liberal interpretations of these rules, independent parties had to both own a minimum 3 percent interest in the SPE and control the SPE. Yet, Enron used its own employees to run some SPEs, and sometimes the independent owners were neither truly independent nor invested the minimum three percent.

Once Enron discovered SPEs, it found that it could engage in still other transactions with these invisible affiliates. As a trading company that was active in volatile markets, Enron needed to hedge. But hedging is costly and sometimes infeasible. Thus, Enron again found an innovative solution that was strikingly short-sighted: it would hedge with itself by using its own SPEs as its hedging counterparties. To give even a colorable legitimacy to these hedges, Enron capitalized its SPEs with large blocks of Enron stock. But the result was an illusory hedge, because if energy prices moved adversely to Enron, it would take more and more Enron stock to provide sufficient collateral to enable the Enron SPE to fulfill its obligation to hedge Enron's risk. These transactions were known, at least in their broader outlines, to Enron's audit committee and its outside auditors, but neither appears to have expressed any serious concerns before Enron's final days.

When these irregularities were finally discovered, Enron was forced in October 2001 to disclose that it had overstated its earnings for 1996 to 2000 by some $613 million (or 23 percent of reported profits over this period).[12] In addition, Enron was required to restate its December 31, 2000 balance sheet so as to increase liabilities by $628 million (or about 5.5 percent of reported equity): similarly, it reduced equity by $1.2 billion (or roughly 10 percent of reported equity). This restatement was the beginning of the end for Enron.

In truth, this outcome was ironic. Enron had tripped over a technical aspect of a highly technical rule and so was placed in default on billions of dollars. If Enron had simply observed the '3 percent rule' properly, it might have been able to continue for some indefinite further period to conceal the true extent of its liabilities. The greater fraud was not that Enron cheated on the '3 percent rule', but that Enron and its gatekeepers collectively rationalized that 'the 3 percent rule' entitled Enron to blind its own investors to some $15 to $20 billion in off-balance sheet financings for which Enron was liable.

Assessing Responsibility: Who Deserves the Blame?

Crimes may have been committed at Enron, but the greater social problem lay in the stupidity it revealed. Why didn't the Enron board realize that management had engaged in far too many risky transactions? Why didn't Enron's auditors place some limits on its use of structured finance and SPEs to hide some $15 to $20 billion off Enron's balance sheet? Were Enron's gatekeepers—its auditors, securities analysts, and the credit-rating agencies—simply asleep? Or were they compromised by conflicts of interest?

A good starting point is to begin with the motives of Enron's management. Looking at Enron's 2001 proxy statement, one finds that within 60 days of its February 15, 2001 date, stock options covering some 12,611,385 of Enron's shares were to become exercisable by its officers and directors, including 5,285,542 by Ken Lay, its then CEO, and 824,038 by Jeff Skilling, who was soon to become its CEO.[13] All told, as of December 31, 2000, Enron had 96 million shares outstanding under stock option plans—or nearly 13 percent of all its common shares outstanding.[14] None of these options appears to have placed restrictions on the subsequent resale of the stock.

Enron was not unrepresentative in this regard, and many Silicon Valley 'high tech' corporations had even higher percentages of their stock covered by stock options, sometimes as high as 20 to 25 percent of outstanding shares. The impact of such an option-based system of executive compensation is to focus management on the short-run. Subject to some potential risk of 'insider trading' liability if the manager clearly was aware of material non-public information, managers can bail out and sell when they sense the firm's stock price is about to decline. In this light, Enron's fervent desire to show immediate earnings growth and to hide problems, liabilities, and money-losing transactions seems a direct consequence of how its management was compensated. They were incentivized to manage for the short-term, and not surprisingly they did.

But if there is no mystery here, why didn't Enron's board or audit committee, or its auditors, or still other gatekeepers stop them? Here, the analysis becomes subtler, more complex, and more important.

The Audit Committee

Viewed from a distance, Enron had an exemplary audit committee with more financial expertise than virtually any contemporaneous audit committees possessed at that time. Its chair, Dr Robert Jaedicke, was an accounting professor who had been the former Dean of Stanford Business School; other members included a CEO of the State Bank of Rio de Janeiro, the former U.K. Secretary of State of Energy, and the former Chair of the U.S. Commodities Futures Trading Commission.[15] Both the Enron board and its audit committee appear to have functioned harmoniously, held regular meetings, and kept detailed minutes, and they were well paid (indeed, at roughly $350,000 per year Enron directors were paid double the U.S. average for directors).[16]

Viewed more closely, however, there were problems. Some audit committee members had low visibility conflicts of interest. For example, Dr John H. Mendelsohn, President of the University of Texas's M. D. Andersen Cancer Center, looked to Enron as a major benefactor for medical research. Dr Wendy Gramm was the wife of the senior Republican Senator from Texas, Phil Gramm, who relied on Enron and its executives for campaign contributions. Still, other corporations had similar conflicts, and conflicts do not adequately explain the audit committee's nonperformance.

Other evidence suggests that Enron's Audit Committee did very little. Enron's board normally held five regularly scheduled meetings a year, which typically lasted between one and two hours.[17] On the day of these meetings, the audit committee would also meet and, at one such meeting, in early February 2001, it considered over the course of a ninety minute meeting:

- a report by Arthur Andersen on Enron's compliance with GAAP and internal controls;
- a report on the adequacy of reserves and related party transactions (which, of course, covered Ken Fastow's very conflicted position at LJM);
- a report on disclosures related to litigation risks and contingencies;
- a report on the 2000 financial statements, which included an update on problems in the broadband division;
- a review of the Audit and Compliance Committee Charter;
- a report on executive and director use of the company aircraft;

- a review of the 2001 Internal Control Audit Plan, which included a review of key business trends and risks; and
- a review of new SEC Regulation Fair Disclosure and a review of the company's policies for communications with securities analysts in light of it.[18]

All this in less than 90 minutes is fast work indeed—and implies a superficial review.

Even better evidence of the Enron Committee's passivity is supplied by New York Times reporter, Kurt Eichenwald, in his detailed study of Enron.[19] A scandal broke at Enron in the late 1980s, when Enron's internal auditors discovered that two rogue employees, both oil traders, were embezzling funds and had far exceeded their trading limits. They prepared a detailed report, but it never reached the Enron board. Instead, senior management called off their investigation and turned the inquiry over to Arthur Andersen, which prepared a much watered down version of the original report that had not gone to the Audit Committee. This 'whitewashed' version caused the Audit Committee to do little more than raise an eyebrow because it seemed to imply that all problems had been satisfactorily solved. In fact, the unauthorized trading continued and Enron later lost $85 million because of trading by these same rogue traders in excess of their authorized limits.

Such an example fits a broader pattern: the Audit Committee was regularly blinded by its professional advisers who fed it only the information that senior management wanted it to receive. In this case, Ken Lay, Enron's CEO, did not want to lose the services of two previously very profitable oil traders and so had the information reaching the committee carefully censored—and later he bluntly instructed the audit committee to essentially drop the matter.[20]

Nor was there much reason for the Audit Committee to upset this equilibrium and insist on greater rigor or more intense review. Until late in 2001, Enron appeared healthy even to its insiders. Management had been uniquely successful, and the directors faced only a remote threat of personal liability even if something did go seriously wrong. As discussed in the next chapter, personal liability for directors and gatekeepers had largely been eliminated by the 1990s. Hence, if nothing seemed broke, the Enron Audit Committee had no incentive to fix it.

The Auditors: Arthur Andersen

If one cannot expect part-time outside directors, who had other pressing business responsibilities, to be skeptical in the face of unbroken success or to investigate diligently their friends and colleagues, the same cannot be said for the auditors. By definition, their job was to be skeptical. Why did they then detect so little?

In addressing this question, it is important to locate Arthur Andersen, both within the accounting profession and in terms of its own rapid transition. Today, after its indictment and dissolution, the name 'Arthur Andersen' has become synonymous with accounting chicanery.[21] But as of even 2000, Andersen was near the top of its profession. Its founder, Arthur Andersen, had carefully cultivated a reputation for unbending integrity. His successor, Leonard Spacek, who took over the firm's management in the late 1940s, became the outspoken conscience of the profession for several decades and frequently criticized lax accounting standards.[22] In short, at least during an earlier era, the Andersen firm had grown and prospered by marketing itself as tougher than its peers. For example, in 1986, Andersen dropped a major, but overly aggressive, client, Lincoln Savings & Loan, because Andersen had lost confidence in the client's honesty.[23] Lincoln Savings and Loan then hired another major firm, Arthur Young, which suffered major losses when Lincoln Savings failed and Charles Keating, its CEO, became the best-known symbol of the S&L meltdown of the 1980s.

Nonetheless, a transition was at work within Andersen. It was the first major auditing firm to enter into the consulting business. Beginning with work it did for General Electric in the mid-1950s, which enabled G. E. to computerize its plant payroll, Andersen developed an expertise, first, in software and computer applications, and, then, more generally, in a host of other consulting specialties.[24] By as early as 1984, well before its peers, consulting revenues had come to exceed auditing revenues at Andersen.[25] With this development, auditing firms, and Andersen in particular, refashioned their business strategy. Auditing became the portal of entry into the large client, through which the firm could market its more lucrative consulting services. The audit partner was to be retrained to become the auditor/salesman, who would be incentivized through compensation formulas that paid as much for cross-selling as for skill at auditing. While this transition affected all the major U.S. accounting firms, Andersen was the extreme example, with the largest consulting revenues on both an absolute and percentage share basis.[26] Consulting income already represented one-half of Andersen's U.S. revenues in 1990, but by 1994 it had climbed to two-thirds.[27]

The rapidness of this transition caused tensions and produced organizational strains within Andersen. As consulting became more profitable than auditing, the consultants first assumed greater authority within the firm and then objected to subsidizing the less profitable audit operations.

Only a decade or so earlier, in 1979, then Andersen CEO Harvey Kapnick had proposed that Andersen spin off consulting to avoid conflicts of interest, but he was forced to resign when the firm's partners rejected his proposal. In 1989, however, the firm gave in to the demands of its consultants and formally split accounting and consulting into separate businesses.[28] Possibly in response to the consultants' objections, Andersen cut back and fired an estimated 10 percent of its partners in the United States in 1992,[29] thereby demonstrating beyond any doubt that a business culture had replaced the older professional culture. Then in 1998, Andersen established a guideline under which its audit engagement partner for a client was expected to double revenues from the client by cross-selling non-audit services.[30] To cross-sell to this extent, the audit partner arguably had to be more a salesman than a watchdog.

Despite these efforts, the consultants could not be placated at Andersen; they demanded a divorce, and the dispute ultimately resulted in an arbitrator permitting them to exit Andersen and form a new consulting firm, Accenture, in return for a $1 billion payment to the accounting side of Andersen in 2000 as the buyout price.[31] Even before this buyout, Andersen had begun to grow a new consulting division to replace the old division that had broken away to become Accenture.

The rise of consulting at Andersen may have caused another internal organizational change that directly contributed to the Enron collapse. Within Andersen, as in other major firms, centralized control was maintained over accounting policies and practices by an internal watchdog body known at Andersen as the Professional Standards Group. Under the leadership of Andersen's founder and his immediate successors, this group had been particularly powerful, even though it was not a profit center. Its essential role was to protect the firm as a whole from the 'capture' of a local Andersen office or audit partner by a powerful client, with the consequence that risky accounting decisions might be approved that could result in liability being imposed on the firm as a whole. Every major firm knew that this was a danger and had such an office. But within Andersen, as the auditor ethic eroded in the 1990s and the auditor/salesman became the new model, the Professional Standards Group was downgraded in power and status. Andersen changed its policy so that local partners could overrule the national Professional Standards Group.[32] No other major firm appears to have done so. Allegedly, Andersen even marketed on this basis, telling clients that Andersen was unique in that the local partner could make a final decision and did not need the national office's approval.[33]

Andersen's Houston office appears to have ignored or overruled the accounting recommendations of the Professional Standards Group with regard to Enron on at least four occasions.[34] Even more importantly, the local Andersen Professional Standards Group representative, Carl Bass, who monitored the Enron account was re-assigned—at the insistence of Enron's Chief Accounting Officer Rick Causey, who believed Bass might interfere with Enron's use of SPEs.[35] Causey, himself, was a former Andersen partner, illustrating the revolving door relationship that had developed between auditors and their clients across the industry. Not only was Bass removed because he disapproved of Enron's risky accounting policies, but Andersen's records were falsified, to mask his disapproval. Internal memos at Andersen that described Bass's views on Enron's accounting were revised to downplay his objections and present him as concurring generally with the views of Andersen's Houston office.[36] In fairness, Andersen did resist early pressure from Enron to have Bass removed and Andersen's CEO even called high-ranking Enron officials to protest.[37] But according to *New York Times* reporter Kurt Eichenwald's detailed account of Enron's fall, the factor that proved decisive and caused Andersen to acquiesce in Bass's removal was not a fear that Enron would drop Andersen as its auditor, but rather the fear that 'the deep-pocketed client would shift its consulting business at the drop of a hat, leaving Andersen only the low-paying audit work. That was a risk that the Andersen partners were simply unwilling to take.'[38]

Causal responsibility for the decline in professional independence at Andersen cannot be exclusively assigned to the rise of consulting services. Andersen had other conflicts as well. In 2000, Andersen earned $25 million in audit fees and $27 million in consulting fees from Enron.[39] Even though the audit fees were less than the consulting fees, they may have meant more to Andersen's Houston office. Enron's audit fees alone accounted for 27 percent of the audit fees of public clients for Andersen's Houston office.[40] Arguably, it was too big a client for that office to lose and survive.

Although Enron was a uniquely large client for Andersen, size appears not to have been a necessary precondition to Andersen's acquiescence in dubious accounting policies. Throughout the 1990s, Andersen was involved in a series of notorious accounting scandals: Sunbeam in 1997, Waste Management in 1999, the Baptist Foundation of Arizona in 1999, and later Global Crossing and Qwest—plus, of course, Enron and WorldCom.[41] Just the Waste Management, Sunbeam and Baptist Foundation cases eventually cost Andersen fines and settlements of over $434 million.[42] Collectively, this rapid succession of scandals, each suggesting auditor involvement in fraud, may explain Andersen's eventual indictment for obstruction of justice in the Enron case. Assistant U.S. Attorney General Michael Chertoff, who made that decision to indict, described Andersen as a 'recidivist.'[43]

Was Andersen really that different from its major competitors? Some think not,[44] and there is evidence that Andersen's competitors in the then Big Five had similar rates of financial statement restatements among their large public clients.[45] Thus, the performance of the other major auditors may have been more or less equivalent, except that Andersen experienced the 'mega-failures.' Arguably, it could be that Andersen was simply unlucky and got caught more often. Still, the latest quantitative evidence does suggest that Andersen did become a lower quality auditor in the 1990s. Examining the auditees of Andersen and the surviving Big Four auditors, Ross Fuerman found that Andersen's audit clients experienced a significantly higher rate of both private and public securities litigation.[46] If one accepts his premise that more litigation about the client's financial statements suggests a lower quality audit, then Andersen does look much like a firm that deteriorated in quality during the 1990s, as its internal culture changed.

Securities Analysts

Even if the auditors were conflicted, one might still expect that securities analysts would warn investors because their professional reputations were dependent on predicting winners and losers in the stock market. Yet, even after Enron announced a major restatement of its financial statements in October 2001, most analysts continued to give Enron a strong buy rating. As of October 31, 2001, Thomson First Call, which collects and tabulates analyst recommendations, found that the mean analyst recommendation for Enron was 1.9 out of a possible 5, where 1 is a 'strong buy' and 5 is a 'sell.'[47] Nor was this pattern simply the result of a sluggish response. After Enron's restatements were announced, and at a time when it was desperately seeking a merger with Dynergy to survive, major broker-dealers such as Merrill Lynch and Lehman Brothers issued 'buy' or 'strong buy' recommendations on Enron.[48]

Again, conflicts of interest seem to explain much of this pattern. Investment banks earned more than $125 million in underwriting fees on Enron offerings over the period from 1998 to 2000.[49] One study has found that analysts working at investment banking firms that engaged in underwriting had significantly higher estimates for Enron's likely stock price appreciation than did the analysts who did not work at investment banks.[50] But there is an anomaly in this story: analysts who worked for investment banks that did not do current business with Enron had even higher price estimates than the analysts who worked for Enron's then current investments banks.[51] Moreover, all analysts surveyed—both independent and affiliated—showed a strongly optimistic bias. Clearly, other forces were at work here besides simply the receipt of current underwriting business.

This persistent optimistic bias may seem surprising because during 2001 the first skeptical studies appeared about Enron, which suggested that its accounting was opaque and its continued earnings growth uncertain. The best known of these studies, written by Bethany McLean for Fortune, appeared in March of 2001 and was bluntly titled, 'Is Enron Overpriced?'[52] The author not only suggests that it was overpriced, but quotes a variety of analysts and fund managers conceding that they found Enron's financial statements 'virtually impenetrable.'

Why did not analysts respond to such warning signals? The answer is shown in its starkest form in the Enron story by Enron's refusal to allow its long-time investment bank, Merrill Lynch, to participate in a major (and highly lucrative) public offering of its stock until it first fired its energy market securities analyst, John Olson, who had downgraded Enron's stock.[53] Eventually, Merrill Lynch gave in and fired Olson. In short, skeptical analysts had to fear retaliation because their employers typically wanted investment banking business. Even if the issuer could not get them fired, they could threaten to exclude a 'disloyal' analyst from their conference calls or from the steady stream of non-public material information that was typically leaked during this era to securities analysts.[54]

Still, even if sell-side analysts were slow to recognize that Enron was overvalued because of their multiple conflicts of interest and their fear of retaliation, why didn't the buy-side wake up? After all, the major mutual and pension funds employ their own analysts, or they hire professional money managers who do. One possibility is that some on the buy-side did detect irregularities at Enron and dumped their stock, but because buy-side research is proprietary and seldom publicly released, the buy-side analysts' discovery of fraud at Enron would not alert others. Indeed, a major institution seeking to liquidate a large and hence illiquid block of stock in Enron would be very careful not to set off alarm bells that would panic other investors. In any event, it is clear that most fund managers did not dump Enron stock until the penultimate moment. As late as October 2001, 60 percent of Enron's stock was held by the major mutual funds, including those managed by Fidelity, Vanguard, Merrill Lynch, Morgan Stanley, and Goldman Sachs.[55] These firms certainly knew that sell-side research was conflicted and should have recognized that Enron's financial statements were opaque and its portfolio of businesses very risky. Why they held Enron when it was trading at price/earnings multiples as high as 70 to 1 (or more) seems best explained by a recurrent tendency that has been much documented: fund managers tend to herd.[56] In part, this tendency exists because fund managers and analysts find it more damaging to their careers to be individually wrong than collectively wrong. In part also, such a tendency is a corollary of a stock market bubble. That is, even if the fund manager or analyst senses that a company is overvalued based on any traditional method of valuation, it remains possible that a 'bubble market' will carry the stock still higher. If the fund manager believes that the 'irrational exuberance' of the market is likely to carry the stock price of Enron up another 20 percent, then the fund manager who sells Enron will underperform the market and appear less successful than his or her competitors. As a result, capital will flow out of the fund and into the funds managed by rivals.

These explanations can account for why credible warning signals would be ignored even in the absence of clearcut conflicts of interest. Supporting this interpretation is the fact that as of October 2001, well after Jeff Skilling had resigned and other warning signals had surfaced, sixteen out of the seventeen analysts covering Enron maintained either 'buy' or 'strong buy' ratings on it.[57] Such a pattern seems strange when others had already determined that Enron was at the least overvalued. But this pattern can be explained on a variety of grounds: conflicts of interest, fear of retaliation, 'herding,' or the bubble. For any of these reasons, analysts may not give the market their unbiased, best judgment.

Attorneys

At least a partial cause of Enron's collapse was the lack of disclosure of material information about the company's activities and liabilities. Both Enron's off-balance sheet liabilities and its related-party transactions with entities controlled by Andrew Fastow, its chief financial officer, were hidden from the market. Normally, the responsibility for ensuring compliance with the corporation's disclosures under the federal securities laws falls on the corporation's attorneys.

What happened? Much attention has focused on the role of Enron's principal outside counsel, Vinson & Elkins. But most criticism of Vinson & Elkins has largely been aimed at their investigation of allegations made by Sharon Watkins, the whistleblower who first called Ken Lay's attention to Enron's accounting problems. Whatever one thinks of this investigation, it was largely a sideshow to the main drama in Enron, and Enron's collapse by this late point was probably inevitable. From a causal perspective, the more central question is who or what was responsible for the inadequate disclosures that allowed Enron to deceive the market for years? Here, the Powers Report (which was prepared by the independent directors of Enron after its bankruptcy and is recognized as an objective account of Enron's implo-sion) describes a disclosure process that was fundamentally dysfunctional.[58] Basically, Enron's disclosures, particularly the most sensitive ones about its liabilities and related-party transactions, were prepared in-house and sub-jected to only minimal outside review by professionals. As the Powers Report concluded with regard to Enron's most suspect transactions:

[I]t appears that no one outside of Enron Global Finance, the entity principally responsible for the related-party transactions, exercised significant supervision or control over the disclosure process concerning those transactions.[59]

In short, gatekeepers were either removed from the process or given no more than a brief opportunity to comment. For example, in the case of Enron's financial statements, the critical footnotes to the financial statements were drafted within the Financial Reporting Group and cir-culated to others, including in-house and outside counsel. According to the Powers Report, Vinson & Elkins claimed 'that they may not have seen all of the filings in advance.'[60] But even when they did review pro-posed disclosures and objected or otherwise commented, their role was modest. Richard Causey, Enron's Chief Accounting Officer who would later be indicted in the same indictment with Ken Lay and Jeffrey Skill-ing, 'was the final arbiter of unresolved differences among the various contributors to the financial reporting process.'[61]

In the case of related-party transactions, the lawyers played a greater role, but still, because of the complexity of these disclosures, the 'accountants and the lawyers relied heavily on—and generally deferred to—the officers and employees in Enron Global Finance who were closer to the transaction and actually knew the details.'[62] In particular, Enron's General Counsel, James Derrick, 'reviewed the final drafts to look for obvious errors, but otherwise had little involvement with the related party proxy statement disclosures.'[63]

The basic picture that emerges then is one in which there was no independent gatekeeper with authority to block or even delay Enron's securities filings if the independent reviewer considered them deficient. Rather, the process was so decentralized and fragmented that in the words of the Powers Report:

There was no systematic procedure in place for ensuring identification of all transactions with related parties that needed to be disclosed in the financial statement footnotes or proxy statements.[64]

Given the lack of oversight, Enron management found it comparatively easy to 'minimize the disclosures about the related-party transactions.'[65]

Of course, it is not surprising (and indeed it was predictable) that Andrew Fastow did not want to disclose his lucrative compensation in related-party transactions to anyone—not to the market, not to Jeffrey Skilling, his boss, and not to the Enron board. But as the Powers Report found, that Fastow was successful in avoiding such disclosure was attributable to 'the fact that the process leading to those disclosures appears to have been driven by the officers and employees in Enron Global Finance, rather than by Senior Management with ultimate responsibility, in-house or outside counsel, or the Audit and Compliance Committee.'[66]

In this light, the lack of transparency surrounding Enron seems attributable less to a gatekeeper that failed and more to the absence of any true gatekeeper in the disclosure process with real responsibility or authority. What was needed—and what was largely absent—was an independent professional—whether an attorney or an accountant—in a position to 'exercise ... independent judgment about the appropriateness of the company's statements.'[67] The absence of such a gatekeeper was not accidental (as Enron's management did not want close oversight). But that the disclosure process could be structured so that the attorneys were placed on the sidelines, where they could comment but not block or delay an inadequate filing, seems a more structural failure that invited abuse. If there is no watchdog, it cannot bark when the thief comes in the night.

Credit-Rating Agencies

Until four days before Enron declared bankruptcy on December 2, 2001, its debt was rated as 'investment grade' by the major credit-rating agencies.[68] This same last-minute recognition of impending insolvency also characterizes the reaction of the credit-rating agencies to the downward spirals at WorldCom and Parmalat as well.

What explains this slowness? Again, one can start with conflicts of interest. The major credit-rating agencies are paid their fees by the very companies that they rate. Although this is problematic, the conflict here is not nearly as intense as it is in the case of the auditor, because the credit-rating agency has thousands of clients, none of which pays a fee that is material to the agency. Nor are the individual raters within the rating agency as dependent upon any individual corporate client or as vulnerable to 'capture' by the client, as are the audit partners of an accounting firm.

Other factors may better explain the apparently poor performance of credit-rating agencies—a performance that, in the case of Enron, Senator

Joseph Lieberman, Chairman of the Senate Governmental Affairs Committee, characterized after his Committee's investigation of the agencies as 'dismally lax.'[69] One factor is pressure on the rating agency because of the devastating consequences of a rating downgrading. In early November 2001, Moody's was approached by prominent persons to warn it that a downgrading of Enron below investment grade would plunge Enron into bankruptcy and disrupt the nation's capital markets.[70] This consequence followed from a downgrading because, under Enron's debt covenants, a downgrading below investment grade triggered a default. The risk that one will trigger a major bankruptcy (and possibly be sued for doing so unjustifiably) has to slow anyone down.

A still more important factor is the lack of competition in the market for credit ratings. Effectively, Moody's and Standard & Poor's share a monopoly, with only modest competition from other raters. Both are highly profitable, but may have little incentive to invest in upgrading their services because they are arguably immune from competition. As will be seen, this immunity partly stems in turn from governmental action that precludes other firms from entering this market. Hence, the absence of competition may be a greater problem than conflicts of interest in the case of this watchdog.

How Was Enron Discovered?

This quick survey has shown that a variety of professionals failed to perform as, in theory, they should have. Conceivably, this failure could be explained by the fact that Enron was a brilliantly conceived, perfectly orchestrated fraud. But it was not. Kurt Eichenwald's account of Enron's collapse bears a simple title that says it all: 'Conspiracy of Fools.'[71]

Despite a soaring bull market, hero worship by an infatuated media, conflicted stock analysts, and fraudulent financial reporting, Enron's problems were detected by those whose self-interest led them to study Enron's activities more diligently than others. Ironically, the 'hero' who discovered Enron's fraud was not a 'gatekeeper' with high reputational capital or significant exposure to liability. Instead, it was a much more unlikely champion of the public interest: the short sellers. Motivated by self-interest and the expectation of high profits, they deduced that Enron had to be a house of cards and slowly spread this message to others.

Jim Chanos, a professional trader who ran Kynikos Associates, a firm that specialized in short-selling, deserves the historical credit for being the first to recognize Enron's hopelessly exposed position. Analyzing Enron's public financial statements, he decided that the company was a 'hedge fund in disguise.'[72] More importantly, he determined that it was earning only a very poor return for a high-risk hedge fund—a 7 percent return on capital.[73] This return could not justify, he realized, Enron's then valuation of six times book value. Add to this picture the hint of fraud and self-dealing created by Enron's voluminous related party transactions, and the stock seemed to him ripe for a fall.

Chanos began to short Enron in November of 2000. Yet, in January 2001, Enron management began to predict publicly that its success at bandwidth trading would add an additional $35 to Enron's then stock price of $90—in effect, a prediction of a $125 market price. In February 2001, Chanos spoke at a national short sellers' conference—known then as 'Bears in Hibernation'—and made Enron one of his two leading picks for a fall. While Chanos sought to educate and convert securities analysts to his position, his real success came when he was able to convince Bethany McLean, a Fortune reporter, that Enron's financial statements raised a host of unanswered questions. Educated to Enron by Chanos, she wrote the now famous Fortune story, 'Is Enron Overpriced?' that began to change the public mood towards Enron.[74] Gradually, Enron's price began to fall, and that decline accelerated when Enron's then CEO Jeff Skilling mysteriously resigned without warning in August 2001. Still, at no point was Chanos aware of the full scope of Enron's fraud, including its extraordinary off-balance sheet liabilities.[75]

Was Chanos simply lucky? The growing evidence is to the contrary. Short sellers appear to have been highly successful at predicting accounting restatements. Researchers have concluded that short sellers can often see through accounting manipulations and profit extensively from this skill.[76]

If they can, why couldn't Arthur Andersen do the same? The critical point here is that Enron's problems were discoverable. Yet, they were not discovered by any of the firm's gatekeepers. Only those whose self-interest led them to search harder—first, the short sellers and, later, Dynergy—discovered the truth. If the truth was discoverable and if, across the board, the professional gatekeepers did not find it, the problems with gatekeepers seem serious.

The WorldCom Smashup

Background

Even more than Enron, WorldCom was a skyrocket that soared and then plunged. Whereas Enron was a long-established and indeed dominant natural gas pipeline that sought to 'morph' itself into a trading company, WorldCom started from scratch. Founded on a shoestring in 1983 as a discount long-distance service provider (then known as LDDS—'Long-Distance Discount Service'), it grew rapidly through a series of mergers, culminating in its 1998 $40 billion merger with MCI Communications Corp. Much of the key to WorldCom's success was its apparent efficiency, which baffled its major rivals, AT&T and Sprint. Somehow WorldCom consistently reported a lower ratio of certain key expenses, known as 'line costs', to its overall revenues than did any of its competitors.[77] 'Line costs' are essentially transmission costs paid to other service providers for the use or the right to use their lines. Line costs were WorldCom's largest single expense and accounted for roughly half of its expenses. They were sufficiently material to be reported on a separate line of its financial statements.[78] This apparent efficiency impressed Wall Street and kept World-Com's stock price high, allowing it to acquire seemingly less efficient rivals in a rapidly consolidating industry.

While impressive, WorldCom's low ratio of line costs to revenues was largely illusory. Ultimately, the key fraud in WorldCom involved the decision of Scott Sullivan, WorldCom's chief financial officer, to cease expensing line costs and instead capitalize them—in order to keep the ratio of line costs to revenues low. But to capitalize a payment made to rival companies for use of their lines and facilities amounts to a mortal sin for accountants. When one capitalizes a payment, one is in effect creating an asset (which will be depreciated at a much slower rate, thereby reducing the current charge to earnings). But no legitimate asset arises out of the payment of such an expense. To see this, imagine an ordinary tenant making a monthly lease payment and seeking to capitalize this payment as if the tenant had acquired an asset by virtue of the payment. In fact, the tenant has acquired nothing and will be forced to move out at the end of the lease. Similarly, WorldCom acquired nothing and was not entitled to capitalize these line costs payments because no colorable asset had been acquired as a result of them.

When WorldCom reported its discovery in June of 2002 that line costs payments had been improperly capitalized, it acknowledged that but for the capitalization of over $3.8 billion in such costs in 2001 and the first quarter of 2002, it would have reported a loss for such periods.[79] Within a month, it was forced into bankruptcy.

Grossly improper as the capitalization of line costs was, it was not the first or the only irregularity in WorldCom's financial statements relating to recognition of expenses. In fact, when a full restatement of WorldCom's financial statements was completed in 2004, some $76 billion in adjustments were recognized, which reduced WorldCom's net equity from

approximately $50 billion to approximately minus $20 billion.[80] The point
then is that the WorldCom fraud was not a one-shot transaction engaged
in by a reckless chief financial officer. Rather, as the federal court hearing
the private securities litigation concerning WorldCom has found:

Before capitalizing the line costs in 2001, WorldCom had engaged in other
strategies to reduce the apparent magnitude of its line costs.[81]

This is important because if the fraud at WorldCom had been limited
to a single occasion, it would be hard to fault WorldCom's gatekeepers,
and all the blame would fall on its chief financial officer and his staff.
But, in fact, as this court further found, WorldCom had cheated earlier,
releasing 'reserves or accruals that had been set aside to cover anticipated costs, and used them to offset line costs.'[82]

In short, in a rapidly consolidating industry, WorldCom was able to
acquire rival long-distance service providers, rather than be acquired
by them, because it manipulated its reporting of expenses to give it the
image of greater efficiency and thereby inflate its stock price.

Why was WorldCom so willing to take these risks and use an accounting treatment that was not even colorably defensible? Here, it is necessary to introduce WorldCom's chief executive, and controlling person,
Bernhard Ebbers. Ebbers became WorldCom's chief executive virtually
at its outset in 1985 and as a result owned a significant percentage of the
company's stock. A true believer in WorldCom, he never diversified his
portfolio by selling significant amounts of his WorldCom stock. Rather,
most of his wealth remained in WorldCom, and his personal net worth
rose and fell with WorldCom's stock price. However, Ebbers did invest
heavily in a variety of other private and illiquid enterprises. He did so
by pledging all his WorldCom stock to secure loans that he used to
acquire private businesses and fund their operations. Most of the loans
to Ebbers were made by affiliates of Citicorp and Bank of America, each
of whom were also major underwriters.

As a result, when WorldCom's stock price began to fall in 2000,
Ebbers faced a personal crisis. Because his WorldCom stock was
pledged to secure loans to him, and because the value of this collateral
had just shrunk, Ebbers received a margin call from Bank of America
in the Fall of 2000. Having no additional shares to pledge, he would
be forced to sell his WorldCom stock in significant quantities, which
in turn would drive WorldCom's price down even further—unless
he could obtain financing elsewhere. He solved his predicament (at
least temporarily) by convincing the WorldCom board of directors
to extend him a $50 million loan in September 2000. The board's

decision has been widely criticized as irresponsible, but the board evidently felt that equivalent sales by Ebbers would cause WorldCom's stock price to crater.

In a sense, they were right. When Ebbers was faced with additional margin calls later in 2000, and when the WorldCom board refused to extend further loans to him, he sold some three million WorldCom shares, and WorldCom's stock price dropped 8 percent on the disclosure of his sales.[83] Following this decline and additional margin calls on Ebbers, the WorldCom board was induced to make additional loans and guarantees to Ebbers, which by May 2001 had reach a grand total of $250 million.[84]

Thus, throughout 2000 and 2001, Ebbers simply could not afford to have WorldCom fail to make its predicted earnings or to lower substantially its earnings forecasts for fear that its stock price would decline and trigger additional margin calls. Nor could he sell much WorldCom stock, as the market would perceive that to be a bail-out and would drop the price faster than he could unload his stock. His position was desperate.

Small wonder then that WorldCom's financial reporting was manipulated. But if the motive for fraud was clear, the question again arises: where were the gatekeepers? After all, far more than Enron, WorldCom was widely recognized to be a high risk client. Its meteoric rise from obscurity through merger after merger fits exactly the profile of a company whose financial statements may conceal more than they reveal. Arthur Andersen, recognizing this, internally assigned WorldCom its highest risk rating.[85]

Assessing Responsibility: Who Deserves the Blame?

Although much less has been written about WorldCom than Enron, some detailed internal studies are available. A special committee of independent directors of WorldCom, assisted by the same outside law firm that drafted the Powers Report for Enron, produced an elaborate study of what had gone wrong,[86] and the WorldCom bankruptcy court appointed as its Examiner, former U.S. Attorney General and Pennsylvania Governor, Richard Thornburgh, who prepared a series of detailed and lengthy reports.[87] To be sure, a bankruptcy examiner is an advocate who typically seeks to frame the case for liability against those who might be induced to contribute to the bankrupt estate. But the facts in the Thornburgh reports tend to speak for themselves.

1 *The Investment Banks*   Even more than Enron, WorldCom was a money machine for the major investment banks because it made large and more frequent offerings to finance its acquisitions and expansion. Between 1997 and 2002, Salomon Smith Barney (SSB) was WorldCom's principal investment bank and received more than $116 million in underwriting and investment banking fees as a result of WorldCom transactions.[88] SSB won and held WorldCom's business by a variety of means, some of which look much like commercial bribery. Specifically, from June 1996 to November 1997, SSB allocated over 748,000 shares in initial public offerings to Mr Ebbers, on which he realized gross profits of about $11 million.[89] This practice—known as 'spinning' in the industry—paid off for SSB, as over the same interval, it was engaged by WorldCom on four engagements on which it received fees of roughly $65 million.[90] The Bankruptcy Examiner, Mr Thornburgh, concluded that, in view of all the related circumstances surrounding these stock allocations in 'hot' offerings, 'they were intended to, and did influence, Mr Ebbers' decision to hire and to continue to hire Salomon ... as WorldCom's lead investment banker.'[91]

SSB's cozy relationship with Ebbers is important for two distinct reasons. First, as underwriter for WorldCom's offerings, SSB bore statutory liability as a gatekeeper. Under the Securities Act of 1933, the underwriter must conduct a 'reasonable investigation' of the statements made by the issuer in its registration statement when the issuer 'registers' securities for public sale. Ultimately, SSB and its parent Citigroup would settle its liabilities under these provisions for a near record $2.575 billion settlement—the second largest securities class action settlement.[92] Yet, despite this risk, SSB proved to be a passive gatekeeper who made no more than perfunctory efforts to conduct 'due diligence' investigations of WorldCom during the two major debt offerings that it underwrote for WorldCom in 2000 and 2001.[93]

Second, SSB was the market's principal source of information about WorldCom, because SSB employed a securities analyst, Jack Grubman, who had become the recognized guru of the telecommunications industry and who quickly became a fervent cheerleader for WorldCom. Indeed, Grubman went well beyond performing simply as a securities analyst and also served as an investment banker and adviser to WorldCom, attending board meetings and acquiring material, non-public information. In so doing, he became the poster boy for reformers who were indignant at the conflicts of interest surrounding securities research. But Grubman cannot be viewed in isolation; he was the employee of an investment banking firm willing to go to great lengths to land and hold a very lucrative client.

2 *The Auditors* Both the Bankruptcy Examiner and the Special Committee of WorldCom directors found that WorldCom's auditor, which once again was Arthur Andersen, committed professional malpractice in performing WorldCom's audit work.[94] Although the examiner (Richard Thornburgh) recognized that WorldCom management had 'deceived' Andersen 'on a number of occasions,' he still concluded that 'Andersen failed to incorporate in its audits the needed testing of the areas where the fraud occurred, such as the "top-side" adjustments directed by former senior management outside of the Company's normal processes for recording revenues and expenses.'[95]

The post-mortem report by the WorldCom Committee of independent directors reached a similar conclusion that 'Andersen's audit approach ... limited the likelihood it would detect the accounting irregularities.'[96] That 'approach,' in their view,

focused heavily on identifying risks and assessing whether the Company had adequate controls in place to mitigate those risks, rather than emphasizing the traditional substantive testing of information maintained in accounting records and financial statements.[97]

This approach allowed Andersen to rely on WorldCom's 'controls without adequately determining that they were worthy of reliance....'[98] Of course, that is precisely the way that a gatekeeper seeking to ingratiate itself with a lucrative client in order to market other services would be likely to behave. One does not undiplomatically challenge or test the client's assertions. But the irony seems obvious: Anderson internally rated WorldCom as a client of the highest risk, yet felt it unnecessary to test the information in WorldCom's accounting records because Andersen deemed WorldCom's accounting controls adequate.

To be sure, these critical assessments may seem self-interested because they come from those who have an interest in holding Andersen liable to the WorldCom estate. But their basic conclusions have also been echoed by the federal district court hearing the private securities litigation over WorldCom, which Court refused to grant summary judgment to Andersen given the 'red flags' surrounding its audit work.[99] In her January 2005 decision, United States District Judge Denise Cote, found that, although WorldCom had concealed its clearly fraudulent decision to capitalize line costs from Andersen, plaintiffs had shown sufficient evidence to justify a trial because 'Andersen appreciated at some level the risk of fraud at WorldCom but did not take adequate steps to detect fraud.'[100] In particular, Andersen's internal records showed, she found, that its audit team was concerned about 'management pressures, specifically

[WorldCom's] desire to "maintain a stock valuation in anticipation of a security offering or a merger." '[101]

Ironically, in June 2001, just after WorldCom had begun to capitalize its line costs, Andersen's audit team, in preparation for its annual audit, held a brainstorming session 'to create a list of how management, assuming it were corrupt, could intentionally manipulate financial statements and conceal it from Andersen.'[102] Their conclusion: World-Com could use 'the improper capitalization of expenses as fixed assets and top-side journal entries' to conceal it.[103] This was prophetic, but Andersen, having figured out how the fraud could be perpetrated, did not audit for the very scenario that it recognized could occur.[104] As the Court concluded:

Without performing this analysis, there was no assurance that the financial statements that were being certified came from the books and records that had been audited.[105]

So why didn't Arthur Andersen look deeper, given the potential for fraud that it clearly recognized? Any answer is speculative, but the Bankruptcy Examiner's conclusion deserves at least serious attention. Mr Thornburgh proposed that

a likely reason [for Andersen's failure to detect fraud] was Arthur Andersen's overriding desire to grow its non-audit business relationship with WorldCom. Consistent with such a desire, it would be natural for Arthur Andersen to wish to trust the representations of ... management rather than press for an increase in corroborating documentation, which could strain the business relationship by increasing the amount of time and fees that may be incurred for the audit.[106]

In short, no one asserts that Andersen knew of Scott Sullivan's fraud, but in a world in which clients needed to be stroked (and not offended) if they were to expand their non-audit consulting relationships, a skeptical attitude and propensity to look behind management's representations was poor marketing. Indeed, after reviewing the email correspondence between Andersen's principal audit partner and Scott Sullivan, Mr Thornburgh found that:

Much of the email correspondence ... appears to relate to potential opportunities for Arthur Andersen to provide consulting services to WorldCom and its subsidiaries.[107]

If the audit partner was focused on marketing, this 'may have served,' as Thornburgh concluded, 'to minimize the importance of ... incidents ... [that Andersen failed to see were] "red flags." '[108]

3 *Securities Analysts*   As noted earlier, WorldCom's leading analyst was Jack Grubman, SSB's expert on telecommunications and a media star of the late 1990s. The Bankruptcy Examiner found that, until April 2002 (which was the same month that Ebbers was fired and the ratings agencies downgraded WorldCom), Grubman and SSB

repeatedly gave WorldCom's stock its highest ratings, enthusiastically urging investors to purchase WorldCom shares, even at times when Mr. Grubman was privately advising WorldCom Management and the WorldCom Board on business strategy, acquisitions and investor relations.[109]

Although other analysts also gave WorldCom a 'strong buy' recommendation, Grubman's reports stood out 'in his rhetorical praise of the Company and in his projected Target Price for its stock, where he was consistently higher than others.'[110] Grubman maintained a 'buy' rating on WorldCom as it slid from $64.50 to $4.00, not downgrading it until one week before the WorldCom board ousted Bernard Ebbers in late April 2002.[111]

Grubman's behavior with regard to WorldCom was not unique. As the Wall Street Journal has reported, he remained 'wildly bullish on many telecommunications company clients of Salomon,' including Global Crossing Ltd., and Winstar Communications, as well as World-Com.[112] Of course, there was a reason for Grubman to remain loyal to SSB's clients: he was paid over $20 million a year for several years at the height of the bubble.[113]

Other securities analysts were paid far less and their employers had much less reason to remain loyal to WorldCom as it declined. But they also moved very slowly to downgrade WorldCom. The Bankruptcy Examiner prepared a schedule of the ratings of all analysts covering WorldCom, showing how they changed over time. Events went downhill quickly for WorldCom in early 2002. On March 11, 2002, WorldCom received a request from the SEC for information relating to its accounting procedures. As of this point, only one analyst (Jeffries & Co., a non-underwriting firm) had less than a buy recommendation on WorldCom (it had a hold).[114] Indeed SSB renewed its own 'buy' rating on March 12. On April 3, 2002, WorldCom announced that it was cutting 3,700 jobs in the U.S. or 6 percent of its staff; on April 22, 2002, Standard & Poor's downgraded WorldCom's credit ratings, and Moody's followed the next day. Only at this point did several firms, including SSB, reduce WorldCom to a 'hold' rating. Yet other firms still maintained a 'buy' rating. On April 30, the WorldCom board fired Ebbers, and on May 9 and 10, Moody's and Standard & Poor's, respectively, downgraded WorldCom's credit ratings to junk status. On May 13, Standard & Poor's removed WorldCom from its S & P 500

Index. Yet, on May 22, Robertson Stephens renewed its 'Strong Buy' recommendation. The Titanic had sunk, but it still received a 'buy' rating from its most loyal analysts.

4 *The Attorneys*   The role of attorneys in the WorldCom collapse has received little attention, but merits more. While there were no serious acts of commission, a pattern of passive omission characterizes the efforts of the attorneys conducting due diligence in connection with WorldCom's securities offerings. In 2000 and 2001, WorldCom made two enormous bond offerings, first a $5 billion offering in May 2000, and then a February 2001 offering of $11.9 billion in notes, which was 'the largest public debt offering in American history.'[115] In both offerings, SSB was the lead underwriter, along with J. P. Morgan Chase & Co.

In the case of the 2000 offering, a considerable time period existed during which counsel and the underwriters could have conducted due diligence. WorldCom filed its registration statement on April 12, 2000 and the date of the offering was May 24, 2000; in fact, this period is considerably longer than what is available in most public debt offerings. Thus, although time constraints can often preclude adequate due diligence, time was not a factor in the WorldCom offerings. Instead, the underwriters appear to have decided to take the business risk that the issuer was withholding material information. To be sure, this is the underwriters' choice, because while the Securities Act of 1933 contemplates a due diligence investigation, it does not mandate it.

Nonetheless, the federal district court hearing the WorldCom class action noted (with apparent surprise) how little due diligence was actually performed:

The only written record of due diligence performed by the Underwriter Defendants for the 2000 offering is a May 26 memorandum prepared by Cravath, Swaine & Moore ('Cravath'), counsel to the Underwriter Defendants. The memorandum reflects due diligence conducted from May 15 to May 23. It describes a May 17th telephone conversation in which Sullivan [WorldCom's CFO] was asked questions about the Sprint merger, whether WorldCom had experienced problems integrating either SkyTel or MCI, and whether there were any other material issues. In that conversation, Sullivan predicted overall growth for the year 2000 would be about 14%, represented that the proceeds for the 2000 offering would be used to repay 'commercial debt,' reported that WorldCom was experiencing a very competitive environment, but that there were no changes in that environment since 1999, and stated that there were no other material issues than the ones that he described in the call.[116]

That appears to have been it. Effectively, Sullivan handled the attorneys for the underwriters much as he would have handled a conference call with second-rank securities analysts—all generalities and few specifics. Yet, a $5 billion bond offering was a very large transaction. The underwriters appear to have relied almost exclusively on the audited financials and the 'comfort letter' that they were to receive from Arthur Andersen, which would cover WorldCom's more recent, unaudited financial statements. In the standard 'comfort letter,' the auditor opines that nothing had come to its attention that would require any material modifications in the issuer's unaudited financial statements. No serious attempt was made to inquire deeper, even though the WorldCom court found that a variety of 'red flags' were present.

By the time of the 2001 offering, WorldCom's situation had deteriorated; its stock price had fallen, and several of the underwriters who were commercial banks had downgraded their internal credit ratings for WorldCom (on a non-public basis).[117] Standard & Poor's had also publicly lowered WorldCom's rating.[118] Even more revealing, some of the underwriters participating in the bond offering had begun to hedge their own WorldCom positions as bank lenders, through the use of credit default swaps.[119] In short, the underwriters were marketing the issuer's debt securities, while simultaneously reducing their own exposure to the issuer's debt.

The 2001 $11.5 billion note offering was the largest public debt offering in history, but nothing special was done. Again, Cravath—possibly the pre-eminent firm in this field—represented the underwriters, and due diligence was conducted from April 19 through to May 16, 2001.[120] While this period was shorter than the time period in the 2000 offering, this roughly four-week interval still left substantial time for a factual investigation of the issuer. A written list of questions was given to WorldCom, and telephone calls were held with Sullivan, WorldCom's CFO, on April 30 and May 9. Finally, a separate telephone call on May 9 was conducted among the underwriters, their counsel, Andersen and WorldCom. In these calls, Sullivan

indicated that WorldCom was comfortable with the current earnings per share, that there were no issues that could affect the company's credit rating, and that the company had nothing material to disclose that had not been discussed with the investment bankers.[121]

Ironically, as of this time, Sullivan had already begun to capitalize WorldCom's line costs.[122] Clearly, the underwriters and attorneys could not have detected this change at this point. But Sullivan was not pressed in any respect in these discussions, despite a variety of recent reversals and S & P's downgrading.

Particularly symptomatic was the response when a problem did surface. Both J. P. Morgan and Cravath noted that Andersen's 'comfort letter' to the underwriters in the 2001 offering failed to give the same assurances as Andersen had given the underwriters in the 2000 offering. Although they were concerned, they were counseled by an SSB banker who 'advised against getting "too vocal" about it since "WorldCom's a bear to deal with on that subject." '[123] In short, the limited due diligence that was conducted appears to have been constrained by the need not to offend the client; the result was a process more perfunctory and formulaic than searching or investigative. To be sure, the underwriters and the attorneys did not suppress any information nor suspect any fraud, but neither did they search for it intensively. As a result, the federal district court hearing the WorldCom class action seems to have implicitly agreed with the plaintiffs' allegation that 'the underwriters did almost no investigation of WorldCom in connection with their underwriting of the bond offerings for the company....'[124]

How Was the WorldCom Fraud Discovered?

The answer is simple, but surprising: the company's internal auditors detected the fraud. WorldCom's capitalization of line costs began in April 2001 and continued through the first quarter of 2002.[125] In May 2002, when WorldCom's internal audit team began its 2002 audit of capital expenditures, it was confused by a new term 'prepaid capacity' that WorldCom managers used to explain the differences between two sets of schedules. The internal auditors had never previously heard this term, which referred to the capital account to which line costs were being transferred. In response, one member of the team—Eugene Morris—used a new software tool to determine how this 'prepaid capacity' account had been created and 'was able to uncover the transfer of line costs to capital accounts in a matter of hours.'[126] In fact, this discovery must have surprised senior management because the internal audit team had not been given access to the corporation's general ledger (precisely to prevent such detection). Thus, the software tool proved critical. But Morse testified that those having access to the WorldCom general ledger 'could also have uncovered the fraud.'[127] The bottom line then is that internal auditors quickly discovered what the outside auditors (who did have access to the general ledger) could not find for over a year. Interestingly, this story parallels a similar incident at Enron where the internal audit team uncovered unauthorized oil trading, which ultimately cost Enron millions in losses, only to see their investigation handed over to Andersen, which whitewashed the events in question.[128]

In fairness, there is no evidence that Andersen knew of the fraudulent capitalization. Nor is there any hard evidence that any other gatekeeper (even Mr Grubman) was willfully blind, but there is evidence that the gatekeepers did not investigate as closely as they might have, had they been better motivated. In particular, it is revealing that Scott Sullivan, World-Com's CFO, was confident that he could deceive his outside auditors, but yet backed away from a proposed merger with Verizon, because he feared that Verizon would conduct serious due diligence efforts that would discover his accounting irregularities.[129] Collectively, the gatekeepers at both Enron and WorldCom missed clues that more motivated actors—short sellers, Dynergy, and possibly Verizon—were able (or would have been able) to find. Their failings involved sins of omission, not commission. When a clear violation was placed before them, they did respond (for example, Andersen did require a restatement at Enron when it was shown that the '3 percent rule' governing special purpose entities had been violated). Yet, even though Andersen could accurately predict how a fraud would most likely occur at WorldCom,[130] it did not see fit to confirm its own hypothesis by inquiring further.

In short, to the extent that Enron and WorldCom are representative, the gatekeepers in these cases appear to have worn blinders. Although not active participants in fraud, they were indifferent watchdogs who conducted largely perfunctory investigations.

Endnotes

1. The size of a corporate bankruptcy is usually rated in terms of the bankrupt corporation's pre-bankruptcy assets. WorldCom, which filed for bankruptcy in July 2002, had $107 billion in such assets; Enron, which filed in December 2001, had $63 billion in pre-bankruptcy assets. By comparison, the third largest bankruptcy was Texaco in 1987, which listed only $36 billion in such assets. See Simon Romero and Riva D. Atlas, 'WorldCom's Collapse: The Overview; WorldCom files for Bankruptcy; Largest U.S. Case,' *New York Times*, July 22, 2002 at A-1.

2. See The Role of the Board of Directors in Enron's Collapse: Report Prepared by the Permanent Subcommittee on Investigations of the Committee on Governmental Affairs, United States Senate, 107th Congress, 2nd Session, Report 107–70 (July 8, 2002) (hereinafter, 'The Role of the Board of Directors in Enron's Collapse') at p 7.

3. See Paul M. Healy and Krishna G. Palepu, *The Fall of Enron*, 17 J. Econ. Perspectives 3 (Spring 2003) (hereinafter, 'The Fall of Enron').

4. Ibid. at 3. Fortune computed Enron's 2000 performance at an 89% return. See Bethany McLean, 'Is Enron Overpriced?', Fortune, March 5, 2001 at 122.

5. See Scott Sherman, 'Enron: Uncovering the Uncovered Story,' *Columbia Journalism Review*, March–April 2002 at 22. This article recites the various awards that Enron won and the uncritical, adoring praise that it received from the business and financial press. Fortune was not alone in its idolization of Enron. Business Week listed Ken Lay, Enron's CEO, on its 2001 list of '25 Top Managers.' Ibid.

6. See Kurt Eichenwald, Conspiracy of Fools (2005) at 623–625.

7. By 1990, 75% of gas sales between pipelines and their utility customers were conducted on a spot market basis. See The Fall of Enron at 5.

8. Ibid. at 7.

9. See The Role of the Board of Directors in Enron's Collapse at 7.

10. Ibid. at 8.

11. See The Role of the Board of Directors in Enron's Collapse at 8.

12. See The Fall of Enron at 11.

13. See The Fall of Enron at 13.

14. Ibid.

15. For a breakdown of the Enron board and their prior backgrounds, see The Role of the Board of Directors in Enron's Collapse at 1–2 and 9.

16. Ibid. at 11. The average compensation for an outside director at the top 200 U.S. corporations in 2000 was $138,747. See also Report of the Blue Ribbon Commission of the National Association of Corporate Directors (2001) at V.

17. See The Role of the Board of Directors in Enron's Collapse at 9–10.

18. See The Fall of Enron at 14.

19. See Kurt Eichenwald, n 6 above, at 34–37.

20. Ibid. at 36–37. Lay did demote one of the officers but saved his job despite clear evidence of embezzlement and fraud.

21. See Christine Earley, Kate Odabashian & Michael Willenborg, Symposium: Crisis in Confidence: Corporate Governance and Professional Ethics Post-Enron: *Some Thoughts on the Audit Failure at Enron, the Demise of Andersen and the Ethical Climate of Public Accounting Firms*, 35 Conn. L. Rev. 1013, 1029 (2003).

22. Ibid; see also Gary John Previts and Barbara Dubis Merino, A History of Accountancy in the Untited States: The Cultural Significance of Accounting (1998) at 310–311.

23. Earley, Odabashian, & Willengborg, n 21 above, at 1018–1019.

24. Ibid. at 1014; see also Stephen A. Zeff, *How the U.S. Accounting Profession Got Where It Is Today?: Part I*, 17 Accounting Horizons 189, 194 (Sept. 2003).

25. See John A. Byrne, 'Fall From Grace,' *Business Week*, August 12, 2002, at 53.

26. Ibid.

27. See Flynn McRoberts, et al., 'A Final Accounting: The Fall of Andersen: Greed Tarnished Golden Reputation,' *Chicago Tribune*, September 1, 2002 at §1, pp 1, 17.

28. See Earley, Odabashian and Willenborg, n 21 above, at 1022–1023.

29. See McRoberts, et al., n 27 above, at 16. Similar partner layoffs occurred at KPMG and Ernst & Young. See Earley, Odabashian and Willenborg, n 21 above, at 1017.

30. See Ken Brown & Ianthe Jeanne Dugan, 'Sad Account: Andersen's Fall From Grace Is a Tale of Greed and Miscues,' Wall St. J., June 7, 2002, at A-1.

31. See Earley, Odabashian and Willenborg, n 21 above, at 1023.

32. See Byrne, n 25 above, at 54; Tom Fowler & Julie Mason, 'Memos: Enron Muffled Auditor; Andersen Urged to Remove Critic,' *Houston Chronicle*, April 3, 2002 at A-1. See also Earley, Odabashian and Willenborg, n 21 above, at 1023.

33. See Mike McNamee et al., 'Out of Control at Andersen,' *Business Week*, April 8, 2002, at 33.

34. See Earley, Odabashian and Willenborg, n 21 above, at 1023.

35. Ibid. at 1024.

36. Ibid.

37. K. Eichenwald, n 6 above, at 426.

38. Ibid.

39. See The Fall of Enron at 15.

40. Ibid.

41. For a list, see Earley, Odabashian and Willenborg, n 21 above, at 1024.

42. In Waste Management, Andersen paid a total settlement of $107 million, including in June, 2001 a then record $7 million fine to the SEC. See *U.S. v. Arthur Andersen*, 374 F.3d 281 (5th Cir. 2004). In the Sunbeam case, it paid $110 million in May 2001, and finally in Baptist Foundation case, it settled for $217 million in May 2002. See Earley, Odabashian and Willenborg, n 21 above, at 1014 and n 3.

43. Ibid.

44. Theodore Eisenberg and Jonathan Macey, *Was Arthur Andersen Different? An Empirical Examination of Major Accounting Firm Audits of Large Clients*, 1 J. of Empirical Studies 263 (2004).

45. This author was the first to point out that, compared to its peer firms, Arthur Andersen had a slightly lower rate of financial statement restatements. While it audited 21% of 'Big Five' audit clients, its clients experienced only 15% of the restatements attributable to 'Big Five' clients between 1997 and 2001. See John Coffee, *Understanding Enron: 'It's About the Gatekeepers Stupid,'* 57 Business Lawyer 1403, 1406 n 16

(2002). Eisenberg and Macey have more fully examined this point and confirmed it. See Eisenberg and Macey, n 44 above.

46. Ross D. Fuerman, *Differentiating Between Arthur Andersen and the Surviving Big Four on the Basis of Auditor Quality: An Empirical Examination of the Decision to Criminally Prosecute Arthur Andersen,* (January 2005) (SSRN Working Paper id = 639644).

47. See The Fall of Enron at 19.

48. Ibid.

49. Ibid.

50. Ibid. at 20. Between January, 2001 and October, 2001 (when Enron announced its major restatement), analysts who worked for investment banks expected a 54% 12-month appreciation in Enron's stock price, while analysts who did not estimated only a 24% appreciation. In short, 'conflicted' analysts predicted more than double the price appreciation that 'unconflicted' analysts predicted.

51. The analysts who worked for investment banks that had no current banking relations with Enron actually had higher estimates of its likely 12-month stock price appreciation (62% versus 53%) compared to the analysts who worked for its current investment banks.

52. Bethany McLean, 'Is Enron Overpriced?', Fortune, March 5, 2001, at 122. The sub-caption to this article summarized its thesis succinctly: 'It's in a bunch of complex businesses. Its financial statements are nearly impenetrable. So why is Enron trading at such a huge multiple?' Ibid. Enron fought to prevent the publication of this article, and its officers met with Fortune's editors but mainly convinced the editors that they, themselves, were disingenuous and confused. See Eichenwald, n 6 above, at 422–425 (describing this visit).

53. See Eichenwald, n 6 above, at 182 to 186. His replacement at Merrill Lynch, Donato Eassey, immediately upgraded Enron (no dummy, he). Ibid. at 194.

54. In response to this problem, the SEC adopted Regulation FD in late 2000 to preclude selective disclosure to analysts, in part to preserve the independence of the analyst.

55. See The Fall of Enron at 16.

56. The term 'herding' was coined in a well-known 1990 article. See David Scharfstein & Jeremy Stein, *Herd Behavior and Investment,* 80 Am. Econ. Rev. 465 (1990). This topic is further discussed in Ch. 6.

57. See 'The Collapse of Enron: The Role Analysts Played and the Conflicts They Face', Hearings Before the Senate Committee on Governmental Affairs, 107th Congress, 2nd Session. (Feb. 27, 2002) (prepared testimony of Frank Torres, Legislative Counsel, Consumer's Union). The 17th analyst had a 'hold' recommendation on Enron.

58. See William C. Powers, Jr., Raymond S. Troubh, Herbert S. Winokur, Jr., Report of Investigation by the Special Investigative Committee of the Board of Directors of Enron Corporation (February 1, 2002) at 181–203.

59. Ibid. at 181.
60. Ibid.
61. Ibid. at 182.
62. Ibid.
63. Ibid. at 183.
64. Ibid.
65. Ibid. at 201.
66. Ibid. at 201–202.
67. Ibid. at 202.
68. See Claire Hill, *Regulating the Rating Agencies*, 82 Wash. U.L.Q. 43, 43 (2004).
69. Ibid. at 79.
70. Ibid. at 69 and n 124. Allegedly, former Secretary of the Treasury Robert Rubin, then Vice Chairman of Citigroup, made such an appeal to the Under-Secretary of the Treasury.
71. See Eichenwald, n 6 above.
72. Jonathan Laing, 'The Bear that Roared: How short-seller Jim Chanos helped expose Enron,' Barron's, January 28, 2002 at 18.
73. Ibid.
74. See McLean, n 52 above.
75. The fullest statement of Chanos's investigation of Enron and its dubious financial statements is contained in his testimony before the House Committee on Energy and Commerce. See 'Lessons Learned from Enron's Collapse: Auditing the Accounting Industry,' Hearings Before the Committee on Energy and Commerce, House of Representatives, 107th Congress, 2nd Session, Serial No. 107–83 (February 6, 2002) at 71–75.
76. See Jap Efendi, Michael R. Kinney and Edward P. Swanson, 'Can Short Sellers Predict Accounting Restatements?,' AAA 2005 FARS Meeting Paper, http://ssrn.com/abstract=591361 (2005). These authors used a sample of 565 firms with restatement disclosures, matched them with a control group of firms not announcing a restatement, and compared the level of the short interest. They concluded that the shorts were able to predict and profit from their anticipation of a restatement. See also, Hemang Desai, Srinivasan Krishnamurthy, Kumar Venkataraman, 'Do Short Sellers Target firms With Poor Earnings Quality?: Evidence From Earnings Restatements' (December 2004, http://ssrn.com/abstract=633283).
77. WorldCom's ratio of line costs to revenues was 43%, whereas AT&T's equivalent ratio appears to have been 46.8% and Sprint's was 53.8%. See *In re WorldCom Securities Litig.*, 2004 U.S. Dist. LEXIS 25155 at *137 n 47.
78. These facts are summarized in *In re WorldCom Securities Litig.*, 2004 U.S. Dist. Lexis 25155 (S.D.N.Y. Dec. 15, 2004) at *19 to *20.
79. Ibid. at *6.
80. Ibid.

81. Ibid. at *21.
82. Ibid.
83. Ibid. at *17.
84. Ibid at *18.
85. Andersen's audit team gave WorldCom its highest risk rating, recognizing that 'there was a "significant" risk of misstatements in the WorldCom financial statements....' See *In re WorldCom Sec. Litig.*, 2005 U.S. Dist. Lexis 710, (S.D.N.Y. January 18, 2005).
86. The committee of independent directors at WorldCom also included a former U.S. Attorney General (Nicholas Katzenbach) and was counseled by Wilmer, Cutler and Pickering (counsel to the Powers Committee) and assisted by PricewaterhouseCoopers. See Dennis R. Beresford, Nicholas deB. Katzenbach and C. B. Rogers, Report of Investigation By The Special Investigative Committee of the Board of Directors of WorldCom, Inc. (March 31, 2003) (hereinafter, 'WorldCom Special Committee Report').
87. See Third and Final Report of Dick Thornburgh, Bankruptcy Court Examiner, January 26, 2004, in *In re WorldCom Inc*, Ch. 11, Case No. 02-13533 (S.D.N.Y. 2004) (hereinafter, 'Bankruptcy Final Report').
88. See Final Report at 137–140. The number $116 million is the result of adding the acquisition fees and underwriting fees received by SSB that were listed on these pages. Additional fees of over $37.5 million were scheduled to be paid by WorldCom to SSB, but were forfeited when several large acquisitions were called off because of antitrust problems (e.g. Sprint and Nextel). Thus, on an ongoing basis, SSB had an even greater anticipated interest in WorldCom.
89. Ibid. at 140.
90. Ibid.
91. Ibid. at 141.
92. See *In re WorldCom Sec. Litig.*, 2004 U.S. Dist. Lexis 22992 (S.D.N.Y. Nov. 12, 2004).
93. See text and notes at nn 113 to 121 below.
94. Bankruptcy final Report at 19 ('The Examiner concludes that Arthur Andersen committed professional malpractice by negligently failing to carry out the kinds of substantive tests that were warranted by the risks of fraud and material misstatements Arthur Andersen identified, as well as by the existence of a number of "red flags" relating to the company's accounting practices.'). The WorldCom Special Committee Report acknowledges that Andersen was deceived by WorldCom personnel but still asserts that Andersen was negligent. See WorldCom Special Committee Report at 25–26.
95. See Bankruptcy Final Report at 19.
96. See WorldCom Special Committee Report at 25.
97. Ibid. at 26.

98. Ibid. In addition, this report specifically found that 'Andersen does not appear to have performed adequate testing to justify reliance on WorldCom's controls.' Ibid.

99. See *In re WorldCom Sec. Litig.*, 2005 U.S. Dist. Lexis 710 (S.D.N.Y. January 18, 2005).

100. Ibid. at *26.

101. Ibid.

102. Ibid.

103. Ibid. at 27.

104. 'Andersen last checked for top-side adjustments in 1999, and found none, or at least no questionable adjustments.' Ibid. Thereafter, Andersen 'simply accepted management's oral representations that no such adjustments had been made.' Ibid.

105. Ibid. at *27 to *28.

106. Bankruptcy Final Report at 345. Andersen had a specific goal for its non-audit business with WorldCom and the audit team was aware of, and discusses, that goal of achieving net fees (both audit and non-audit) of $18.5 million by 2001. Ibid. at 346. In fact, Andersen's total fees for audit and non-audit services went from $17,923,000 in 1999 to $26,688,000 in 2000, and then fell to $16,790,000 for 2001, as World-Com began to encounter difficulties. Ibid. at 346 n 320.

107. Ibid. at 346.

108. Ibid. at 347.

109. Ibid. at 113.

110. Ibid. at 128.

111. See Charles Gasparino, et al., 'Wild Card: Citigroup Now Has A New Worry: What Grubman Will Say,' Wall Street Journal, Oct. 10, 2002 at A-1.

112. See Charles Gasparino, 'Salomon Probe Includes Senior Executives,' Wall Street Journal, September 3, 2002, at C-1.

113. Ibid.

114. See Bankruptcy final Report, Appendix 7 ('WorldCom Analyst Reports – Ratings') at pp 1–6.

115. See *In re WorldCom Inc. Sec. Litig.*, 346 F. Supp. 2d 628, 650 (S.D.N.Y. 2004).

116. Ibid. at 647–648.

117. Ibid. at 650 (noting that both Bank of America and J. P. Morgan internally downgraded WorldCom just prior to this offering).

118. Ibid.

119. Ibid. at 651–652. J. P. Morgan in particular used this technique.

120. Ibid. at 652–653.

121. Ibid. at 653.

122. The capitalization of line costs began on April 20, 2001 when some $771 million was transferred from an expense account to a capital

account. Ibid. at 641. Days later, the first due diligence conference call was held on April 30. Ibid. at 653.

123. Ibid. at 654.
124. Ibid. at 634. The Court further noted that in other cases in which the underwriters were found to have satisfied their due diligence defense, they and their counsel had held as many as 20 meetings with the issuer's management. Ibid. at 676.
125. Ibid. at 642.
126. Ibid.
127. Ibid. at 642 n 15.
128. See text and notes at nn 19 to 20 above.
129. Scott Sullivan has recently testified at the criminal trial of Bernhard Ebbers that he advised Ebbers to call off merger talks with Verizon 'because if they proceeded further, WorldCom would have to show Verizon financial documents that could have revealed illegal accounting changes.' See Ken Belson, 'Key Witness On WorldCom Tells Jury He Broke Law,' *New York Times*, February 18, 2005 at C-3.
130. See text and notes at nn 102 to 105 above.

3

Explaining Gatekeeper Failure

Although the collapse of Enron and WorldCom make fascinating stories, they are, by themselves, just anecdotes. Alone, they are simply additional chapters in the long and spectacular history of business failure in the United States.[1] Yet, Enron and WorldCom do not stand alone; rather, they were the best-known examples in a sudden and massive eruption of financial irregularity that occurred at the end of the longest sustained bull market in U.S. history. Some firms failed, but more simply acknowledged the inflation of their financial results and then endured the painful process of stock market decline, managerial transition, and public and private litigation that follows once shareholders learn they have been misled. Surprisingly, all this occurred in the absence of any economic depression or major adverse macroeconomic change. Investors lost confidence in the market and re-evaluated stock prices downward because they learned that reported financial results could not be trusted—in part, because the gatekeepers had failed.

This chapter will seek to understand what broader forces caused gatekeepers to fail. It will begin with the aggregate evidence on financial irregularity and then turn to three leading explanations for that sudden failure. In overview, those explanations are:

1 *The decline in deterrence hypothesis.* During the 1990s, the legal threat facing gatekeepers for involvement in securities fraud declined dramatically. Suddenly less deterred by the threat of either private litigation or SEC enforcement, gatekeepers could more easily acquiesce in managerial efforts to inflate their corporation's reported results;

2 *The increased managerial pressure hypothesis.* During the 1990s, rapid changes in executive compensation made corporate managers far more interested in maximizing their firm's short-term stock market price—even if the resulting stock price spike could not be sustained for long. So incentivized, corporate managers found

ways to pressure or seduce their gatekeepers into acquiescence in
progressively riskier accounting policies; and

3 *The stock market bubble hypothesis.* In a bubble, investors lose their
skepticism, and may come to expect stock prices to escalate annually.
In this atmosphere of market euphoria, gatekeepers become irrelevant—or, even worse, shareholders reinforce the pressure on them
for the use of risky and/or improper accounting policies in order to
sustain hyperbolic earnings growth. Caught between the pressure of
managers and stockholders for constantly increasing profits, auditors
and analysts may learn to tell their audience what they want to hear.

All these stories are, of course, complementary. If, for example,
auditors confronted at the same time increased benefits from managers
eager to seduce them and reduced legal costs as a result of deregulation,
then their willingness to acquiesce in financial irregularity should predictably increase, as should the aggregate amount of such irregularity.
As will be seen next, that aggregate amount soared.

The Crescendo of Financial Irregularity in the 1990s

Publicly-held companies in the United States are required by the
federal securities laws to file an annual disclosure document, known as
the Form 10-K, with the SEC, which document must contain financial
statements certified by an independent public accountant. In addition,
quarterly reports, known as the Form 10-Q, containing uncertified
financial statements, must also be filed after the end of the fiscal year's
first three quarters. In effect, these rules convert the independent public accountant into a mandatory gatekeeper.

Now, suppose the corporation does something improper: for example,
it fails to close its books at year's end and instead keeps including revenues
received in January of the next year in the prior year's revenues—in order
to meet its previously announced earnings estimate.[2] This impropriety
could initially escape the independent accountant's attention, but it will
have a distorting effect on future years. For example, unless the corporation again fails to close its books on time in the next year, it will have
only eleven months earnings to report, resulting in an earnings shortfall.
Predictably, it will be driven to again extend the covert closing date for its
fiscal year beyond the year's end to make up this shortfall. Eventually, the
fraud will be caught—in large part because otherwise the company is facing the hopeless prospect of greater and greater distortions.

Experience with financial statement restatements suggests that most
result from marginal practices that are not necessarily fraudulent at the

outset, 'but in time they become increasingly questionable until finally someone steps over the line.'[3] At this point, under duress, the company will restate its financial statements, publicly acknowledging that the prior financial statements (whether annual or quarterly) were inaccurate. This step may be taken at the company's own volition, at the insistence of the auditor (who otherwise threatens to resign and disaffirm its prior certification), or in response to prodding by the SEC.

This step will, however, not be taken lightly and may encounter stiff resistance from corporate management, because restatements tend to trigger stock drops, class action lawsuits, and SEC investigations. In addition, shareholder or regulatory pressure may cause the board to replace some financial executives. Hence, corporations do not lightly restate their financial statements, because such restatements are stigmatizing. As a result, financial statement restatements serve as a good proxy for the incidence of fraud. A year-to-year plotting of financial statement restatements provides us with a fever chart roughly indicating managerial willingness to engage in financial irregularity.[4]

In this light, it is revealing that financial statement restatements soared during the last half of the 1990s. Although individual studies use different measures and produce somewhat different results, the overall data is remarkably consistent. One such initial study conducted in 2001 by Moriarty and Livington, found that the number of earnings restatements by publicly-held corporations averaged 49 per year from 1990 to 1997, next increased to 91 in 1998, and then skyrocketed to 150 and 156 in 1999 and 2000, respectively.[5] A fuller study conducted by the United States General Accounting Office in October 2002, examined all financial statement restatements (not just earnings restatements) and also found a similarly sharp, discontinuous spike in 1999 that continued through 2002.[6] The GAO Study's data (Figure 3.1) shows the following trend line:[7]

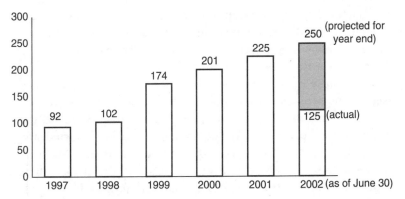

Figure 3.1   Total number of restatement announcements identified, 1997–2002

Even these numbers may understate the hyperbolic rate of increase, as later studies have found even higher numbers of restatements.[8] A skeptic might object that such a trend line could be misleading. After all, not all restatements are equal. Some may involve small, infrequently traded companies or involve only trivial changes or trigger only modest stock price reactions, while others may be on a scale with Enron or WorldCom. In fact, some restatements over this period actually involved increases in earnings, rather than declines. Given this potential diversity of restatements, it is necessary to focus more precisely on financial statement restatements by companies listed on the NYSE, Amex, and Nasdaq, thereby excluding smaller companies that trade only on regional exchanges or over the counter. Between 1997 and 2001, the proportion of listed companies on the NYSE, Amex and Nasdaq that restated their financial statement approximately tripled, increasing from less than 0.89 percent in 1997 to approximately 2.5 percent in 2001.[9]

Most importantly, the GAO Study found that from January 1997 to June 2002, approximately '10 percent of all listed companies announced at least one restatement.'[10] On this basis, Enron and WorldCom do not look like deviant outliers; nor can such a high incidence of irregularity be dismissed by corporate apologists as a 'few bad apples.' Something more systematic was in progress. Particularly noteworthy was the fact that the size (in terms of market capitalization) of the typical restating company rose rapidly over this period.[11] Indeed, in 2002, companies listed on the NYSE or Nasdaq accounted for over 85 percent of all restatements identified in that year.[12] Hence, restatements no longer reflected mistakes made by small, new or inexperienced companies (as they had in the past), but instead indicated behavioral changes and increased risk-taking at large, mature firms.

Still, a thorough-going skeptic could argue that the increase in restatements might be more the product of changed behavior by regulators. Arguably, as regulators tightened their rules, more restatements followed. For a time, the accounting industry made this argument. But the premise of this argument is undercut if the market is surprised by the restatement and reacts with a sharply downward price movement. Here, the GAO Study found that restating companies over the 1997 to 2001 period suffered an immediate market-adjusted stock price decline equal to 10 percent on average of the restating firm's market capitalization, measured on the basis of the stock's three-day price movement, from the trading day before the announcement through the trading day after the announcement.[13] Between 1997 to 2002, restating firms lost over $100 billion in market capitalization just over this three-trading day period surrounding a restatement announcement.[14] In short, even if there were some trivial restatements caused by increased regulatory formalism,[15] the typical restatement surprised the market. Although 'technical' restatements may have been made simply to comply with the SEC's new activism on earnings management,[16] these should have produced only an indifferent yawn from the stock market. Instead, an average market drop of 10 percent following a restatement clearly shows that the market was on average keenly disappointed.[17]

The available data shows that, during the late 1990s, the magnitude of the typical financial restatement increased, both in absolute terms (nearly doubling) and as a percentage of the issuer's rapidly increasing market capitalization.[18] This suggests that managers became progressively willing over this period to take greater risks. Moreover, as the decade of the 1990s wore on, earnings restatements increasingly began to be experienced by large, mature, publicly-held firms, rather than by smaller, or newly public, companies that might be expected to be more inexperienced or rash.

The GAO Study's data corroborates this picture of managerial behavior changing over the 1990s, because it shows a significant change in the cause of restatements. Although there are many reasons why a company may restate its financial statements (e.g. to adjust costs or expenses, revalue assets, or to recognize liabilities), one particular reason dominated during the period from 1997 to 2002. The GAO study found that revenue recognition issues accounted for almost 39 percent of the 919 announced restatements that it identified over the 1997 to 2002 period.[19] In effect, attempts by management to prematurely recognize income had become the most common cause of restatements. Earlier in the decade and during prior decades, earnings management was more a game of 'smoothing out' the peaks and valleys in a corporation's income flow in order to reduce the apparent volatility in the corporation's returns. Thus, managements characteristically held back 'excess earnings,' hiding them in 'rainy day reserves,' in order to use such funds later to smooth out any subsequent declines in the firm's earnings.

Despite this earlier preference for income-smoothing, by the end of the 1990s, managers at these same firms were robbing future periods for earnings that could be recognized immediately. In short, 'income smoothing' gave way to more predatory behavior. Symptomatically, restatements involving revenue recognition produced disproportion-ately larger stock market declines.[20] In particular, the market responded more negatively to revenue recognition restatements than to any other form of restatement.[21] Seemingly, the market feared revenue-timing restatements because of the apparent signal they carried that reported earnings could not be trusted. Yet, despite the market's antipathy for them, revenue recognition restatements became the most common form of restatement. At a minimum, this suggests that the interests of man-agement and shareholders were not well aligned, and that gatekeepers became progressively less able to serve shareholders, who deeply feared revenue recognition errors.

Explaining the Changes in Gatekeeper Behavior

If restatements rose so rapidly, some deeper cause must explain this phenomenon. Three complimentary explanations all seem highly plausible.

1 The Under-Deterred Gatekeeper   This deterrence hypothesis focuses on the decline in the expected liability costs that faced auditors who were considering whether or not to acquiesce in aggressive accounting policies favored by managers. Prior to the 1990s, auditors faced a very real risk of civil liability, principally from class action litigation.[22] How did the legal risks decrease during the 1990s? The list of legal changes is lengthy, but all were in the same direction of reducing the legal threat. Among the most important were:

1 The Supreme Court's 1991 decision in *Lampf, Pleva, Lipkind, Prupis & Petigrow v. Gilbertson*,[23] which significantly shortened the statute of limitations applicable to securities fraud;[24]
2 The Supreme Court's 1994 decision in *Central Bank of Denver, N.A. v. First Interstate Bank of Denver*,[25] which eliminated private 'aiding and abetting' liability in securities fraud cases;[26]
3 The Private Securities Litigation Reform Act of 1995 (PSLRA), which:
   (a) raised the pleading standards for securities class actions to a level well above that applicable to fraud actions generally;[27]
   (b) substituted proportionate liability for 'joint and several' liabi-lity;[28]

(c) restricted the sweep of the RICO statute so that it could no longer convert securities fraud-class actions for compensatory damages into actions for treble damages;[29] and

(d) adopted a very protective safe harbor for forward-looking information;[30] and

4 The Securities Litigation Uniform Standards Act of 1998 (SLUSA), which abolished state court class actions alleging securities fraud.[31]

Although the rapid succession of these developments prevents us from calculating their individual impacts, their aggregate impact is easily susceptible to measurement. The available data shows that class-action plaintiffs virtually ceased suing secondary defendants (such as auditors) during the latter half of the 1990s. Following the passage of the PSLRA in 1995, Congress instructed the SEC to undertake a study of the legislation's apparent impact on securities litigation.[32] As its baseline, the SEC study began with the number of audit-related suits filed against the then Big Six accounting firms from 1990 to 1992.[33] For those three years, the relevant numbers were 192, 172, and 141, respectively.[34] In 1996, however, the first year following the passage of the PSLRA, the SEC found that, out of the total of 105 securities-class actions filed in that year, accounting firms were named in only six cases, corporate counsel in zero cases, and underwriters in nineteen cases.[35] It thus concluded that '[s]econdary defendants, such as accountants and lawyers, are being named much less frequently in securities class actions.'[36]

Corroborating this picture is another source of evidence. Accounting studies have found that in the early 1990s, the major auditors adopted increasingly cautious risk-management policies to reduce their exposure to litigation; in particular, they adjusted their client portfolios to eliminate riskier clients.[37] But once the auditors' legal exposure was reduced by the passage of the PSLRA, they reversed themselves, and risk-management policies were relaxed, resulting in riskier client portfolios and less conservative reporting strategies in the late 1990s. In short, litigation exposure and accounting conservatism seem to be positively correlated.

To evaluate litigation exposure and how it changed during the 1990s, one must also consider the likelihood of public enforcement. Here, the unique fact about the 1990s is that the prospect of both public and private enforcement declined simultaneously. From some point in the 1980s until the late 1990s, the SEC shifted its enforcement focus away from actions against the Big Five accounting firms towards other priorities.[38] These other priorities included Internet fraud, which boomed in the early 1990s, insider trading, penny stock fraud, and limited partnership syndications. This shift was partly a product of the high cost of suing a major accounting firm. During the 1990s, the SEC's budget was largely frozen by an increasingly conservative Congress, and the SEC had to husband a small budget that was increasingly dwarfed by an exponentially growing stock market. The collective impact of these changes was to reduce the risk of liability for auditors. Indeed, auditors were the special beneficiaries of many of these statutory changes. For example, the pleading rules and the new standard of proportionate liability introduced by the PSLRA protected them far more than it did most corporate defendants.[39] Even though auditors continued to be sued, the number of suits declined and, more importantly, the settlement value of cases against auditors decreased significantly in the wake of these developments.[40]

2 Increased Managerial Pressure: The Impact of Equity Compensation   Not only did the deterrent threat facing gatekeepers weaken during the 1990s, but even more importantly the pressures on them to acquiesce in dubious or risky accounting policies increased. This increased pressure was a product of a fundamental shift in executive compensation in the United States during the 1990s. Executive compensation changed dramatically and rapidly during the 1990s, shifting from being primarily cash-based to being primarily equity-based. In 1990, only 8 percent of the total compensation of a chief executive of a large industrial corporation included within the S & P index was paid in equity, but by 2001, equity-based compensation had risen to approximately two-thirds of the median annual compensation of such a chief executive.[41] Figure 3.2 shows the swiftness of this transition.[42]

Another measure of this shift is the growth in stock options. Over the decade of the 1990s, stock options rose from 5 percent of shares outstanding at major U.S. companies to 15 percent—a 300 percent increase.[43] The value of these options rose by an even greater percentage and over a dramatically shorter period: from $50 billion in 1997, in the case of the 2,000 largest corporations to $162 billion in 2000—an over 300 percent rise in three years.[44] Stock options create an obvious and potentially perverse incentive to engage in short-run, rather than long-term, stock price maximization because executives can exercise their stock options and sell the underlying shares on the same day.[45] To illustrate the impact of this change, assume a CEO holds options on two million shares of his company's stock and the company is trading at a price-to-earnings ratio of 30 to 1 (both reasonable

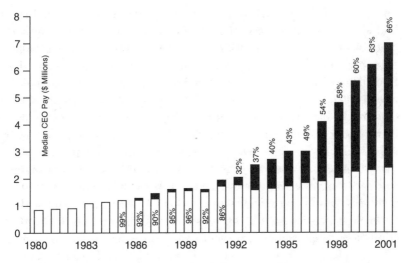

Figure 3.2   CEO compensation at S & P index companies, 1980–2001
Source: Brian J. Hall, Harvard Business School.

assumptions for this era). On this basis, if the CEO can cause the 'premature' recognition of revenues that result in an unexpected increase in annual
earnings by simply $1 per share, the CEO has caused a $30 price increase
that should make him $60 million richer. No small incentive!

Obviously, when one pays the CEO with stock options, one creates incentives for short-term financial manipulation and accounting
gamesmanship. Indeed, financial economists have found a strong statistical correlation between higher levels of equity compensation and both
earnings management and financial restatements. One recent study by
Efendi, Srivastava and Swanson utilized a control group methodology
and constructed two groups of companies, each composed of 100 listed
public companies.[46] The first group's members had restated their financial statements in 2001 or 2002, while the control group was composed
of otherwise similar firms that had not restated. What characteristic
most distinguished the two groups? The leading factor that proved to
influence most the likelihood of a restatement was the presence of a
substantial amount of 'in the money' stock options in the hands of the
firm's CEO. The CEOs of the firms in the restating group held on average 'in the money' options of $30.9 million, while CEOs in the non-
restating control group averaged only $2.3 million—a nearly 14 to 1
difference.[47] Further, if a CEO held options equaling or exceeding 20
times his or her annual salary (and this was the 80th percentile in their
study—meaning that a substantial number of CEOs did exceed this
level), the likelihood of a restatement increased by 55 percent.

Other studies have reached similar results. Denis, Hanouna, and Sarin find a significant positive relationship between a firm's use of option-based compensation and securities fraud allegations being leveled against the firm.[48] Further, they find in their study of 358 companies charged with fraud between 1993 and 2002 that the likelihood of a fraud charge is positively related to 'option intensity'—namely, the greater the amount of the options, the higher the likelihood.[49] Similarly, Cheng and Warfield have documented that corporate managers with high equity incentives who sell more shares in subsequent periods, are more likely to report earnings that just meet or exceed analysts' forecasts, and more frequently engage in other forms of earnings management.[50] As stock options increase the managers' equity ownership, they also increase their need to diversify the high risk associated with such ownership. This produces both more efforts to inflate earnings to prevent a stock price decline, and increased sales by managers in advance of any earnings decline. In short, there is a 'dark side' to option-based compensation for senior executives: absent special controls, more options means more fraud.

The hidden problem here is not that stock options provide excessive compensation, but that they provide excessive liquidity.[51] This excess liquidity was, in turn, partially the product of deregulatory reform at the SEC in the early 1990s, which relaxed the rules under Section 16(b) of the Securities Exchange Act of 1934 to permit officers and directors to exercise stock options and sell the underlying shares without holding the shares for the previously required six-month period.[52] Thus, executives could view stock options as the equivalent of cash, because they were not required to bear the risk of holding the underlying stock for even six months. As a result, even a short-term inflation of the stock price that could not be sustained for long could still benefit the firm's executives—if they exercised their options and sold the stock (as they commonly did).

3 Applying Pressure: The New Techniques of the 1990s   If corporate managers had greater reason to pressure their gatekeepers (and particularly their auditors) into accepting dubious accounting policies, it still remains open to question whether they could do so successfully. This problem is subtler than it first sounds. A public corporation cannot lightly fire its auditor, because SEC rules require the issuer to explain any disagreement with the auditor that arose during the two fiscal years prior to the auditor's dismissal or resignation (and then permit the auditor to comment on the issuer's explanation).[53] These rules effectively empower the auditor, because if the real dispute is over a risky accounting policy and the auditor is fired or resigns, the issuer must give a public explanation. In turn, the auditor has every incentive to disclose its view of the truth in response to an issuer's self-serving claim that dismissal was the result of excessive fees. Still, if the issuer cannot easily threaten the auditor, it can attempt to seduce it with highly lucrative consulting contracts. Bribes work better than threats for a variety of reasons, beginning with the fact that they trigger no special disclosure obligation. Indeed, a key advantage of this approach is that the issuer can suspend the flow of highly lucrative consulting income to the audit firm at any time and without disclosure, thereby outflanking the SEC's attempt to protect auditor independence with disclosure.

Nor did issuers have to struggle to interest auditors in consulting income. The 1990s were the decade in which the major accounting firms learned how to use their auditing role to cross-sell consulting services. Prior to the mid-1990s, the provision by audit firms of consulting services to their audit clients appears to have been infrequent and insubstantial in the aggregate.[54] But by 2002, the typical large public corporation had come to pay its auditor an amount for consulting services that was typically three times what it paid the same firm for audit services.[55] Given the rapidity of this shift and its coincidence with the transition in executive compensation that made senior executives intensely more interested in maximizing reported earnings, it is a tempting inference that one purpose of directing consulting income to the firm's auditors was to induce them to defer to management on issues of accounting policy. Consider again the hypothetical CEO who has options on two million shares of his firm's stock, which is trading at a price/earnings ratio of 30 to 1. An additional dollar of earnings per share seemingly makes him $60 million richer. Would he be willing to spend shareholders' money on unnecessary but lucrative consulting contracts to obtain this additional dollar of earnings? In truth, the empirical evidence does not clearly corroborate this hypothesis that consulting income was used as a bribe,[56] but it certainly leaves open the possibility that such inducements were sometimes used in this fashion.

Another interpretation seems superior to this simple theory that consulting revenues were used by managers as a bribe to secure auditor acquiescence. Although some studies have found that an audit firm that received high consulting revenues from its audit client was more likely to acquiesce in earnings management,[57] more recent studies have reached inconsistent results, generally failing to find any pronounced relationship between the receipt of consulting income and involvement in earnings management.[58] At best, the evidence seems inconclusive.[59] Where then are we left? A very plausible answer is that the foregoing studies are measuring the wrong potential conflict. The common methodology in these studies has been to identify a proxy variable (typically, a high ratio of non-audit fees to audit fees) and then investigate whether corporate issuers with this characteristic experienced a disproportionate number of restatements or other indications of earnings management. Underlying this approach is the assumption that an audit firm might be rigorous and skeptical towards a firm that did not pay it high non-audit fees, but very flexible and acquiescent toward a client that did. But, whether or not this happened, these studies cannot disprove a subtler hypothesis. That subtler and more plausible hypothesis is that the prospect of consulting income caused the auditor to bend the rules for both sets of clients. Put differently, if accounting firms were intent on maximizing consulting revenues, they should be prepared to acquiesce to the demands of any client in a position to potentially direct consulting business to them. Thus, a comparison between clients with a high ratio of consulting-to-audit income and clients with a low such ratio wholly misses this danger that the audit firm was increasingly acquiescing to the demands of both.

In short, the alternative hypothesis is that the real conflict lies not in the actual receipt of high fees, but in their expected receipt. Even the client currently paying low consulting revenues to its auditor might reverse this pattern if the auditor proved more cooperative. The case for this alternative hypothesis begins from the fact that the accounting industry is an extremely concentrated one (with today only four major firms). These firms are necessarily aware of their principal rivals' business models and strategies, and a tendency to consciously follow parallel paths is likely.[60] In common, these firms all changed their business strategy in the 1990s to move in the direction of becoming diversified conglomerates that offered a broad range of financial consulting services. The key attraction of this strategy was that accounting firms were uniquely positioned so that they could use auditing as a portal of entry by which to cross-sell other more lucrative consulting services to their audit clients. Unlike other consulting firms (for example, management consultants), auditors necessarily had the attention of the chief financial officer who had to be in constant contact with them; thus, having a captive audience, auditors were better positioned to cross-sell other services than was an outsider offering the same services.

Audit firms also knew that auditing revenues would continue to be relatively flat, while consulting revenues in other fields (particularly in respect to software and computer networks) could grow exponentially. Thus, they changed their business model, using incentive fees to encourage the audit partner to market the firm's consulting services and sometimes pricing their audit services virtually on a 'loss leader' basis. These changes are detailed more fully in Chapter 5, but the relevant point here is that major changes were instituted on an across-the-board basis, and not selectively in terms of individual or special clients. Senior management of the Big Five informed their audit partners that they were expected (and would be compensated in terms of their ability) to market consulting services.

Given this transition, a client who was not currently paying consulting revenues represented an unfulfilled opportunity, and the anticipation of consulting revenues produced the same conflict as did their actual receipt. As a result, studies that show little difference in the likelihood of earnings management or financial statement restatements, based on the actual receipt of consulting revenues, prove little and are actually consistent with this latter hypothesis under which the expectation of consulting income compromises the auditor.

4 The Market Bubble Story   A final causal explanation for gatekeeper failure posits that Enron's and WorldCom's downfalls, and the host of other sudden stock collapses in 2001 to 2002, can be seen as the consequence of a classic bubble that overtook the equity markets in the late 1990s and produced a market euphoria.[61] But what exactly is the connection between a market bubble and gatekeeper failure? Here, a hypothesis needs to be advanced that cannot be rigorously proven, but that is consistent with modern behavioral economics: in a bubble, gatekeepers become less relevant and hence experience a decline in both their leverage over their client and the value of their reputational capital. That is, in an atmosphere of market euphoria, investors rely less on gatekeepers, and managements in turn regard them as more a formality than a necessity. Gatekeepers provide a critical service only when investors are cautious and skeptical and therefore rely on their services. Conversely, in a market bubble, caution and skepticism are by definition suspended or even abandoned. In such an environment, auditors continue to be used, but this is more because SEC rules mandate their use than that investors demand their use. As a result, because gatekeepers have reduced relevance in such an environment, they also have reduced leverage with their clients. For example, if we assume that the auditor will be largely ignored by euphoric investors, the rational auditor's best competitive strategy (at least for the short term) is to become as acquiescent and low cost as possible.

The key element in this story involves the question of why investors cease to care about the gatekeeper's reputation. After all, the rise of auditing as a profession in the 19th century was originally the product of investors' own concerns about fraud and irregularity, not regulatory requirements. What then caused this concern to weaken? Here, behavioral economics supplies a plausible answer. Modern economics recognizes that individuals, including investors, have 'bounded rationality' and do not pursue all information relevant to an optimal decision.[62] The Nobel Prize-winning research of Professors Kahneman and Tversky has in particular demonstrated that individuals typically make decisions by using heuristics—that is, rules of thumb—rather than by incorporating all obtainable information. A heuristic that they find to be pervasively used by individuals and that has particular relevance to the context of securities markets is the 'availability heuristic.'[63] It asserts that individuals estimate the frequency of an event by recalling recent instances of its occurring (even if these instances are normally rare or infrequent, when viewed from a longer term perspective). Hence, if the stock market has recently experienced extraordinary returns for several years, it becomes predictable that individuals will overestimate the likelihood of such extraordinary gains continuing.[64] In effect, there is a status quo or persistence bias: what has recently occurred is expected to continue. Thus, as the market soared in the early and mid-1990s, investors, operating on heuristics, came to assume that this pattern would continue. Further aggravating this tendency is the deep-seated bias displayed by many individuals towards optimism in predicting future events.[65]

Thus, from the perspective of behavioral economics, 'bubbles' are not irrational moments of speculative excess or frenzy, but are more the product of the predictable expectations of individuals who tend to assume that whatever has recently occurred will persist. To trigger this persistence bias, it is arguably only necessary that market returns have in fact been extraordinary for a few successive years in order to cause investors to treat this phenomenon as normal and likely to continue. Such an explanation helps us understand why bubbles have re-occurred throughout history. Their re-occurrence is explained less by the hypothesis that investors are inherently gullible than by the explanation that a period of extraordinary returns creates an expectation that such returns are normal and will persist.

If one accepts (even to a degree) this premise of a persistence bias, it is clear that the 1990s represent a unique period in which market returns had climbed exponentially for a record length of time. Assessing this era, Yale economist, Robert Shiller, points out that the Dow Jones Industrial Average stood at 3,600 in early 1994, but by 1999, it had passed 11,000, and by early 2000 it peaked at around 11,700.[66] Indeed, from a longer-term perspective, he observes that the stock market had risen 'fairly uniformly ever since it bottomed out in July, 1982.'[67] Eighteen straight years of a rising market could make even the most rational investors unduly optimistic and cause them to suspend disbelief.

The impact of a market bubble is not limited to the heuristic biases it creates in investors; it also directly impacts the gatekeepers. For one gatekeeper—the securities analyst—a market bubble presents a special challenge: during a bubble, those who are cautious and prudent will be outperformed by those who recklessly predict extraordinary returns. Hence, in a bubble, extreme optimism for analysts becomes less a heuristic bias than a competitive necessity. Put more bluntly, it is dangerous to be sane in an insane world. As a result, the securities analyst who prudently predicted reasonable growth and stock appreciation during the 1990s was increasingly left in the dust by the investment guru who prophecized a new investment paradigm in which revenues and costs were less important than the number of 'hits' on a website. As will be seen in Chapter 7, these pressures could result in the phenomenon of 'herding'—under which analysts protect themselves by concurring with the consensus of the 'herd,' rather than expressing their own individual views.

Institutional factors further compounded this problem. As the initial public offering (or IPO) market soared in the 1990s, securities analysts became celebrities and valuable assets to their firms; indeed, they became the principal means by which investment banks competed for IPO clients, as the underwriter with the most popular 'star' analyst could produce the greatest first day stock price spike in an IPO. But as their salaries thus soared, analyst compensation came increasingly from the investment banking side of their firms. Hence, just as in the case of the auditor, the analyst's economic advancement required the subordination of the analyst's professional values to the firm's interest in satisfying its major clients.

Conclusion

This chapter has explained that during the 1990s the cost of acquiescence went down for gatekeepers, while the benefits went up. In response, financial irregularity, as measured by financial statement restatements, soared. In such an environment, the gatekeeper's natural desire to preserve its reputational capital could diminish. Either the gatekeeper could willingly risk that capital for high short-term returns, or the gatekeeper could decide that the value of this capital had simply declined in a bubble (and thus could not justify the same level of zealous protection if it cost the firm clients).

To present this hypothesis that reputational capital can cease to be protected is not to consider it proven, but it is to set the stage for a more intensive examination of each of these gatekeepers in later chapters.

Endnotes

1. For an overview of America's most spectacular business failures, see David Skeel, Icarus in the Boardroom: The Fundamental flaws in Corporate America and Where They Came From (2005).
2. This is an example of a 'revenue recognition timing' error, which became the most common form of accounting irregularity in the 1990s. Daniel Dooley, an expert on forensic accounting at PricewaterhouseCoopers, describes the typical 'revenue recognition timing manipulation' as follows:

   The situation usually involves (a) pressure to meet revenue targets as the accounting period (i.e. quarter) comes to a close; (b) a known or expected short-fall of sales transactions actually consummated through period-end; (c) the potential existence of sales that are expected to be consummated shortly after the period-end; (d) opportunity—either unilaterally or in collusion with the customer (i.e. counter-parties)—to alter the dating of these post period-end transactions in order to make such transactions appear to have been consummated prior to the period-end close of business.... A necessary result of any such "timing" accounting irregularity is that the current accounting period "borrows" revenues from the next period or periods, thus starting off these subsequent periods "in the hole." If these next periods also are beleaguered by flat or declining actual sales ..., then even more premature revenue recognition accounting irregularities will be needed ....

   See Daniel V. Dooley, *Financial Fraud: Accounting Theory and Practice*, 8 Fordham J. Corp. & Fin. L. 53, 64–65 (2002).

3. See Michael R. Young, Accounting Irregularities and Financial Fraud: A Corporate Governance Guide (2000).
4. The term 'restatement' is defined by Accounting Principal Board Opinion No. 20 as any restatement of financial statements that was the result of error, thus excluding restatements due to changes in accounting principles. The studies discussed in this chapter count only restatements that resulted from errors, not permissible changes in accounting principles.
5. See Moriarty and Livingston, *Quantitative Measures of the Quality of Financial Reporting*, 17 Financial Executive 53, 54 (July/August 2001).
6. See United States General Accounting Office, Report to the Chairman, Committee on Banking, Housing, and Urban Affairs, U.S. Senate, Financial Statement Restatements: Trends, Market Impacts, Regulatory

Responses and Remaining Challenges (October 2002) (GAO-03–138) at 4–5 (hereinafter, 'GAO Study').

7. See GAO Study at 15. Although the results for 2002 are only estimated in this study, the later Huron Consulting Group found 330 restatements in 2002. See n 8 below.

8. A more recent study by the Huron Consulting Group finds an even higher rate of restatements: 216 in 1999; 233 in 2000; 270 in 2001; 330 in 2002, and 220 in 2003. On this basis, roughly one-in-eight publicly-held companies restated their financial statements. See Huron Consulting Group, *2003 Annual Review of Financial Reporting Matters*, at 4. The number of restatements fell modestly to 323 in 2004, but has since risen again. If one wishes to focus only on restatements of annual financial statements (and thereby exclude quarterly statements), Huron Consulting found these numbers to be: 2000: 98; 2001: 140; 2002: 183; 2003: 206; 2004: 253. See Press Release 'New Report by Huron Consulting Group Reveals Financial Statements Increased at a Record Level in 2004' (January 19, 2005).

9. See GAO Study at 4.

10. Ibid. However, this figure rises to around 12.5% (or one-in-eight) if one instead relies on the Huron Consulting Group's study. See Huron Consulting Group, n 8 above.

11. Specifically, the average (median) size by market capitalization of a restating company rose from $500 million ($143 million) in 1997 to $2 billion ($351 million) in 2002. See GAO Study at 4.

12. Of the 125 actual restatements identified through mid-2002, 54 were listed on Nasdaq, and 53 were listed on the NYSE (for a total of 107 or 85% of all restatements). Ibid.

13. Ibid. at 5. The GAO Study also found a longer term market-adjusted decline of 18% over the period from 60 trading days before the announcement to 60 trading days after the announcement. Ibid. at 29.

14. Ibid. at 28.

15. Accounting firms have sometimes attempted to explain this increase in restatements on the basis that the SEC tightened the definition of 'materiality' in the late 1990s. This explanation is not convincing, in part because the principal SEC statement that tightened the definition of materiality—Staff Accounting Bulletin No. 99—was issued in mid-1999, after the number of restatements had already begun to soar in 1998. Also, SAB No. 99 did not truly mandate restatements, but only advised that any rule of thumb employed by auditors and issuers that assumed that amounts under 5% were inherently immaterial could not be applied reflexively. See Staff Accounting Bulletin No. 99, 64 F.R. 45150 (August 19, 1999).

16. The SEC's prioritization of earnings management as a principal enforcement target can be approximately dated to SEC Chairman Arthur Levitt's now famous speech on the subject in 1998. See Arthur

Levitt, 'The Numbers Game, Remarks at NYU Center for Law and Business' (Sept. 28, 1998).

17. See text and notes at nn 13 to 14 above.

18. According to Moriarty and Livingston, n 5 above, companies that restated earnings suffered market losses of $17.7 billion in 1998, $24.2 billion in 1999, and $31.2 billion in 2000. Ibid. at 55. Expressed as a percentage of the overall capitalization of the market (which was ascending hyperbolically over this period), these losses for 1998 through 2000 came to 0.13%, 0.14% and 0.19%, respectively, of market capitalization. Although these percentages are much lower than those found by the GAO study, the losses still increased significantly over this period.

19. See GAO Study, n 6 above, at 5. Revenue recognition was also the leading reason for restatements in each individual year over this period. Ibid.

20. While revenue recognition restatements accounted for 39% of restatements over the 1997 to 2002 period, they were associated with $56 billion (or roughly 56%) of the $100 billion in market capitalization that restating companies lost over this period. Ibid. at 28.

21. See Kirsten L. Anderson and Teri Lombardi Yohn, *The Effect of 10K Restatements on Firm Value, Information Asymmetries, and Investors' Reliance on Earnings* (September 2002) (http://ssrn.com/abstract=332380) at p 13.

22. See *Private Litigation Under the Federal Securities Laws: Hearings Before the Subcomm. on Sec. of S. Comm. on Banking, Hous., and Urban Affairs*, 103rd Cong. 347 (1993) (statement of Jake L. Netterville, Chairman, Board of Directors of the American Institute of Certified Public Accountants) (noting that the six largest accounting firms' potential exposure to loss was in the billions). One major auditing firm, Laventhol & Horwath, did fail as a result of litigation and associated scandals growing out of the S & L scandals of the 1980s. See *What Role Should CPAs Be Playing in Audit Reform?*, Partner's Report for CPA firm Owners (Apr. 2002) (discussing the experience of Laventhol & Horwath).

23. 501 U.S. 350 (1991).

24. See ibid. at 359–61 (creating a federal rule requiring plaintiffs to file within one year of when they should have known of the violation underlying their action, but in no event more than three years after the violation). This one-to-three year period was typically shorter than the previously applicable limitations periods, which were determined by analogy to state statutes and often permitted a five-or-six year delay.

25. *Cent. Bank of Denver v. First Interstate Bank of Denver*, 511 U.S. 164 (1994).

26. See ibid. at 164.

27. See Private Securities Litigation Reform Act of 1995, Pub. L. No. 104–67 §101, 109 Stat. at 737–49 (codified as amended at 15 U.S.C. §78u–3).

28. See ibid. §201, 109 Stat. at 758–762.
29. See ibid. §107, 109 Stat. at 758.
30. See ibid. §102, 109 Stat. at 749–756.
31. Securities Litigation Uniform Standards Act of 1998, Pub. L. No. 105-353, 112 Stat. 3227 (codified in scattered sections of 15 U.S.C.). For an analysis and critique of this statute, see generally Richard W. Painter, *Responding to a False Alarm: Federal Preemption of State Securities Fraud Causes of Action*, 84 Cornell L. Rev. 1 (1998).
32. See Office of the Gen. Counsel, U.S. Sec. & Exch. Comm'n, Report to the President and the Congress on the first Year of Practice Under the Private Securities Litigation Reform Act of 1995 (1997), http://www.sec.gov/news/studies/lreform.txt [hereinafter Practice Under the Private Securities Litigation Act of 1995].
33. The Big Six firms were Arther Andersen LLP, Deloitte & Touche LLP, Ernst & Young LLP, KPMG LLP, Price Waterhouse, and Coopers Lybrand. See *In re IKON Office Solutions, Inc.*, 277 F.3d 658, 662 n 1 (3d Cir. 2002). The Big Six became the Big Five in 1998 when Price Waterhouse and Coopers Lybrand merged to form PricewaterhouseCoopers. Ibid.
34. Practice Under the Private Securities Litigation Act of 1995, n 86 above, at 21–2. The figures for the years 1990 to 1992 were reported to the SEC by the Big Six and include all class actions against them; thus, potentially some non-securities class actions could be included in this total. Nonetheless, the number of such nonsecurities actions seems likely to have been small. As the above SEC study further noted: '[D]uring the period 1991 through June 1996, accountants were defendants in 52 reported settlements (as opposed to complaints), ... and law firms were defendants in 7. Thus, there seems to be a real decline in the number of lawsuits against secondary defendants.' Ibid. at 22.
35. Ibid. at 21–2.
36. Ibid. at 4. As this study expressly noted, both the PSLRA and the Supreme Court's decision in *Central Bank of Denver* in 1994 that ended private 'aiding and abetting' liability under Rule 10b-5 could have caused decline. See n 24–29 and accompanying text.
37. See Jere R. Francis and Jagan Krishnan, *Evidence on Auditor Risk-Management Strategies Before and After the Private Securities Litigation Reform Act of 1995*, Asia Pacific Journal of Accounting and Economics, Vol. 9, No. 2 (December 2002) (http://ssrn.com/abstract=328701).
38. Several former SEC officials, including Stanley Sporkin, the former longtime head of the SEC's Division of Enforcement, have made this point to me. They believe that the SEC's enforcement action against Arthur Andersen, which was resolved in June 2001, was one of the very few (and perhaps the only) enforcement actions brought against a Big Five accounting firm on fraud grounds during the 1990s. See *SEC v. Arthur Andersen LLP*, SEC Litigation Release No. 17039 2001 Sec Lexis 1159 (D.D.C. June 19, 2001). Although the SEC did bring charges during the

1990s against individual partners in these firms, the high cost and man-power required bring suits against the Big Five, and the expectation that these defendants could zealously resist appears to have deterred the SEC from bringing suits against them. In contrast, during the 1980s, especially during Mr. Sporkin's tenure as head of the Enforcement Division, the SEC regularly brought enforcement actions against the Big Five.

39. At a minimum, plaintiffs in a securities fraud action today must plead with particularity facts giving rise to a ' "strong inference of [fraudulent intent]." ' See 15 U.S.C. §78u–4(b)(2). At the outset of a case, it may be possible to plead such facts with respect to the managers of the corporate defendant (for example, based on insider sales by such persons prior to the public disclosure of the adverse information that caused the stock drop), but it is rarely possible to plead such information with respect to the auditors (who by law cannot own stock in their client).

40. Although little systematic data exists, recent cases have noted that, after the enactment of the PSLRA in 1995, the odds facing plaintiffs in class actions climbed, particularly when they were suing secondary defendants. As one federal court has recently observed: 'Clearly, in any securities case where a plaintiff must prove that a professional acted with knowledge and/or recklessness with regard to material misstatements and omissions, a successful outcome can never be regarded as a sure thing.' See *In re Rite Aid Corp. Sec. Litig.*, 269 F. Supp. 2d 603, 608 (E.D. Pa. 2003). Compare *In re Ikon Office Solutions, Inc.*, 277 F.3d 658 (3d Cir. 2002) (affirming dismissal of securities class action against auditors when corporate defendant had earlier settled for $111 million) with *In re Ikon Office Solutions, Inc. Sec. Litig.*, 194 F.R.D. 166 (E.D. Pa. 2000) (approving $111 million settlement by the corporation). If the auditors can escape without paying anything in a fraud case in which its corporate client settled for $111 million, this suggests that the PSLRA had a very different impact on these two classes of defendants.

41. See Brian J. Hall, 'Six Challenges in Designing Equity-Based Pay,' in 15 Accenture Journal of Applied Corporate finance 21, at 23 and figure 1 (Spring 2003).

42. Ibid. at 23.

43. See Gretchen Morgenson, 'Corporate Conduct: News Analysis; Bush Failed to Stress Need to Rein in Stock Options,' New York Times, July 11, 2002 at C-1; see also Gretchen Morgenson, 'Market Watch: Time For Accountability At the Corporate Candy Store,' *New York Times*, March 3, 2002, Section 3, p 1.

44. Ibid. (citing study by Sanford C. Bernstein & Co.). Thus, if $162 billion is the value of all options in these 2,000 companies, aggressive accounting policies that temporarily raise stock prices by as little as ten percent create a potential gain for executives of over $16 billion—a substantial incentive.

45. See Hall, n 41, at 24–29 (surveying misincentives in stock options). This point has also been made by a variety of commentators who have called

for minimum holding periods or other curbs on stock options. These include Henry M. Paulson, Jr., chief executive of Goldman, Sachs, and Senator John McCain of Arizona. See David Leonhardt, 'Corporate Conduct: Compensation: Anger At Executives' Profits Fuels Support for Stock Curb,' *New York Times*, July 9, 2002, at A-1.

46. See Jap Efendi, Anup Srivastava, and Ed Swanson, *Why Do Corporate Managers Misstate Financial Statements: The Role of Option Compensation, Corporate Governance, and Other Factors*, (August 2004) (http://ssrn.com/abstract=547920). For similar studies, see Shane A. Johnson, Harley E. Ryan Jr., and Yisong S. Tian, *Executive Compensation and Corporate Fraud*, (April 2003) (http://ssrn.com/abstract=395960); Jared Harris and Philip Bromiley, *Incentives to Cheat: The Influence of Executive Compensation and Firm Performance on Financial Misrepresentation*, (Working Paper, Carlson School of Management, University of Minnesota, March 2005) (finding strong correlation between high level of CEO compensation on stock options and financial misrepresentations).

47. Efendi, Srivastava, and Swanson, n 46 above, at 2.

48. See David J. Denis, Paul Hanouna and Atulya Sarin, *Is There a Dark Side to Incentive Compensation?* (March 2005) (http://ssrn.com/abstract=695583). For an earlier study finding that the greater use of option-related compensation results in greater private securities litigation, see Lin Peng and Ailsa Roell, *Executive Pay, Earnings Manipulation and Shareholder Litigation*, (December 2004), AFA Philadelphia Meetings (http://ssrn.com/abstract=488148).

49. Denis, Hanouna and Sarin, n 48 above, at 4.

50. See Qiang Cheng and Terry Warfield, *Equity Incentives and Earnings Management* (November, 2004) (http://ssrn.com/abstract=457840).

51. See Hall, n 41 above, at 24–29. It should be noted here that other forms of equity compensation, such as restricted stock, do not give rise to this same conflict because management must either hold the stock longer or can only sell a modest percentage of it in any given year, thus precluding the possibility of a bail-out.

52. Rule 16b-3(d) expressly permits an officer or director otherwise subject to the 'short-swing' profit provisions of Section 16(b) of the Securities Exchange Act of 1934 to exercise a qualified stock option and sell the underlying shares immediately 'if at least six months elapse from the date of the acquisition of the derivative security to the date of disposition of the ... underlying equity security.' See 17 C.F.R. 240.16b-3(d). The SEC comprehensively revised its rules under Section 16(b) in 1991, in part to facilitate the use of stock options as executive compensation and to 'reduce the regulatory burden' under Section 16(b). See Securities Exchange Act Release No. 34–28869, 1991 Sec Lexis 171 (February 8, 1991). A premise of this reform was that 'holding derivative securities is functionally equivalent to holding the underlying equity security for purpose of Section 16.' Ibid. at *35 to *36. But it is not 'equivalent' if the executive would have

to borrow funds to acquire the shares and then be subject to the loss of the collateral securing that loan if the stock price declined during the six months that the executive was required to hold the stock.

53. Item 4 ('Changes in Registrant's Certifying Accountant') of SEC Form 8-K requires a publicly-held or 'reporting' company to disclose any 'disagreements with the former accountant on any matter of accounting principles or practices, financial statement disclosure, or auditing scope or procedure.' See also 17 C.F.R. 229.304 (detailing the substantive disclosures that must be made).

54. According to the Panel on Audit Effectiveness, which was appointed in 1999 by the POB at the request of the SEC to study audit practices, 'audit firms' fees from consulting services to their SEC clients increased from 17% ... of audit fees in 1990 to 67% ... in 1999.' The Panel on Audit Effectiveness, Report and Recommendations (Exposure Draft) 102 (May 31, 2000). The Panel further found that, in 1990, 80% of the Big Five auditing firms' SEC clients received no consulting services from their auditors, and only one percent of those SEC clients paid consulting fees exceeding their auditing fees to Big Five auditors.

55. A 2002 survey by the *Chicago Tribune* found that the one hundred largest corporations in the Chicago area (determined on the basis of market capitalization) paid average consulting fees to their auditors that were over three times the audit fee they paid to the same auditor. See Janet Kidd Stewart & Andrew Countryman, 'Local Audit Conflicts Add Up: Consulting Deals, Hiring Practices in Question,' *Chicago Tribune*, February 24, 2002 at C1. The extreme example was Motorola, which had an over sixteen-to-one ratio between consulting fees and audit fees. Ibid.

56. See text and notes at nn 57 to 59 below. This topic is also addressed more fully in Ch. 10.

57. The best known of these studies is Richard M. Frankel, Marilyn F. Johnson and Karen Nelson, *The Relation Between Auditors' Fees For Nonaudit Services and Earnings Management*, 77 Accounting Review 71 (Supp. 2002). For studies reaching results similar to this study, see Carol Callaway Dee, Ayalew A. Lulseged, and Tanya S. Nowlin, *Earnings Quality and Auditor Independence: An Examination Using Nonaudit Fee Data*, (January 28, 2002) (http://ssrn.com/abstract=304185); Michael J. Ferguson, Gim-Seong Seow and Danqing Young, *Non-Audit Services and Earnings Management: U.K. Evidence*, 21 Contemporary Accounting Research No. 4 (2004) (http://ssrn.com/abstract=570034).

58. For studies that reach inconsistent results with Frankel, Johnson and Nelson, n 57 above, see Hollis Ashbaugh, Ryan LaFond and Brian Mayhew, *Do Nonaudit Services Compromise Auditor Independence? Further Evidence*, 78 Accounting Review 611 (2003); Hyeeso Chung and Sangay Kallapur, *Client Importance, Non-Audit Services and Abnormal Accruals*, 78 Accounting Review 931 (2003); William R. Kinney, Zoe-Vonna Palmrose and Susan Scholz, *Auditor Independence, Non-Audit Services*

and Restatements: Was the U.S. Government Right?*, 42 J. Accounting Res. 561 (2004) (finding little relationship between purchase of non-audit services and earnings restatements).

59. Professor Roberta Romano reviews some 26 statistical studies of the relationship between non-audit services and earnings management, restatements, accounting quality or other potential dependent variables. She finds some ten studies that find some positive association (but in some cases both positive and negative associations) and sixteen studies in which no association is present or is exclusively negative. See Roberta Romano, *The Sarbanes-Oxley Act and the Making of Quack Corporate Governance* (September 2004) (http://ssrn.com/abstract=596101).

60. In suggesting conscious parallelism, which is lawful, it is not intended to suggest that actual collusion occurred, which is not lawful.

61. The literature on bubbles is now burgeoning. Perhaps the best-known scholar in this field was Charles Kindleberger, who viewed bubbles as 'demand determined' and the product of irrational investors. See Charles P. Kindleberger, Mania, Panics and Crashes: A History of Financial Crises (2000) at 76–78. See also Robert J. Shiller, Irrational Exuberance (2001); Andrei Schleifer, Inefficient Markets (2000); Kenneth A. Froot & Maurice Obstfeld, *Intrinsic Bubbles: The Case of Stock Prices*, 81 Amer. Econ. Rev. 1189 (1991). While most of these recent accounts focus on and assign causal responsibility to 'noise traders,' the account offered here focuses more on a behavioral phenomenon: 'persistence bias' and the tendency of investors to expect recent exceptional returns to continue.

62. For overviews of behavioral economics, see Christine Jolis, Cass Sunstein, and Richard Thaler, *A Behavioral Approach to Law and Economics*, 50 Stan. L. Rev. 1471 (1998); Cass Sunstein, *Behavioral Analysis of Law*, 64 U.Chi. L. Rev. 1175 (1997). The term 'bounded rationality' was coined by Herbert Simon, a Nobel prize winner, and is broadly accepted by most economists. See Herbert A. Simon, *Rationality As Process and Product of Thought*, 68 Am. Econ. Rev.: Papers & Proceedings 1 (1978).

63. See Jolis, Sunstein and Thaler, n 62 above, at 1477–1478. See also, Amos Tversky and Daniel Kahneman, 'Judgment Under Uncertainty: Heuristics and Biases' in Judgment Under Uncertainty 3 (Daniel Kahneman, Paul Slovic, and Amos Tversky eds. 1982).

64. This is by no means the only way to explain bubbles without resorting to claims of mass delusion. An alternative theory is that institutional money managers have rational incentives to engage in 'herding behavior,' preferring a common wrong decision to a risky correct one. This tendency for herding is discussed in Chapter 7.

65. See Jolis, Sunstein and Thaler, n 62 above, at 1524–1525; see also Neil D. Weinstein, *Unrealistic Optimism About Future Life Events*, 39 J. Personality & Soc. Psychology 806 (1980).

66. See Robert J. Shiller, Irrational Exuberance (2000) at 4.

67. Ibid. at 5.

4

A Comparative Perspective

To this point, the focus has largely been on the U.S. capital markets. Yet, gatekeepers—auditors, investment bankers, securities analysts, credit-ratings agencies—function in all the world's major capital markets. Do they behave the same across all environments? Logically, their behavior and performance should vary depending on the factors present in the local environment. For example, the legal threat that gatekeepers face for inadequate performance differs vastly across legal regimes. Only in the United States do auditors, investment bankers and other gatekeepers face robust private enforcement of law. In the United States, the combination of the class action and the contingent fee, under which the successful plaintiff's attorney is typically awarded a percentage (usually around 25%) of the recovery that the attorney obtains for the class, results in the existence—unique to the United States—of an entrepreneurially motivated bar of plaintiff's attorneys, eager to act as 'private attorneys general' for alleged victims of securities fraud.[1] Add to this picture the consensus of opinion that the SEC is the most aggressive enforcement agency among the world's capital market regulators, and it would seem to follow that gatekeepers would be more deterred, and hence more law compliant, in the United States.

Logical as this prediction may sound, however, it runs into immediate problems. Although there is evidence of tougher enforcement in the United States, there is also evidence of more systematic violations. Other factors beyond the level of enforcement must be factored into any overall equation. Potentially, the incentive to engage in securities fraud could be stronger in the United States. Alternatively, other non-legal mechanisms for restraining potential violators might be stronger in Europe.

Evaluating the pressures and incentives facing gatekeepers across different legal regimes is critical to our understanding of how they are likely to behave and what reforms are needed. But it is no easy task. One cannot simply count the number of enforcement proceedings brought or lawsuits filed in different jurisdictions, because this measures only the differing levels of enforcement. Nevertheless, a natural experiment is available from which some lessons can be learned. A global stock market bubble burst in 2000 affecting economies around the world. Historically, in the wake of a bubble's burst, scandals come to light and the authorities have prosecuted them aggressively—a tradition that dates back at least to the South Seas Bubble in the early 18th century.[2] The burst of the 2000 bubble was truly a worldwide phenomenon, with the percentage decline in stock market valuations being greater in a number of European countries than it was in the United States.[3]

Thus, one would logically expect an increased number of corporate financial scandals in both the U.S. and Europe to come to light, following the 2000 market crash, and to be prosecuted. But that prediction proves to be only half correct. In the United States, as earlier discussed, a wave of financial irregularity crested, resulting in scores of civil and criminal prosecutions and ultimately the Sarbanes-Oxley Act of 2002. One measure of the intensity of this outburst was the crescendo of financial statement restatements that began to rise in the early 1990s and crested in 2002.[4] The United States General Accounting Office found that over 10 percent of all listed companies in the United States announced at least one financial statement restatement between 1997 and 2002.[5] Later studies have placed the number even higher.[6] Because a financial statement restatement is a serious event in the United States which, depending on its magnitude, often results in a private class action, an SEC enforcement proceeding, a major stock price drop, and changes in senior management, one suspects that these announced restatements were but the tip of the proverbial iceberg in terms of the total amount of financial irregularity—with many more companies negotiating changes in their accounting practices with their outside auditors in order to avert a formal restatement.

In contrast, in Europe, very few public companies announced restatements. To some degree, this could be a result of lesser oversight in Europe, where the threat of private litigation is less intimidating and where governmental regulators are arguably more tolerant. Also, European accounting rules differ so that restatements may not even be permitted in some jurisdictions. However, even if restatements are not possible, financial scandals would still erupt if managers were caught manipulating stock prices by inflating earnings. The reality is, however, that few managements in Europe were detected in such conduct, suggesting that they had less motivation to cheat—at least in this fashion. In addition, because large European companies tend to be audited by the same Big Four auditing firms that audit most U.S. firms, both populations of companies were being monitored by common scorekeepers, suggesting that roughly similar auditing standards should have been applied. The inference thus arises that European managers did not feel the same pressure to 'cook the books' as did American managers over this same period.

To be sure, Europe has experienced recent financial scandals (with Lernout and Hauspie[7] and Parmalat[8] being the most notorious). But these were characteristically different from the U.S.-style financial collapse, which, as earlier noted, tended to involve earnings manipulation and the premature recognition of income. Revealingly, only European firms cross-listed in the United States appear to have experienced similar episodes of earnings management.[9]

What explains these differences—both the different character to corporate scandals and their difference in frequency? Here, a basic hypothesis must be advanced: the structure of share ownership fundamentally determines who is likely to commit securities fraud and in what fashion. Differences in share ownership account for differences in corporate scandals, both in terms of the nature of the fraud, the identity of the perpetrators, and the seeming disparity in the number of scandals at any given time. Worldwide, corporate governance subdivides into two alternative, but overlapping, systems. The U.S., the U.K. and, to a slightly lesser extent, Japan can be characterized as 'dispersed ownership' systems of corporate governance. At most public corporations within this environment, no single shareholder or allied group of shareholders owns sufficient shares to ensure its ability to elect directors; as a result, a 'separation of ownership and control' arises in the classic phrase of Adolf Berle and Gardiner Means.[10] In this environment, the shareholder–manager relationship is the sensitive one.

In contrast, Europe (and most of the world) fits the model of a 'concentrated ownership' system of corporate governance.[11] Corporate control is typically located in a single shareholder or family group, and contests for control are not feasible. As a result, corporate managers do not enjoy the same broad discretion and opportunities for self-dealing that they have in dispersed ownership systems. Instead, controlling shareholders have that discretion and are the instigators of most frauds. Although this point may seem obvious, its corollary is less so: the modus operandi of fraud is also characteristically different. Corporate managers tend to engage in earnings manipulation, while controlling shareholders tend to exploit the private benefits of control. In general, corporate managers do not possess the financial resources or absolute control necessary to be able to buy or sell assets to or from the corporation or to insist that the corporation obtain its supplies or sell its output to their affiliates.[12] Such practices—known as 'tunneling'—requires that one control the board, which the individual managers rarely do to this degree. Put differently, controlling shareholders in concentrated ownership regimes can exploit their company without necessarily manipulating its financial statements. Conversely, managers in dispersed ownership systems either cannot do so or can only to a much lesser degree.

Given these differences, the role of gatekeepers in these two systems is necessarily different. Arguably, gatekeepers may play a more central role in dispersed ownership systems. To be sure, gatekeepers are needed in both systems and they have regularly failed in both. But, although the gatekeepers failed both at Enron and Parmalat, they failed in revealingly different ways, as will be seen. In turn, different reforms may thus be necessary. The panoply of reforms adopted in the United States, culminating in the Sarbanes-Oxley Act of 2002, may not be the appropriate remedy in Europe—and indeed may not work well in any concentrated ownership system. Still, this does not mean that gatekeepers face lesser problems in Europe. In fact, the dominance of controlling shareholders in European corporations may make it even harder to design a system in which gatekeepers reliably perform their intended roles.

Additional complexity arises, because companies with dispersed ownership and companies with concentrated ownership co-exist in all major markets and jurisdictions.[13] Thus, the U.S. has recently witnessed the Adelphia scandal in which a controlling family looted the corporation it had founded of several hundred million dollars in a style that closely resembles Parmalat,[14] and France has seen the Vivendi scandal, in which an American-style media conglomerate actively inflated its stock price (and thereby approached insolvency) in order to make repeated acquisitions.[15] Yet, in any jurisdiction, one structure of shareholder ownership will typically be dominant. Depending on which system is dominant, the legal and institutional infrastructure surrounding the public corporation will tend to fit one of the two following patterns:

1 *The dispersed ownership system*, which is characterized by strong securities markets, high disclosure standards, rapid share turnover, and overall market transparency, with banks exercising only limited oversight and with the market for corporate control constituting the ultimate disciplinary mechanism; or

2 *The concentrated ownership system*, which is instead characterized by controlling blockholders, weaker securities markets, high

private benefits of control, limited potential for hostile control contests, and lower disclosure and market transparency standards, but often with active oversight being exercised by a principal bank.[16]

In the 'dispersed ownership' system, small shareholders cannot easily take coordinated action, and thus managers have enhanced power and discretion, which they may use in low-visibility ways to further their own interests. In contrast, in concentrated ownership systems, the controlling shareholder or control group can favor their own interests over those of the minority or 'public' shareholders by engaging in self-dealing transactions with the firm. In both systems, public shareholders depend on gatekeepers to protect them. In both systems, however, gatekeepers sometimes fail. But the ways in which they characteristically fail also differ, as next examined.

Styles of Fraud and Irregularity: Comparing Dispersed Versus Concentrated Ownership

Fraud in Dispersed Ownership Systems

In dispersed ownership systems, the largest shareholder in a typical public corporation will own well under 10 percent of the stock.[17] Although institutional investors today collectively own a majority of the stock of U.S. public corporations, a variety of factors—including conflicts of interest, the need to maintain liquidity, and fear of liability—constrain their potential ability to take concerted action and cause them not to place their own representatives on the board of directors.[18] Shareholders as a result have little direct access to management and cannot directly monitor corporate affairs. In such an environment, they are dependent upon the corporation's public disclosures. Precisely for this reason, the securities laws in these jurisdictions (e.g. the U.S., the U.K., and Japan) tend to regulate closely what the public corporation must disclose and specifically mandate elaborate, periodic disclosures to the market, even when the corporation is not issuing securities. In contrast, in concentrated ownership systems, the controlling shareholder has direct access to management and is less dependent upon the corporation's public disclosures in evaluating the value of its investment. Not surprisingly, the securities laws in these jurisdictions have historically been less demanding and, in particular, have required little continuing disclosure when the corporation was not selling its own securities.

Because of the dependency of public shareholders in a dispersed ownership system on the company's public disclosures, a financial statement restatement has long been an adverse event that, at least in the United States, often elicits a sharp market penalty. For example, the earlier noted GAO study of financial statement restatements in the United States between 1997 and 2002 found that the typical restating firm lost an average 10 percent of its market capitalization over a three-day trading period surrounding the date of the announcement.[19] Even this average figure understates the severity of the penalty in cases where the restatement signals fraud or managerial over-agressiveness. Because many restatements are technical and insignificant (and some even increase reported earnings), the average market reaction to a restatement groups together the insignificant and the serious.

When a restatement calls management's credibility into question, however, the market reaction is more severe. For example, studying earnings restatements by public corporations from 1971 to 2000, Richardson, Tuna and Wu found that, over a window period extending from 120 days prior to the announcement of the restatement to 120 days after the announcement, restating 'firms lose on average 25 percent of market value over the period examined and this is concentrated in a narrow window surrounding the announcement of the restatement.'[20] Twenty-five percent of market value represents an extraordinary market penalty. It implies that the market often interprets a restatement as a signal of fraud that requires a complete revaluation of the corporation. For example, in the cases of Cendant, MicroStrategy, and Sunbeam, three major U.S. corporate scandals in the late 1990s, they found that 'these three firms lost more than $23 billion in the week surrounding their respective restatement announcements.'[21]

Other studies have found that the intensity of the market's negative reaction varies with the cause of the restatement, with the most negative reactions being associated with restatements involving revenue recognition issues.[22] In short, at least in the United States, where the small shareholder in a dispersed ownership system depends on publicly disclosed information, a company's admission that it has prematurely recognized income implies to the market that its management has cheated and elicits a severe market penalty. Yet, despite the market's fear of such practices, the frequency of revenue recognition errors rose, and they became the dominant cause of restatements, in the period from 1997 to 2002. The GAO Report found that revenue recognition issues accounted for almost 38 percent of the restatements it identified over that period,[23] and the Huron Consulting Group study also found it to be the leading accounting issue underlying an earnings restatement between 1999 and 2003.[24]

What explains the prevalence of revenue recognition problems, in the face of the market's hypersensitivity to them? Here, it is necessary to return to the point made in the preceding chapter that senior executive compensation changed abruptly in the United States during the 1990s, shifting from a cash-based system of compensation to a predominantly equity-based system. As this shift occurred, managerial behavior changed. During earlier periods, when managers were primarily compensated on a cash basis, U.S. financial managers had traditionally employed 'rainy day reserves' to hold back the recognition of income that was in excess of the market's expectation in order to defer its recognition until some later quarter when they faced a shortfall in expected earnings.[25] As they did not hold much stock, managers then saw little need to beat the market's expectation, and holding earnings in reserve assured them that they would be able to meet the market's expectations in the future. Such defensive behavior protected them from ouster, which was only likely if the market became truly dissatisfied. Thus, managers engaged in income-smoothing, rolling the peaks in one period over into the valley of the next period. This traditional form of earnings management was also intended to mask the volatility of earnings and reassure investors who might have been alarmed by rapid fluctuations in earnings.

In contrast, managers in the late 1990s appear to have reversed their course, not only ceasing to save earnings for the future, but prematurely recognizing income—in effect, 'stealing' earnings from future periods in order to create an earnings spike. Why did they do so? An over-simple answer is that they needed to meet earnings projections set for their company by securities analysts. But this answer ignores that analyst predictions were largely based on management projections privately given to the analyst.[26]

The bottom line is that U.S. managements became increasingly optimistic in their projections as the 1990s wore on. This takes us back, in turn, to the one critical explanation that distinguishes the U.S. from Europe most. In overview, as executive compensation abruptly shifted in the United States during the 1990s, moving from a cash-based system to an equity-based system, it created powerful pressures to overstate income in order to inflate the firm's stock price—but this happened only in the case of U.S. companies and a relatively few European firms that also incentivized managers with stock options.

Obviously, when one pays the CEO with stock options, one is using a high octane fuel that creates incentives for short-term financial manipulation and accounting gamesmanship. Not surprisingly, financial economists have found a strong statistical correlation between higher levels of equity compensation and both earnings management and financial restatements.[27] At this point, the contrast between managerial incentives in the U.S. and Europe comes into clearer focus. These differences involve both the scale of compensation and its composition. In 2004, CEO compensation as a multiple of average employee compensation was estimated to be 531:1 in the U.S., but only 16:1 in France, 11:1 in Germany, 10:1 in Japan, and 21:1 in nearby Canada. Even Great Britain, with the most closely similar system of corporate governance to the U.S., had only a 25:1 ratio.[28] Even more important is the shift towards compensating the chief executive primarily with stock options. Although stock options have been coming into wider use in recent years in Europe, equity compensation still constitutes a much lower percentage of total CEO compensation in Europe (even in the U.K., it was only 24% in 2002).[29] European CEOs not only make much less, but their total compensation is also much less performance related.[30]

Why is there this extraordinary difference in compensation between the U.S. and Europe? Here, we need to return to the central issue of dispersed versus concentrated ownership. The conventional wisdom in the United States attributed the U.S.'s shift towards greater use of equity compensation to its tax laws, which were amended in the early 1990s to restrict the corporate deductibility of high cash compensation.[31] Although this was a factor in inducing many corporations to use equity in preference to cash, it is only part of the fuller story. Another and larger part of that story is that institutional investors in the U.S. increasingly pressured companies in the 1990s to shift towards equity compensation. Why? Institutional investors, who hold the majority of the stock in publicly-held companies in the U.S., understand that, in a system of dispersed ownership, executive compensation is probably their most important tool by which to align managerial incentives with shareholder incentives. They had long wanted U.S. managers to be more attentive to the market. Throughout the 1960s and 1970s, they had seen senior managements of large corporations manage their firms in a risk-averse and growth-maximizing fashion, retaining 'free cash flow' to the maximum extent possible.[32] Such a style of management produced the bloated and inefficient conglomerates of that era (for example, Gulf & Western and IT&T). In short, a system of exclusively cash compensation creates its own perverse incentives, motivating managers to avoid risk and bankruptcy and to pursue inefficient growth maximization, because a larger firm size generally implied higher cash compensation for its senior managers.

Once the U.S. tax laws and institutional pressure together produced a shift to equity compensation in the 1990s, managers' incentives changed. Predictably, managers began to focus more on maximizing share value (as the institutions had wanted). But what the institutions failed to anticipate was that there can be too much of a good thing. Aggressive use of these incentives in turn encouraged the use of manipulative techniques to maximize stock price over the short-run. Although such price spikes may not be sustainable, corporate managers can exploit the material, non-public information that they inherently possess. In short, when managers recognize that a high rate of earnings growth can no longer be sustained, they can exercise their stock options and bail out—well before the same information reaches the market.

In summary, the basic point about dispersed ownership systems is that managers possess discretion and will predictably manipulate the firm's financial and accounting policies in their own interest. Under cash-based compensation systems, they favored a policy of 'empire building,' because by maximizing firm size they not only reduced the risk of a hostile takeover or a bankruptcy but they could also justify a larger salary in the case of a larger firm. When executive compensation shifted from cash to equity, these incentives also shifted. The incentive to maximize firm size gave way to an incentive to maximize its stock price. Although this was a more rational goal, it could be carried to excess—for example, through premature revenue recognition. In principle, boards and auditors should have recognized and adjusted their behavior to control these perverse incentives, but changes in corporate governance often lag behind those in the market.

Fraud in Concentrated Ownership Regimes

The pattern in concentrated ownership systems is very different, but not necessarily better. In the case of most European corporations, there is a controlling shareholder or shareholder group.[33] This is important for two very different reasons. First, a controlling shareholder does not need to rely on indirect mechanisms of control, such as equity compensation or stock options, in order to incentivize management. Rather, it can rely on a 'command and control' system because, unlike the dispersed shareholders in the U.S., it can directly monitor and replace management. Hence, in a concentrated ownership system, corporate managers have both less discretion to engage in opportunistic earnings management and less motivation to create an earnings spike (because it will not benefit a management that is not compensated with stock options).

Second, the controlling shareholder also has much less interest in the day-to-day stock price of its company. In concentrated ownership systems, controlling shareholders seldom, if ever, sell their control blocks into the public market. Rather, if they sell at all, they enter into privately negotiated transactions at a substantial premium over the market price, selling to an incoming, new controlling shareholder. Such control premiums are characteristically much higher in percentage terms in Europe than in the United States.[34] As a result, controlling shareholders in Europe do not obsess over the day-to-day market price and rationally do not engage in tactics to prematurely recognize revenues to spike their stock price. Either they do not sell or they sell at prices that are not closely related to the current stock market price. These two explanations—lesser use of equity compensation and lesser interest in the short-term stock price—provide a logical explanation for why there were less accounting irregularities in Europe than in the U.S. during the late 1990s.

This generalization may seem subject to counter-examples. Some well-known European companies—for example, Vivendi Universal, Royal Ahold, Skandia Insurance or Adecco[35]—did experience accounting irregularities. But these are exceptions that prove the rule. Most were U.S.-listed companies whose accounting problems emanated from U.S.-based subsidiaries[36] or that had transformed themselves into American-style conglomerates (the leading example being Vivendi) that either awarded stock options or needed to maximize their short-term stock price in order to make multiple acquisitions. Even when a European company that experienced financial irregularities did not trade extensively on U.S. exchanges, it still may have learned the practices that produced the scandal from a U.S. source. Thus, Skandia Insurance Co. became embroiled in a major scandal in Sweden involving undisclosed bonus packages paid to its senior managers. In the end, senior management and the auditors were forced to resign, a criminal investigation ensued, partial restitution of the bonuses was made, and the board was reconstituted.[37] All told, the equity incentive program that Skandia implemented between 1997 to 2000 paid out some 600 million kroner (or roughly $80 million),[38] and it appears to have followed a largely American template and may have copied from its American subsidiary, American Skandia. Skandia was both a firm with relatively dispersed ownership and one that had aggressively expanded into the U.S. market and was copying a variety of other U.S. practices. All in all, the controversial incentive payments, which caused a major scandal in Sweden, appear tame by the standards of Tyco or Adelphia.[39]

Ultimately, what does the relative infrequency of financial reporting or accounting controversies in Europe imply? Arguably, it could be the product of less rigorous regulatory oversight of public companies in Europe or, alternatively, the consequence of the lesser litigation risk in Europe. European issuers might not feel it necessary to restate their financial statements, even when they discovered a past error, for a variety of reasons, including the lesser prospect of litigation or enforcement. But even if this is true, this explanation still does not supply a motive for financial manipulation. That is, even if European issuers could inflate their financial statements with impunity, they had less reason to do so (and they could expect at least some potential resistance from their auditors). Finally, financial statement inflation can lead to the ultimate collapse of the corporate issuer when the market eventually discovers the fraud (as Enron and WorldCom illustrate). Here, European examples of similar collapses are conspicuously absent. Many of Europe's recent financial disasters have involved not venal managers, but simple blunders (usually involving derivatives).[40]

What this lesser frequency does not imply, however, is either that European managers are more ethical or that European shareholders are better off than their American counterparts. Concentrated ownership simply encourages a different type of financial overreaching: the extraction of private benefits of control. Professors Dyck and Zingales have shown that the private benefits of control vary significantly across jurisdictions, ranging from -4 percent to $+65$ percent, depending in significant part on the legal protections given minority shareholders.[41] In general, higher private benefits seem to be extracted from European corporations (particularly those incorporated under French civil law legal regimes) than from either U.S. or U.K. corporations.

Significant variations are evident in how private benefits are extracted from a public corporation. In emerging markets, the expropriation of private benefits typically occurs through financial transactions. Ownership may be diluted through public offerings, and then a coercive tender offer or squeeze-out merger is used to force minority shareholders to tender at a price below fair market value. These techniques have been analyzed in detail by other authors, and in their crudest forms they have been given the epithet 'tunneling' to describe them.[42] A classic example was the Bulgarian experience between 1999 and 2002, when roughly two-thirds of the 1,040 firms on the Bulgarian stock exchange were delisted, following freeze-out tender offers for the minority shares at below market, but still coercive, prices.[43]

In more developed economies, such blatantly coercive transactions may be precluded. Instead, 'operational' mechanisms can be used: for example, controlling shareholders can compel the company to sell its output to, or buy its raw materials from, a corporation that they independently own. In emerging markets, growing evidence suggests that firms within corporate groups engage in more related party transactions than firms that are not members of a controlled group.[44] In essence, these transactions permit controlling shareholders to transfer resources from companies in which they have lesser cash-flow rights to ones in which they have greater cash-flow rights.[45]

Although it may be tempting to deem 'tunneling' and related opportunistic practices as characteristic only of emerging markets where legal protections are still evolving, much evidence suggests that such practices remain prevalent in more 'mature' European economies.[46] Indeed, some students of European corporate governance claim that the dominant form of concentrated ownership (i.e. absolute majority ownership) is simply inefficient because it permits too much predatory misbehavior.[47]

One must be careful here not to overgeneralize. If European corporate governance were as vulnerable to opportunistic behavior by controlling shareholders as some critics suggest, then one wonders why minority shareholders would invest at all and why even 'thin' securities markets could survive. Perhaps, the answer is that other actors substitute for the role that litigation and gatekeepers play in dispersed ownership legal regimes. For example, some argue that the universal banks, which typically hold large, but non-controlling blocks of stock as well as advancing debt capital, play such a protective role.[48] Others point to the impact of co-determination, which gives labor a major voice in corporate governance in some European countries that it lacks in Anglo-Saxon legal systems.[49] Still others point to cross-monitoring by other blockholders.[50] All these answers encounter problems, which need not be resolved here. For present purposes, no claim need be made that dispersed ownership systems are more efficient than (or otherwise superior to) concentrated ownership systems. Rather, the more relevant (but still controversial) assertion is that there is less reason to believe that gatekeepers—that is, professional agents serving shareholders but selected by the corporation—can work as well in concentrated ownership regimes as they can in dispersed ownership regimes; nor perhaps, are they relied upon as much.

To understand this contention that gatekeepers may play a less central role in concentrated ownership systems, it is useful to examine some representative scandals that have characterized concentrated ownership systems because they seem to show a distinct and different pattern of gatekeeper failure. Two recent scandals are illustrative: Parmalat and Hollinger. Parmalat is the paradigmatic fraud for Europe (just as Enron and WorldCom are the representative frauds in the United

States). Parmalat's fraud essentially involved the balance sheet, not the income statement. It failed when a 3.9 billion euros account with Bank of America proved to be fictitious.[51] Overall, some $17.4 billion in assets appear to have mysteriously vanished from its balance sheet. Efforts by its trustee to track down these missing funds have led him to allege that at least 2.3 billion euros were paid to affiliated persons and shareholders.[52] In short, private benefits appear to have been siphoned off to controlling shareholders through related party transactions. Unlike the short-term stock manipulations that occur in the U.S., this was a scandal that had continued for many years, probably for over a decade.

At the heart of the Parmalat fraud lies a crucial failure by its gatekeepers. Parmalat's auditors for many years had been an American-based firm, Grant Thornton, whose personnel had audited Parmalat and its subsidiaries since the 1980s.[53] Although Italian law uniquely mandated the rotation of audit firms, Grant Thornton found an easy evasion. It gave up the role of being auditor to the parent company in the Parmalat family, but continued to audit its subsidiaries.[54] Among these subsidiaries was the Caymans Islands-based subsidiary, Boulat Financing Corporation, whose books showed the fictitious Bank of America account, the discovery of which triggered Parmalat's insolvency.[55]

The recent Hollinger scandal also involved overreaching by controlling shareholders. Although Hollinger International is a Delaware corporation, its controlling shareholders were Canadian, as were most of its shareholders. According to the report prepared by the counsel to its independent directors, former SEC Chairman Richard Breeden, Hollinger was a 'kleptocracy.'[56] Its controlling shareholders allegedly siphoned off more than $400 million from Hollinger—or more than 95 percent of the company's adjusted net income from 1997 to 2003.[57] On sales of assets by Hollinger, its controlling shareholders secretly took large side payments, which they directed be paid to themselves out of the sales proceeds.[58] But bad as the Hollinger case may be, little evidence suggests that Lord Black and his cronies manipulated earnings through premature revenue recognition. No one suggests that they were above doing this; rather, they had little motive to do so. To inflate Hollinger's stock price, its controlling shareholders would have had to convince the market that they would no longer consume significant private benefits of control. This would have required a level of parsimony that Lord Black and his colleagues probably could not have afforded.

What is the message then? This contrast suggests two tentative conclusions. First, although controlling shareholders may misappropriate assets, they have much less reason to inflate the stock price. Fabricating earnings will not benefit them much if the market expects the controlling shareholders to still consume 'excessive' private benefits of control. Second, when controlling shareholders are able to choose their own auditors (as they appear to have done at both Parmalat and Hollinger), the watchdog has even less incentive to bark. At both Parmalat and Hollinger, the auditors appear to have been implicated in the misconduct far more than in the typical earnings restatement case. This assessment does not mean that business ethics are better (or worse) within a concentrated ownership regime, but only that the modus operandi for fraud is different. The real conclusion is that different systems of ownership encourage characteristically different styles of fraud. The next question becomes whether gatekeepers can play a functionally equivalent protective role in both legal regimes.

Implications

Both ownership regimes—dispersed and concentrated—show evidence of gatekeeper failure. The U.S.–U.K. system of dispersed ownership proved vulnerable to gatekeepers acquiescing in (or at least not detecting) inflated earnings, and concentrated ownership systems have failed to detect or restrain the expropriation of private benefits of control. A key difference, of course, is that in dispersed ownership systems the villains are managers and the victims are shareholders, while, in concentrated ownership systems, the controlling shareholders overreach minority shareholders.

In turn, this raises the critical issue: can gatekeepers in concentrated ownership systems monitor the controlling shareholder who hires (and potentially can fire) them? Although there clearly have been numerous failures by gatekeepers in dispersed ownership systems, the answer for these systems probably lies in redesigning the governance circuitry within the public corporation so that the gatekeeper does not report to the managers that it is expected to monitor. Thus, the auditor or attorney can be required to report to an independent audit committee, rather than corporate managers. Unsurprisingly, this is precisely what the Sarbanes-Oxley Act mandated. But this same answer does not work as well in a concentrated ownership system. In such a system, any audit committee will probably serve at the pleasure of the controlling shareholder. Thus, Sarbanes-Oxley-style reforms may do little good in a concentrated ownership system (where they might provide only an illusory promise of reform).

Similarly, some gatekeepers who play a significant role in dispersed ownership systems may be more peripheral to a system of concentrated ownership. For example, the securities analyst is inherently a gatekeeper for dispersed ownership regimes. In concentrated ownership regimes, the volume of stock trading in its thinner capital markets may be insufficient to generate brokerage commissions sufficient to support a profession of analysts covering all publicly-held companies. But even if analyst coverage in concentrated ownership regimes were equivalent to that in dispersed ownership systems, the analyst's predictions of the firm's future earnings or value would still mean less to public shareholders if the controlling shareholder remained in a position to squeeze-out (or otherwise exploit) the minority shareholders.

Even the role of the auditor differs in a concentrated ownership system. The existence of a controlling shareholder necessarily affects auditor independence. In a dispersed ownership system, corporate managers might sometimes 'capture' the audit partner of their auditor (as seemingly happened at Enron). But the policy answer was obvious (and Sarbanes-Oxley quickly adopted it): rewire the internal circuitry so that the auditor reported to an independent audit committee. However, in a concentrated ownership system, this answer works less well because the auditor is still reporting to a board that is, itself, potentially subservient to the controlling shareholder. Thus, the auditor in this system seems less independent because it can never truly escape the control of the party that it is expected to monitor. Although diligent auditors could have presumably detected the fraud at Parmalat (at least to the extent of detecting the fictitious bank account at the Cayman Islands subsidiary), one suspects that they would have been quietly replaced at the point at which they began to monitor earnestly. More generally, auditors can do little to stop squeeze-out mergers, coercive tender offers, or even unfair related party transactions. These require statutory protections if the minority's rights are to be protected. In fairness, shareholders in a concentrated ownership system may receive some protection from other gatekeepers, including the large banks that typically monitor the corporation.

There is an important historical dimension to this point. As will be seen in the next chapter, the independent auditor arose in Britain in the middle of the 19th century, just as industrialization and the growth of railroads was compelling corporations to raise capital from a broader audience of investors.[59] Amendments in 1844 and 1845 to the British Companies Act required an annual statutory audit with the auditor being selected by the shareholders.[60] This made sense, because the auditor was thus placed in a true principal–agent relationship with the shareholders who relied on it. But this same relationship does not exist when the auditor reports to shareholders in a system in which there is a controlling shareholder. Finally, even if the auditor were asked to report on the fairness of inter-corporate dealings or related party transactions, this is not its core competence. Other protections—such as supermajority votes, mandatory bid requirements, or prophylactic rules—may be far more valuable in protecting minority shareholders when there is a controlling shareholder. This may explain the slower development of auditing procedures and internal controls in Europe.

What reforms would work to make gatekeepers effective in concentrated ownership economies? If the controlling shareholder can potentially dominate the selection of the auditor or other gatekeepers at any shareholder election, then the auditor should not be elected by all the shareholders, but only by the minority shareholders who are truly relying on it. In effect, the auditor would be converted into the agent of the minority shareholders. Implementing this recommendation would not be easy, but only if the minority shareholders can select their own auditor would a true principal–agent relationship arise.

Summary

Across different legal regimes, the structure of share ownership is likely to determine the nature of financial fraud directed against investors. Public policy thus needs to start from the recognition that dispersed ownership creates managerial incentives to manipulate income, while concentrated ownership invites the low-visibility extraction of private benefits. As a result, governance protections that work in one system may fail in the other. Indeed, the optimal gatekeeper for concentrated ownership systems may yet remain to be designed.

Endnotes

1. For an overview of this system, see John C. Coffee, Jr., *Understanding the Plaintiff's Attorney: The Implications of Economic Theory for Private Enforcement of Law Through Class and Derivative Actions*, 86 Colum. L. Rev. 677 (1986).
2. For a pre-Sarbanes-Oxley review of the last 300 years of this pattern, see Stuart Banner, *What Causes New Securities Regulation? 300 Years of Evidence*, 75 Wash. U.L.Q. 849 (1997).
3. See Bengt Holmstrom and Steven Kaplan, *The State of U.S. Corporate Governance: What's Right and What's Wrong*, 15 Accenture J. of App. Corp. Fin. 8, 9 (2003) (showing that from 2001 through December 31,

2002, the U.S. stock market returns were negative 32%, while France was negative 45% and Germany negative 53%).

4. See text in Ch. 3 at nn 5 to 10.

5. See U.S. Gen. Accounting Office, Pub. No. 03-138, Financial Statement Restatements: Trends, Market Impacts, Regulatory Responses and Remaining Challenges (2002) at 4.

6. See Huron Consulting Group, An Analysis of Restatement Matters: Rules, Errors, Ethics, for the Five Years Ended December 31, 2002 (Jan. 2003) (discussed in text in Chapter 3 at nn 8 to 10). Under Huron's numbers, it would appear that roughly one-in-eight public corporations restated their financial statements over this period.

7. Lernout & Hauspie Speech Products, a high-tech Belgian company making speech software that could turn the spoken word into a written text, proved to be a notorious fraud in which a significant proportion of the assets simply disappeared. Listed on Nasdaq in 1995, it had by March 2000 a market value of $10 billion. In June 2000, L & H reported 1999 revenue of $143.2 million from South Korea and Singapore, up incredibly from less than $300,000 the prior year. Newspaper stories began to report suspicions that this revenue had been fabricated, and by November 2000, an internal audit at L & H reported that the company had overstated its sales by $277 million (or 45%) from 1998 to 2000. Some $100 million in assets in South Korea were also found to be non-existent. The fraud was so pervasive that the company could not be re-organized and was simply liquidated. See Brad Spurgeon, 'After a "Macho" Flameout, Lernout Seeks Second Chance,' *International Herald Tribune*, May 28, 2005 at 13. Uniquely, this episode has features of American earnings management and European asset misappropriation.

8. For a detailed review of the Parmalat scandal, see Andrea Melis, *Corporate Governance Failures. To What Extent is Parmalat a Particularly Italian Case?* (September 30, 2004) (http://ssrn.com/abstract=563223). See also text at nn 53 to 58 below.

9. Lernout and Hauspie Speech Products clearly fits this pattern. See text and note at n 7 above. So also do the financial irregularities uncovered at Adecco, Royal Ahold and Vivendi. See at n 37 below.

10. See Adolf A. Berle, Jr. and Gardiner C. Means, The Modern and Private Property, 4 (1932).

11. For the leading recent empirical survey making this point, see Rafael La Porta, Florencio Lopez-de-Silanes, Andrei Shleifer and Robert W. Vishny, *Corporate Ownership Around the World*, 54 J. Fin. 471 (1999).

12. Management buyouts and 'going private' transactions are an exception to this generalization, but these transactions are heavily regulated in the United States and subjected to close judicial scrutiny.

13. See Lopez-de-Silanes, Shleifer and Vishny, n 11 above (finding some firms with dispersed ownership in all European markets and many firms with concentrated ownership in the U.S. market).

14. Adelphia Communications went into bankruptcy after it was discovered that it had made undisclosed loans and loan guarantees of at least $3.1 billion to its founder's family. As will be seen, this closely resembles the Parmalat scandal in that the fraud involved the balance sheet and asset diversions to the founder's family, rather than earnings manipulation. In bankruptcy, Adelphia has sued its former auditors, Deloitte & Touche, for allegedly failing to disclose or investigate Adelphia's loans to the Rigas family. See Robert Frank, 'Adelphia Sues Deloitte & Touche, Accusing Former Auditor of Fraud,' Wall St. J., Nov. 7, 2002 at A2.

15. Under the control of its 'imperial' chief executive officer, Jean-Marie Messler, Vivendi Universal inflated its financial results between October 2000 and April 2002, apparently to make multiple acquisitions. Mr Messler was fined $1 million by the SEC (and barred from being a director of a public company for ten years) and later was additionally fined 1 million euros by the French financial markets regulator, the Autorité des Marches Financiers, which found him to have engaged in an intentional fraud. In 2002, he was forced to resign when the Vivendi board discovered that he had propped up its stock price by secretly using corporate funds to repurchase its shares. The extent of these undisclosed repurchases brought about a liquidity crisis that nearly forced Vivendi into insolvency. See Jo Johnson, 'Vivendi Probe Ends with Euros 1 million Fine for Messier,' *The Financial Times*, December 8, 2004 at p 31. Such CEO behavior has much in common, both in style and substance, with that of the U.S. CEOs at WorldCom, Tyco or Global Crossings.

16. For an overview of these rival systems, see John C. Coffee, Jr., *The Rise of Dispersed Ownership: The Roles of Law and the State in the Separation of Ownership and Control*, 111 Yale L. J. 1 (2001).

17. For the fullest study of shareholder ownership in the U.S., which finds ownership to be highly dispersed, see Harold Demsetz and Kenneth Lehn, *The Structure of Corporate Ownership: Causes and Consequences*, 93 J. Pol. Econ 1155, 1157 (1985). Using data from 1980, Professors Demsetz and Lehn do find that the five largest shareholders in a U.S. corporation typically own 24.8% of the voting power, thus suggesting that some coordination is possible and that investors are not powerless. Today, the largest holders will typically be institutional investors, who for independent legal reasons seldom, if ever, seek to elect their officers or agents to the board.

18. For a detailed description of the factors that dissuade institutional investors from participating in control or placing representatives on corporate boards in the United States, see John C. Coffee, Jr., *Liquidity Versus Control: The Institutional Investor As Corporate Monitor*, 91 Colum. L. Rev. 1277 (1991).

19. See GAO Report, n 4 above, at 5.

20. See Scott Richardson, Irem Tuna, and Min Wu, *Predicting Earnings Management: The case of earnings restatements*, (October 2002) (http://ssrn.com/abstract=338681) at p 16.

21. Ibid.

22. See Kirsten L. Anderson and Teri Lumbardi Yohn, *The Effect of 10K Restatements on Firm Value, Information Asymmetries, and Investors' Reliance on Earnings* (September, 2002) (http://ssrn.com/abstract = 332380).

23. See GAO Report, n 4 above, at 28.

24. See Huron Consulting Group, n 6 above, at 4.

25. The term 'rainy day reserves' was made famous by then SEC Chairman Arthur Levitt in a 1998 speech criticizing the looseness of accounting principles and practices. See Levitt, 'The "Numbers Game": Remarks at the N.Y.U. Center for Law and Business' (Sept. 28, 1998).

26. Since late 2000, Regulation FD has limited the ability of corporate managers to make selective disclosure of material information to favored investors. See 17 CFR 243.100 et seq. Prior to 2000, however, selective disclosure of forecasts and projections to large institutional investors just prior to their release to the market was a standard practice. To this extent, projections made by analysts often originated with the company.

27. For example, see Jap Efendi, Anup Srivastava, and Ed Swanson, *Why Do Corporate Managers Misstate Financial Statements: The Role of Option Compensation, Corporate Governance and Other Factors*, (August 2004) (http://ssrn.com/abstract=547920) (finding in a control group study that the leading difference between firms that did and did not restate their earnings was the amount of 'in the money' stock options held by the CEO). Other studies were discussed or cited in Ch. 3 at nn 46 to 50.

28. See Gretchen Morgenson, 'Explaining (Or Not) Why the Boss Is Paid So Much," *New York Times*, Jan. 25, 2004, §3, at 1.

29. See Guido Ferrarini, Niamh Moloney and Cristina Vespro, Executive Remuneration in the EU: Comparative Law and Practice (ECGI Working Paper 2003) at 7 n 21.

30. Ibid. at 6–7 (noting that performance related pay is in wide use only in the U.K. and that controlling shareholders tend to resist significant use of incentive compensation).

31. In 1993, Congress enacted Section 162(m) of the Internal Revenue Code, which denies a tax deduction for annual compensation in excess of $1 million per year paid to the CEO, or the next four most highly paid officers, unless special tests are satisfied. Its passage forced a shift in the direction of equity compensation. For a fuller account of this change, see Coffee *What Caused Enron? A Capsule Social and Economic History of the 1990s*, 89 Cornell L. Rev. 269, 274–275 (2004).

32. Professor Michael Jensen coined the term 'free cash flow' in course of articulating his well-known critique that corporate managers in large conglomerates excessively retained earnings in order to maximize the

firm's size in their own self interest. See Michael Jensen, *The Agency Costs of Free Cash Flow, Corporate Finance and Takeovers*, 76 Am. Econ. Rev. 323 (1986). Managers, he argues, had incentives to direct excess cash flow to marginally profitable ventures rather than pay out excess cash flow to shareholders as dividends.

33. For excellent overviews of European ownership patterns, see Franks and Mayer, *Corporate Ownership and Control in Germany, the U.K. and France*, 9 J. Applied Corp. Fin. 40 (1997); The Control of Corporate Europe (Fabrizio Barca & Marco Becht, eds. 2001); La Porta, Lopez-de-Silanos, Shliefer & Vishny, n 11 above.

34. See Alexander Dyck and Luigi Zingales, *Private Benefits of Control: An International Comparison*, 59 J. fin. 537 (2004) (discussed in text at n 41 below); see also Tatiana Nenova, *The Value of Corporate Votes and Control Benefits: A Cross-Country Analysis*, (2000) (http://ssrn.com/abstract=237809) (finding significantly higher control premiums in countries relying on French civil law and high, but lower, premiums in countries using German civil law; these control premiums were significantly above the average premiums in common law countries); Luigi Zingales, *What Determines the Value of Corporate Votes*, 110 Q. J. Econ. 1047 (1999).

35. Both the financial scandals at Adecco and Royal Ahold originated in the United States and, at least initially, centered around accounting at U.S. subsidiaries. See Haig Simonian, 'Europe's First Victim of Sarbanes-Oxley? Corporate Governance: Adecco was pilloried for its poor handling of U.S. accounting problems,' *Financial Times*, January 29, 2004, at p 14; Kevin McCoy, 'Prosecutors Charge Nine More in Royal Ahold Case,' *USA Today*, January 14, 2005 p 1B (noting that Royal Ahold's accounting problems began at U.S. Foodservices, Inc., a subsidiary of Royal Ahold, where the U.S. managers were compensated with stock options); Vivendi Universal can be described as a U.S.-style acquisitions oriented financial conglomerate. See Jo Johnson, 'Vivendi Probe Ends With Euro $1 Million fine for Messier,' *Financial Times*, December 8, 2004 at p 31.

36. This characterization certainly applies to Adecco and Royal Ahold.

37. See 'Skandia Calls Special Meeting to fill Board Seats,' BestWire January 8, 2004.

38. See Heather Timmons, 'Insurance Company Chairman Steps Down,' *New York Times*, December 2, 2003, Section W-1.

39. The company renovated some apartments for senior managers and provided free leased housing for some of their children. See Carl Mortished, 'Do We Stick With Carrots?' *The Times* (London), December 3, 2003, p 2B. As a reform, Skandia eliminated all bonuses for managers.

40. One of the most prominent such financial disasters in Europe was the Metallgesellschaft fiasco in 1994, which at bottom involved the mishandling of derivatives. See Andrew Fisher, 'Metallgesellschaft: The

Oil Deals That Crippled a German Metal-Trading Giant,' *Financial Times*, March 20, 1995 at 20. Metallgesellschaft's financial distress seems more to have been more the product of the negligent mishandling of derivatives than any fraudulent desire to inflate earnings. See also Franklin Edwards & Michael Canter, *The Collapse of Metallgesellschaft: Unhedgeable Risks, Poor Hedging Strategy, or Just Bad Luck*, 15 J. Futures Mkts., 211, 235–6 (1995). Such accounting scandals as have occurred in Germany—for example, the fraud at Klockner-Humboldt-Deuta or the collapse of the Jurgen Schneider real estate empire—involved longstanding frauds in which assets were overstated and liabilities understated with the apparent acquiescence of both auditors and sometimes the principal lending bank. The monitoring failures in these cases, which more closely resemble Parmalat than Enron, are reviewed in Ekkehard Wenger and Christoph Kaserer, 'German Banks and Corporate Governance—A Critical View,' in Klaus Hopt et al., Comparative Corporate Governance—The State of the Art and Emerging Research, 499 (1998).

41. See Dyck and Zingales, n 34 above; see also Nenova, n 34 above.

42. For the article coining this term, see Simon Johnson, Rafael La Porta, Florencio Lopez-de-Silanos, and Andrei Schleifer, *Tunneling*, 90 Amer. Econ. Rev. 22 (2000).

43. See Vladimir Atanasov, Conrad S. Ciccotello, and Stanley B. Gyoshev, *How Does Law Affect Finance? An Empirical Examination of Tunneling in an Emerging Market*, William Davidson Institute Working Paper Number 742 (January 2005) (http://ssrn.com/abstract=423506). These authors estimate that these coercive transactions were effected at about 25% of the shares' intrinsic value.

44. See Jian Jane Ming and T. J. Wong, *Earnings Management and Tunneling through Related Party Transactions: Evidence from Chinese Corporate Groups*, EAA 2003 Annual Conference Paper No. 549 (June 2003) (http://ssrn.com/abstract=42488).

45. See Marianne Bertrand, Paras Mehta and Sendhil Mullainathan, *Ferreting Out Tunneling: An Application to Indian Business Groups*, MIT Dept. of Econ. Working Paper No. 00–28 (Sept. 2000) (http://ssrn.com/abstract=246001).

46. Many commentators have criticized German corporate governance on the grounds that it permits controlling shareholders to diverge from a pro rata distribution of enterprise cash flows, for example, through onesided transfer pricing arrangements with affiliated companies, or asset sales on favorable terms to affiliates. See Jeffrey N. Gordon, *Pathways to Corporate Convergence?: Two Steps On the Road to Shareholder Capitalism in Germany*, 5 Colum. J. Eur. L. 219, at 222 (1999). If this is the problem, an independent auditor is probably not the answer, as it cannot stop such transactions. For a more recent overview of the means by which controlling shareholders currently divert value to themselves

in Europe, see Tom Kirchmaier and Jeremy Grant, *Financial Tunneling and the Revenge of the Insider System: How to Circumvent the New European Corporate Governance Legislation* (October 2004) (http://ssrn. com/abstract=613945).

47. See Tom Kirchmaier and Jeremy Grant, *Corporate Ownership Structure and Performance in Europe*, CEP Discussion Paper No. 0631 (April 2004) (http://ssrn.com/abstract=616201).

48. This was once the consensus view. But more recently, skeptics have demonstrated that the universal banks in Germany have few representatives on the supervisory board, tend to do no more monitoring than banks in dispersed ownership regimes, and largely defer to the managing board's decisions. See Jeremy Edwards and Klaus Fischer, Banks Finance and Investment in Germany (1994).

49. The impact of co-determination on corporate governance has been much debated. See, e.g. Mark J. Roe, *German Co-determination and German Securities Markets*, 1998 Colum. Bus. L. Rev. 167 (1998).

50. See Gary Gorton and Frank A. Schmid, 'Universal Banking and the Performance of German firms' (National Bureau of Economic Research Working Paper No. 5453) (1996) (suggesting role of nonbank blockholders in monitoring the controlling shareholder).

51. This summary of the Parmalat scandal relies upon the Wall Street Journal's account. See Alessandra Galloni and David Reilly, 'How Parmalat Spent and Spent,' Wall Street Journal, July 23, 2004.

52. Ibid. Parmalat's former CEO, Mr. Tanzi, appears to have acknowledged to Italian prosecutors 'that Parmalat funneled about Euro 500 Million to companies controlled by the Tanzi family, especially to Parmatour.' See A. Melis, n 8 above, at 6. Prosecutors appear to believe that the total diversions to Tanzi family-owned companies were at least euros 1,500 million. Ibid. at 6 n 2.

53. Ibid. at 10.

54. Ibid. at 9–10.

55. Ibid. at 10.

56. See 'Report of Investigation by the Special Committee of the Board of Directors of Hollinger International Inc' (August 30, 2004) at 4.

57. Devin Leonard, 'More Trials for Lord Black,' Fortune, October 4, 2004 at p 42.

58. Ibid.

59. See A. C. Littleton, Accounting Evolution to 1900 (1988) at 260–262.

60. See text and notes in Ch. 5 at nn 10 to 17.

Part II

The Development of Gatekeepers

An Overview

Three principal professions: accounting, law, and securities analysis, have evolved to offer gatekeeping services to investors. A fourth gatekeeper, the credit-rating agency, also merits examination, even if the few entities engaged in this work do not amount to a full-scale profession, because their specialized services are much relied upon by investors and because their different institutional arrangements and legal status furnish an instructive counterpoint.

The histories and political economies surrounding these four gatekeepers are very different. Law is an ancient profession, which only recently has recognized that its members may owe some duties to investors; in general, the legal profession continues to resist attempts to impose broader gatekeeping obligations on it. Accounting is the paradigmatic gatekeeping profession, and it successfully distinguished itself from the more clerical task of bookkeeping only by stressing its need for independence and its duties to third parties. Yet, from its earliest days, auditors have debated and divided over their ability to serve two masters, assisting managements by providing a multitude of services while also monitoring them in the service of investors. As will be seen, the Sarbanes-Oxley Act resolved, albeit only partially, a debate that had continued for over a century, often dividing the accounting profession.

Securities analysts (or 'financial analysts' as they formerly were called) constitute the newest of these professions. Once, it seemed the most independent of the professions serving investors, but, even more than its fellow professions, it has recently experienced a crisis that has thinned its ranks and challenged its claims to professional independence. Originally, analysts—unlike attorneys or accountants—were in fact compensated by investors (through the mechanism of brokerage commissions). Thus, a simple and genuine principal–agent relationship

existed between the gatekeeper and the parties it served (i.e. investors). But, as competition eroded brokerage commissions, analysts
were forced to find alternative sources of compensation. The resulting
transition placed them in the same conflicting position as attorneys and
accountants, receiving their compensation, albeit indirectly, from the
parties that they were expected to monitor.

As with securities analysts, credit-rating agencies were once compensated by investors, but now have their fees paid by the corporations that
they rate. While this creates a conflict, there is some evidence that the
credit-rating agencies have been better able to control these conflicts
and monitor their agents than other gatekeepers. However, the more
important fact about credit-rating agencies is that they inhabit a market
almost devoid of competition. Increasing criticism, particularly post-
Enron, has focused on the modest level of scrutiny exercised by these
agencies and the limited depth of their investigations. Their lackluster performance seems best understood as the traditional preference
of the monopolist to under-invest and enjoy the quiet life. The level of
competition in the marketplace for gatekeeper services thus may rank
co-equal with conflicts of interest in determining overall gatekeeper
performance. But, as will be seen, the impact of competition is complex:
too little competition and the gatekeeper underperforms: too much and
it may feel compelled to acquiesce to corporate management's preferences, for fear that it will be replaced.

Although the institutional histories of these four professions are
different, they share some important common denominators. First and
foremost, the first three professions have fought zealously to protect
their professional autonomy and resist efforts of both state and federal regulators to mandate the standards and norms applicable to them.
Second, at least in the case of attorneys and accountants, they have
stubbornly resisted any obligation to be judgmental about their clients,
seeking in common to exercise only a 'weak' gatekeeping responsibility.
This 'minimalist' definition of their roles poses, of course, the ultimate
policy question: how much greater responsibilities could or should they
assume? Third, as noted earlier, each of these professions appears to have
lost considerable leverage vis-à-vis their clients over recent decades—to
the point that their professional independence is now more in question
than it arguably was during the middle of the 20th century.

This shift in the balance of power between the gatekeeper and the
corporate client is the product of different forces: economic changes,
reduced legal liability, technological developments that call into question the basic assumptions of their discipline, and, above all else,
increased pressures on the corporate client (or its managers) to maximize

earnings or meet the market's expectations. But the common result is that gatekeepers are under pressure and perceive themselves less able to dictate the terms of their relationship with the corporations that they monitor. This common loss of leverage is the premise that sets the stage for the inquiry in this book's final section of how gatekeepers can best be empowered and motivated to protect investors.

Before examining any individual profession, a prefatory generalization is useful about all professions and the unique role and status they possess in the United States. Beginning at some point in the latter half of the 19th century, professions in a rapidly secularizing United States came to represent an occupation with a moral calling. Whereas, early in the 19th century, the young man who wished to lead a moral career might have entered the ministry, by the end of that century he would have been more likely enter a profession. The attraction of a professional career was in no small part that a person entering the profession could honorably offer his services to society, while also improving his economic position. This ability to do good and do well at the same time entitled the professional to aspire to loftier ambitions (or pretensions) and enjoy a higher sense of self worth than the mere merchant or employee. In addition, entering a profession offered the prospect of professional independence, including the ability to choose and reject clients, which possibility was simply not open to a corporate employee. Particularly for the attorney, this definition of professional independence was attractive, and it received its fullest, most aspirational expression during the Progressive Era when public figures, such as Louis Brandeis, presented the attorney as the guardian of liberty and the values of legality.

A cultural historian of this era uses the example of a symptomatic transition that one modest occupation underwent during the late 19th century to illustrate this pattern. Undertakers started the century, he notes, as humble coffin-makers, but emerged as providers of a professional service. As he observes: 'In the 1890s, the title 'mortician' appeared, suggested by the word 'physician,' and the subject 'mortuary science' soon entered the curriculum of accredited colleges.'[1] Behind this new terminology lay a professional metamorphosis: the traditional undertaker had transformed himself into the more prestigious 'funeral director,' someone providing specialized and quasi-scientific services to the bereaved's family that were based on training, expertise and professional standards. Snicker as one might at the pretensions of the undertaker to professional status, his ambitions were, more or less, the same ambitions that led bookkeepers of the same era to seek to elevate themselves into 'accountants' or, at a slightly later point, into 'financial analysts.'

More generally, these were the ambitions of an emergent middle class that came to dominate political and economic life in the United States during the late 19th century. With such transformations into professionals came not only economic advancement, but also social prestige and personal satisfaction. Not surprisingly, during the late 19th century, professions proliferated. But their rise coincided with a political development: During the Progressive Era, which peaked in the first two decades of the 20th century, the aspirations of the middle class for professional status fused with a reformist political movement that sought to address and constrain the vices that had accompanied rapid industrialization and industrial concentration: oligopolistic 'trusts', egregious corporate misconduct, political corruption, and suddenly aggravated economic inequality. Not only was the Progressive Era led by professionals (for example, Louis Brandeis), but many of its reforms sought to activate the professions as watchdogs for broader society. For both the professions of law and accounting, this was the formative era in which their professional associations were shaped, and the Progressive Era's calls for greater disclosure and transparency for a time seemed about to transform them.[2]

In fact, no radical transformation actually transpired. Instead, during the Progressive Era and the later New Deal, the professions of law and accounting were both challenged to respond and accept a quasi-public role. Predictably, both professions equivocated, and ultimately retreated from their high watermarks of activism reached during the Progressive Era. Competitive pressures, economic opportunities, and the fear of loss of professional autonomy explain much of their behavior.

However, for many contemporary critics of the professions, the Progressive Era represents a Golden Age when professionals combined private practice with a pursuit of the public interest. The era thus offers for them a normative model for how the professions should behave. But the forces that frustrated the Progressive Era's reformers remain and are no less powerful today. In this light, the following encapsulated histories of three professions try to locate the professional within a rapidly changing political and economic environment. To the extent that the gatekeeper is found to be seeking to minimize the obligations it undertook to investors, or appears less able to exercise independent judgment, these conclusions are presented not so much to demonstrate the futility of a more normative theory of the professions, but to identify the forces and barriers that will predictably resist reforms. This analysis is ultimately intended to set the stage for a serious discussion in the final section of this book of the re-engineering that would be realistically necessary for the professions to play a more active role as gatekeepers.

Simply wishing or advocating that professionals should act more like independent gatekeepers will accomplish little—as history will show.

Endnotes

1. See Burton J. Bledstein, The Culture of Professionalism: The Middle Class and The Development of Higher Education in America (W. W. Norton & Co. 1976) at p 5. Professor Bledstein argues that in the United States, the professions were open to the middle class, whereas in contrast in Great Britain of the same era, equivalent access was generally denied to them. Bledstein also points out that most professional societies in the United States were organized during a relatively short time frame in the 1880s and early 1890s. Ibid. at 88–92.
2. While our focus is exclusively on the 'gatekeeping' professions, it should be noted that the Progressive Era profoundly affected other professions as well. For a review of its impact on the American Medical Association, see Paul Starr, The Social Transformation of American Medicine (1982).

5

The Rise, Fall, and Redefinition of the Auditor: From Bookkeeper to Professional to Information Consultant

Accounting is an old art, but a relatively modern profession. Conventional histories of accounting usually begin with the formalization of double-entry bookkeeping, which is credited to an Italian monk, Fra Luca Pacioli, who in 1494 published the first work explaining the accounting practices that Italian merchant houses had probably already used for at least a half-century.[1] Yet, early accountants were basically bookkeepers; they assisted the proprietors of a business in developing a more or less systematic approach for recording exchanges or understanding the economic consequences of a specific venture. As the historians of accounting have explained,[2] a business was not then viewed as an entity separate and distinct from its owners. Not until the 19th century did accounting achieve the intellectual synthesis that the owners' capital contribution, plus or minus subsequent profits and losses, equaled the net worth of the business.[3]

With the advent of this later 'entity theory' of accounting (and also with the acceptance of limited liability for corporations), the business became separate from its owners. In principle, third parties could now examine and rely on financial statements of the business in determining whether to advance credit or capital to the business. However, before third parties could rely on these business-based financial statements that appeared in the 19th century, they needed some means by which to verify and evaluate the reliability of those statements. At this point, which appears to have been reached only in the mid-19th century, the bookkeeper began to evolve into the auditor.[4]

The significance of this transition needs to be underscored. The most important economic transition in the corporate world during the 20th century was probably the separation of ownership and control. This is the idea made famous by Adolf Berle and Gardiner Means, who discovered in the early 1930s that corporate managements had become relatively autonomous.[5] Yet, it seems unlikely that this separation could have occurred, or widely dispersed share ownership been achieved, unless and until dispersed shareholders had first gained confidence in professional agents upon whom they could rely to assure them as to the accuracy of the financial statements prepared by corporate promoters and managers. In short, the Berle/Means corporation depended upon, and had to await, the development of auditing.

The British Experience: Inventing the Auditor

The evolution of modern accounting occurred largely in Great Britain, probably because it was both the principal mercantile power of the 19th century and the location of the Industrial Revolution. The actual nature of this evolution was, however, very path-dependent and shaped by a long-standing British tradition that dated back to the medieval era. The special British contribution to modern accounting involved its unique experience with the concept of an auditor. The traditional bookkeeper did not in any meaningful sense perform an audit. After all, he was an employee of the owner of the business, not an independent professional, and no one realistically expected the bookkeeper to behave in an objective, independent fashion or to challenge the accuracy of his employer's financial statements.

But in Great Britain, there already was a pre-existing concept of the auditor. It dated back to the 13th century, and in its most public form it involved a close-knit community electing trusted persons to act as 'awdytours' to verify, typically on an annual basis, that public funds had been properly applied.[6]

While this system of auditing appears to have first developed to hold the fiscal officers of public enterprises accountable, it was widely copied within the great manors of medieval England. There, the auditor would be a trusted senior servant, before whom all other servants having control over money or property would orally present their records of how they had handled the funds entrusted to them.[7] The bookkeeping involved in this activity was only a primitive 'charge and discharge' system that added up the expenditures listed by the servant to ensure that no funds had been embezzled. If the auditor found any 'arrearages' in accounts, the delinquent servant could be sent to prison on the testimony of the auditor[8]—a power that even the Sarbanes-Oxley Act does not give the auditor or the audit committee today. The relevant point here is that the medieval English auditor was an inspector, not a bookkeeper, someone checking another agent's financial records for the benefit of the persons appointing him (either the lord of the manor or the members of a guild or other commercial or public body).

Consistent with this history, when Great Britain came in the 1840s to remove the prohibition it had passed a century earlier on free incorporation, it conditioned the ability of private citizens to form corporations (without the permission of Parliament or the Crown) on the mandatory use of an annual audit, with an independent auditor being elected each year by the shareholders. To appreciate this development, one needs to understand that, a century earlier, English law had responded to the first great stock market bubble in history—the South Seas Bubble—by deliberately discouraging the use of the corporation. Although the availability of the corporate form was not entirely forbidden, the Bubble Act, passed in 1720, prohibited new corporations from forming or 'presuming to act as corporate bodies' without a royal charter or a special act of Parliament.[9] In effect, private citizens could only form a corporation if they could convince Parliament or the Crown to authorize them. Although this prohibition could be evaded by a variety of techniques, public skepticism of the private corporations, based on its assumed responsibility for the South Seas Bubble, retarded use of the corporate form in both Great Britain and the United States for the next century.

Eventually, as Great Britain entered the Industrial Revolution, the cost of this sweepingly prophylactic rule was recognized to be excessive. Financing the construction of railroads across England required that their securities be marketed to the public, which was also eager to invest. Yet, under the Bubble Act, a special act of Parliament was necessary for each new firm to incorporate. In 1825, the Parliament repealed the Bubble Act,[10] and, in the wake of its repeal, England quickly experienced a 'railroad mania' during the 1830s and 1840s, as railroad stocks were aggressively marketed to the public. Many failed under circumstances suggesting either that the original promotion was fraudulent or that dishonest managers had pocketed much of the proceeds.[11]

The resulting scandals—in effect, a mini-Bubble—convinced Parliament that some controls had to be placed on the ability of promoters to form and syndicate private corporations. The upshot was a series of statutes, of which the Joint Stock Companies Act,[12] adopted in 1844, and the Companies Clauses Consolidation Act,[13] adopted in 1845, stood out. The first applied to 'private' corporations (i.e. those companies incorporated without a special act of Parliament or a royal charter), and the second largely extended its new protections to 'statutory' corporations (i.e. those companies that were created by a special act of Parliament). Although these two statutes differed in a number of respects, both required an annual statutory audit with the auditor being elected by the shareholders.[14] Neither statute required that the statutory auditor actually be an accountant (there being precious few at the time), but the 1845 Companies Clauses Act showed Parliament's intent by authorizing the elected auditor to pay professional accountants to assist him and to charge their expense to the corporation.[15] Moreover, the 1845 Act further provided that the auditor could not 'hold any office in the company'—hence, from the outset, there was a statutory requirement of independence.[16]

The statutory requirement of an audit and the express authority to hire accountants at the corporation's expense unquestionably spurred the growth of the profession of accounting in England.[17] In truth, demand preceded supply, as the profession grew to handle the statutory audit. As of 1799, there were only 11 practicing accountants in London, but, within fifty years, this number had risen to 210.[18] Professional societies began to form and receive royal charters, thereby permitting its members to use the term 'chartered accountant.' The first such 'Societies of Accountants' were formed in Scotland, with the Edinburgh society receiving the initial royal charter in 1854.[19]

Spurring the formation and growth of these professional organizations was the understandable desire of their members to distinguish themselves from mere bookkeepers and clerks. As a result, each royal society's first step was usually to establish examinations for admission and then to promulgate standards of professional conduct. Then as now, exclusivity carried cachet.

In overview, what stands out most about the British experience (and distinguishes it from the American experience discussed next) is that statutory law in Britain mandated a specific form of gatekeeper. The relationship between the auditor and its client was not simply a matter of private contracting; rather, the law required this gatekeeper to be independent and selected by a shareholder vote—in order to ensure that the agent would be faithful to its principal. Although British law did not require that the auditor be an accountant, any person who occupied the position of auditor, and who did not hire competent accountants to assist him, probably faced a high prospect of liability at common law if he failed to detect fraud or inflation of the company's accounts. Hence, once accounting firms developed in response to the new laws, the practice quickly developed that the stockholders would elect an accounting firm as their statutory auditor.

By so mandating a gatekeeper, British law effectively created a profession, in effect creating an 'artificial' demand for accounting services that would not have existed (at least to the same extent) in the absence of such legislation. Although some have objected to such a mandatory approach on the ground that it 'commodifies' a service that should instead be left to the market and private choice,[20] the English experience seems to show that such a strategy can work, as in its wake a strong profession quickly arose—and then spread to the United States.

The American Experience

Accounting as a profession developed much more slowly in the United States than in Great Britain. A number of reasons can explain the slower trajectory in the United States, including the earlier progress of the Industrial Revolution in Great Britain and the initially smaller size of the capital markets in the U.S. But all these factors eventually reversed themselves by the early 20th century, as the U.S. capital markets came to overshadow the London market and the pace of technological progress in the U.S. vastly outstripped that in Great Britain. Even then, however, the profession grew slowly in the U.S. during the early 20th century, and did not truly blossom until federal legislation—first the income tax and later the federal securities laws—created a demand for its services.

This contrast between accountants as public gatekeepers in Great Britain, mandated by statute, and accountants as private gatekkeepers in the U.S., used only to the extent that clients retained their services to assure others as to the reliability of their financial statements, suggests a hypothesis. That the profession developed more rapidly in Great Britain implies that private incentives for companies to provide assurances to investors were insufficient to induce companies to appoint an independent gatekeeper. The demand for accounting services in Britain was jumpstarted by legislation, whereas in the U.S. only private incentives induced corporate managers to hire accountants. These exclusively private incentives produced slow growth in the U.S. profession until the Progressive Era when federal legislation pumped up demand and caused the U.S. profession to overtake in size its British ancestor.

From a law and economics perspective, private corporations (and their promoters) will logically attempt to 'bond' with their shareholders by voluntarily imposing restraints on self-regarding behavior by managers in order to obtain a higher price for their shares.[21] Subjecting oneself to the scrutiny of an independent auditor seems a paradigmatic example of such 'bonding.'[22] But how much bonding will occur in an unregulated market is an open question. Also, behavior that resembles 'bonding' may prove on closer inspection to be largely illusory because shareholders cannot directly observe the actual relationship between the auditor and the corporate client. Self-interested managers gain the best of both worlds if they can convince shareholders that adequate controls are in place to prevent opportunistic behavior by managers (thereby maximizing share value), while still continuing to extract undisclosed private benefits of control from the company. Some evidence suggests that such illusory bonding was prevalent in the U.S. market during the early 20th century.

In any event, the U.S. experience with accounting represents a natural experiment in the functioning of a private market for such services. From the late 19th century until the New Deal, accountants were largely unregulated in the U.S., either by federal law or by the common law of torts. Within this private market, demand for accounting services was limited, and accountants proved to be relatively weak gatekeepers, possessing little power to discipline their own members and exercising even less control over their clients. Not until the passage of the federal securities laws in the 1930s, which made the use of independent auditors a condition of access to the capital markets (as in Great Britain), and also imposed significant liabilities on accountants, did accountants became 'public' gatekeepers—as they had been for nearly a century in Great Britain. Accordingly, this chapter will initially focus on the period prior to the passage of the federal securities laws because it is the 'test case' example of a free market in which the relationship between gatekeepers and client was largely a matter of private contracting—an era that had no corollary in Great Britain.

The Early Days

As of 1850, when the City of London alone already had 210 public accountants,[23] only 19 accountants in the aggregate were listed in the city directories of New York, Chicago, and Philadelphia.[24] Indeed, well into the 1870s, it was common practice for teams of shareholders to visit corporate offices periodically to verify the company's financial reports (or other information).[25] While seemingly impractical, such a self-help remedy was the only alternative, given the absence of professional auditors.

During the last quarter of the 19th century, British capital began to be attracted by the high rates of return available in the United States, and British auditors in consequence began to cross the Atlantic to monitor their clients' investments, which were chiefly in railroads, insurance and mortgage companies.[26] Eventually, British accountants came to establish resident offices. The first national accounting firm organized in the U.S. was Barrow, Wade, Guthrie & Co., in 1883, and several of its principal partners were British accountants.[27] Price Waterhouse & Co., already well established in Great Britain, sent agents to the United States, beginning in 1890, and soon thereafter established a permanent office.[28] Its early senior partners—first, A. Lowes Dickinson and, later, George O. May, both British expatriates—dominated the American profession until the Second World War.

The arrival of chartered accountants from Britain enhanced the prestige of the discipline in the United States, but also attracted intense hostility, as native American accountants quickly sensed that bankers and the most lucrative clients preferred the British chartered accountant to his domestic cousin. This hostility surfaced in the first efforts of the new profession to secure legislative recognition. All sides recognized that accountants had to distinguish themselves from mere bookkeepers to achieve true professional status. The British migrants looked to the professional societies that had received royal charters in Great Britain as their model, and urged the founding of a national professional association of accountants in the United States. In 1887, the American Association of Public Accountants (AAPA) was formed, largely at the instigation of British accountants. Over time and after various mergers in the 20th century, it would ultimately grow into the American Institute of Certified Public Accountants (AICPA). But at its inception, it has been described as a hybrid, in equal parts a guild and a London's men club.[29] Although the AAPA's formation followed the organization in 1880 of the Institute of Chartered Accountants in England and Wales by only seven years, two major differences distinguished the two bodies. First, the Institute in England had started in 1880 with over 1,000 members, while the AAPA counted only 31 members (many of them British) as of its founding in 1887.[30] Second, lacking anything equivalent to a royal charter, the AAPA had neither legal recognition nor the power to exclude incompetent or unqualified persons from the practice of accountancy. Put simply, the AAPA lacked licensing authority, and in the absence of such authority, a professional society could have only limited power over its own members and even less influence over the profession in general.

The AAPA's founders recognized that legislative recognition and licensing procedures were prerequisites to true professional stature.

Beginning in 1894, a coalition of industry groups lobbied the New York legislature for the nation's first CPA licensing law. The effort was not immediately successful, in large part because of divisions within the industry. Although bills were introduced that would have prohibited practice as a public accountant in New York without a license (and made such a license dependent upon passing an examination), the New York legislature would not go this far, fearing probably the exclusionary consequences of such legislation. Instead, the bill that finally passed in 1896 simply provided for the issuance of a certificate conferring the title 'certified public accountant' upon qualified persons and prohibited the use of that title by unlicensed persons.[31] Moreover, licensing authority was given not to the professional association, but to the New York State Board of Regents. Similar permissive legislation, following the same model, passed within a few years in Pennsylvania (1899), Maryland (1900), California (1901), Illinois (1903), New Jersey (1904), Florida (1905), and Michigan (1905).[32] As a result, weaker professional control characterized the U.S. profession from the outset, because it lacked control over both entry and exit—that is, control over admission of new members and expulsion or discipline of existing members. Under these state statutes, unlicensed persons could engage in any activity that a 'certified public accountant' could, but simply could not use that title. Even if suspended or disbarred from the professional association for misconduct or incompetence, a licensed certified public accountant could continue to practice, using that title, because his license came from the state.

This inability to control entry challenged the profession. Some favored federal licensing legislation in order to generate uniform national standards; more preferred state control, possibly because it was weaker. Eventually, the profession found a substitute for the royal charter on which the British profession was founded. It developed a nationwide licensing examination and eventually convinced virtually all the states to allow it to design and administer this exam. In so doing, the profession at least achieved control over entry—but this development did not come until the mid-20th century.[33]

Although it eventually gained substantial control over entry, the profession never won control over exit. It could not bar an expelled member from practicing accounting. The one professional sanction that the profession could employ was adverse publicity. Under its bylaws, the AAPA could expel or suspend a member found 'guilty of an act discreditable to the profession.'[34] Although this power was broadly construed and occasionally invoked, its deterrent effect was undercut by a corollary AAPA policy, adopted in its early days, never to publish the names of persons or firms found guilty of professional misconduct.[35] In effect, from its earliest days, the profession undertook only a relatively toothless form of self-policing.[36]

If the AAPA was a weak watchdog, it was a more effective guild. During the early 20th century, it opposed competitive bidding for audit engagements,[37] condemned advertising by accountants,[38] favored fixed fee schedules,[39] and constantly fought proposals for the federal licensing of accountants or the creation by the federal government of an internal audit bureau to perform auditing services with governmental employees. The AAPA united the profession when it enjoined rival associations that were selling C.P.A. certificates on a mail order basis,[40] but the profession divided again whenever the topics of national standards or uniform CPA examinations arose.

On one level, the division within the accounting profession mirrored broader political divisions within the larger society, ones that separated Progressive Era reformers who tended to support a strong national government from traditionalists who favored states' rights and decentralization. Underlying even this deep-seated political dispute, however, was an even more basic economic division within the new profession. Smaller CPA firms simply could not support themselves based on audit work for publicly-held corporations.[41] Not only were the opportunities for such work limited, as well into the 20th century few public firms published audited financial statements,[42] but such audit work as was available typically went to larger firms, usually those with British origins.

Smaller firms survived by designing and implementing bookkeeping and internal control systems for corporate clients. As a result, they were suspicious of the AAPA, which they saw as a captive of an Eastern Establishment of large firms that specialized in audit work, wanted strict national standards, and envisioned, in the words of one critic, 'a professional body above the regulatory laws of any state.'[43] Practitioners in smaller firms resisted both its emphasis on auditing and on auditor independence, because they needed to provide broader accounting services to their corporate clients, including bookkeeping, tax, and consulting services. Because they worked as virtual employees of the corporations they served, rather than as an outside inspector, their position inherently raised questions about their independence. In response, the smaller firms viewed independence as an overrated virtue—one that they saw as the product of an unthinking emulation of British standards.

Eventually, a rival organization to the AAPA was founded in 1921 to represent smaller firms and to shift the profession's focus from auditing to the provision of broader accounting services.[44] Known as the

American Society of Certified Public Accountants (ASCPA), it engaged in a bitter rivalry with AAPA, at least until midway during the Depression, when both organizations' common desire to avoid federal control of the accounting profession compelled them to accept a merger and form the American Institute of Certified Public Accountants (AICPA). Both before and after this merger, however, attempts to propose national standards or ethical rules of conduct were certain to exacerbate the rivalry between large and small firms and between the 'federalists' and the 'states righters.' As a result, during its formative period and extending until well into the 1930s, accounting was often a profession divided against itself.[45]

The early impact of the profession on the amount of financial information disclosed by American business corporations appears to have been positive, but modest. Prior to 1900, corporate disclosure of financial information was rare.[46] Corporate secrecy was the norm, either for fear of alerting competitors or based on the then standard justification that the shareholder needed only to know the amount of dividends paid. Even in the case of the few corporations with broadly dispersed shareholders, little financial information was disclosed to shareholders. For example, the American Sugar Refining Company, which had over 10,000 shareholders and was among the most actively traded stocks on the New York Stock Exchange, made no information available other than its dividend record and capitalization; similarly, between 1897 and 1905, Westinghouse neither published an annual report to shareholders nor held an annual meeting of shareholders.[47] All this was in sharp contrast to the British practice, where the Directors Liability Act of 1890 had made directors liable to investors for false statements in prospectuses and thus had already given rise to a system of mandatory disclosure.

After 1900, the level of financial disclosure increased, but the pattern was far from uniform. Companies such as American Tobacco Company and General Electric led the way, even before 1900.[48] In 1902, U.S. Steel, the product of a mega-merger engineered by J. P. Morgan, set a new standard in detailed annual financial reports (with Price Waterhouse serving as its auditor).[49] Still, the driving forces in this process of reform were the New York Stock Exchange and the investment bankers (with the unquestioned leader, J. P. Morgan & Co., being an Anglo-American firm and thus likely to be influenced by British practice). The New York Stock Exchange obviously had an interest in increasing investor confidence and its own listings; similarly, because underwriters were the principal reputational intermediaries upon whom investors relied in this era,[50] investment bankers wanted audited financial records for their own due diligence purposes and to minimize blame and reputational injury if an offering soured.

The accounting profession did push consistently for audited financial statements, even seeking legislation, but it showed little concern for the comparability of financial statements,[51] and, as next discussed, it actively opposed efforts to seek greater uniformity in accounting principles.

The Impact of the Progressive Era

The principal factors that accountants had stressed to justify their claims to professional status—their independence and their obligations to third parties—endeared them to Progressive Era reformers. Inherently, the Progressive Movement believed in social justice, progress, expertise, and the perfectibility of social institutions.[52] Correspondingly, its leaders distrusted corporate power, free markets, and the impact of great wealth on the political process. Given this starting point, and in particular a technocratic inclination to rely on experts, the Progressive Era reformers quickly came to view the accounting profession as the natural watchdogs of large corporations. The profession, itself, responded more opportunistically, accepting support to the extent it increased the demand for its services, but rejecting any attempt at regulation or public oversight.

To a modest degree, the reformers' hopes for the profession were realized, as accounting reformers did demonstrate that state and municipal accounting could be improved in ways that promoted transparency and restricted some forms of political corruption.[53] But the reformers' larger vision was unrealistic, and even quixotic, because they conceived of the accountant as a watchdog more for the public interest than for the interests of investors. In their normative vision, accountants would detect and report excessive profits as a signal that competition was failing and oligopoly was imminent. Investors, however, wanted no such warning that profits were excessive, but rather assurances that they were real.

Beyond even this incongruence between the Progressive Era's normative goals and the actual needs of investors, the fundamental irony about the Progressive Era was that its principal reforms greatly exacerbated the conflicts within the accounting profession and rendered it far less able to play the reformers' intended watchdog role. This is because the major reforms of the Progressive Era—the progressive income tax, authorized by the Sixteenth Amendment and enacted in 1913, and the powerful federal regulatory agencies created during that era, especially the Federal Trade Commission and the Federal Reserve Board—greatly increased the demand for accountants to perform consulting services for their corporate clients. Once accountants accepted and became dependent upon employment as tax advisers and consultants for their clients, their independence from their clients was compromised. Arguably, the result was a Faustian bargain: the profession at last prospered, but sacrificed its cherished independence in the process.[54]

The Progressive Era's high hopes for the accounting profession as a guardian against corporate power were first clearly exhibited in the 1902 report of the Industrial Commission.[55] Created by Congress in 1898 to investigate the impact of the new trusts that dominated the U.S.'s economic landscape, the Industrial Commission mobilized the critics of industrial concentration and held extensive hearings that elaborately documented seeming abuses of corporate power. Its final report, issued in 1902, recommended that 'the larger corporations— the so-called trusts—should be required to publish annually a properly audited report, showing in reasonable detail their assets and liabilities, with profit and loss; such a report and audit under oath to be subject to governmental regulation.'[56] A minority report went considerably further, concluding that an office or bureau should be established under the Treasury Department to register all corporations involved in interstate commerce and to require from each a detailed financial report that would be audited by accounting professionals employed by the Treasury Department.[57] The purpose of this disclosure was less to inform investors than to protect the public from the dangers of monopolization and exorbitant profits.[58]

For the accounting profession, the recommendation of mandatory audits for large corporations represented a potential Full Employment Act that they heartily endorsed, but the concept of a federal audit bureau implied federally subsidized competition—an idea that threatened them to their core. In response to the Industrial Commission's recommendations, a Bureau of Corporations was established in 1903 within the then new Department of Commerce, and for over a decade it regularly and futilely proposed legislation to require federal incorporation of most public corporations.[59] Otherwise, the Bureau of Corporations largely focused on its preferred remedy of 'efficient publicity' and conducted numerous corporate investigations. Even before Brandeis used the term, reformers of this era instinctively understood that sunlight was the best disinfectant.[60]

Although the AAPA endorsed the idea of mandatory audits for public corporations and even lobbied for legislation that would require such audits,[61] its members were far from convinced about the wisdom of federal controls on corporate power. Conservatives actively opposed expansion of federal power over the economy; others saw such expansion as necessary and/or inevitable. Robert Montgomery, an early and outspoken leader of the profession, who delivered the Presidential address at the 1912 annual meeting of the AAPA on the topic of 'Federal Control of Corporations,' told his membership where its own self-interest lay:

Foolish laws, and more foolish laws, relating to taxation and regulation will not diminish the income of the professional accountant; on the contrary, the more involved and unscientific the law, the more our profession will benefit financially.[62]

As he bluntly recognized, the profession's self-interest coincided with the Progressive Era's agenda.

The enactment of a federal income tax law in 1913 did immediately and substantially increase the demand for accounting services, but the sudden availability of tax practice also raised an ethical question: on tax issues, was the professional accountant to act as a neutral expert, taking neither the taxpayer's side nor the Government's side?—or, was the accountant permitted to be an advocate for its client? For a brief period, the profession actually debated this question earnestly, with editorials appearing in its professional journal, before it predictably decided that it could take its client's side as an advocate.[63]

The Progressive Era also witnessed the first promulgation of generally accepted accounting standards, in which process the accounting profession cooperated—but as a less than enthusiastic participant. Both the Federal Trade Commission and the Federal Reserve Board, each a creation of this era, favored the development of uniform systems of accounts, but for different reasons. The FTC curiously believed that a lack of knowledge of true costs caused businessmen to underprice their products and engage in ruinous 'cut-throat' competition.[64] It proposed to work with the AAPA to develop and promote uniform cost standards and, ultimately, uniformity of accounting rules. Initially, the AAPA was happy to endorse the development of uniform cost systems, probably because it implied work for accountants in helping corporate clients to design and implement such systems. Then, in 1916, the FTC's chairman suggested that such uniform standards should be verified by accountants registered by the Federal Reserve Board, so that creditors could have confidence in them.[65] This idea of mandatory registration or licensing was plainly unacceptable to the profession. The AAPA also became skeptical of uniform accounting rules as an infringement on their professional autonomy. The conventional wisdom within the profession was that uniform rules reduced the stature of accountants.

From prior experience with uniform accounts, the profession believed that their implementation would lead to a 'rulebook' mentality that could be implemented by clerks.[66]

The proposal for a federal registry of auditors had 'the effect of a bombshell' on the Council of the American Institute of Accountants, which met with the FTC chairman and adamantly opposed federal registration as threatening a federal takeover and de facto licensing of accountants.[67] Faced with such hostility, the FTC chairman looked for a compromise, and turned to the Federal Reserve Board for support, quietly shelving the auditor registration proposal, which sank out of sight until it resurfaced later in the New Deal.

In contrast to the FTC, the Federal Reserve Board had a different reason for favoring uniform accounting rules. The newly-formed Federal Reserve Board continuously faced the problem of discounting the commercial paper of large corporations. More reliable audits, it believed, would reduce its credit risk, and it hinted that it might apply a more favorable discount rate to corporate customers whose audits met its standards. Always eager to encourage independent audits, the AAPA had long recommended independently audited financial statements for companies whose commercial paper was to be discounted by the Federal Reserve.[68] More generally, federal minimum standards for audits were far less offensive to the profession than restrictions on the inventory of permissible accounting rules. In any event, after much discussion, the AAPA agreed to cooperate with the Federal Reserve Board and in 1917 submitted to the Federal Reserve Board a memorandum on auditing standards that largely derived from a pre-existing in-house study prepared by a Price Waterhouse partner as a means of specifying minimum audit standards for that firm.[69] With no expertise of its own to draw upon, the Federal Reserve adopted the document intact as a set of model audit rules and published it as a Federal Reserve Bulletin under the poorly chosen title, 'Uniform Accounting.'[70]

Widely circulated and highly influential, this publication set forth model formats for both the balance sheet and the income statement, that gradually were adopted as the prevailing format (thereby replacing highly individual and idiosyncratic styles of presentation used by many public companies).[71] Nevertheless, the publication set off a controversy. The Price Waterhouse memorandum that was largely adopted by the Federal Reserve Board treated the verification of receivables and the observation of inventories as optional procedures, which the auditor did not necessarily have to perform.[72] Possibly, this position was intended only as confidential internal advice within one firm as to what positions they could live with, if necessary. Corporate clients seized on this language from a now official government document to resist efforts by their auditors to engage in such costly, but 'optional' procedures. For this and other reasons, much of the accounting industry viewed the 1917 publication of Uniform Accounting as lowering, rather than raising, standards.[73]

In any event, the practical impact of this effort was to incline banks and other conservative users of financial statements to rely only on the certificates of the large Eastern auditing firms that they already knew—thereby deepening the divisions between large and small firms and increasing the small firms' suspicions of the industry's principal accounting association.

Back to Normalcy: The 1920s

The reform aspirations of the Progressive Era were quickly and quietly abandoned in the 1920s, as the market boomed and politicians agreed that the business of America was business. Although the AAPA (now renamed the American Institute of Accountants (or AIA)) continued to recommend national legislation that would require independent audits for public corporations, Congress had no interest in such reforms. Even the New York Stock Exchange, long an ally of the AIA, refused to endorse an AIA proposal to require independent audits by all its listed companies.[74]

Within the profession, the 1920s saw a shift away from the prior preoccupation with auditing. Tax work was proving highly lucrative, and managements had a new interest in cost accounting. As two leading accounting historians have explained:

[I]n the 1920s, the political sector asked CPAs to serve as advisers to, not monitors of, corporate clients. The rapid increase in the tax and cost areas, combined with the growth of advisory services, forced the profession to walk a fine line in maintaining its claim to professional status.[75]

The loss of enthusiasm for auditor independence in the 1920s was at least in part the product of changes in the political and economic environment that the profession inhabited. Bankers had long been the leading proponents and consumers of independent audits, but in the 1920s bankers shifted from being lenders to being investment bankers underwriting equity offerings. From this altered perspective, they saw little demand among investors for audits.[76] Corporate managements made clear their expectation that auditors should work with them 'to ensure that every firm received a fair return on its investment.'[77] This concept of a 'fair return' on investment was also picked up by the governmental agencies, most notably the Department of Commerce and the FTC, which encouraged the gathering of cost data and the use of depreciation and accrual accounting to reduce taxes.[78] Assembling such data, of course, employed accountants. Unchanged was the basic fact that, at least prior to the enactment of the federal securities laws, 'most small CPA firms and practitioners in non-industrial areas survived by providing a wide range of advisory services to their clients.'[79]

In overview, the important point here is that the 1920s represented the final era of the free and unregulated market in auditing services. In theory, accountants could have competed as reputational intermediaries, with the most competent and respected becoming dominant. Little evidence suggests that that happened. Instead, throughout this period, which was, of course, a bubble era equaling that of the 1990s, accounting firms pursued consulting and advisory income and generally ignored issues of independence (which had been heatedly debated during earlier periods). Although newly listed companies did comply with the New York Stock Exchange's requirement of annual financial reports (and their number soared in the 1920s), it was not until 1932, after the Crash and with more intrusive reforms looming, that the New York Stock Exchange first required listed companies to file audited financial statements, prepared by an auditor 'qualified under the laws of some state or country.'[80]

Historians of the era have divided over whether financial reporting truly improved over this period, and some accounting scholars have expressed particular doubt that auditing in the manner it was then conducted 'improved the perceived quality of financial reports.'[81] Possibly, this was because (as virtually all contemporaneous observers agreed) the investors of this era were still too unsophisticated to review or rely on financial statements.[82] The free market did not spur the reputational competition among market participants that theory was to predict. In this respect, the 1920s presaged the 1990s.

The Crash and the New Deal: The Struggle to Protect Autonomy

The 1929 Crash changed everything—but less so for the accounting profession than virtually any other affected group. Uniquely, accountants successfully preserved their professional autonomy, whereas other private actors—the New York Stock Exchange, for example, and broker-dealers in particular—were forced to surrender much of theirs.

Perhaps this should not be surprising, because the public recrimination after the Crash did not primarily focus on accountants. Rather, the Pecora Hearings focused national attention and anger on such poster boy targets, as (1) stock pools, which were thought to be engineered by Wall Street insiders, (2) pyramid-style holding companies, as exemplified by Samuel Insull and the ever-secretive Ivan Krueger, and (3) short selling by executives in their own companies, as vividly illustrated by Albert Wiggins, the president of Chase National Bank.[83]

Of course, accountants did not escape unscathed. The Securities Act of 1933 imposed presumptive liability on accountants (and other experts) if they had audited the books of a company engaged in a public offering. Both the Securities Act of 1933 and the Securities Exchange Act of 1934 also gave the Securities and Exchange Commission authority to regulate accounting (and auditing) and mandated that the auditor be independent of the client.

So how then does one conclude that the profession preserved its autonomy? Here, it is useful to focus on the period just prior to the Congress's consideration of federal securities legislation. Following the Crash, it was obvious to any informed observer that legislative reforms were likely. Anticipating such regulation, J. M. B. Hoxsey, Secretary of the New York Stock Exchange and the official most responsible for its listing rules, initiated a correspondence with the AIA in 1931, candidly writing that 'if we act now ... we may retard unwarranted intrusions.'[84] Hoxsey invited the AIA to form an alliance with the NYSE to propose sensible reforms, and the AIA formed a committee to develop a joint position. Specifically, Hoxsey invited the AIA to indicate that (1) it would take responsibility for reviewing the propriety of the accounting principles management selected, (2) income statement data should be disclosed in annual reports, and (3) earnings management through the use of reserves to artificially smooth income should be discouraged.[85] Given the temper of the times, these were modest reforms that did not impose uniform or standardized accounting rules on an unwilling profession.

Nonetheless, the AIA, through George O. May, who was both chair of the AIA's committee appointed to consult with the NYSE and also the senior partner of Price Waterhouse, rejected any responsibility for these determinations, insisting that it was entirely management's responsibility to choose its accounting principles, disclose income data, or engage in earnings management. In light of the far more sweeping reforms, including a federal audit bureau and uniform accounting standards, that were already being proposed, this was a tough, unyielding stance that left the profession defining its gatekeeping responsibilities in minimal terms. As Hoxsey had probably recognized, assigning some responsibility to the accountants for approving management's choice of accounting principles was a compromise that might hold off regulators from adopting uniform accounting principles (which had always been the reform that the profession most feared). Still, the AIA replied to the NYSE that at least so long as the auditor had 'no reason to doubt ... [management's] competence or good faith,' the auditor 'may properly certify accounts without qualification even though his own preference would be for a different treatment.'[86] This rejection of any role for the profession in making 'preferability' decisions continued throughout the decade, with the AIA similarly informing the SEC that this prerogative belonged only to management.[87]

Why did the profession reject out of hand a compromise that struck even the NYSE as moderate and likely to forestall more intrusive legislative interventions? Fear of liability cannot supply more than part of the answer, because the profession had not yet experienced any significant exposure to liability and the stricter liability rules of the federal securities laws were not yet in view.[88] Hence, the more likely answer is that the profession rejected any role for itself in making 'preferability' decisions because acceptance of such a role would have placed it in an adversarial relationship with its clients.[89] Even though auditors might seem to be naturally in an adversarial (or at least monitoring) relationship with their audit clients, the fear was that subjecting management's choice of accounting principles to any form of preferability review by the auditing firm would exacerbate the relationship. Possibly, this suggests that the profession was already too deeply affected by the receipt of tax, advisory and consulting income for it to accept voluntarily any responsibility that could antagonize corporate managements. Alternatively the profession may have feared that any acceptance of enhanced discretion by auditors would have resulted in auditor-shopping and a proverbial 'race to the bottom,' as firms would be forced to compete in terms of their willingness to acquiesce in management's choice. In any event, the pattern that emerges clearly in the 1930s was that of a gatekeeper that wished to define its gatekeeping obligations as narrowly as possible.

The AIA similarly rejected Hoxsey's inquiry on behalf of the NYSE as to whether it should mandate disclosure of income statement data. While the AIA did not deny that income was of 'cardinal importance to investors,' it replied that the auditor had no right to instruct the client to disclose it.[90] More surprisingly, the AIA also rejected Hoxsey's suggestion that the profession should condemn the intentional understatement of assets and income. Earnings management and income smoothing was defensible, the AIA committee responded, because 'measurement of profits as between years is necessarily in large measure conventional.'[91] In short, one had to adopt some 'conventions' to measure income, and an 'income smoothing' convention represented good social policy in their judgment.

The interaction between the AIA and the NYSE over this period is instructive because it shows the NYSE understandably committed to reforms that it believed would restore investor confidence—for example, audit certificates, quarterly reporting, changes in capital stock accounting to restrict stock watering, changes in depreciation policy and disclosure of accounting for foreign subsidiaries.[92] Because the NYSE's revenues came primarily from brokerage commissions, it had greater reason to seek to restore investor confidence and increase trading volume. But the AIA, which received its revenues from corporate clients, had less incentive, and it took a decidedly more conservative tone. The AIA's Special Committee submitted its final report in 1932,[93] and, although it agreed to some reforms, its principal stress was on reducing the public expectations of accountants by (1) educating the public that balance sheets did not show present values of assets and liabilities, and (2) insisting upon 'the right of corporations to select methods of accounting deemed by them to be best adapted to the requirements of their business.'[94] Much as the profession had earlier cooperated with the FTC and the FRB in preparing 'Uniform Accounting' in 1917, so similarly it cooperated with the NYSE in 1932—eager to encourage audits, but reluctant to see any imposition of new responsibilities or judgmental discretion upon it.

Even after the SEC was established, the AIA held to the same positions that it had expressed to the NYSE. Indeed, as late as 1936, it still urged the SEC to allow issuers not to disclose much income statement data (such as sales) on the grounds that disclosure would place many issuers at a competitive disadvantage and would only be beneficial to speculators.[95] Even the non-disclosure of executive salaries in the AIA's view could be justified on this ground. Surprisingly, this dismissal of the income statement's importance seems roughly the equivalent of a gatekeeper arguing that its own gate could be left unattended. In some respects—such as in rationalizing income smoothing or the understatement of assets—the profession may have been motivated by liability considerations, but in lobbying for the omission of sales data it was virtually renouncing the value of its own professional services. Such a position seemingly reveals a deep allegiance to the client's interests that is in obvious tension with the idea of professional independence.

Once the drafting of the Securities Act of 1933 began, the profession stayed well in the background.[96] The AIA never testified and instead left the representation of the industry to go by default to Colonel A. H. Carter, President of the New York State Society of Certified Public Accountants. Carter urged Congress to revise the proposed legislation to provide instead that all registration statements be audited, and Carter testified before the Senate Committee that 85 percent of all listed companies were already audited.[97] Yet, the Committee's response to this information was lukewarm at best. Rather, the Committee's chairman, Senator Duncan Fletcher, understandably wondered why it was necessary to require by law what was already the prevailing practice. His views were echoed by Senator Gore, who pointed out that the fact that 85 percent of the NYSE's companies were audited had not prevented the 1929 Crash. Auditing, they were implying, was no panacea.

The practical political explanation of Colonel Carter's testimony may have been that he was seeking to confine Congress to symbolic legislation that would do no harm, but only codify current best practices. In any event, the Senate Committee appears to have largely ignored Carter, never including his proposed audit requirement in their bill. That such a requirement did enter the final legislation was more the product of the substitution of a different drafting team that had been assembled by then Harvard Law School Professor Felix Frankfurter, with the blessing of President Roosevelt, to draft the House version of the same legislation. Written by Frankfurter protégés, James Landis and Benjamin Cohen, the House bill used the English Companies Law as its principal model,[98] and under the active sponsorship of House Speaker Sam Rayburn, it quietly replaced the Senate draft bill on which Colonel Carter had testified.

Under the Landis/Cohen draft, the FTC (and later its successor, the SEC) did gain authority to define the accounting concepts used in registration statements.[99] Indeed, Section 19(a) of the Securities Act expressly gave the SEC authority to resolve many of the accounting issues that had been exploited by aggressive managements during the 1920s.[100] Although this represented a major defeat for the profession, the profession did gain a compensating provision requiring independent audits for all public offerings of securities.[101]

Although the SEC gained authority over accounting, this did not imply that the SEC could exercise that authority easily or without political cost. Indeed, from its creation in 1934, the SEC went to great lengths to assure the accounting profession that it would only reluctantly use its authority to set accounting standards.[102] The priority of its first Chairman, Joseph Kennedy, was to induce Wall Street to accept the SEC and file registration statements with it, thereby increasing capital flotation and encouraging economic recovery. To realize this goal, he sought to avoid bruising confrontations with the accounting profession. This policy resulted in the Kennedy-led Commission largely abandoning accounting reform. The issue first arose in a clear-cut fashion in October 1934, when a Minnesota public utility sought to sell securities under a registration statement whose financial statements wrote up its fixed assets by $16 million. Predictably, two Commissioners insisted that the issuer should be forced to restate its balance sheet on a historical cost basis.[103] After all, this was precisely the type of risky accounting practice that in their view had led to the 1929 Crash. But the Kennedy-led majority accepted a compromise that permitted the inflated financial statements to be used, provided that disclosure was made in footnotes as to the impact of the write-up.[104] Although arguably politically expedient, this decision began a long and undistinguished history of SEC acquiescence in dubious accounting positions that the accounting profession itself was able to justify, mainly on the grounds that issuer management should have the discretion to choose the accounting principles it wanted.

The next SEC Chairman, James Landis, had agreed with Kennedy's position that encouraging issuers to register securities and raise capital was more important than revising accounting rules, but, as Chairman, he came to be highly and publicly critical of what he saw as the accounting profession's excessive servility to its clients.[105] His skeptical comments had one demonstrable impact: the American Institute of Accountants (AIA) and the American Society of Certified Public Accountants (ASPCA), long fierce rivals, decided that they feared the SEC more than each other, and so they merged in 1937 in order to better resist the dangers of a federal takeover. Landis was followed as SEC Chairman by William O. Douglas, who characteristically was an activist who wanted to use the SEC's powers to reform accounting principles. But Douglas never went beyond instructing the Commission's staff to prepare studies of existing practices.[106] Other crises, most notably his struggle with the New York Stock Exchange, and his campaign to enact trust indenture and bankruptcy bills, took precedence.

Meanwhile, the Commission's chief accountant, Carman G. Blough, quietly undercut the public activism of Landis and Douglas and, within the Commission, advocated an accommodation with the profession. Eventually, he convinced a majority of the Commission's members in December 1937 that his office lacked the staff, time, and resources to formulate correct accounting principles.[107] Although some Commissioners wished the SEC to be more proactive on accounting, the Commission was both preoccupied with other matters and sufficiently divided to make compromise seem necessary. In April 1938, the Commission announced its compromise in Accounting Series Release No. 4, a very brief two-sentence statement, whose final sentence said it all:

In cases where there is a difference of opinion between the Commission and the registrant as to the proper principles of accounting to be followed, disclosure will be accepted in lieu of correction of the financial statements themselves only if the points involved are such that there is substantial authoritative support for the practices followed by the registrant and the position of the Commission has not previously been expressed in rules, regulations or other official releases of the Commission, including the published opinions of its chief accountant.[108]

What these words meant was that, unless the SEC had earlier published a release or opinion rejecting a particular accounting practice or convention, the Commission would defer to the industry position. The one exception to this general rule of deference arose if a position taken by the registrant lacked 'substantial authoritative support'; in that case the Commission or its staff could reject that accounting position and require a correction of the issuer's financial statements. Experience soon proved, however, that the Commission would seldom find such 'substantial authoritative support' lacking.[109] Although the Commission had not abandoned its right to revise accounting rules, it had imposed on itself an obligation to act prospectively and to grant presumptive weight to any position followed by a substantial segment of the profession.

In retrospect, the accounting profession survived the 1930s with remarkably little loss of professional autonomy, given the intensity of the national crisis that the 1929 Crash precipitated. To be sure, federal statutes had given the SEC authority to define accounting concepts and, if it had desired, even to impose uniform accounting rules. But the SEC quickly showed little inclination to move in that direction. Moreover, the same legislation contained benefits as well as costs for the profession, as it imposed independent audits on all issuers of securities in the public markets, which had been the profession's legislative goal since the Progressive Era. Although the profession had been subjected to a deliberately punitive standard of liability by the Securities Act of 1933, the impact of the 1933 and 1934 Acts was not felt in the 1930s—and indeed did not truly materialize until the class action was perfected as a procedural device in the 1970s.

Finally, even in the face of pressure from its natural allies, such as the NYSE, to assume a greater gatekeeping responsibility, the profession resisted and successfully stood firm. Its position of not being able to make 'preferability' decisions hardened as the decade wore on.[110] When the AIA and the ASCPA undertook merger talks in the mid-1930s, they recognized the need to subscribe to a common set of basic principles—a common ideology for the profession. Essentially, they agreed on three principles: (1) resistance to uniform accounting principles, (2) consistency, and (3) conservatism. Consistency was the logical alternative to preferability. Its attraction was that it limited the profession's responsibilities. Under a consistency-oriented system of accounting, the accountant did not determine if an accounting principle was wise or appropriate, but only that it had been used in practice and had been consistently applied by the issuer.[111] Conservatism as a principle entitled the issuer to write down fixed assets to nominal amounts, thus opting to take a bath in one period, but thereby becoming able to report positive income (freed of depreciation charges) in the next period. During the 1930s, this tactic enabled some issuers to make an accounting recovery faster than they made a financial recovery. Both principles—consistency and conservatism—maximized management's discretion and thus were popular with corporate clients. Ultimately, the profession had defined its core values so as to minimize conflicts with corporate clients.

Two lessons are suggested by this experience. First, despite the intense pressures of the 1930s focus on the accounting profession, the profession consistently resisted expansion of its gatekeeping responsibilities. Second, professions are difficult to regulate, even when the political will to do so exists. Few agencies—then or now—can claim to possess the broad expertise necessary to adopt comprehensive rules governing a profession, and thus regulators are predictably forced to defer to the profession on most technical questions.

Standard Setting: From the CAP to the APB to the FASB

The SEC's de facto delegation in 1938 of control over accounting rules to the profession necessarily raised the question of how the industry would formulate its own 'authoritative' standards. The initial response of the AICPA was to expand and strengthen its Committee on Accounting Procedure (or CAP), which had long maintained at least a nominal supervision over accounting orthodoxy. As of 1938, the CAP had become virtually moribund and had not offered any specific advice on accounting issues in years.[112] The AICPA, recognizing that self-regulation could not survive without a more serious effort, sought to revive CAP in 1938, expanding its membership, and adding several prominent academics, along with Carman Blough, the SEC's chief accountant, who had been a leading advocate of SEC deference to the industry.[113]

Within a year, CAP began to issue its first Accounting Research Bulletins. While its work was respected, CAP was always closely constrained. Its rules provided that its pronouncements had to be adopted by a two-thirds vote of its members and could not be retroactive.[114] Dissents would also be published.[115] This meant not only that it took a broad consensus to change the rules, but that accountants who wished to depart from a rule could rely on the dissenting position contending that it also constituted 'substantial authoritative support' in the now all-important language of Accounting Series Release No. 4.[116] In truth, dissents were seldom needed, because the Accounting Research Bulletins promulgated by CAP typically contained numerous exceptions and recognized that in special circumstances other accounting treatments were permissible. Thus, as John Carey, the friendly historian of the accounting profession, recognized:

As a consequence, except as the SEC or the New York Stock Exchange insisted on compliance, individual companies and auditors were at liberty to deviate if they chose to assume the burden of justifying their departure.[117]

Permissive and toothless, CAP was inevitably destined to be the target of criticism. World War II delayed that criticism, but it came relentlessly in the 1950s. Some of the criticism came from within the industry, most notably from Leonard Spacek, the managing partner of Arthur Andersen & Co, who in a 1956 speech attacked the AICPA's 'antiquated accounting principles' and analogized its methodology for determining accounting principles based on past practices to a medical profession that relied primarily on the views of coroners.[118]

Faced with criticism from a variety of fronts, the AICPA responded with the creation of the Accounting Principles Board (APB) in 1959 as a replacement for CAP. Unlike CAP, the APB was to base its pronouncements on professional research, and an accounting research program was simultaneously begun. Once again, however, a two-thirds vote of its members was required before an opinion could be issued by the APB, and dissents would be published.[119] Because the APB's membership was set at 21 members, the need to obtain the concurrence of 14 members, most of whom would have contentious clients to whom they had to answer, ensured that compromises would have to be struck and multiple exceptions recognized.[120]

In truth, the APB did attempt to address difficult issues in an independent way. When it did so, however, it encountered fierce opposition both from within the profession and from without. A well-known controversy illustrates its vulnerability. In 1962, as a device for encouraging economic recovery, Congress enacted an investment tax credit for investment in certain depreciable assets placed in service after 1961; obviously, Congress intended an incentive to spur investment in plant and equipment. In December 1962, however, the APB ruled that the tax credit had to be spread over the productive life of the depreciable asset[121]—thereby dulling the incentive to businesses which had hoped to use an immediate 'flow through' accounting treatment and receive the full effect of the credit in the first year. The result was a political firestorm, with industry, the profession, and Congress all objecting. The denouement came in early 1963 when the SEC effectively overruled the APB, advising auditors that they could follow any of several alternative approaches not approved by the new APB opinion.[122]

This outcome both encouraged industry and dissident firms to orchestrate similar attacks on later controversial APB opinions and undercut the SEC's own position, which had previously been to insist that issuers conform to, and seldom depart from, APB opinions. In addition, the crisis made the two-thirds approval rule an even greater obstacle to reform, because it seemingly showed that controversial rules would weaken the APB.

The APB's supporters, recognizing that the APB's credibility had been weakened and seeking to enhance its authority, lobbied the AICPA's Council at its 1964 meeting to adopt a motion to the effect that '[a] pronouncement of the [APB] constitutes the only generally accepted accounting principle for purposes of expressing an opinion on financial statements, unless and until rescinded by the Council.'[123] This was a risky strategy that backfired when the APB's critics substituted and adopted a weaker motion calling only for further study by a special committee.[124] A year later, the special committee reported its much watered-down conclusion that, although opinions of the APB constituted 'substantial authoritative support,' 'substantial authoritative support' could also exist for positions that deviated from APB opinions.[125] The result was to leave the APB as little more than a source of advisory opinions on which the profession could rely, but was not required to follow.

Predictably, the SEC was dissatisfied with this outcome (which they had indirectly caused), as were securities analysts who, probably for the first time, entered the debate seeking greater comparability of earnings. Nonetheless, the bottom line as at the end of the 1960s was, in the candid words of John L. Carey, the profession's friendly historian, that despite decades of effort 'there was still no authoritative, comprehensive code of accounting principles in existence.'[126] Nor was there yet significant pressure driving the profession towards comparability of financial statements.

If the APB was weakened by its theoretically sound, but politically naïve, attempt to address the investment tax credit, it suffered even greater injury in attempting to restrict 'pooling of interest' accounting for mergers and acquisitions.[127] Under pressure from the press, Congress, the SEC, the FTC, and academia, the APB considered abolishing pooling, which the FTC had called a 'tool of deception' and which the popular press, led by the acerbic accounting critic Abraham Briloff, regularly described in colorful phrases, such as 'pooling-fooling' or 'dirty pooling.'[128] But the APB could not muster the necessary two-thirds vote, and could only circulate a weak compromise opinion that would prohibit poolings when the size ratio of the acquiring and acquired firms was no greater than three to one. This proposal galvanized the financial industry into opposition, as it threatened to chill some mergers. Even this milder proposed opinion proved unable to gain two-thirds support.[129] A third opinion suggested a nine-to-one ratio as the outer limit on pooling, but it encountered the formal opposition of four of the 'Big Eight' accounting firms. After it too was withdrawn, the APB circulated APB Opinion No. 16 in August 1970 that lacked any size criterion to limit poolings. It received withering criticism, in part because virtually any transaction could be structured to satisfy its relaxed test. At various points in this controversy, some of the Big Eight firms threatened to withdraw from the APB; one (Arthur Andersen) threatened an antitrust suit against the APB, and the SEC inconsistently gave and withdrew support for various drafts.

Given the seeming impotence of the APB, the AICPA formed a special committee, headed by former SEC Commissioner Francis Wheat, to review the APB's status and the possible alternatives for the formulation of accounting principles. In 1972, the Wheat Committee recommended that the APB be abolished and replaced by a standard-setter that was more broadly representative and autonomous. The acrimonious debate over pooling was not the sole cause of the APB's demise; other financial scandals, most notably the bankruptcy of the Penn Central, had added to the general sense that accounting principles were being written by, and for the benefit of, corporate clients. The APB's on-going inability to take, and hold to, a clear position is the strongest explanation for its downfall. Whatever it proposed, the profession sought to (and usually did) weaken to the point that the change became virtually irrelevant.

In the place of the APB, the Wheat Committee proposed the creation of a Financial Accounting Standards Board (FASB). The members of the FASB would be indirectly appointed by the AICPA Board of Directors (who would actually appoint the nine trustees of a Financial Accounting Foundation (FAF), which would in turn appoint the seven members of

FASB). While this structure provided some marginally greater insula-
tion from industry pressures, the real difference between FASB and the
APB was that each FASB member would be full-time and could have
no other business affiliation.[130] FASB began operations in 1973, and to
facilitate its commencement, the SEC issued Accounting Series Release
No. 150 in December 1973, which required registrants to comply with
SEC rules and releases when the SEC had taken a position on a specific
issue, but otherwise to prepare financial statements in accordance with
the "principles, standards and practices promulgated by the FASB."[131]

FASB got off to a slow start and initially became the target of criticism
for its dilatory pace, as a series of financial scandals had led Congress
to again consider the option of directly mandating the accounting principles for publicly-owned corporations.[132] Ironically, however, FASB's
greatest crisis arose not from any foot-dragging on its part, but from an
honest and well-motivated attempt to deal with an obvious accounting
issue. Possibly because FASB was better insulated from industry pressures than its predecessors, it did not anticipate the firestorm that its
actions would touch off—or that, once again, an accounting standard-
setter would be abandoned by the SEC in its hour of need.

In 1993, FASB issued a proposed opinion that would have required
companies to recognize some expense for stock-based compensation,
including stock options.[133] To an accounting purist, FASB's position
simply said what the vast majority of economists considered obvious:
options are dilutive, conferring real value on executives, but at a real cost
to shareholders. However self-evident these truths were to economists,
the resulting controversy generated by this proposal far dwarfed anything that the APB had experienced in 1962 in the investment tax credit
controversy. The business community felt personally threatened, and
even 'liberal' Democratic Senators, such as Joseph Lieberman, Diane
Feinstein and Barbara Boxer, were mobilized to save Silicon Valley's stock
options. In May 1994, a 'sense of the Senate' Resolution was adopted
by a vote of 88 to 9 expressing opposition to the FASB proposal. Arthur
Levitt, then a very new SEC Chairman, lobbied FASB to abandon its
rule (but later confessed his regret at doing so).[134] Facing insurmountable opposition, FASB finally abandoned its proposal in 1994.

The industry, however, was unforgiving, and in 1995 it sought still
greater control over the FAF (through which it could control the nomi-
nation of FASB members). The Financial Executives Institute (FEI),
which was composed of chief executives of Fortune 500 firms, proposed
to reduce the size, staff, and budget of FASB, to give control of its agenda
to an external body, and to require a supermajority vote of 80 percent
for approval of all standards.[135] Here, the SEC at last dug in its heels and

mounted a largely successful defense of FASB. Although SEC Chairman Levitt was able to secure the addition of four 'public' members to the FAF board, he failed to gain the right that he had sought for SEC approval of all FAF nominees.[136] In any event, the deeper problem was that industry contributions funded the FASB's work, and that spigot had been turned off when FASB seemingly bit the hand that fed it. Nor was the reduction in funding simply a coincidence. The same tactic was similarly employed against the Public Oversight Board (POB), a self-regulatory body that was entrusted with oversight of the profession's internal disciplinary process, when that body began to show signs of activism.[137] As a result, the FASB, the POB and other self-regulatory bodies could see a clear handwriting on the wall by the late 1990s: activism meant the end of funding.[138]

Symptomatically, throughout the bruising fight between Corporate America and the SEC over the independence of FASB, the accounting profession largely stood on the sidelines. Arthur Levitt was disappointed at their passivity:

[I] was shocked when I saw how the auditors behaved in these dustups. They failed to rally to the cause of investors, and instead supported the demands of their corporate clients. They had become advocates.[139]

Levitt's perceptions of the accounting profession, formed in this initial confrontation over FASB, changed his priorities as SEC Chairman, prompting the strong views he articulated in his celebrated 1998 speech, 'The Numbers Game.'[140] In that speech, which marked the beginning of Levitt's increasingly adversarial relationship with the accounting profession, Levitt catalogued a variety of tactics (most notably, 'cookie jar reserves' and 'big bath' restructuring charges) that managements used, and in which accountants had acquiesced, to manage earnings. Having described the means of manipulation, Levitt then turned to the purpose of these tactics and articulated his basic sense of what had gone wrong:

Too many corporate managers, auditors, and analysts are participating in a game of nods and winks. In the zeal to satisfy consensus earnings estimates and project a smooth earnings path, wishful thinking may be winning the day over faithful presentation. As a result, I fear that we are witnessing an erosion in the quality of earnings, and therefore, the quality of financial reporting. Managing may be giving way to manipulation; integrity may be losing out to illusion.[141]

These were strong words, possibly the strongest that an SEC Chairman had ever levied at any profession. In overview, a short, straight line connects the fight over FASB to Levitt's growing concern with accounting gamesmanship in 1998 and then to his attempt, which began a year later, to restrict the consulting activities of the accounting profession. Along the way, the confrontation escalated from a dispute of intermediate size and gravity to a total war between the industry and the SEC, with a commensurate increase in the rhetoric on both sides. Although the industry forced Levitt to abandon his original proposed prophylactic rule and accept a weak compromise instead,[142] the industry ultimately won the battle but lost the war, because it was thereafter perceived, both in Washington and in the nation, less as an objective profession bearing neutral expertise and more as a bare-knuckled political interest group. Its political capital expended, it was vulnerable when the next crisis struck—as it did when the Enron scandal broke in late 2001.

Viewed dispassionately, the AICPA's handling of the FASB provides an illustration of how a profession can dominate self-regulation, even when it is forced to create a reasonably independent body. For much of its early career, the FASB, unlike the APB, operated by a simple majority vote, but then in 1991, as the industry was becoming suspicious of its activism, the voting rule was changed back to a supermajority rule (five of the seven members having to vote for a change).[143] The goal was clearly to slow the FASB down.

This use of a high supermajority rule, however, created a problem for the profession and its clients, who constantly needed interpretations, clarifications, and special rulings involving unique facts or 'emerging' issues. To address this need for the constant revision of rules that would otherwise become rigid and inflexible, the AICPA prevailed upon FASB to establish an Emerging Issues Task Force (EITF), which was staffed with CPAs from the major firms. The EITF was empowered to issue authoritative pronouncements interpreting and extending Generally Accepted Accounting Principles, but not to overrule or contradict FASB's own statements.[144] In the view of at least one former FASB member, the EITF was used by the major firms 'more as a forum to argue a specific client's fact situation than as a forum to achieve a professionally oriented solution.'[145] In effect, its role was to grant dispensations and exemptions. The relative productivity of the FASB and the EITF seems consistent with this view. From its inception in 1973 to August 2003, FASB has issued some 150 Statements of Financial Accounting Standards, but the EITF, formed more recently in 1984, has issued hundreds of pronouncements.[146] Thus, the industry had the best of both worlds: a constrained self-regulator that could only change the rules when it could act with a very high consensus, but an active, indeed prolific interpretive arm that could address new and 'emerging' issues, chiefly to grant exemptive relief. Phrased differently, FASB issued principles, but the EITF produced rules—context-specific rules with bright lines that solved the day-to-day problems of practitioners. Revealingly, it was the EITF (not the FASB) that liberalized the treatment of 'special purpose entities,' which were the mechanism that Enron used in record numbers to mask its liabilities.

To the extent that the FASB could still be an activist (as it was in 1993 when it sought to expense stock options), the AICPA always had the residual power, inherent in its control of FASB's budget, to check it. Only with Sarbanes-Oxley has this control over the purse strings been ended, by allowing FASB to tax its clientele of financial statement producers.

The puzzling question is whether the profession truly understood its own self-interest. Given its de facto control over FASB, did it help itself by opposing a stronger, more consistent body of accounting principles—or, rather, did it shoot itself in the foot? A cohesive and authoritative body of accounting principles protects the profession in two important ways.[147] First, it allows the professional to better withstand pressure from clients to sign off on misleading financial statements. If a client were to threaten to fire the honest professional for a refusal to acquiesce, the professional would know that strong and clear mandatory rules protected him or her because no other honest professional could approve the requested treatment. The clearer that GAAP principles are, the more that the established professional is protected from the deviant firm or other outlier who is willing to acquiesce in dubious positions in order to win clients. Second, the more mandatory and less permissive that GAAP principles are, the more the professional is protected in litigation, because it can accurately assert that it had no discretion. Rather, it was required to follow the treatment that it approved. In short, the more discretion and latitude that the inventory of generally accepted accounting principles gives the client, the less the leverage possessed by the professional when they disagree.

Yet, despite these advantages, the AICPA fought adamantly for over 75 years to resist 'uniform' accounting principles. To be sure, 'uniform' principles may be too rigid and may sometimes mislead (although they certainly do maximize the comparability of financial statements). Originally, back in the Progressive Era, the profession fought 'uniform' accounting standards because it saw such standards as denigrating the professional to the status of a mere technician, unable to exercise discretion or judgment. But the battle for professional status and recognition had long since been won by the 1980s, and the AICPA's insistence on keeping FASB weak and inactive cannot be rationally explained on such a basis. Indeed, narrowing the issuer's ability to pick and choose accounting principles would have seemingly protected the profession's own interests. That the profession did not do so suggests less a lais- sez-faire philosophy than an inability to resist pressure from clients. In a competitive marketplace, the profession seemed unable to accept the short-term costs in terms of client-switching in order to establish a tighter, more cohesive body of accounting principles that would have better protected its long-term interests.

The Reform of Auditing

Although the debate over accounting principles has frequently generated controversy over the last half-century, exactly the opposite has charac- terized the evolution of auditing principles. At least prior to the debate over the Sarbanes-Oxley Act, the development of authoritative audit- ing standards was, in John Carey's phrase, 'a steady orderly process.'[148] Carey, the profession's principal historian, attributes this to the alleged fact that audit standards 'are the responsibility of the accountants alone,' whereas accounting principles necessarily involve the interests of management and regulators as well.[149] This assessment may, however, be more revealing than accurate. In the wake of every major account- ing scandal over the last century, suspicion has been expressed that the auditors did not do their job. Even if such suspicions were sometimes unjustified, they at least showed the public to be skeptical about the adequacy and integrity of the auditing process. From time to time, Congress has held elaborate hearings after audit failures to ask simi- lar questions: Did the auditors look hard enough? Did they miss clear signs of fraud? Were they sufficiently independent of their clients? In contrast, prior to Enron,[150] neither Congress nor the public at large has shown much interest in the substance of accounting principles, defer- ring instead to the profession's presumed expertise.

Why then (at least before Sarbanes-Oxley) did auditing standards attract little attention or controversy when the public has long been skeptical about the integrity of auditors? Several answers provide over- lapping and complementary explanations.

First, auditors and regulators have long shared a common interest in enhancing auditing standards. The profession's economic interest is to promote higher standards and more exacting controls, because the more demanding the audit, the more the auditor is paid.[151] Thus, the profession prospers to the extent either that it can convince its clients to accept the need for greater testing of internal controls, or that it can convince regulators to mandate such testing. Not surprisingly then, for

four decades before Sarbanes-Oxley mandated such a testing requirement for internal controls, the accounting profession had advocated
formal auditing and testing of internal financial controls.[152]

Second, the rise of internal controls coincided with the ascendancy
of the 'monitoring model' as the basic paradigm for understanding
the role of the board of directors.[153] During the late 1970s and 1980s,
boards of directors absorbed a normative lesson taught to them first by
academics, and later by the courts: namely, that their principal obligation was to monitor management, and not to formulate business strategy themselves. Because outside directors are part-time performers,
they were inherently dependent on other agents to engage in the 'nuts
and bolts' surveillance and testing that would alert them to impending problems. Hence, as boards became more outsider-dominated and
more convinced that their fundamental task was to monitor management, public corporations became ever greater consumers of internal
controls and control testing.

A third, more historical explanation of the rapid development of auditing standards over recent decades begins from the fact that accounting
reform is usually scandal-driven. Given a scandal, the industry realizes
it must offer some reform (or face even greater federal intrusion), and
the enhancement of auditing has always been the industry's preferred
reform. The first great accounting scandal after the creation of the SEC
was the McKesson & Robbins case in 1938.[154] Despite an annual audit
by Price Waterhouse & Co., senior managers of that company succeeded
in siphoning away millions of dollars in cash, primarily by overstating
its inventory and accounts receivable by approximately $20 million.[155]
Although the McKesson case showed the near complete ineffectiveness
of audits in detecting fraud that involved collusion among managers,
the SEC concluded that no evidence demonstrated that Price Waterhouse was a knowing participant, and it escaped censure by the SEC.

Realizing that it had barely dodged the bullet and that self-reforms
were necessary if SEC auditing standards were to be avoided,[156] the
AICPA responded to the McKesson & Robbins crisis by promulgat-
ing revised auditing standards that required the physical observation
of inventories and the confirmation of accounts receivable[157] (thereby
filling a void in the original 1917 auditing standards that had been
ironically drafted by Price Waterhouse for the Federal Reserve Bank).[158]
Under further SEC prodding following the McKesson & Robbins scandal, the profession adopted Generally Accepted Auditing Standards that
addressed—belatedly to be sure—how much reliance could be placed
on clients' records and when more detailed checking was necessary.[159]
SEC rules, adopted on the eve of World War II, also required the auditor

to describe in its audit opinion the scope of its audit and any omission from generally recognized auditing procedures, and to represent that the audit was made in accordance with generally accepted auditing standards.[160] As a result, even if comparability of financial statements still remained a distant goal (because of the ability of managements to pick and choose accounting principles from a large inventory), comparability in auditing procedures had largely been achieved by the time of World War II.

Other scandals brought similar reforms. In the 1970s, accounting scandals dominated the business headlines of the decade: the wreck of the Penn Central at the beginning of the 1970s, then the National Student Marketing[161] and Equity Funding[162] cases in the mid-1970s. Then came the major scandals of the mid-1980s (of which the Savings and Loan crisis, as particularly exemplified by the case of Charles Keating and his Lincoln Savings and Loan,[163] stood head and shoulders over the rest). Public cynicism about the integrity of the auditing process was reinforced by the post-Watergate temper of the time. For a brief time, legislative intervention seemed possible in the late 1970s when Senator Metcalf and Representative Moss offered a draft bill to register accounting firms.[164]

These fears led the profession to organize two private commissions to study the auditor's role in fraud detection: first, the Cohen Commission[165] in 1974 and then, in 1985, the even more important Treadway Commission.[166] The Cohen Commission candidly recognized that since the end of the 19th century, '[t]he straightforward recognition ... of the detection of fraud as an object of an audit has been steadily eroded.'[167] The modern auditor had come to see itself as more a provider of financial information than as an investigator seeking fraud. Although recognizing that the profession had quietly repressed the topic of fraud, the Cohen Commission was less certain as to the specific steps it should recommend. On one hand, it concluded that 'the independent auditor should be expected to detect those illegal or questionable acts that the exercise of professional skill or care would normally uncover.'[168] But it also stressed the right of auditors, at least if they took reasonable care, to rely on management's representations. Essentially, its compromise viewed the auditor 'as a watchdog, and not a bloodhound.'[169] This was colorful, but not very precise. Finally, the Cohen Commission emphatically supported the promulgation of auditing standards through private self-regulation and rejected the claim that the provision of consulting services by auditors had compromised their independence or performance—precisely the conclusions one expected from an industry-organized private commission.

The Treadway Commission, which was sponsored by the AICPA and a coalition of other private accounting bodies, focused even more narrowly on fraud detection, and its work led the AICPA to specify in more detail the fraud detection responsibilities of auditors, emphasizing their obligation to report illegal acts to the board.[170] At the same time, however, the Treadway Commission also popularized the idea of an 'expectations gap': namely, the idea that the public expects more of auditors than they can possibly perform. This concern over unrealistic public expectations in turn led the profession to tinker with the form and content of the auditor's report in the hopes of downsizing the public's expectations (and the auditor's potential liability).

Definitionally, whenever there is an 'expectations gap,' it can be closed either by increasing the profession's commitment or decreasing the public's expectations. Although the Treadway Commission sought to strike a balance that required greater efforts by auditors aimed at fraud detection, the profession's overall reaction to the Treadway Commission has been more to stress the need to downsize public expectations than to accept any increase in auditor responsibilities.[171] In its view, the best reform was to more clearly define the auditor's duties in a more limited fashion.[172] Understandable as this desire was to curb litigation by downsizing expectations, the profession resisted upgrading auditing standards as part of any integrated compromise. Rather, it sought primarily to reduce the scope of its auditing obligations.

In 1998, the POB at the request of SEC Chairman Arthur Levitt appointed a blue-ribbon panel of experts to conduct a comprehensive review and evaluation of 'the current audit model.' The POB was, itself, a self-regulatory body with relatively uncertain and ambiguously defined authority that had been created within the AICPA in 1978 as part of a successful effort to hold off legislation proposed by Senator Metcalf and Congressman Moss to register the accountants who audited public companies. After a two-year study, the Panel reported. While it divided predictably on some issues (such as the impact of consulting services on auditor independence), it did find that:

[E]ven in the face of the strengthened auditing standards issued over the past 15 or so years, audit firms may have reduced the scope of audits and level of testing, at least in part as a result of redesigning their audit methodologies.[173]

In particular, the Panel still found auditors expressing 'uncertainty about their responsibility to detect fraud.'[174] It specifically recommended the adoption of 'stronger and more definitive auditing standards to effect a substantial change in auditors' performance and thereby improve the likelihood that auditors will detect fraudulent financial reporting.'[175] Most controversially, it recommended the mandatory introduction of a 'forensic-type fieldwork phase' in all audits.[176] This unpopular rec- ommendation implied actual surprise examinations that sought to catch fraud, as opposed to more cerebral evaluations of the audit risk and control risk. The proposal drew sharp objections from within the profession, and an unsuccessful attempt was made to delete this recom- mendation from the final report.[177]

While the Panel's 2000 report received little public attention (because it was soon overtaken by the storm of accounting restatements that would crest in 2001 and 2002), its assessment of the state of auditing was simi- lar to that of the Cohen Commission over 25 years earlier: fraud pre- vention had remained a peripheral concern of the profession. Instead, much of the profession preferred a methodology under which the audi- tor made an initial risk assessment of the client's financial statements and then concentrated its fieldwork in those areas perceived to involve high risk. The approach economized on actual forensic fieldwork. Why was this approach more popular? In part, friction with the client was feared. Adding a mandatory 'forensic' component to the audit placed the auditor in the highly visible position of disbelieving the client and thus strained the auditor–client relationship. Economically, forensic work of this kind was not particularly lucrative, because most 'foren- sic' work would be field work performed by junior personnel within the auditing firm. Overall, the reluctance of the auditor to undertake a 'forensic' or anti-fraud review as part of its standard audit suggests again that the leverage in the auditor–client relationship remained very much on the client's side.

This short history of auditing brings us to the present and to a larger question: Given that the profession had largely retained its autonomy in the aftermath of scandal after scandal throughout the 20th century, why did the 2001–2002 crisis, dominated by the Enron and WorldCom sagas, produce an entirely different result and culminate in the con- gressional creation of a public regulatory body—the Public Company Accounting Oversight Board (PCAOB)—to replace the AICPA as the private regulator of auditing? An initial answer is that, unlike the 1929 Crash, which the Pecora Hearings presented as being essentially about stock manipulation, the 2001 crisis was unmistakably about accounting. Arthur Andersen inadvertently symbolized the failure of accounting, becoming the co-equal symbol (with Enron) of financial chicanery and misdeeds in high places.

This is only a partial explanation. Equally important, the accounting profession had discredited itself. In its strong-armed lobbying efforts to overcome Arthur Levitt's proposals to restrict consulting activities by auditing firms, it had implicated and embarrassed Congress. Congress in turn had considerable reason to overcompensate in structuring reform proposals—if only to show its new-found independence from the accounting lobby. Arthur Levitt swiftly moved from the status of a controversial activist in a deregulatory era to an unheeded prophet who had seen the future and been abused precisely for that vision.

Finally, once Congress and its staff looked closely at the state of self-regulation within the profession, it found a convoluted system of governance, so complex and divided as to easily justify the adjective, Byzantine. On the few occasions that private self-regulatory bodies had attempted to show independence or leadership, they had been bullied into submission by the threat of reduced funding. Both the FASB and the POB had seen their funding reduced or threatened, and other bodies—the Auditing Standards Board (ASB) and the Independence Standards Board (ISB)—did not even attempt to be independent of the industry or to have majority public membership.[178]

As a result, the centerpiece of the Sarbanes-Oxley Act was the creation of the PCAOB, as a body empowered and instructed 'to oversee the audit of public companies ... in order to protect the interests of investors and further the public interest in the preparation of informative, accurate and independent audit reports.'[179] PCAOB's powers are ample; it is today the unquestioned regulator of auditing, and all early signs suggest that it is independent and will use its new powers aggressively.

But the SEC also received fully adequate powers in 1934. Thus, the real issue is what the PCAOB should seek to do with its new powers. Sarbanes-Oxley contemplates a particular direction in which auditing should evolve: namely, toward the design and testing of enhanced systems of internal control. Specifically, Section 404 of Sarbanes-Oxley imposes special duties on both corporate managers and their independent auditors in this regard.[180] But, this again raises in a new form the old issue of the 'expectations gap.' How much can enhanced internal controls realistically be expected to accomplish?

⸱ Here, a cynic might observe that requiring the profession to design and evaluate more adequate internal controls for its clients is a reform roughly equivalent to throwing Brer Rabbit into the briar patch. Just as Brer Rabbit wanted to be thrown into the briar patch, so too did the profession covet a new source of revenues that could replace the loss of consulting services. Indeed, this new emphasis on internal controls, at least in part, continued and amplified a pre-existing transition that was well underway. At some point in the mid-1980s, the major accounting firms each decided to diversify their auditing activities and offer far broader attestation and assurance services than simply the traditional financial audit.[181]

Historically, the modern focus on internal controls derives from another epic scandal concerning corporate misbehavior, but one only tangentially related to financial reporting. The pervasive foreign bribery and corporate political contribution scandals of the 1970s focused the corporate world's attention on the need for greater internal control—in part to protect shareholders, but mainly to prevent illegal acts. Needing to respond in the 1970s to a pervasive, foreign bribery crisis that had caused the fall of foreign governments, Congress enacted the Foreign Corrupt Practices Act, and the SEC pressured the New York Stock Exchange to require audit committees for listed companies.[182] The result was to redirect auditing towards the prevention of illegality.

Besides criminalizing foreign bribes to gain or retain business, the Foreign Corrupt Practices Act (FCPA) amended the Securities Exchange Act of 1934 to require public companies to 'devise and maintain a system of internal accounting controls sufficient to provide reasonable assurances that,' among other things, 'transactions are recorded as necessary ... to maintain accountability for assets.'[183] While the FCPA spoke the language of auditing, its motivating concern was the prevention of off-book accounts (or 'slush funds') that could be used to fund bribes (or other questionable activities). Auditors were thus conscripted in a war on foreign bribery. In this light, Section 404 of Sarbanes-Oxley only seeks to implement and enforce the obligations that were created a quarter of a century earlier by Section 13(b)(2) of the Securities Exchange Act (which the FCPA added). Essentially, Section 404 belatedly imposes a duty on the auditor to examine and report on the issuer's internal controls.[184] Such a duty may be burdensome for the issuer, but it is highly profitable for the auditor.

The FCPA's basic strategy of using internal controls as a supplement to prohibition was copied by regulators almost reflexively in the wake of later scandals. When insider trading scandals broke in the mid-to-late 1980s, which scandals made famous the 'notorious' names of Ivan Boesky and Michael Milken, Congress responded by adopting the Insider Trading and Securities Fraud Enforcement Act of 1988 (ITSFEA), which mandated compliance codes and internal controls at broker dealers and investment advisers.[185] When Congress mandated the promulgation of federal sentencing guidelines in the 1980s, the Justice Department responded by adopting a system of 'Organizational Sentencing Guidelines' that included powerful incentives in the form of sentencing credits for those corporations that installed and maintained internal compliance programs designed to prevent unlawful conduct.[186] Delaware in due course followed in the wake of these developments and defined the fiduciary duties of directors to seemingly mandate a similar system of compliance.[187] In response to September 11, 2001 and the sudden appearance of domestic terrorism, Congress adopted the USA Patriot Act,[188] which imposed detailed controls on the financial services industry to combat the free flow of funds among terrorist groups and which further mandated audits of these controls. Finally, in 2002, Congress enacted Sarbanes-Oxley, including Section 404, which followed precedent by again imposing internal control requirements. Put simply, the reflexive response from regulators to any new crisis had become to demand better internal controls.

Does such an approach really work? In truth, no one knows, as there is little research on the efficacy of internal controls. To express a note of skepticism is not to imply that internal controls are without value. But the accounting profession much prefers to be instructed to implement better internal controls (at the issuer's expense) than to accept a greater responsibility for the detection of fraud.

Some critics suspect that this new emphasis on internal controls has become a knee-jerk regulatory response that is empty of actual content, serving a function more symbolic than substantive.[189] From this perspective, a regulatory preoccupation with internal controls allows the profession to escape what it least wants to do: namely, focus on the 'forensic' task of hunting for fraud. Designing and testing internal controls is intellectually stimulating and lucrative work; 'forensic' auditing is often neither.

What alternative priority, other than enhanced internal controls, should PCAOB emphasize? The alternative has already been framed. In August 2004, PCAOB's Standing Advisory Group held its initial meeting with the PCAOB board. This Standing Advisory Group, appointed by PCAOB, consisted of leading academics, former regulators, and representatives of interested groups. Following that meeting, ten members of the Standing Advisory Group wrote a joint letter to PCAOB, which urged that PCAOB's agenda needed to be 'prioritized ... based on what is needed to correct the failures that resulted in investors losing confidence in independent auditors.' They suggested that two deficiencies merited priority status: (1) 'detection of fraud by independent auditors,' and (2) 'conflicts impacting the independence of the auditor arising from non-audit related services such as those provided in connection with tax shelters and tax consulting services to executives.'[190] Specifically, they advised PCAOB 'to write a new auditing standard to clarify the fact that auditors should have the obligation to detect material fraud.'[191] They further suggested that the Panel on Audit Effectiveness had already provided sufficient guidance to enable PCAOB to draft such a standard.

This was not the advice that the profession wanted to hear, and PCAOB has been largely silent in response. But this advice is entirely consistent with the earlier research conducted by the Panel on Audit Effectiveness, which stressed the need for greater emphasis on 'forensic' fieldwork.[192] Thus, the battle lines seem to have been drawn: the profession is content with an emphasis on internal controls, while reformers want enhanced standards requiring the auditor to recognize a responsibility to detect material fraud. For the profession, this latter priority carries the prospect of greater litigation exposure.

Changes Within the Profession

Until this point, this chapter has focused primarily on historical and legal developments that impacted on the accounting profession. But internal organizational developments may be at least as important in explaining the phenomenon of 'gatekeeper failure' and the inadequate performance of auditors in the late 1990s. Four such developments will be examined in this section: (1) the rise of consulting services and their impact on the culture of the professional firm; (2) the decline in the threat of litigation; (3) the failure of professional discipline; and (4) the trend toward consolidation and increased competition. All these influences interacted in the 1990s to increase the auditing firm's incentive to acquiesce in client demands and to reduce its fear of liability or sanctions.

Initially, however, it is useful to gain a broader sense of the growth of the profession. As of the end of World War II, the AICPA had 9,500 members in 1945; as of 1973, this number had grown to 95,000, and by 1995 had risen to 320,000.[193] The profession was no longer a tight-knit club whose members knew each other, but rather a vast constituency with the population of a medium-sized city. Underlying this growth is the democratic status of accountancy as fundamentally a middle-class profession, accessible to most without the often prohibitive cost of a graduate school education or the potential class, racial, or religious barriers that once constituted barriers to entry to older professions. While this absence of elitism seems commendable, it may also imply that the accounting profession had little of the sense of *noblesse oblige* that characterizes a profession with more aristocratic aspirations. The accounting profession seems to have responded to economic incentives far more quickly than did the older, slower legal profession.

The Rise of Consulting Services

The growth of consulting revenue as a proportion of accounting firms' overall revenues during the 1990s was dramatic. If we look simply at the 'Big Five' firms, the following chart, derived from the Report of the Panel on Audit Effectiveness, shows a major swing in the revenue mix:[194]

'Big 5' Revenues from All Clients		
	1990	*1999*
Accounting and auditing	53%	34%
Tax	27%	22%
Consulting	20%	44%
Total	100%	100%

In short, consulting revenues more than doubled over this period and had come to exceed auditing revenues by a healthy 10 percent. Moreover, the expected future growth of consulting income was unlimited, while audit revenues were historically flat. That is, one audit firm might steal several clients from rivals in one year and lose several others in the next year, but the competition was largely zero-sum because the number of large public corporations needing lucrative audits was limited and only modestly increasing.

Yet, before one can conclude that the rise of consulting income compromised the accounting profession, one must recognize that the empirical literature has produced conflicting studies with most finding, no statistically significant association between a higher level of consulting income and a higher likelihood of a financial statement restatement. Initially, the first of these studies found a 'significant positive association' between indicators of earnings management and the size of non-audit fees.[195] This positive association between non-audit fees and earnings management seemed at least consistent with the hypothesis that managers who wish to engage in earnings management seduce their auditors with higher non-audit compensation.

The majority of later studies, however, have reached contrary findings, most (but not all) finding that a high ratio of non-audit fees to audit fees does not correlate with a higher risk of restatements or earnings management.[196] At first glance, such data seemingly refutes Sarbanes-Oxley's premise that the pursuit of consulting income compromised auditors. Although a more detailed examination of these studies will be undertaken in Chapter 9, their basic flaw is to assume that auditors were seeking to distinguish between audit clients that paid them high non-audit fees and those that did not, acquiescing more to those that paid the higher bribe. In reality, as next discussed, the profession did not act in this selective fashion. Rather, it strategically repositioned itself to market non-audit services by using audit services as a virtual loss leader. To do so, it changed its internal compensation and promotion policies to compel all its audit personnel to cross-sell non-auditing services. Once this happened, the audit partner became part auditor and part salesman. At this point, it was in the audit partner's self-interest to defer to all clients.

In short, the mistake in focusing primarily on whether firms that paid a higher level of non-audit fees to their auditor had a higher rate of earnings restatements is that this perspective ignores that there can be an across-the-board change over the entire accounting industry. During the late 1990s, that industry was highly concentrated with the principal firms consciously pursuing a common strategy of exploiting cross-selling opportunities at audit clients. If their basic strategy was to market consulting services to the audit client, then it mattered little whether the client was currently paying significant consulting fees to the auditor or not. Either way, the auditor's intent was to maximize prospective consulting revenues from the client. The auditor's independence was compromised not by the threat that existing consulting revenues from the audit client would be withdrawn, but by the anticipation that additional consulting revenues were obtainable—if the auditor 'cultivated' management and acquiesced to it.

Although it is clear today that the industry has abandoned its attempt to transform itself into diversified consulting firms,[197] it is still useful to retrace the rise and fall of this attempted redefinition of the profession. Historically, non-tax consulting income appeared relatively late in the development of the accounting profession. The profession's own historians now see the era from the 1940s to the mid-1960s as the Golden Age of Accounting, when the profession was at its peak, having achieved full recognition of its professional status.[198] During this period, non-tax consulting services rendered only a modest contribution to the total mix of firm revenues, and accounting firms were first and foremost auditing firms.

The first fissure under this citadel appeared with the advent of the computer, as accounting firms thereafter began to compete to offer information-processing services. Leading this race was Arthur Andersen & Co, which in the mid-1950s, designed and installed the first business application of the computer, a payroll system for General Electric at a Kentucky plant.[199] By the end of the 1960s, Arthur Andersen's administrative division had grown to a staff of 1,150 and its 'management advisory' fees accounted for 25 percent of the firm's total revenues.[200] Uniquely, it was becoming a conglomerate of management advisory services.

By the mid-1970s, the SEC had begun to express concern over the potential conflicts of interest that auditors' expanded scope of services created. In fact, in 1979, Harvey E. Kaprick, then the chief executive of Arthur Andersen, believed he saw the writing on the wall (after private conversations with then SEC Chairman Harold Williams) and proposed to his partners that his firm be split into two related firms: auditing and consulting.[201] His shocked partners rebuffed his proposal, and, after 1980, during the deregulatory Reagan era, the SEC grew less vocal in its concerns. Alone, the POB continued to voice its fears, but it was too powerless to take on the industry that funded it.[202] Meanwhile, the profession developed a party line that by rendering management advisory services to an audit client the accounting firm became a better auditor, because it learned more about its client and could bring this deeper knowledge to bear in auditing the client.

During the 1980s, consulting revenues grew rapidly, rising in the case of the then Big Eight accounting firms to a range of between 11 percent and 28 percent in 1984.[203] By this point, Arthur Andersen was already the largest U.S. consulting firm,[204] and six of the Big Eight also placed in the top 10 U.S. consulting firms in terms of gross revenues.[205] By the end of the decade, consulting income at Arthur Andersen had risen to 44 percent of total revenues.[206]

While Arthur Andersen clearly led this race, the rest of the Big Eight did not lag far behind. Even Price Waterhouse, long the premier auditing firm and traditionally the firm least interested in consulting services, transformed itself abruptly during the 1980s. Although its consulting revenues rose only from 6.8 percent in 1980 to 13.3 percent in 1985 (roughly a 100% increase, but well behind Andersen in overall terms),[207] the staff of its Management Advisory Services Department increased from 337 to 1,300 (or from 8.2% to 18% of total firm personnel).[208] Moreover, this new personnel had a characteristically different background. By 1988, only one out of four consultants at Price Waterhouse had a CPA, and a non-CPA joined the firm's Policy Board for the first time in 1980.[209] Although it started well behind Arthur Andersen, Price Waterhouse's historians report that by 1986, its mission had become to transform itself into a 'full-service business advisory firm.'[210]

Such a transition implied wrenching organizational changes within the firm. In a much quoted remark, Michael Cook, then the newly-elected chief executive of Deloitte, defined his goal in the mid-1980s as being 'to change Deloitte's self-image from that of a professional firm that happened to be in business ... to a business that happened to market professional services.'[211] This transition implied an abrupt change in organizational culture, including both the forced resignations of partners who did not meet marketing goals (thereby ending the old norm that partnership implied a form of tenure) and the use of new criteria for promotion to partner that deemphasized technical knowledge in favor of marketing prowess.[212] It also implied a very significant presence of non-CPAs in the senior management structure of the accounting firm.

During the latter half of the 1980s, this change in the major firms' self-image was manifested in a variety of ways.[213] Many firms dropped the reference to CPA or Certified Public Accountants from their letterhead. Instead, they saw the accountant of the future as an 'independent information professional.'[214] Similarly, the term 'auditing' was downplayed; the Elliott Committee in a 1995 report to the AICPA sought to popularize as its replacement the broader term 'assurance services'—a term it defined to mean 'services that improve the quality of information or its context for decision-makers through the application of independent professional judgment.'[215] So defined, auditors were more consultants than bean counters.

Driving this desire to expand beyond traditional auditing services was the fact that audit income had stagnated. In 1995, in his introduction to the Elliott Committee's report, which recommended that the profession expand aggressively into this new field of 'assurance services,' Robert Elliott noted that:

Over the past six years inflation-adjusted accounting and auditing revenues have been flat for the 60 largest firms, while Gross Domestic Product had risen by 28% in real terms.[216]

Of course, consulting income had soared over this same period. As a result, tensions arose within firms, because the audit partners were either being subsidized by the consulting partners or were earning much lower salaries. Eventually, these tensions would explode at some firms—most notably, Arthur Andersen where the consulting division seceded and, after much litigation, became Accenture, an independent firm that is now the world's largest consulting firm.[217]

The disparity in revenues generated by consulting versus auditing not only produced organizational stresses, it also gave rise to new practices that undercut the traditional professional culture of these firms. To justify their subsidization by the more lucrative consulting divisions, audit partners increasingly became marketers of consulting services. In some cases, audit services may have been provided on such a discounted basis that auditing in effect became a 'loss leader.'[218] Inherently, few things are more destructive to a watchdog culture that demands professional skepticism than to learn that its services are so little valued as to be given away below cost. Worse yet, another development probably had even more perverse effects: some firms compensated their audit partners with incentive fees or other bonuses based on the consulting services that they cross-sold.[219] After the fact, the SEC has expressed its strong view that 'such incentives programs ... [are] inconsistent with the independence and objectivity of external auditors that is necessary for them to maintain, both in fact and appearance.'[220]

Even where such incentive fees were not used, the audit partner now knew that if he displeased the client, not only might the firm be replaced as auditor, but, even earlier and more likely, the flow of consulting revenues, often involving much more money, would be reduced or cut off. Thus, loyalty to the firm and fellow employees whose jobs were at stake seemingly dictated acquiescence.

Cross-selling became accounting firms' primary tactic for increased revenues in the 1990s. As Arthur Wyatt, once a FASB board member and long a senior partner at Arthur Andersen, recalled in a 2003 speech to the American Accounting Association that attempted a post-mortem assessment of the causes underlying Andersen's fall:

Cross-selling of a range of consulting services to audit clients became one of the most important criteria in the evaluation of audit partners. Those with the technical skills previously considered so vital to internal firm advancement found themselves with relatively less important roles.[221]

As a result, the culture of the accounting firm changed. As Wyatt argued, these cultural changes in the end may have been more important than the economic incentives:

The core values of the professional firm were undermined by primarily commercial interests.

The issue was not how the delivery of a particular consulting service might affect the auditors' judgment. The issue was not how the existence of consulting fees that were even greater than the annual audit fees might affect the auditors' judgment. The issue was how the increasing infusion of personnel not conversant with, or even appreciative of, the vital importance of delivering quality accounting and audit service affected the internal firm culture, its top level decisions and the behavior patterns of the impressionable staff personnel. It wasn't that consulting personnel were unprofessional in performing their work, but their actions and behavior were far more commercially driven than were auditor actions. Auditors were more willing to take on additional risk in order to maintain their revenue levels. Many long-standing audit procedures that put audit personnel in touch with recurring transactions were scaled back. Clients were more easily able to persuade engagement partners that their way of viewing a transaction was not only acceptable but also desirable. Audit partners too often acquiesced to the client views in the current period, agreeing to fix the problem next year ... Healthy skepticism was replaced by concurrence. The audit framework was undermined.... The gradual changes in internal firm culture effectively altered the long-standing value systems of firm leaders ....[222]

In short, culture counts. In Wyatt's view, a culture developed in the 1990s that did not highly value auditing knowledge or accounting theory, and disaster predictably followed.

Although Mr. Wyatt's inside-the-firm perspective may well provide the most insightful assessment of all the ex post critiques of the profession, its implications are sweeping. If professional culture is critical, then 'bean counters' may have to stay 'bean counters' to preserve that culture, and expansion or diversification into related fields may need to be resisted or banned. Arguably, the accounting profession has already recognized this, as the major accounting firms have sold or spun off their non-tax consulting divisions.[223] In addition, proxy advisory firms have advised their institutional clients to vote as shareholders against rehiring auditors who collected consulting fees from audit clients that exceeded the fees for their audit-related work.[224] Probably in consequence, a sharp drop is evident in the number of corporations paying consulting fees to their auditor that exceeded their audit fees. *Business Week* has reported that, among the corporations included in the Standard & Poor's 500-stock index, the number of corporations paying consulting fees to their auditors in excess of their audit fee fell from 60 percent in 2002 to just 2 percent in 2004.[225] This is an overnight transition, which suggests that the market has already imposed a non-statutory ceiling on the consulting revenues that the auditor may receive.

The Decline of Deterrence

Accountants have long complained that they were the victims of a relentless tide of litigation that threatened their existence. Such predictions of imminent demise have a long history and can be traced back to the profession's shocked reaction to then Chief Judge Cardozo's decision for the New York Court of Appeals in *Ultramares Corp.* v. *Touche*.[226] In truth, that decision, which upheld liability to third parties for fraud, actually steered a middle course and absolved the merely negligent accountant from liability to third parties whose relationship to the auditor did not approach privity.

A liability wave did in fact crest in the 1980s and early 1990s, and then receded equally rapidly during the 1990s. Nor was this shift in liability accidental; rather, the accounting profession lobbied hard for the passage of the Private Securities Litigation Reform Act in 1995, which did uniquely ease the litigation pressure on secondary participants (such as attorneys and accountants). Not only did the accounting profession's exposure to private litigation decline sharply in the late 1990s, but this decline coincided with a reduced ability on the part of an under-funded SEC to pursue large enforcement cases over the same period.

To understand this transition, one needs to begin with the cresting wave of litigation that the profession faced in the 1970s and 1980s. Here, the starting point was the amendment of the Federal Rules of Civil Procedure in the late 1960s to perfect the class action as an efficient means for litigating small or 'negative value' claims. Shareholders who lose, for example, $10,000 or less as the alleged result of securities fraud cannot sue individually as a practical matter because the cost of litigation would exceed any possible recovery. They hold what is often termed a 'negative value' claim: that is, one that may be legally meritorious, but too costly to enforce. A class action solves this problem, however, by permitting the aggregation of small claims, and Federal Rule of Civil Procedure Rule 23(b)(3) was amended to facilitate such a 'small claimant' class action in 1966.[227]

Thereafter, cases and settlements began to mount. In its 1973 annual report, Arthur Andersen estimated that there were then 500 claims in process involving auditors.[228] That was just the start. During the four years ended August 31, 1984, Arthur Andersen alone paid $137,089,359 in the settlement of private lawsuits.[229] One 1984 study estimated that 'more lawsuits had been filed against accountants in the last decade and a half than in the entire history of the profession.'[230]

It was only to get worse. Between 1989 and 1994, the then Big Six firms settled 35 securities class actions for $395.8 million, and the entire profession settled 50 class actions for $482 million.[231] Even this number understates, because the total costs to the profession included its litigation expenses on all cases, those both won and lost. In 1993, the profession told Congress that those total costs had amounted to $783 million in the prior year for simply the Big Six—or more than 14 percent of their audit revenues.[232] Another study, prepared in 1997 by a consulting firm retained by the AICPA, found that the annual costs of judgments, settlements and legal defense for just the Big Six firms between 1990 and 1993 ranged from $367 million to $1.1 billion.[233] When the costs of insurance were added on, this study concluded that aggregate "audit protection costs" for the Big Six amounted to between 7.7 percent and 11.9 percent of their gross revenues over this period, or between 10 percent and 88 percent of average earnings for firm partners.[234] Even assuming that such evidence from retained consultants may be to a degree massaged or exaggerated in order to enhance the profession's sense of a litigation crisis, there is little doubt that litigation expenses clearly represented the major cost of doing business that was not under the profession's control. In addition, beyond the annual costs, there was always the less quantifiable risk that an individual case could result in an adverse judgment that would exceed insurance resources and be bankrupting.

Given their increasing exposure, it was no surprise that the profession made 'litigation reform' its major priority and lobbied for it over an extended period. Then, in 1994, Republican majorities were elected in both Houses of Congress, and the profession's wishes were answered in 1995 with the passage of the Securities Litigation Reform Act of 1995 (PSLRA). Although the PSLRA has proven to be far less than the death sentence for the securities class action that some had feared (indeed, after a brief decline in 1996, federal securities class actions increased to record numbers by the end of the decade), accountants did uniquely gain from the PSLRA.

Two provisions particularly benefited accountants: (1) the substitution of proportionate liability for the former rule of joint and several liability,[235] and (2) a special pleading rule that required the plaintiff at the outset of the case, and before discovery, to plead with particularity facts giving rise to a 'strong inference of fraud.'[236] Under proportionate liability, even if an auditor were found liable in a securities fraud case, the auditor would normally be liable only for its 'percentage of responsibility.' Because the aggregate of the 'percentages of liability' of all the defendants (and other responsible persons) could not exceed 100 percent, a decision by the fact finder, for example, that the issuer's CEO was 60 percent responsible and its CFO 20 percent responsible implied that the auditor could not be responsible for more than the remaining 20 percent (unless it had 'knowingly committed' the violation). Similarly, the 'strong inference of fraud' pleading standard also particularly protected the auditor defendant because at the outset of the case the plaintiffs typically possess little information about the auditor's involvement. Thus, for example, plaintiffs might know at the outset that the CEO defendant had sold his stock and bailed out before material adverse news was disclosed by his company (thus allowing them to successfully plead such a 'strong inference of fraud'). But plaintiffs will typically lack similar information about the auditor at the outset of the case. The upshot is a Catch 22-style dilemma: one cannot plead a 'strong inference of fraud' against the auditor until one has obtained discovery, and one cannot obtain discovery until one has pleaded a strong inference of fraud.

Securities litigation against auditors and other secondary participants dropped off abruptly after the PSLRA's passage. In 1996, the SEC undertook a congressionally mandated study and found that out of 105 securities class actions filed in that year, accounting firms were named in only six cases and law firms in none.[237] This decline was probably attributable to more than the PSLRA. Several Supreme Court decisions in the early- to mid-1990s had also altered the litigation landscape in a way that protected auditors, most notably by abolishing 'aiding and abetting' liability under Rule 10b-5.[238] Litigation against auditors did not disappear; indeed, by the end of the decade the profession was hit with several of the largest judgments ever entered against it.[239] Still, the prerequisite for such litigation in the minds of the plaintiffs' bar had become whether they believed they could ultimately demonstrate that the auditor was a knowing and active participant in a virtual criminal fraud (such as in the *Cendant* case where individual accountants had pleaded guilty to criminal fraud charges at the outset). Overall, not only did the volume of litigation against auditors decline, but so did the settlement value of such litigation. In turn, this made liability insurance easier to obtain and less costly.

This decline in private litigation against auditors was matched by a similar decline in SEC enforcement actions. Throughout the 1990s, the SEC's budget was effectively frozen, and it also had other enforcement priorities. As a result, it appears to have been reluctant to charge the Big Six firms in an action against the firm itself (as opposed to an individual partner or partners), because such actions would be costly, both in money and staff time. The SEC could expect that a defendant auditing firm would be unlikely to settle without an extended fight, and it could not afford to undertake more than a few such actions.[240]

Can one therefore conclude that because accountants were underdeterred they therefore committed fraud? This seems too cynical and simplistic. Law is not the only force that restrains professionals from committing fraud. Nevertheless, faced with less litigation risk, accounting firms probably had less reason to invest in internal controls. The position and power of the internal audit partner, who supervised quality control, also likely declined vis-à-vis those partners who handled marketing or who cross-sold other services. Indeed, the Enron case furnishes the clearest example of this pattern. Carl E. Bass, an Andersen internal audit partner, warned other Andersen partners in 1999 that Enron's accounting practices were dangerous. In conjunction with Enron executives, David Duncan, the lead Andersen partner (who was later convicted of obstruction of justice charges), quietly arranged his replacement from the Enron account within weeks after his protest.[241] With the threat of liability reduced, institutional memories grow short, and the usual processes of rationalization can justify auditor acquiescence in risky accounting practices—without any conscious involvement in fraud.

The Absence of Professional Discipline

In principle, professional discipline could substitute for private or public enforcement in order to maintain professional standards. Any of three bodies could effectively sanction an individual CPA who engaged in fraudulent or simply flawed audit work for public companies: the AICPA, a state board of accountancy in a jurisdiction where the CPA was licensed, or the SEC. Although the AICPA would seem the most logical body to bring disciplinary charges (as its position roughly corresponds with that of the NASD in the securities industry), the AICPA seldom disciplined, or even censured, its members. One survey found that over an eleven-year period, the AICPA disciplined less than 20 percent of those accountants that had already been publicly sanctioned by the SEC.[242] The AICPA's justification for this laxity seems to have been that it lacked the resources to investigate members' professional misconduct and would have been subject to counter lawsuits if it acted without due process or good cause.[243]

State boards of accountancy proved even more irrelevant. While they do suspend accountants who commit crimes or steal client funds, they have consistently shown limited interest in cases of professional misconduct, even when alerted by a formal SEC investigation.[244] In contrast, the SEC did take action against individual accountants, but the number of such cases was small in proportion to either the size of the profession or the number of audits that the SEC criticized.[245] In general, even when the SEC criticizes a company's accounting practices, it rarely takes action against the outside accountant who attested to the company's results and in fact appears to have taken no such action between July 1, 1997 and December 31, 1999.[246] In short, during the 1990s, the public enforcement risk seemed minimal.

If any meaningful mechanism for quality control existed within the profession, it was the AICPA's procedures for peer review. Under AICPA rules, each member audit firm had to have its quality control system reviewed by a peer firm every three years.[247] In theory, the peer reviewer examines both the design of the system and its actual operations, including a review of internal firm documents, audit reports and working papers. At the end of the process, the peer reviewer issues a report and the subject firm responds, and both documents are sent to the Peer Review Committee of the SEC Practice Section of the AICPA.[248] In principle, the Peer Review Committee could require corrective measures by the subject firm to ensure that detected quality control deficiencies are corrected. Also, the POB, in its capacity as overseer, could review both the peer reviewer's report and the subject firm's response and comment to the Peer Review Committee.

What actually happened? The Panel on Audit Effectiveness in its 2000 report found that the process was toothless, producing just review and more review, with no meaningful sanctions being imposed. The following table (5.1) taken from that report shows both the range of actions taken by the Peer Review Committee both over the year ended June 30, 1999 and since the inception of the peer review process:[249]

In short, the most severe sanction available under the peer review system was more peer review (either in the form of mandated outside consultants, continued oversight, or, at most, accelerated peer review).

Table 5.1   *Actions of the Peer Review Committee*

Action	Year Ended June 30, 1999	Since Inception
1 Accelerated Peer Review	1	54
2 Employment of an Outside Consultant	11	110
3 Oversight by the peer reviewer or a Peer Review Committee member to monitor progress in implementing corrective actions	11	220
4 Oversight of firm's internal monitoring program	32	402
5 Changes made in firm's quality control document or other guidance materials	1	44
6 Continuing professional education in specified areas	4	62

Source: Panel on Audit Effectiveness Report, 2000.

No one appears actually to have flunked peer review. Although it is possible to be skeptical of most forms of self-regulation, peer review within the accounting profession pales in comparison to the real penalties and real suspensions levied by the NASD in its oversight of broker-dealers.

Peer review is, of course, today defunct, having been replaced by the PCAOB, which seems destined to behave in a much more activist fashion, much like the NASD. However, in assessing the behavior of gatekeepers, one is forced to conclude that peer review approached a charade, a Potemkin Village of competitors examining each other, but always mindful that they too would be examined in the same fashion. What goes around comes around, and in a very concentrated industry, no major audit firm wanted to make enemies by flunking a rival—particularly a rival who could retaliate.

Consolidation: And Then There Were Four

From an industrial organization perspective, the most striking fact about accounting as an industry is the degree to which it has recently consolidated. The profession was long dominated by eight firms—the 'Big Eight.' In the late 1980s, they began to merge, and six of the 'Big Eight' participated in mergers, beginning with Peat Marwick & Mitchell's merger with KMG-Main Hurdman, a non-'Big Eight' affiliate of the largest European firm, in 1987. In 1989, Ernst & Whinney merged with Arthur Young to form Ernst & Young, and Deloitte Haskins & Sells merged with Touche Ross to form Deloitte & Touche. Then, in 1998, Price Waterhouse merged with Coopers & Lybrand to become the second largest firm, PricewaterhouseCoopers. This last merger deserves special attention because it married the accounting firm with the unique 'Tiffany' reputation for integrity and professionalism (i.e., Price Waterhouse) with a firm that had frequently been sued and clearly ranked much lower on the prestige pecking order. Such a merger not only produced a very uncertain organizational culture, but showed that maintenance of one's reputation was not a paramount consideration for management. Instead, globalization and the concomitant desire to grow quickly to a global scale seemed to have justified mergers, even when they diluted a firm's reputational capital.

Finally, in 2002, Arthur Andersen dissolved, after a mass exodus of its clients, partners and staff in the wake of its criminal conviction (later overturned) in connection with Enron.[250] The surviving Big Four today audit over 78 percent of all U.S. public companies and 99 percent of all public company revenues.[251] Although competitors may take smaller clients from the Big Four, there is little prospect that they can grow to the global scale necessary to compete for large public companies. The General Accounting Office has found that significant barriers to entry exist.[252] Indeed, because each of the Big Four tends to have a different specialization, focusing on different industries, there is even less competition than the name 'Big Four' implies. Within a particular industry, the dominant firm may have only one true rival—if that.

What does the oligopolistic structure of the accounting industry imply for the performance of accountants as gatekeepers? Here, a seeming paradox surfaces: the more that the profession is an oligopoly, then the more leverage that an individual accounting firm would seem to have over its clients. That is, if firms face only limited competition, then the client's threat to fire its auditor if it did not acquiesce in the client's preferred accounting treatment seems less than credible. Where would the client go? Of course, this difficulty in firing the auditor could be one reason why clients instead gave lucrative consulting contracts to their auditors. Arguably, the carrot works better than the stick, precisely because the threat to take the carrot away was more credible.

Conversely, the consolidation of the industry has another, less obvious significance that may explain auditor acquiescence. In a competitive industry with a dozen or more competent firms available, any firm's involvement in a major financial scandal might inflict severe reputational damage on it with lasting consequences. Thus, the firm should rationally invest in internal controls to avoid such a scandal. But in a heavily consolidated industry, the client has limited options. There may be no adequate substitute firm or all firms may have experienced a similar level of embarrassing episodes.

If the other firms in this concentrated industry will also predictably suffer reputational losses, they may prefer not to compete over this issue. More specifically, if each of the Big Four audits roughly 25 percent of all large public companies, it seems predictable that each will experience one or more clients who will engage in fraudulent financial reporting. But if each suffers a similar level of reputational damage, none is worse off vis-à-vis its competitors. Hence, the auditor may conclude that the occasional scandal is tolerable—so long as its existing competitors behave similarly and new entrants face formidable barriers to entry. Ultimately, reputational injury is a relative concept. As the market became more consolidated (and possibly as accounting firms became more interested in maximizing consulting income), management at each of the major firms could observe on an ongoing basis that they were not falling significantly behind their rivals in terms of reputational injury. To the extent that they were not falling behind their peers, they could accept the risk of an occasional embarrassment as a cost of doing business. In addition, as firms merged, their reputations and cultures became so blended that real differences among them (which once were obvious to the market) may have ceased to exist or at least became less visible. In short, reputations became 'noisy'—too much so for firms to compete on this basis.

The Loss of Intellectual Rationale

Any profession has its accepted dogma that defines its self-image. Challenge that orthodoxy in a manner that shakes the profession's convictions, and the profession itself becomes less confident and self-assured. Orthodoxy within the accounting profession reached its peak with the 1940 publication of William Patton and A. C. Littleton's monograph, 'An Introduction to Corporate Accounting Standards'.[253] Essentially, these respected accounting professors presented a 'matching model' that sought to relate revenues and expenses in a way that, they argued, best enabled investors to evaluate managerial performance. By deliberately shifting the focus of accounting from the balance sheet to the income statement, this model armed investors with a measure (namely, earnings per share) by which managements could be held accountable. As a result, it gave accounting a *raison d'être*: their methodology could empower investors, enabling them to evaluate, grade, and monitor management.

However, as time went by, Patton and Littleton's reliance on historical cost made their model increasingly vulnerable in an increasingly inflationary world. To the extent that income in their methodology was based on historical cost, it simply overstated the earnings power of the business—at least if assets could not be replaced at historical cost. By the mid-1970s, their model had come under increasing attack, as both theorists and the FASB saw a need to restore the balance sheet as the fundamental pivot of accounting in an inflationary world.[254]

Also in the 1970s, the value of accounting data faced an even more fundamental challenge, as the 'efficient capital market hypothesis' (ECMH) became the dominant model of financial economics. The ECMH's rise represented a basic paradigm shift that made many of the key issues in accounting seem fundamentally irrelevant. While accountants had, for example, long debated whether one accounting presentation was superior to another (for example, purchase accounting versus pooling of interests), the financial economist could now yawn at this debate, insisting that it made no difference because an efficient market could see behind these formal differences and determine intrinsic value. By the early 1990s, there was a growing consensus in the words of the then AICPA President that 'financial reporting should be re-engineered, as we move from an industrial to an information era.'[255]

Valid as this intellectual debate was, it also provided a rationalization for economically expedient choices. Where once accounting principles had been the subject of fierce debate within the profession, it now could be reasonably argued (in the words of one prominent academic) that standard setters 'need not spend undue time worrying about limiting choices of accounting methods.'[256] Accountants could defer to any choice that corporate management made and publicly disclosed, because the choice of principles simply didn't matter. Once this intellectual rationale for deference to management's choice of accounting principles became respectable, a slippery slope led quickly downhill to increased acquiescence in earnings management. More generally, as the profession entered the 'Information Age' of the 1990s, there was increasing uncertainty as to what its tools could validly purport to accomplish, and the old certainty as to the accountant's role, which had peaked with the Patton and Littleton 1940 monograph, had largely come undone.

Symptoms of Breakdown

When a profession loses its moorings, some dramatic episodes often may signal the decline of professional values. In 2001, an SEC investigation uncovered a startling 8,000 violations by PricewaterhouseCoopers of the prohibition against owning stock in its audit clients.[257] Some 31 of the top 43 partners in the firm were found to own stock in audit clients.[258] While many of these violations involved small amounts, they were clear-cut violations of a long-established rule that lies at the core of the concept of auditor independence. Nor was PricewaterhouseCoopers unique. Even after PricewaterhouseCoopers had been disciplined, the SEC later found that Ernst & Young had engaged in a series of business ventures with audit clients, and it imposed an unprecedented sanction on E & Y under which E & Y was barred from accepting any new clients for six months.[259] The independence rules seem to have become rules that the major firms thought they could ignore—repealed in effect by the decision of the regulated.

Over this same interval, the Big Four began to market massive and risky tax shelters to their audit clients and their senior managements. In retrospect, it now appears that many of these shelters were dubious long shots, having no more than a colorable chance of passing muster with the IRS—if the shelter was discovered. As a result, KPMG, which made the aggressive marketing of tax shelters a major firm priority, for a time faced criminal indictment because of its role in these 'abusive' tax shelters (and a number of its senior partners were indicted). But, having destroyed Arthur Andersen, the Department of Justice could not risk reducing the Big Four to the Big Three and so permitted KPMG to enter into a deferred prosecution agreement in 2005 under which it publicly acknowledged its guilt.[260]

KPMG's marketing of dubious tax shelters did not distinguish it from its compatriots in the then Big Five, as both Ernst & Young and PricewaterhouseCoopers also settled similar charges with the Department of Justice. But KPMG's example illustrates better than the others the impact of such behavior on the culture of the firm. KPMG appears to have entered the tax shelter marketing business late and only after a failed merger with Ernst & Young gave it an opportunity to see E & Y's books and realize how rapidly its competitor was growing and profiting from this new line of business.[261] In response, KPMG made it a top priority to expand its tax practice and quickly developed a more aggressive marketing approach to compensate for its late entry. Although tax shelters involved high risk and close judgments, management of this division demanded complete loyalty from its tax partners and tolerated no questioning within the firm of a tax strategy approved by its leaders. Skeptics were told that you were 'either on the team or off the team.'[262]

By 2002, KPMG was deriving nearly $1.2 billion of its $3.2 billion total revenues from tax services—or nearly 38 percent, a level far exceeding that of its rivals.[263] As a result, the executives running tax services were promoted to higher positions within KPMG; one executive became the firm's deputy chief executive; another, its chief financial officer.[264] Both have now been indicted. But with their rise within the firm came an inevitable culture shift. KPMG's experience underlines the loss of professional values—objectivity and detachment—in favor of 'hell-bent-for-leather' marketing. In such a culture, the traditional professional—objective, cautious, skeptical—can only feel as if he or she were an alien.

From a profession-wide perspective, this pattern of auditors marketing business ventures to clients (even when they were not questionable tax shelters) is more troubling than simply the provision of consulting services. In principle, the consultant can be objective, but the salesman never is. Necessarily, such a development strains the profession's historic independence from the client. Indeed, some of these practices involved fairly flagrant violations of the profession's own self-generated rules. For some time, the profession had promulgated its own standards for auditor independence through the Independence

Standards Board (ISB), which was a tame self-regulatory panel within the AICPA. Had the major firms considered its mild standards overly constraining, they probably could have caused them to have been relaxed further on request. But instead, they were simply ignored and disobeyed. Throughout the late 1990s, accounting firms entered into a host of business relationships with their audit clients, including strategic alliances, co-marketing arrangements, and joint ventures, and regularly offered equity interests in their own business ventures to audit clients.[265] The idea of professional distance and detachment from the client appears to have been treated as an ancient and obsolete concern. The tax shelter cases present the most obvious conflict, because the audit firm marketing the long-shot tax shelter would also have to opine later on the adequacy of the issuer's tax reserves in giving its audit opinion. In effect, what the tax advisory arm of the firm marketed to the audit client, the audit arm would have to uphold—or embarrass the firm.

Why were such obvious conflicts tolerated? The only plausible answer is that the major firms feared neither regulatory sanctions nor reputational injury from violation of such 'technical' rules. Reputational injury was less of a consideration because their business strategy was to develop their relations with existing clients, rather than market themselves to new clients based on a reputation for high integrity. In this light, accounting firms had little to fear from the disclosures that they had grown too close to their clients. This would not offend their clients, who by definition already knew of these relationships.

Although some have asserted that the major firms viewed auditing as a 'loss leader,'[266] this involves a pejorative characterization that ultimately is unimportant. All that can be fairly concluded is that some firms kept their audit fees low for clients purchasing very high levels of non-audit services.[267] Better evidence of the erosion in professional values probably lies in the firms' internal compensation policies. For example, in the late 1990s, Ernst & Young established a target level that each audit partner was expected to meet for the purchase of non-audit services by the audit client. Failure to achieve that level resulted in an automatic 10 percent reduction in salary.[268] Arthur Andersen similarly had a program, adopted in 1998, that set a target level for audit partners: they were expected to generate double the audit revenues from their audit client by cross-selling non-audit services.[269] In such an environment, the audit partner skilled at marketing prospered and rose within the firm, while the more technically skilled partner who was a lesser salesman lost stature and faced dismissal.

Post Sarbanes-Oxley: the latest developments

In the wake of scandals, some developments are predictable, but others are counter-intuitive. Logically, one would have predicted that the increasing rate of financial statement restatements, which began to soar hyperbolically in the mid-1990s, would have subsided after the passage of Sarbanes-Oxley in 2002, as corporate managements became more cautious (or at least more deterred). But, to the contrary, restatements have continued to increase even after Sarbanes-Oxley—and exponentially. The number of restatements announced by U.S. publicly-traded companies increased 20 percent in 2004, rising to 619 from 514 in 2003.[270] On a percentage basis, 5.4 percent of all U.S. public companies announced a restatement in 2004, up from 5.3 percent in 2003 and exactly double the 2000 rate of 2.7 percent.[271] Obviously, this raises a question: if Sarbanes-Oxley and stricter enforcement are working, why has the rate of restatements not declined? The best, but tentative, answer would appear to be that better, less conflicted watchdogs find more errors. Once Sarbanes-Oxley rewired the auditor–corporate interface so that the auditor reported directly to an independent audit committee, the auditor became less inhibited and found more errors. Nor was a risk-averse committee of outside directors as likely to resist, or attempt to talk the auditor out of its position, that a restatement was necessary.

A less optimistic possibility must also be recognized, however. Executive compensation in the United States (and uniquely there) continues to increase at an extraordinary rate. In the case of the largest companies that comprise the S & P 500 index, median total chief-executive compensation rose by 30.2 percent in 2004, compared with a more modest 15 percent rise in 2003.[272] If the scandals slowed CEO pay increases for a year or two, their effect seems to have worn off. Moreover, the ratio of chief executive compensation to the pay of the average production worker has also begun to increase again, rising to 431:1 in 2004, up from a more modest 301:1 in 2003.[273] The peak year was 2000, when this ratio hit 525:1. After Enron's fall, the gap seemed to be closing,[274] but now the prior pattern has reasserted itself. Thus, if much has changed in the wake of recent scandals, some things have remained constant. Executive compensation in the U.S. appears to be governed by the rules of a tournament system in which the winner comes close to taking all. In turn, this implies that chief executives, compensated in such a fashion, will predictably seek to inflate income—and hence gatekeepers will remain under pressure.

In the wake of Sarbanes-Oxley, new sources of data about auditor performance have become available. One of Sarbanes-Oxley's more controversial provisions is its Section 404, which requires an annual evaluation of a public company's internal controls by its independent auditor. The first year in which the impact of this provision became observable was 2004, when a flood of companies began to disclose internal control deficiencies. Between January 1, 2004 and May 2, 2005, some 11 percent of large public corporations (i.e. those having a market capitalization of over $75 million) disclosed internal control deficiencies.[275] This number almost certainly understates the full extent of the problem, because smaller companies (to whom the internal controls disclosure requirement does not yet apply) have even higher rates of financial statement restatements and internal control deficiencies. Eventually, this percentage should decline, but in the near future, improved controls are likely to produce more restatements, as long-buried problems are uncovered.

As data on restatements and material weaknesses becomes available, differences among auditors emerge. In both 2003 and 2004, the clients of Deloitte & Touche had the highest average restatement rate (7%), while the clients of Ernst & Young had the lowest (3%) among the Big Four. Alone, this statistic may be misleading, because different auditors specialize in different industries, and the rate of restatements is very industry-specific. But, when the rate of restatements and the disclosures of 'material weaknesses' are compared, the same pattern persisted: Deloitte & Touche and BDO Seidman had the highest level of restated financials as a percentage of companies audited, and each ranked high in rates of both 'material weaknesses' and 'qualified audit opinions' among their clients.[276]

The point here is not to rate the major auditors, but to note that comparative ratings do become more feasible and meaningful in the future. This may in turn make feasible more meaningful competition on the basis of professional reputation. For the future, those audit committees that want to know 'who is best' will have a metric available to them for comparison.

Another basis for comparison has become available in the form of the PCAOB's annual reports detailing its inspection of the major auditors.[277] These PCAOB Inspection Reports are publicly available (minus some confidential material). Although written in the quietly understated prose of a bureaucratic body, the initial round of reports, released in 2005, were highly critical of all the major audit firms.[278] All told, the initial round of inspection reports suggested that the major audit firms had serious internal control problems of their own, with very divergent practices being followed in different audits.[279]

Scandals lead inevitably to a loss of confidence in an affected profession, and this in time translates into a difference in judicial attitude.

Thus, even though Sarbanes-Oxley did nothing to change the balance of advantage in securities litigation, that balance has changed in response, shifting at least modestly in the plaintiff's direction. Post-Enron, litigation against auditors is less likely to be dismissed and more likely to proceed to trial. Yet, although the number of securities class actions filed rose sharply in 2003 and 2004, the number of actions in which auditors are named as defendants continues to fall, and to record low levels.[280] Today, the PCAOB probably represents a greater threat to the negligent auditor than private litigation. But whether it can escape capture by the industry it regulates remains an open question for the future.

How would the profession respond to these new pressures? The emerging answer is that the profession has taken a number of steps, but none noticeably in the direction of assuming a greater obligation to detect fraud. The most obvious responses fall under three headings, as seen below.

1 Purging the Client Inventory   In the wake of scandals, the Big Four have re-evaluated their client portfolios and largely decided that they will attempt to service only the larger, less risky client. During 2004, more than 1,600 public companies announced that they had changed their outside auditors.[281] This was a 78 percent increase from 2003. Overall, for the years 2003 and 2004 (the first two complete years after the passage of the Sarbanes Oxley Act), some 2,514 public companies switched auditors—a number that represents more than one-fourth of publicly listed companies in the U.S.[282] One other fact about this transition stands out: of those firms switching auditors in 2004, more than 85 percent were small firms with $100 million or less in revenues.

What is behind this pattern? Although in some of these cases the client may have fired the auditor, in the majority of cases it was the reverse. Why? Once auditors could no longer market consulting services (at least as a practical matter) to their auditor clients, it made sense to reevaluate the audit client: was the litigation risk that it posed justified by its audit fees? In the case of the smaller, younger or higher-risk client, the risk–reward ratio no longer made sense to the Big Four. Even though audit fees have risen sharply, they seldom could justify accepting any significant risk of major class action securities litigation (particularly at a time when the settlement value of such litigation has also begun to rise). Smaller, higher-risk clients may have been worth the risk earlier when they offered the prospect of high consulting income, but in the absence of such income, their risk exceeded their expected value—and they have been dropped.

Although the Sarbanes-Oxley Act only bars an accounting firm from providing a limited number of consulting services to an audit client, the market appears to be enforcing a considerably broader prohibition. Institutional Shareholder Services, the principal proxy adviser servicing institutional investors, opposes auditors receiving more in consulting fees from its corporate client than it receives for audit and audit-related work.[283] This norm has rapidly become accepted. Although, in 2002, some 60 percent of the S & P's 500-stock index failed this test and paid more in consulting fees to their auditor than they paid in audit fees, the percentage of firms failing this test fell from 60 percent in 2002 to just 2 percent in 2003.[284] For the future, as consulting revenues decline and the threat of litigation continues, additional firms may also be dropped by their auditors.

These developments have two implications: first, the business model that the major auditing firms collectively followed in the 1990s has now largely been abandoned. Audit fees, supplemented by tax services, will have to support the Big Four for the future, and the ability of the Big Four to market even tax services to audit clients is also coming under increasing scrutiny and is likely to be curtailed by the PCAOB.[285] Second, as the Big Four sheds audit clients, smaller audit firms, particularly those in the second-tier just below the Big Four, gain them.[286] Thus, a curiously serendipitous development may be at hand: as the result of scandals, the prospect of greater competition among audit firms has at last become imaginable. It is too soon to conclude that this will happen, but the possibility is growing.

2 Capping Liability   A quiet response to the threat of liability has been a concerted effort by the accounting profession to contract out of substantial liability to their audit clients. In their agreements with their audit clients, the major auditors are attempting to negotiate provisions that preclude either a court action by the client or punitive damages.[287] Instead, the contract calls for alternative dispute resolution procedures, which typically would refer any dispute to an arbitration panel that would lack the power to award punitive damages.

Corporate managements have little reason to resist such a provision. The corporation is only likely to sue its auditor after a major financial scandal, which scandal would typically result first in management's ouster. Moreover, the less the liability facing the auditor, the more likely it is to acquiesce in demands from corporate managements. Hence, corporate management might also wish to minimize the pressure on its auditor.

These changes do not affect the securities class action, which is brought instead by investors, not the corporation. But a broad political lobbying effort may be developing to place some cap on securities class action liability. At present, the prospect of legislative change still seems remote, but gradually the memory of Enron may fade.

3 Cutting Back on the Auditor's Obligation   Historically, underwriters and directors have turned to the auditor to fulfill their own due diligence responsibilities under the federal securities laws. To this end, they have traditionally asked auditors for representations and/or negative assurances on a variety of topics. Facing a growing threat of liability, auditors have begun to resist. In a 2005 draft white paper prepared by the AICPA, the position was taken that auditors should not even respond to 'questions from the underwriters regarding the auditor's awareness of any instances of fraud or illegal acts?'[288] The draft concluded that even if the auditor heard management issue misinformation to the underwriters, the auditor should not correct that misinformation. Paradoxical as it sounds, the audit profession in the wake of Enron seems to be retreating from any broad obligation to report fraud.

Why? The fear of liability is clearly the driving force. The audit profession fears that it is being excessively relied upon by others. In particular, underwriters and directors want to rely on the auditor in order to establish their own due diligence defense.[289] Understandably, auditors fear that if underwriters and directors can rely on them broadly, auditors will become the residual bearers of liability at whom everyone else points their finger when a fraud is discovered. The result has been a turf war between, on one side, the financial industry's principal trade groups—the Securities Industry Association and the Bond Market Association—and the AICPA, on the other side. But if the audit profession feels that others are setting it up to be the scapegoat, the fact remains that its growing refusal to discuss the prospect for fraud or illegality with other gatekeepers represents a disappointing retreat. The Treadway Commission had urged the profession to accept a greater responsibility for fraud detection and prevention, but, perversely, the threat of liability has seemingly made auditors reluctant even to consult with other professions about the risk of fraud.

A Preliminary Evaluation

Auditing developed in the United States in a series of stages. First, British auditors crossed the Atlantic to assist British investors making investments in American corporations; next, auditing was marketed to U.S. corporate managements to enable them to discover frauds and misappropriations by their employees. By the beginning of the 20th century, the actual principal served by most auditors was senior management, not dispersed shareholders. This association with senior management increased with the adoption of the federal income tax and the rise of tax planning. Probably not before the 1920s, at the earliest, did auditing become seriously concerned with protecting public investors from their managers. Not until the 1930s did the SEC appear on the scene to attempt to monitor the auditor's performance of this responsibility, and not until the 1970s did class action litigation generate a serious deterrent threat that enforced this duty. As a result, the history of auditing as a gatekeeping profession is relatively brief. During the 'Golden Age' of 1940s through 1960s, audit firms—or at least some of them—did compete based on their reputations. But by the 1980s at the latest, the desire to become global players changed their competitive strategy and induced a desire for growth; then, in the 1990s, the rise of consulting services changed everything.

Over its century-long evolution, the accounting profession in the United States has worked hard to achieve two goals: (1) to acquire and preserve professional autonomy, and (2) to limit its gatekeeping responsibilities. To the latter end, it has sought to 'close the expectations gap' by downsizing investor expectations, perpetuating a toothless system of professional discipline, and avoiding 'preferability' decisions as to the choice of accounting principles. Post-Enron, this resistance to expanded responsibilities has continued, with the profession disclaiming any responsibility to underwriters or other professionals.

By not taking more serious precautions, the profession exposed itself to repeated audit failures and waves of scandals. For most of the 20th century, auditors survived these scandals by asserting—with varying degrees of credibility—that their clients had deceived them. This strategy worked for a time, but gradually the profession paid for its passivity. In successive stages, each involving scandals, the profession surrendered much of its original professional autonomy: first, with the passage of the federal securities laws; second, with the substitution of the more independent FASB for the easily controlled APB as the standard-setter for accounting; and third, with the loss of its authority over auditing with Sarbanes-Oxley's recent creation of the PCAOB.

While the accounting profession's behavior has been consistent and stable over the long term, the 1990s do stand out as a marked discontinuity in its history. Initially, the profession had great success in the 1990s, winning long-sought legislative victories and extending its range of services exponentially. Politically, it became a major lobbying force that neither party wished to offend.[290] Yet, ultimately, the profession overreached. Despite the long history of audit failures over the last century, it adamantly opposed all meaningful reforms and won a costly Pyrrhic victory over SEC Chairman, Arthur Levitt, in 1999 and 2000 when he sought to protect auditor independence from consulting income. But as a result, the profession had little political capital left to expend when the Enron crisis broke in 2001.

More generally, the profession resisted exercising even minimal control over its members, either by placing any meaningful restrictions on the client's choice of accounting principles or by creating a credible system of self-regulation. By tolerating a disciplinary system that amounted to little more than a charade, the profession ensured that eventually such a system of private self-regulation would become politically unacceptable. If short-sighted, this attitude should not surprise us. As will be seen next, the bar behaved very similarly over the same period.

In terms of its own self-image, the accounting profession experienced an enormous transition, beginning in the 1980s and climaxing in the 1990s, during which the organizational culture of the major accounting firms underwent wrenching changes. Unfortunately, this transition devalued the 'watchdog' ethos of the auditor. Part of the transition was caused by the rise of consulting services, and part by a rapid series of mergers that began in the 1980s. But, even independent of these changes, as the profession sought to redefine itself as 'information professionals,' it blurred its gatekeeping responsibilities. In the course of refashioning its image to escape the narrow stereotype of 'bean counters,' the profession's characteristic attitude shifted from skepticism to optimism. By the time of Enron and WorldCom, the profession had come to view its key role as that of assisting corporate management to explain itself to investors. In so doing, it moved close to midway between the traditional skeptical posture of the auditor and the newer, problem-solving posture of the public relations specialist.

Clearly, the Sarbanes-Oxley Act has sought to address these deeper problems in the agency relationship between accountants and investors by insisting upon a more pristine relationship between auditor and client. To achieve this, it has transferred virtually all control over auditor compensation, oversight and retention to a more independent audit committee. In addition, the Sarbanes-Oxley Act mandated a new emphasis on internal controls. Finally, an increased threat of litigation will also restore a greater degree of skepticism to the accounting profession. Whether these answers will prove sufficient or whether corporate managements will continue to be able to dominate the relationship remains an open question. Still, the accounting profession continues to resist accepting a greater responsibility for the detection of fraud, and it remains unwilling to oversee management's choice of accounting principles. Given existing systems of executive compensation, the more management retains complete discretion over the choice of accounting principles (as it does even after Sarbanes-Oxley), the more further scandals seem inevitable.

Endnotes

1. For the standard account of the development of accounting, see A. C. Littleton, Accounting Evolution to 1900 (Garland Publishing, Inc. 1988) (hereinafter, "Littleton"), at 12–21.

2. Besides Littleton, this chapter chiefly relies on the three standard institutional histories of accounting: John L. Carey, The Rise of the Accounting Profession: From Technician to Professional, 1896–1936 (A.J.C.P.A. 1969) (hereinafter "Carey"); Gary John Previts and Barbara Dubis Merino, A History of Accountancy in the United States: The Cultural Significance of Accounting (Ohio State Press 1998) (hereinafter, 'Previts and Merino'); and P. Miranti, Jr., Accountancy Comes of Age: The Development of an American Profession, 1886–1940 (1990). A more recent history by Professor Stephen A. Zeff has great topical relevance and carries the history of the profession to the present date. See Stephen A. Zeff, *How the U.S. Accounting Profession Got Where It Is Today?*: Part I and Part II, 17 Accounting Horizons 189–205, (2003) and 267–286 (2003).

3. See Carey at 15–16. For a concise discussion of the books of account that a 19th century merchant typically maintained and their limitations, see Alfred D. Chandler, Jr., The Visible Hand: The Managerial Revolution in American Business (1977) at 38–39. The typical merchant, Chandler concludes, could determine from his books his operating income and his working capital, but not his net gain or loss or net worth. Only with the development of the railroads did there arise businesses that gave 'systematic attention to capital accounting' and depreciation. Ibid. at 111.

4. Littleton argues that true systems of accounting did not arise until the 19th century. He stresses the development of auditing as a key factor that enabled this transition. See Littleton at 165; see also Carey at 17–19.

5. See Adolf A. Berle and Gardiner C. Means, The Modern Corporation and Private Property (1932).

6. Littleton at 260–261. Littleton gives the example of an English statute, adopted in 1310, that required the election of 'six good men of the city' to audit the Chamberlain of the City of London.

7. Littleton at 261–261.

8. Littleton cites a statute of Edward I, adopted in 1285, stating that servants found 'in arrearages upon the account could be sent to prison by the testimony of the auditor.' Littleton at 262.

9. 6 Geo., ch. 18 (1791). For an overview, see Stuart Banner, Anglo-American Securities Regulation: Cultural and Political Roots, 1690–1860 (1998) at pp 76–78.

10. See Bubble Companies Act of 1825, 6 Geo. 4, ch. 91 (1825).

11. For an overview, see John Richard Edwards, 'Financial Accounting Practice 1600–1970: Continuity and Change,' in Accounting History from the Renaissance: A Rembrance of Luca Pacioli (T. A. Lee, A. Bishop and R. H. Parker, eds.) (Garland Publishing Inc. 1996) at 35–40.

12. 7 & 8 Vict., ch 110 (1844).

13. 8 & 9 Vict., ch 16 (1845). For a more detailed overview of this and related legislation enacted during this era, see Sean M. O'Conner, *Be Careful What You Wish For: How Accountants and Congress Created the Problem of Auditor Independence*, 45 Boston College L. Rev. 741 (2004).

14. See Joint Stock Companies Act, 7 & 8 Vict., ch 110, art. XXXVIII (1844); 1845 Companies Clauses Act, 8 & 9 Vict., ch 16, art. 102 (1845).

15. See 8 & 9 Vict., ch 16, art. 108 (1845).

16. On this point, see Carey at 17.

17. Carey finds that these statutes 'made inevitable the development of an organized profession of accounting whose practitioners were identified as competent and independent.' Ibid. at 19.

18. Ibid.

19. Ibid.

20. Professor O'Connor has in particular raised this objection, although he does approve and stress the fact that British law required the shareholders to elect the auditor, whereas the federal securities laws in the United States do not. See O'Connor, n 13 above.

21. This is, of course, one of the key insights to the standard economic model of the firm. See Jensen and Meckling, *Theory of the Firm: Managerial Behavior, Agency Costs, and Ownership Structure*, 3. J. Fin. Econ. 305 (1976).

22. Use of an independent auditor is also a form of monitoring (as is, for example, the creation of an independent board of directors). But the original commitment of the promoter to use an independent auditor is a self-imposed restraint by the manager or the promoter in order to assure investors, and is thus an example of bonding.

23. See text at n 18 above.

24. See Previts and Merino at 131 (summarizing the findings of Professor Littleton).

25. Ibid. at 131–132.

26. Ibid. at 138. Previts and Merino suggest that a boom in the U.S. breweries industry attracted British capital in the 1890s and brought a special influx of British accountants. Chandler places the migration a decade earlier and cites investment bankers bringing chartered accountants from Britain to assist in railroad reorganizations. See Chandler, n 3 above, at 464.

27. Ibid. at 144.

28. See Carey at 27–28.

29. Previts and Merino at 138.

30. See Carey at 38. Five years later, in 1892, the AAPA's membership had grown from 31 to 35. Ibid. at 39. In short, early growth was slow.

31. See Carey at 44.
32. Ibid. at 45.
33. By 1950, every state but one had adopted the AICPA's Uniform CPA Examination. See Zeff, n 2 above, at 193.
34. See Previts and Merino at 206.
35. Ibid.
36. Although the AAPA was formed in part to compel 'the observance of strict rules of conduct as a condition of membership,' Carey found that no such rules were adopted during its first twenty years. Carey at 47.
37. See Carey at 87 ('Competitive bidding for audit engagements was frequently deplored'). The AIA's Code of Professional Ethics (and later the AICPA's code) forbade competitive bidding for auditing assignments, most forms of advertising, and the direct, uninvited solicitation of clients. This position persisted until the Federal Trade Commission objected in the late 1970s and forced the deletion of these rules. See Zeff, n 3 above, at 202–203.
38. Previts and Merino at 247–248.
39. Carey at 87.
40. Previts and Merino at 242–243.
41. Ibid. at 243–245.
42. This began to change in 1913 when the New York Stock Exchange, under pressure from Progressive Era reformers in New York State, initiated a requirement that newly-listed firms would have to publish annually audited financial statements. See Previts and Merino at 250. But even this rule did not apply to existing corporations, which were grandfathered by it.
43. Previtz and Merino at 244 (quoting Homer Dunn in an 1923 article, entitled 'Reforming the Institute' published in the Certified Public Accountant).
44. Ibid. at 243–244.
45. John L. Carey coined the term the 'Great Schism' to refer to the long-standing rivalry between the American Institute of Accountants (which name the AAPA took after a 1916 reorganization) and the American Society of Certified Public Accountants, which was formed in 1921. Although their quarrel was generally about CPA certificates and admission standards, the AIA favored national, uniform standards and the ASCPA favored state control.
46. For the fullest review of disclosure practice circa 1900, see David F. Hawkins, *The Development of Modern Financial Reporting Practices Among American Manufacturing Corporations*, 37 Business History Review 135–168 (1963).
47. Ibid. at 136–137. Practices among banks, insurance companies and railroads were better than those of manufacturing companies, probably because the former were more closely regulated.
48. Ibid. at 140.

49. Ibid. at 147.

50. Ibid. at 144 ('The first test of a security was the reliability of the investment bankers involved, not the financial condition of the issuing company').

51. In contrast, the Investment Bankers Association of America sought to standardize the disclosures relating to industrial securities and during the 1920s regularly recommended minimum standards for financial disclosure in prospectuses. Ibid at 151. These efforts may have been in response to the Blue Sky Laws, which were widely adopted in the 1920s, but clearly the investment bankers adopted a more public and activist posture during this era than did the accountants.

52. For broad overviews of this era and its goals, see Richard Hofstadter, The Progressive Movement, 1900–15 (1963); see also Richard Hofstadter, The Age of Reform: From Bryan to F.D.R. (1955); Arthur S. Link, Woodrow Wilson and the Progressive Era, 1910–17.

53. The AAPA (and later its successor, the AIA) was a leader in the movement to establish uniform systems for municipal industries and public service corporations, an effort that dated back at least to 1906. See Previts and Merino at 229–230. Accounting practitioners also found common cause with Progressive reformers, in particular the National Civic Federation and the National Municipal League, in asserting that inefficiency and waste lay at the heart of the problems in the public sector. In response, accounting practitioners developed a variety of monitoring systems to tighten internal controls within public and municipal bodies. Ibid. at 177–178.

54. Accounting firms grew rapidly in the period following 1890, after a slow start in the prior decades, as the result of an active merger movement that increased demand for auditing services. See Chandler, n 3 above, at 464. This merger boom was ironically a defensive response to the Sherman Anti-Trust Act of 1890, which outlawed price-fixing but seemingly permitted oligopolistic mergers.

55. Previts and Merino at 184–186.

56. See U.S. Congress, House of Representatives, Final Report of the Industrial Commission, H. Doc. 380, 57th Congress, 2d Session (1902) at 650. (hereinafter, 'Final Report of the Industrial Commission').

57. See Previts and Merino at 185–186.

58. For a further review of the Industrial Commission view of disclosure as a means of protecting consumers, see Barbara Merino and Marilyn Neimark, Disclosure Regulation and Public Policy: A Sociohistorical Reappraisal, Journal of Accounting and Public Policy 33–57 (1982).

59. Such legislation was introduced annually between 1903 to 1914 and occasionally thereafter, but never was seriously debated. See Previts and Merino at 186.

60. See Louis D. Brandeis, Other People's Money and How Bankers Use It, 62 (Richard M. Abrams, ed., 1967) (1914) ('[S]unlight is said to be the best ... disinfectant; electric light the most efficient policeman.').

61. As early as 1905, President Theodore Roosevelt had proposed legislation requiring mandatory audits for public companies, and in 1906 the AAPA had lobbied the New York state legislature in Albany to require an annual independent audit for insurance companies. See Carey at 57–58.

62. See Carey at 72. Robert Montgomery was both an eventual President of the American Institute of Accountants and a founder of Lybrand, Ross Bros., & Montgomery, which became one of the largest U.S. accounting firms.

63. See Previts and Merino at 182.

64. Ibid. at 230.

65. See Carey at 129–132; Previts and Merino at 231.

66. Carey reports that, in 1913, the Interstate Commerce Commission prescribed a system of uniform accounts for railroads, which apparently resulted in one railroad thereafter discontinuing its annual independent audit by its auditors. Carey at 60. The Federal Power Commission and state utility regulators had also mandated uniform accounts from time to time, but the profession's collective experience with such systems led it to disfavor any system of mechanical rules as potentially rendering them superfluous. See B. Merino and T. Coe, *Uniformity in Accounting: A Historical Perspective*, Journal of Accountancy (August 1978) 62–69. A choice of accounting principles was perceived as protecting the profession from decline into a clerical activity performed by technicians and bookkeepers. See also Previts and Merino at 275.

67. See Carey at 130–131; Previts and Merino at 231–232.

68. Carey at 129.

69. Ibid. at 133; see also Hawkins, n 46 above, at 155.

70. A year later, it was republished by the FRB in 1918 as 'Approved Methods for the Preparation of Balance Sheet Statements,' and in 1929 it was further revised by the AIA for the FRB and published again, this time under the title 'Verification of financial statements.' See Hawkins, n 46 above, at 155. These latter titles correctly indicated that the focus of the publication was principally on auditing.

71. Hawkins, n 46 above, at 156.

72. Carey at 134; Previts and Merino at 232–233.

73. Ibid. at 233.

74. Previts and Merino at 267 (noting that '[t]he reaction of the stock exchange was disinterest when the AIA attempted to devise a plan for audits of all corporations').

75. Ibid. at 236.

76. Ibid. at 250 (noting lack of increased demand for audits despite influx of retail investors in 1920s).

77. Ibid. at 249. Auditors, it was thought, might assist the issuer in pursuing such a fair return by certifying to utility regulators or other rate-makers that certain assets should be included in the rate-base or as to the return on invested capital. Such advocacy efforts obviously raised

issues as to the auditor's independence that were ignored or repressed throughout this era.

78. Ibid. at 251.
79. Ibid.
80. See Carey at 169.
81. Ibid. at 250. See also Merino and Neimark, n 58 above. Some research does suggest that accounting practice improved in some areas during the 1920s. See Gadis J. Dillon, *Corporate Asset Revaluations: 1925-1934*, Accounting Historian Journal (Spring 1978) 1–17. Unlike the impact of the federal securities laws, which has been much studied and debated by historians and economists (who have tended to reach opposite conclusions), far less research has focused on whether financial audits and accounting presentations became more accurate or informative in the decade before the 1929 Crash. Professor George Benston has asserted that financial reporting had improved to a stage that was adequate before the 1929 Crash, but his conclusion is largely based on the fact that data about sales, cost of sales, depreciation and net income was provided to investors by most NYSE listed companies. But, as Merino and Neimark observe, such an approach ignores the quality of the accounting numbers. They point to a variety of prevalent abusive practices during this period, such as inclusion of large executive bonuses in the cost of sales or recording stock dividends from controlled affiliates in sales revenues at the market price of the stock so received, that cast a serious cloud over the quality of this information. Ibid. at 43–44. Also, prior to 1932, the NYSE did not require the financial reports filed with it to be audited. See Carey at 169.
82. Merino and Neimark, n 58 above, claim that investors did not see, consult, or rely on financial statements in the 1920s. It is likely that the draftsmen of the federal securities laws had a similar view that investors would not directly rely on financial statements. For example, their intellectual mentor and the patron saint of disclosure, Louis Brandeis, had doubted that financial statements could ever adequately inform investors. See Brandeis, n 64 above, at 7 ('For a small investor to make an intelligent judgment from these many corporate representations ... is ordinarily impossible').
83. The Pecora Hearings is the title generally given to hearings held by the Senate Banking and Currency Committee between 1932 and 1934, which led to the enactment of the Securities Act of 1933 and the Securities Exchange Act of 1934. Ferdinand Pecora, the Committee's counsel and a former prosecutor, effectively stage managed the hearings in a theatrical manner that focused national anger on its principal targets, which included the Insull public utility pyramid, Charles Mitchell, the chairman of National City Bank, and Albert Wiggin, President of the Chase National Bank, who became notorious for his short sales of his own bank's stock. See Joel Seligman, The Transformation of Wall Street (3rd edn 2003) (hereinafter, "Seligman") at 1–2, 20–24, 78.
84. Previts and Merino at 459 n 113; see also Hawkins, n 46, at 137–138.

85. Previts and Merino at 276–7; see also Carey at 174–80.

86. Previts and Merino at 277.

87. Ibid.

88. The scope of the accountant's duty to non-clients was not truly laid out in U.S. law until Chief Judge Cardozo's decision for the New York Court of Appeals in *Ultramares v. Touche*, 255 N.Y. 170, 174 N.E. 441 (N.Y. 1931). In *Ultramares*, Cardozo found that the accountant could only be liable in negligence to a non-client where a special relationship existed that closely approximated privity of contract. While this rule went marginally beyond strict privity and frightened some in the profession, it was intended by Cardozo as a compromise that protected the accountants from astronomic liability to non-clients in cases involving only negligence, and not fraud or recklessness.

89. This is also the conclusion of Previts and Merino. Ibid. at 278 (concluding that '[c]lose allegiance between most practitioners and their managerial clients … made an adversarial relationship unattractive').

90. Previts and Merino at 278.

91. Ibid.

92. See Hawkins, n 46 above, at 158.

93. See Report of the Special Committee on Cooperation with Stock Exchanges of the American Institute of Accountants to the Committee on Stock Lists of the New York Stock Exchange, September 22, 1932.

94. See Hawkins, n 46 above, at 158.

95. Ibid. at 279.

96. Carey suggests that the AIA did not wish to testify publicly because it feared hostile questioning and adverse publicity. Carey at 183.

97. See Hearings on s.875 Before the Senate Comm. On Banking and Currency, 73rd Cong. 56–62 (1933). See also Carey at 185–190; Previts and Merino at 273.

98. For an analysis of the Landis/Cohen bill, which largely became The Securities Act of 1933, see Seligman at 61–65.

99. Ibid. at 65.

100. Section 19(a) of the Securities Act of 1933 gave the Commission (originally, the FTC) the 'authority from time to time to make, amend and rescind such rules and regulations as may be necessary to carry out the purposes of this title, including rules and regulations … defining accounting, technical and trade terms used in this title.' Section 19(a) then went on to authorize the Commission to 'prescribe … the items or details to be shown in the balance sheet and earnings statements and the methods to be followed in the preparation of accounts, in the appraisal or valuation of assets and liabilities, in the determination of depreciation and depletion, in the differentiation of recurring and non-recurring income, in the differentiation of investment and operating income, and in the preparation … of

consolidated balance sheets or income accounts ....' See 15 U.S.C. §77.

101. The Landis/Cohen team quietly put this provision in Schedule A to the Act ('Schedule of Information Required in Registration Statement'), based on advice that Congress paid little attention to schedules. See Seligman at 64–65, 70. Paragraph 25 of Schedule A required a balance sheet, 'certified by an independent public or certified accountant, of a date not more than one year prior to the filing of the registration statement.'

102. Seligman at 116.

103. Ibid. at 117.

104. Ibid.

105. Ibid. at 198. In December, 1936, then Chairman Landis publicly criticized the profession's leaders in a speech before the Investment Bankers' Association of America: 'The impact of almost daily tilts with accountants, some of them called leaders in their profession, often leaves little doubt that their loyalties to management are stronger than their sense of responsibility to the investor.' Ibid. See also Carey at 201. Landis implied that close regulation of the profession might therefore be necessary. The speech evoked a heated reaction from the profession, which Carey viewed as the end of the 'honeymoon' between the SEC and the profession. Ibid.

106. Seligman at 198–199.

107. Ibid. at 200. Carey also viewed Blough as the profession's ally at the SEC. See Carey at 201.

108. Ibid. at 200.

109. In 1939, two SEC staff attorneys noted that the Commission had left unresolved most of the major accounting issues by failing to define 'substantial authoritative support.' See Maurice Kaplan and Douglas Reaugh, *Accounting, Reports to Shareholders and the SEC*, 48 Yale Law Journal 965, 978 (1938), see also Seligman at 201.

110. While professing cooperation with the SEC, the AIA by the middle of the 1930s was resisting disclosure of sales and the cost of sales on the grounds that it disadvantaged U.S. issuers and helped their foreign competitors. See Carey at 196–197. Even Carey describes this as 'an astonishingly conservative position.' Ibid. at 197.

111. For precisely this analysis, see Previts and Merino at 275–276.

112. Carey at 12.

113. Ibid. at 13.

114. Ibid. at 14–15.

115. Ibid.

116. Carey notes that those wishing to rely on the positions set forth in a published dissent would have the 'burden of proof for justification.' Ibid. at 15.

117. Ibid. at 88.

118. Ibid. at 75.
119. Ibid. at 96.
120. Ibid.
121. Carey at 99–101.
122. See SEC Accounting Series Release No. 96; see also Carey at 103.
123. See Carey at 113.
124. Ibid. at 117.
125. Ibid. at 119–121.
126. Ibid. at 143.
127. For a detailed history of these attempts, see Seligman at 418–430.
128. Ibid. at 421.
129. Ibid. at 422–423.
130. Ibid. at 554.
131. Consistent with its 1938 position in Accounting Series Release No. 4, Accounting Series Release No. 150 said that departures from FASB statements would be deemed to lack 'substantial authoritative support.'
132. A comprehensive and scathing critique of the accounting profession was prepared in 1977 by Senate staff working for Senator Lee Metcalf. See 'The Accounting Establishment,' Staff Study prepared by the Senate Government Operations Subcommittee on Reports, Accounting and Measurement, Senate Doc. No. 95–34, 95th Cong. 1st Sess. [1977]. No House or Senate Committee actually endorsed its criticisms, but at least for a time it hung like a Sword of Damocles over the profession. By 1980, however, the nation had entered the Reagan era, deregulation had become the political watchword, and the crisis for the profession was past.
133. For an overview of this controversy, see Seligman at 714–719. After FASB was reformed by the Sarbanes-Oxley Act and given assurances of adequate funding, it has once again taken this same position that stock compensation should be expensed by the issuer. FASB has, however, again encountered opposition from within Congress and has announced an intent to delay the effective date of its expensing requirement until some time in 2006. See Mark Jaffee, 'Board May Delay Rule on Options Expensing,' Washington Post, June 30, 2004 at E-1.
134. Arthur Levitt in his SEC memoir relates that:

> I worried that, if the group continued to push for the stock-option rule, disgruntled companies would press Congress to end the FASB's role as a standard-setter. To me, that would have been worse than going without the stock option rule.

See Arthur Levitt, Take on the Street (2002) (hereinafter, "Levitt") at 110. Levitt has graciously conceded error on this point, saying:

> I was wrong, I know the FASB would have stuck to its guns had I not pushed it to surrender. Ibid.

In fact, however, he may have been right. FASB might have been terminated or at least its independence might have been significantly reduced, given the climate at this point, had it not given in.

135. Seligman at 717.

136. At the time, only two of FAF's 14 members could be legitimately considered public representatives. The accounting profession had the right to nominate four FAF trustees; the Financial Executive's Institute had two seats, and the Securities Industry Association had another seat. See Levitt at 113; Seligman at 718. Levitt was able to add four public representatives to FAF's board, but he had to back down on his demand that the SEC approve all nominees to FAF's board. Levitt at 114.

137. See Seligman at 718.

138. This problem was finally addressed by the Sarbanes-Oxley Act, whose Section 109 authorizes both FASB and the Public Company Accounting Oversight Board (PCAOB) to establish annual budgets, subject to SEC approval, and then fund these budgets from annual accounting support fees from issuers. In effect, FASB can today tax the industry that it regulates.

139. Levitt at 114–115.

140. Remarks by Arthur Levitt, The Numbers Game, NYU Center for Law and Business, N.Y., N.Y., Sept. 28, 1998.

141. Ibid. at 2.

142. Under this compromise, reached after a long fight in 2000, the SEC identified nine categories of services which it 'deemed inconsistent with an auditor's independence' and also required audit clients to disclose fees paid for non-audit services. See Securities Act Release No. 33–7919 (Nov. 21, 2000); for an overview, see William McLucas and Paul Eckert, *The Securities and Exchange Commission's Revised Auditor Independence Rules*, 56 Bus. Law. 877 (2001).

143. See Previts and Merino at 382.

144. U.S. GAAP has a hierarchical structure consisting of four levels of guidance. Level A consists of official accounting principles promulgated by FASB. The consensus positions taken by the EITF are two levels down on Level C and rank equally with, for example, the AICPA's Accounting Standards Executive Committee's Practice Bulletins. See Wiley's GAAP 99: Interpretation and Application of Generally Accepted Accounting Principles, (Patrick E. Delaney et al. (eds) 1999). Still, the application of an EITF consensus position is mandatory for accountants.

145. This was the view of Arthur Wyatt, a long time partner of Arthur Andersen and a FASB member, stated as far back as 1988. See A. R. Wyatt, *Professionalism in Standard-Setting*, The CPA Journal, (July 1988) at 58.

146. See George J. Benston, *The Regulation of Accountants and Public Accounting Before and After Enron*, 52 Emory L. J. 1325, 1334 (2003).

147. Professor Benston has made this point very cogently. Ibid. at 1335–1336.

148. See Carey The Rise of the Accounting Profession: To Responsibility and Authority, E 1937–1969 (hereinafter "Carey II") at 145.
149. Ibid.
150. Uniquely, Enron has focused public attention on the ability of accounting principles to ignore liabilities that were hidden just off the issuer's balance sheet through the use of 'special purpose entities' (SPE). In particular, the bizarre rule under which the liabilities of a SPE with a 5% independent ownership arguably did not have to be set forth on a consolidated balance sheet of the parent, even when the parent guaranteed the SPE's debts, has fascinated the public. See, e.g. George J. Benston & Al L. Hartgraves, *Enron: What Happened and What We Can Learn From It*, 21 J. Acct. & Pub. Pol'y 105 (2002); Benston, n 146 above, at 1337–1338.
151. See David N. Ricchiute, Auditing and Assurance Services at 640–1 (7th edn. 2003) ('[P]ublic accounting firms have compelling economic incentives to enter—rather than ignore—the assurances services market.'). See also, Lawrence Cunningham, *The Appeal and Limits of Internal Controls to Fight Fraud, Terrorism, Other Ills*, 29 Iowa J. Corp. L. 267 (2004).
152. See Ricchiute, n 151 above, at 200; Cunningham, n 151 above, at 283. Section 404 of the Sarbanes–Oxley Act today requires the auditor of a public company to assess and report publicly on its client's internal controls.
153. The fountainhead of the monitoring model was Professor Melvin Eisenberg's The Structure of the Corporation (1976). Begun in 1980, the American Law Institute's Principles of Corporate Governance: Analysis and Recommendations (1982) was also a major influence in the acceptance of the monitoring model. Professor Cunningham has first made the observation that the rapid growth of internal controls followed the acceptance of the monitoring model. See Cunningham n 151 above, at 282.
154. See Carey at 22–41.
155. See SEC, Report on Investigation, McKesson & Robbins, Inc (1940). See also, 2 L. Loss & J. Seligman, n 152 above, at 717–19.
156. As a technical matter, the SEC always possessed statutory authority to regulate auditing. Sections 19(a) of the Securities Act and 13(b) of the Securities Exchange Act authorize the SEC to prescribe 'the methods to be followed in the preparation of accounts.' See 2 L. Loss and J. Seligman, Securities Regulation (3rd edn 1989) (hereinafter, "Loss & Seligman"), at 715–16. Nonetheless, the SEC never vigorously asserted its authority over auditing, and the AICPA assumed its own authority. In 1939, the AICPA created a Committee on Auditing Procedure, which functioned until 1972 and issued some 54 Statements on Auditing Procedure. Eventually, it evolved into the Auditing Standards Board, which was created within the AICPA in 1978. Ibid. at 721 n. 276.
157. See Carey II at 146–147.

158. See text and notes in this chapter at notes 69 to 73.
159. See Carey II at 150.
160. Ibid. at 158.
161. See *SEC v. National Student Marketing Corp.*, 402 F. Supp. 641 (D.D.C. 1975); *SEC v. National Student Marketing Corp.*, 457 F. Supp. 682 (D.D.C. 1978). The episodes of audit failure listed in the text are by no means exhaustive. Other major scandals in this era included Penn Square Bank, Continental Illinois, Drysdale Government Securities, Baldwin United, and ESM Government Securities. See 1–2 SEC and Corporate Audits, Hearings before Subcomm. on Oversight & Investigations, House Comm. on Energy & Commerce, 99th Congress, 1st Sess. (1995).
162. The Equity Funding case broke in 1973 when a securities analyst, Ray Dirks, learned from a whistle-blower inside the company that it was insolvent and actually counterfeiting bogus insurance policies to fool its auditors. See *Dirks v. SEC*, 463 U.S. 646 (1983). By the time that the Equity Funding fraud was exposed, over $120 million in fictitious or inflated assets were listed on the company's balance sheet. See 2 L. Loss and J. Seligman, Securities Regulation (3rd edn 1989) at 720 n 274. Eventually, independent public accountants working on the Equity Funding audit were criminally convicted. See *United States v. Weiner*, 578 F. 2d 757 (9th Cir. 1978).
163. See *In re American Continental Corp./Lincoln Sav. & Loan Sec. Litig.*, 794 F. Supp. 1424 (D. Ariz. 1992) (addressing liability of accountants who may have aided fraud).
164. The two Congressmen drafted a 'Public Accountancy Regulatory Act,' which would have established a National Organization of Securities and Exchange Commission Accountancy, with which accounting firms would be required to register in order to furnish audit reports for public companies. See Previts and Merino at 380–381. In effect, the bill proposed a precursor to the Public Company Accounting Oversight Board, which was later established by Sarbanes-Oxley.
165. Formed in 1974, the Cohen Commission produced its report in 1978. See the Commission on Auditor's Responsibilities, Report, Conclusion, and Recommendations (1978) ('Cohen Commission'). Manuel Cohen, a former SEC Chairman, served as chair of this commission. See also, 2 L. Loss and J. Seligman, n 162, at 721.
166. Report of the National Commission on Fraudulent Financial Reporting (1987). A formed SEC Commissioner, James Treadway, also served as chair of this Commission.
167. Cohen Commission at 33.
168. Ibid. at 47. The Cohen Commission recommended, and the AICPA accepted its recommendation, that an Auditing Standards Board (ASB) be created within the AICPA, and it came into existence in 1978. Essentially, it paralleled the APB, which adopted accounting principles until it was replaced by FASB.

169. See Previts and Merino at 367 (discussing Cohen Commission's impact).

170. The Treadway Commission made a number of important recommendations, including that (1) when a public company changed its independent auditor, it should be required by SEC rule to disclose any material accounting or auditing issue discussed by them within a three-year period preceding the change, (2) the SEC should require all public accounting firms that audit public companies to undergo periodic peer review, and (3) the SEC should have enhanced administrative sanctions and penalties for use against professional firms. For an overview, see 2 L. Loss & J. Seligman, supra note 162, at 725.

171. For example, in 1987, the year that the Treadway Commission issued its report recommending mandatory peer review for auditors of publicly held companies, the membership of the AICPA refused to approve a rule that effectively mandated it. Although 61% of the AICPA membership voted in favor of the change, a two-thirds vote was required and so the proposed change failed. See 2 L. Loss & J. Seligman, n 162 above, at 725–726 n 283.

172. For a review of the various rule modifications proposed or adopted to close the expectations gap, see Erica B. Baird, 'Legal Liability Under the Expectations Gap Statements on Auditing Standards,' in Accountants' Liability (1991) at 63–66 (PLJ Litig. & Admin. Practice Course Handbook Series No. 415, 1991); see also Michael Young, *The Liability of Corporate Officials to Their Outside Auditor For Financial Statement Fraud*, 64 Fordham L. Rev. 2155, 2159–2160 (1996).

173. See The Panel on Audit Effectiveness Report and Recommendations, 31 August, 2000 (hereinafter, "Panel Report"), at 82.

174. Ibid. at 84.

175. Ibid. at 87.

176. Ibid. at 88.

177. Some modest cosmetic rephrasing of this proposal was accepted. Ibid. at 254.

178. The Panel on Audit Effectiveness specifically requested a reconstitution of the ISB to give it a majority of public members and a new charter for the POB to give it clear jurisdiction over both the ASB and ISB. See Panel Report, n 173 above, at xii to xiii and 140–141.

179. See s 101(a) of the Sarbanes-Oxley Act.

180. Sarbanes-Oxley Act Section 404 ('Management Assessment of Internal Controls'), 15 U.S.C. §7672, first requires in subsection (a) that management must accept responsibility 'for establishing and maintaining an adequate internal control structure and procedures for financial reporting' and then provides in subsection (b) that the outside auditor 'shall attest to, and report on, the assessment made by the management of the issuer on this issue.' Section 404(b) also gives the PCAOB authority to adopt standards governing this attestation, and it has done so in its Auditing Standard No. 2 (2004), which requires the auditor to

conduct a formal audit (and not simply a review) of the client's internal controls and to give an adverse opinion if there is 'more than a remote' likelihood of a material failure.

181. See Cunningham, n 151 above, at 283.

182. In 1977, the NYSE approved a rule change requiring audit committees for listed companies after a 'request' from then SEC Chairman Roderick Hills that it do so. See 2 Loss & Seligman, n 162 above, at 722–723.

183. See Section 13(b)(2) of the Securities Exchange Act of 1934, 15 U.S.C. §78(m)(b)(2).

184. Originally, following the FCPA's enactment, the SEC proposed in 1979 to require such a report from the auditor on internal controls, but backed off this proposal in 1980 under industry pressure. See Sec. Ex. Act Rel. No. 15, 772 (1979); see also 2 L. Loss and J. Seligman, n 162 above, at 724 n 282.

185. See Pub. L. No. 100–704, 102 Stat. 4677 (codified at 15 U.S.C. §78(o)). ITSFEA specifically amended Section 15(f) of the Securities Exchange Act to impose upon broker/dealers an affirmative duty to 'institute, maintain and enforce written policies and procedures reasonably designed' to prevent misuse of material information—in effect a system of internal control.

186. For an overview, see Richard Gruner, *Towards An Organizational Jurisprudence: Transforming Corporate Criminal Law Through Federal Sentencing Guidelines*, 36 Ariz. L. Rev. 407 (1994). The organizational sentencing guidelines were first issued by the U.S. Sentencing Commission in draft form in 1988 and took effect on November 1991.

187. See *In re Caremark Int'l Inc. Derivative Litig.*, 698 A.2d 959 (Del. Ch. 1996) See also Lowell Brown, *The Corporate Director's Compliance Oversight Responsibility in the Post-Caremark Era*, 26 Del. J. Corp. L. 1 (2001).

188. The USA Patriot Act is an acronym for its full title, 'Uniting and Strengthening America by Providing Appropriate Tools Required to Intercept and Obstruct Terrorism Act of 2001' (codified at 18 U.S.C. 1, et seq. (2001)).

189. For a strong such critique, see Kimberly Krawiec, *Cosmetic Compliance and the Failure of Negotiated Governance*, 81 Wash. U.L.Q. 487 (2004).

190. See letter, dated August 27, 2004, to Douglas Carmichael, Chief Auditor, PCAOB. This letter was signed by ten members of the Standing Advisory Group, including former SEC Chief Accountant Lynn Turner.

191. Ibid.

192. See text and notes at nn 172 to 177 above.

193. See Previts and Merino at 348–349.

194. See Panel Report, n 173 above, at 112.

195. See Richard M. Frankel, Marilyn F. Johnson, and Karen K. Nelson, *The Relation Between Auditors' Fees for Non-audit Services and Earnings*

Management, 77 Acct. Rev. 71, 81 (2002). This study also found a significant negative association between these same indicators and the size
of the audit fee, suggesting that more auditing discouraged earnings
management.

196. The literature on the impact of non-audit fees is growing prodigiously,
but remains divided. For another study finding that high non-audit
fees correlate with earnings management, see Carol Callaway Dee,
Ayalew A. Lulseged, and Tanya Nowlin, 'Earnings Quality and Auditor Independence: An Examination Using Non-Audit Fee Data' (finding a correlation between a high proportion of non-audit fees and high
income-increasing discretionary and total accruals that constitute a
proxy for earnings management) (2002) (SSRN id=304185). More
studies, however, find no association between high non-audit fees and
restatements. See, e.g. Kannan Raghunandan, William Read, Scott
Whisenant, 'Are Non-Audit Fees Associated With Restated financial
Statements: Initial Empirical Evidence (2003) (SSRN id=394844);
William Kinney, Zoe-Vonna Palmrose, and Susan Scholz, 'Auditor
Independence and Non-Audit Services: What Do Restatements Suggest?' (Working Paper 2003).

197. According to a study by Glass, Lewis & Company, an institutional
advisory firm, non-audit fees paid to audit firms by audit clients
declined in 2003. Although the fees paid for tax work by the audit firm
fell as a percentage of the audit fee from 57% in 2002 to 43% in 2003,
tax work remains the second line of business of the major audit firms.
Some large firms paid tax advisory fees to their auditor as much as four
times their audit fee. Glass, Lewis's study gives the example of Cisco
Systems, which in 2003 paid PricewaterhouseCoopers $2.8 million for
audit work and $12.9 million for tax work. See Gretchen Morgenson,
'Counting the Hats on Auditors,' *New York Times*, June 27, 2004, Section 3, p 1.

198. See Stephen A. Zeff, *How the U.S. Accounting Profession Got Where It
Is Today: Part I*, 17 Accounting Horizons 189, 193 (September 2003)
(noting that during this era it was the unquestioned arbiter of accounting policies, to whom the SEC deferred, and that '[n]owhere else in
the world did the organized accounting profession possess such a large
degree of influence in setting the norms of professional practice').

199. Ibid. at 194.

200. Ibid.

201. Ibid. at 204.

202. Ibid. at 205. In 1979, the POB issued a study, entitled 'Scope of Services
by CPA firms,' which expressed its strong view that 'there is potential
danger to the public interest and to the profession in the unlimited
expansion of [management advisory services] to audit clients.' Ibid. As
usual, the POB's warnings went unheeded, and it remained throughout the 1980s a lone voice crying out in a wilderness of deregulation.

203. See G. J. Previts, The Scope of CPA Services (1985) at 134.

204. Ibid. at 154.

205. See T. C. Hayes, 'Accountants Under Scrutiny: Consulting Jobs Called Risk to Independence,' *New York Times*, June 25, 1979 at D-1, D-4.

206. See Zeff, n 198 above, at 269.

207. Ibid. at 270.

208. Ibid.

209. See D. G. Allen and K. McDermott, Accounting for Success: A History of Price Waterhouse in America, 1890–1990 (1993) at 235.

210. Ibid. at 233.

211. M. Stevens, The Big Six: The Selling Out of America's Top Accounting firms (1991) at 170.

212. See Zeff, n 198 above, at 271–272.

213. Ibid. at 275.

214. Ibid. One high ranking AICPA official seriously suggested that the initials CPA should stand instead for 'certified professional adviser.' See Stuart Kahan, 'Running With the Winds of Change,' Practical Accountant, (December 1997).

215. Ibid. at 278.

216. Ibid.

217. For a detailed review of this bitter divorce, see Barbara Ley Toffler with Jennifer Reingold, Final Accounting: Ambition, Greed and the Fall of Arthur Andersen (2003). They report that the consulting partners' chief grievance was that they were subsidizing the audit partners. PricewaterhouseCoopers and Ernst & Young similarly sold or spun off their consulting operations, both to avoid the appearance of conflicts and to resolve internal tensions. Today, only the Deloitte firm continues to market consulting services (other than tax services) to its clients on a significant scale.

218. It cannot be concluded that auditing services were in fact provided at a loss (although this was frequently alleged). However, a practice of 'low balling' or offering audit services at a very low profit margin in order to gain a portal of entry into the corporate client (through which more lucrative services could be marketed) was observed by many. See Lee Berton, 'Audit Fees Fall as CPA firms Jockey for Bids,' Wall St. J., January 28, 1985 at 33.

219. See Arthur Levitt, Take on the Street (2002) at 116 and 139. For a further discussion of such compensation formulas, see text at nn 279 to 280 below.

220. See Securities Act Release No. 33–8154 ('Strengthening the Commission's Requirements Regarding Auditor Independence'), (December 2, 2002), 2002 SEC LEXIS 3075 at * 95 to * 96.

221. Arthur R. Wyatt, 'Accounting Professionalism—They Just Don't Get It!' Speech before the American Accounting Association Annual Meeting in Honolulu, Hawaii, August 4, 2003 at p 6.

222. Ibid.

223. The one exception to this generalization is the Deloitte firm, which continues to market consulting services aggressively, believing in part that retaining this capacity allows it to hire superior personnel who would not be interested in a career path focused solely on auditing.

224. See Amy Borrus, 'Auditors: The Leash Gets Shorter,' Business Week, December 27, 2004 at 52.

225. Ibid.

226. In *Ultramares Corp.* v. *Touche*, 255 N.Y. 170, 174 N.E. 441 (N.Y. 1931), the New York Court of Appeals held that before an accountant could be held liable for negligent misrepresentation, the accountant had to be in privity of contract with the plaintiff or there must be a 'bond so close as to approach that of privity, if not completely one with it.'

227. See generally 7A Charles Alan Wright and Arthur R. Miller, Federal Practice and Procedure, s 1753 (1986).

228. See L. Loss & J. Seligman, n 162 above, at 720 n 273.

229. Ibid. This total of $137 million apparently did not include another case in which it was ordered to pay $17 million as a result of its audit of Drysdale Government Securities Corp. Ibid.

230. See Minow, *Accountants Liability and the Litigation Explosion*, 158 J. Acct. 70 (Sept 1984).

231. See Steven P. Marino & Rence D. Marino, *An Empirical Study of Securities Class Action Settlements Involving Accountants, Attorneys, or Underwriters*, 22 Sec. Reg. L. J. 115, 148 (table 8) (1994).

232. See Private Litigation Under the Federal Securities Laws: Hearings Before the Subcomm. on Securities of the Senate Committee on Banking, Housing and Urban Affairs, 103d Cong., 1st Sess. (1993) (statement of Jake L. Netterville).

233. See Law & Economics Consulting Group, 'An Economic Analysis of Auditor Independence for a Multi-Client, Multi-Service Public Accounting firm' (1997) at 9–10 (quoted in Susan P. Shapiro, *Bushwacking the Ethical High Road: Conflicts of Interest in the Practice of Law and Real Life*, 28 Law and Social Inquiry 87, at 188 (2003).

234. Ibid.

235. See Section 21D(f) of the Securities Exchange Act of 1934, 15 U.S.C. §78u-4(f). By its terms, this provision is, however, inapplicable if the defendant 'knowingly committed' a securities law violation.

236. See Section 21D(b)(2) of the Securities Exchange Act of 1934, 15 U.S.C. §78u-4(b)(2).

237. The SEC's study compared these six cases in 1996 with the number of audit-related suits filed against the then Big Six accounting firms from 1990 to 1992. For those three years, the relevant numbers were 192, 172, and 141, respectively. See Office of the Gen. Counsel, U.S. Sec. & Exch. Exch. Comm'n, Report to the President and the Congress on the First Year of Practice Under the Private Securities Litigation Reform Act of 1995 (1997) at 21–2.

238. See *Central Bank of Denver v. First Interstate Bank of Denver*, 511 U.S. 164 (1994). See also text and notes at nn 25 to 26 to Chapter 3.

239. The largest recovery against an accounting firm was the $335 million settlement paid by Ernst & Young in 2000 in the *Cendant* case where several Cendant officers and employees who were former employees of E & Y were convicted of fraud. See *In re Cendant Corp. Litig.*, 264 F.3d 286, 294 (3d Cir. 2001). Also, in 2000 and 2001, Arthur Andersen paid $110 million in connection with its settlement of the *Sunbeam* case and $75 million in connection with the *Waste Management* case. For a list of the largest recoveries against auditors, see Coffee, *Gatekeeper Failure and Reform: The Challenge of Fashioning Relevant Reforms*, 84 B.U.L. Rev. 301, 342 (2004).

240. The SEC's pre-Enron action against Arthur Andersen in connection with its audit of Waste Management was one of the very few (and possibly the only) fraud action brought against a major accounting firm in its own name during the decade before Enron's collapse. See *SEC v. Arthur Andersen LLP*, SEC Litigation Release No. 17039 (D.D.C. June 19, 2001).

241. See Robert Manor & Jon Yates, 'Faceless Andersen Partner in Spotlight's Glare,' Chi. Trib. April 14, 2002, at C-1.

242. See David S. Hilzenrath, 'Auditors Face Scant Discipline,' Wash. Post., December 6, 2001 at A-1.

243. See Benston, n 146 above, at 1345–1346.

244. For example, the New York State Board of Accountancy was reported by the Washington Post to have disciplined only 17 out of 49 New York accountants sanctioned by the SEC. See Hilzenrath, n 242, at 1.

245. The General Accounting Office (GAO) found that between January, 2001 and February 2002, 39 CPAs were suspended or barred from appearing before the SEC. See General Accounting Office, financial Statement Restatements: Trends, Market Impacts, Regulatory Responses and Remaining Challenges (2002) 3, 53.

246. A recent study of 204 randomly selected cases out of the 300 SEC Accounting and Audit Enforcement Releases issue between July 1, 1997 and December 31, 1999, found no instance in which the SEC took action against the individual auditor or its firm. See Mark S. Beasley et al., Fraudulent Financial Reporting 1987–97: An Analysis of U.S. Public Companies (1999); see also Benston, n 146 above, at 1346.

247. See Panel Report, n 173 above, Appendix C, p 192.

248. Ibid. at 192–193.

249. Ibid. at 193.

250. For a fuller discussion of this wave of mergers (and all the reasons therefore), see United States General Accounting Office, Report to the Senate Committee on Banking, Housing and Urban Affairs and the House Committee on Financial Services, Public Accounting Firms: Mandated Study on Consolidation and Competition (GAO-03–864) (July 2003) at pp 10–11.

251. Ibid. at 21–2. If one defines the 'large client' as a public company with over $250 million in sales, the Big Four today audit 97% of such companies. Ibid. at 22.

252. Ibid. at 45–51.

253. For an overview of the significance of this monograph to the profession, see Previts and Merino at 281–283, 384–385.

254. Ibid. at 384.

255. Ibid. at 391 (quoting in part and paraphrasing AICPA President Philip B. Chenok in a 1990 statement).

256. Ibid. at 347 (paraphrasing advice to FASB of Professor William Beaver, a Stanford economist and accounting professor).

257. See Jerry W. Markham, III, A Financial History of the United States: From the Age of Derivatives Into the New Millennium (1970–2001) at 257 (2002).

258. Ibid.

259. E&Y was banned by the SEC in April, 2004 from accepting any new clients for six months as a result of alleged conflicts in its audit relationship with PeopleSoft, a high-tech software company. See Adrian Michaels 'Top Auditors Lose More Listed Company Clients,' *Financial Times*, July 22, 2004, at p 24. Interestingly, this was well after Enron and Sarbanes-Oxley.

260. See Lynnley Browning, 'How an Accounting Firm Went from Resistance to Resignation,' *New York Times*, August 28, 2005 at A-1.

261. Ibid. at A-16.

262. Ibid.

263. Ibid.

264. Ibid.

265. The variety of these co-ventures are detailed in Securities Exchange Act Release No. 42994 ('Revision of the Commission's Auditor Independence Requirements') (June 30, 2000).

266. This claim has been repeatedly made in journalism on Enron and Arthur Andersen. See Noam Scheiber, 'How Arthur Andersen Got Away With It: Peer Revue,' The New Republic, January 28, 2002 at 19.

267. An internal memorandum at Arthur Andersen announced the imposition of a ceiling on the firm's audit charges for Waste Management Company because it was a 'crown jewel' with regard to the purchase of non-audit services. See 'Arthur Andersen LLP Agrees to Settlement,' SEC News Release No. 2001–62 (June 19, 2001).

268. See Ianthe Jeanne Dugan, 'Depreciated: Did You Hear the One About the Accountant? Its Not Very Funny,' Wall Street Journal, March 14, 2002 at A1.

269. See Ken Brown & Ianthe Jeanne Dugan, 'Sad Account: Andersen's Fall From Grace is a Tale of Greed and Miscues,' Wall Street Journal, June 7, 2002 at A1.

270. See Glass Lewis & Co., 'Restatements – Traversing Shaky Ground: An Analysis for Investors' (June 2, 2005) at 1. This analysis includes U.S. domestic companies traded on an exchange or Nasdaq, but excludes foreign private issuers. The number of restatements for 2005 is not yet known, but Glass Lewis & Co. has preliminarily reported that it will exceed 1,000—or a roughtly 50% increase over 2004.

271. Ibid. at 5. Indeed, this rate has climbed steadily from 1.3% in 1997, 1.7% in 1998, 2.5% in 1999, 2.7% in 2000, 3.4% in 2001, 4.4% in 2002, 5.3% in 2003, to 5.4% in 2004. Ibid.

272. See 'Executive Pay: Too Many Turkeys,' *The Economist*, November 24, 2005.

273. Ibid. Again, this extraordinary ratio is a fairly recent development. The ratio of CEO to average production employee compensation was 107:1 in 1990 and only 42:1 in 1982. Ibid.

274. Ibid.

275. See Glass, Lewis & Co., n. 270, at 33. Some 586 public companies disclosed 'material weaknesses' in internal controls between January 1, and May 2, 2005; earlier, in 2004, some 313 companies made similar disclosures.

276. Ibid. at 51.

277. Sarbanes-Oxley requires the PCAOB to conduct an annual inspection of each public accounting firm that audits more than 100 issuers.

278. None of the Big Four escaped sharp criticisms. But some reports stood out. For example, the KPMG's report stated: 'In some cases, the deficiencies were of such significance that it appeared to the inspection team that the firm had not, at the time it issued its audit report, obtained sufficient competent evidential material to support its opinion on the issuer's financial statements.' See PCAOB Release No. 104–2005–088 ('Report on 2004 Inspection of KPMG LLP, September 29, 2005') at p 3. Although quietly stated, this is still a sharp rebuke.

279. The Inspection Reports do not publicly disclose defects in a firm's quality control system, as criticisms of these systems remain non-public under Sarbanes-Oxley unless the auditor fails to respond to them to the PCAOB's satisfaction within 12 months of the date of the report. But the general tenor of these reports suggests that criticisms of internal control systems at the Big Four were recurrently made.

280. Cornerstone Research has found that auditors were named as defendants in only five cases filed in 2005 and only eight cases filed in 2004. This came to three and four percent, respectively, at all securities class actions filed in those two years. See Cornerstone Research, '2005: A Year in Review', at 16 (2006).

281. See Diya Gullapalli, 'Number of Firms that Switched Auditors Jumped 78% in 2004,' Wall Street Journal, February 7, 2005 at C-3

(reporting results of a study by Glass Lewis & Co., a proxy advisor firm). For an earlier study, see Phyllis Plitch and Lingling Wei, 'Auditor–Client Breakups Rise, While Disclosure Often Lags,' Wall Street Journal, 3 August, 2004 at C-3.

282. Gullapalli, n 281, at C-3.

283. See Amy Borrus, 'Auditors: The Leash Gets Shorter,' Business Week, December 27, 2004 at 52.

284. Ibid.

285. Ibid.

286. Glass Lewis & Co. reports that the more than 1,600 auditor changes in 2004 produced a net loss of 400 clients for the Big Four; in contrast, the largest winner was BDO Seidman, LLP, which gained 109 new clients in 2004. See Gullapalli, n 281, at C-3.

287. The press has reported that Sun Microsystems Inc. and Silicon Graphics Inc. have recently entered into such agreements with Ernst & Young. See Michael Rapoport, 'Auditing Liability Caps Face Fire', Wall Street Journal, November 28, 2005 at C-3.

288. See Floyd Norris, 'Are Auditors Not Doing Due Diligence?', *New York Times*, 7 October, 2005 at C-1. The draft white paper further concluded that the auditor should not respond even if the corporate client authorized the auditor to do so.

289. Under Section 11(b)(3)(C), 15 U.S.C. §77k(b)(3)(C), underwriters and directors can escape strict liability for a material misstatement or omission in a registration statement by reasonably relying upon an expert whose report covered the matters in question.

290. Between 1997 and 2001, the accounting industry spent $41 million on lobbying activities, and each of the Big Five were among the top 20 contributors to George Bush's 2000 presidential campaign. See James Cox, *After the Sarbanes-Oxley Act: The Future Disclosure System: Reforming the Culture of Financial Reporting: The PCAOB and the Metrics for Accounting Measurement*, 81 Wash. U.L.Q. 301, 316 (2003).

6

Corporate Attorneys as Gatekeepers: The Short History of a Developing Concept

Introduction

Law is an old profession, but the idea of the attorney as a gatekeeper for parties other than the attorney's direct client is far more recent. Indeed, the concept has never truly been accepted by the organized bar, which prefers to view the attorney as an advocate, whose sole duty is the zealous representation of the client.[1] Few attorneys probably consider themselves gatekeepers. Still, presenting the attorney as primarily an advocate profoundly misrepresents the functional activity of the corporate lawyer.

The corporate lawyer functions in a very different capacity from the advocate in at least two important respects. First, the corporate lawyer acts principally as a transaction engineer. Corporate lawyers (including in this category tax and other business planning specialists) rarely appear in court and have little direct contact with litigation. Essentially, their real work is the planning, structuring and negotiation of transactions for their largely corporate and institutional clientele. Second, the special skill of the corporate lawyer has been drafting and disclosure, including the special verification skills—known as 'due diligence' work within the profession—that accompany the preparation of disclosure documents. Traditionally, the corporate lawyer prepared or reviewed the disclosure documents and shareholder communications that, from the New Deal on, the Securities and Exchange Commission increasingly required the public corporation to file and disseminate. Because these documents carried a risk of liability, it was natural that the corporation would want them vetted by their attorneys. But, over time, the process of preparing disclosure documents for public offerings evolved into an often elaborate 'due diligence' investigation, jointly conducted by counsel for the issuer and counsel for the underwriters. Characteristically, both counsel approached this task not as 'zealous advocates,' but as careful factfinders, seeking to reduce the risk of liability by verifying the essential facts. From this starting point, investors too came to rely on the corporation's outside counsel to assure full disclosure. But while investors may have expectations, they have few, if any, rights against the attorneys for the corporation.[2]

The differences between the corporate lawyer and the litigator all suggest that the corporate lawyer is well positioned to serve as a gatekeeper. As transaction engineers, corporate lawyers have a skill set focused on negotiation, drafting, business planning, and the ability to maintain a comprehensive, almost encyclopedic, understanding of extremely complex and integrated business transactions. Skill at oral advocacy and verbal fluency are less required, but the litigator's tendency toward hyperbole is also less common. Corporate lawyers are also more likely to view themselves as value neutral technicians, not embattled advocates sharing the same foxhole with their clients. In truth, the world of the corporate lawyer probably more closely borders on that of the accountant than that of the litigator/advocate. For example, in practice, corporate lawyers are likely to be far more familiar with 'generally accepted accounting principles' than with the Federal Rules of Civil Procedure (which is the bible for litigators).

The litigator and the corporate lawyer also differ in their characteristic relationship to the corporate client. Litigators see themselves as guardians and protectors, the shield between the client and an oppressive state or an extortionate plaintiff's attorney. Not only do litigators inhabit a more adversarial environment, but they generally are consulted by their clients on an *ex post* basis after trouble has arisen. In contrast, corporate lawyers tend to advise on an *ex ante* basis and accordingly envision themselves as 'wise counselors,' who gently guide their clients toward law compliance by pointing out the risks of alternative courses of action. Because the corporate attorney traditionally had a continuing relationship with the client, often having been relied upon for many years, the corporate attorney arguably enjoyed more discretionary ability to influence the client's strategic choices than did an attorney hired for a one-shot transaction (such as the typical litigator). Indeed, the bar's own self-image has long cast the independent counsel as a force for law compliance,[3] and this role represents at least a modest form of gatekeeping.

This picture is changing, and it is increasingly debatable whether the corporate lawyer can either monitor the corporate client to the same extent as in the past or gently dissuade it from illegal or reckless action.[4] For over a generation, the bar has insisted that the professional independence of the elite law firm partner promoted law compliance.[5] 'Independent' professionals, it was argued, would counsel against and quietly prevent rash and reckless actions by employees and agents of the corporate client. The more one accepts this premise, however, the more one is compelled to recognize that recent structural changes within the bar may have diminished the ability of the outside attorney to exercise any constraining influence over the corporate client.

In particular, the economic relationship between the corporate lawyer and its client has changed, probably beginning in the 1970s, as corporations found it more cost efficient to expand their in-house legal staffs than to pay the increasingly high fees of outside counsel. As a result, large corporations internalized a legal staff capable of handling most recurring matters, and the outside corporate lawyer increasingly came to be hired on a transaction-specific basis. This implies both that such an attorney must compete actively against other firms who also serve the same client, and that the attorney will generally possess less detailed knowledge of the client's overall activities. Nor can it be assumed that such an attorney enjoys any reservoir of good will that would enable the attorney to offer paternalistic advice. Hence, it is far less certain today that the outside attorney in the corporate law firm can play the traditional 'wise counselor' or 'statesman' role.

By no means, however, has the corporate lawyer in private practice suffered economically or in professional prestige; nor has the large law firm become less powerful. To the contrary, the last half century has essentially seen the large law firm grow to dominate the bar. In 1960, of the 206,000 lawyers then in private practice, some 64 percent were in solo practice. By 2000, there were some 700,000 lawyers in private practice, of whom some 53 percent (or roughly 370,000) were in firms.[6] More to the point, in 1960, only 38 law firms employed 50 or more lawyers, and the total number of attorneys so employed in large firm practice numbered only a few thousand. By 2000, well over 100,000 lawyers were employed in law firms having 50 or more attorneys. Within these large, hierarchical organizations, corporate practice is the dominant activity—and increasingly so.[7]

At first glance, this may seem a paradox. The legal profession is today dominated by large, powerful and ever expanding firms of as many as 1,000 or more lawyers, which essentially specialize in serving large corporations. Yet, law firms probably have substantially less leverage over their corporate clients, and their relationship with their largest corporate clients is probably less intimate, ongoing or fully informed than is the relationship between the same corporation and its outside auditor. There is, however, a second side to this coin: the law firm is probably more independent of the client than in the past because a single corporation's billings are no longer material to most law firms. Nor is any one partner in the law firm as exposed to 'capture' by the client as is the audit partner of a major audit firm.

In overview, the market for corporate legal services is a highly competitive and much less concentrated market than is the market for auditing services. The key actor in this process is the in-house general counsel, who has every incentive to break down the traditional one-to-one relationships between his client and its primary outside counsel. From our perspective, this relative shift in the balance of power between outside and inside counsel raises a basic question: can the in-house counsel replace the outside lawyer/statesman as a gatekeeper? Here, it is difficult to be optimistic. While the outside attorney has been increasingly relegated to a specialist's role and is seldom sought for statesman-like advice, the in-house general counsel seems even less suited to play a gatekeeping role. First, the in-house counsel is less an independent professional—indeed he is far more exposed to pressure and reprisals than even the outside audit partner. Second, the in-house counsel is seldom a reputational intermediary (as law and accounting firms that serve multiple clients are) because the in-house counsel cannot easily develop reputational capital that is personal and independent from the corporate client.

This does not mean that the inside counsel is a mere lackey. Indeed, the inside counsel is uniquely positioned to specialize in preventive law. The enhanced professional status of the in-house counsel depends to a considerable degree on accepting and promoting this responsibility, thereby staking out turf in the internal tug-of-war over authority and jurisdiction within the large public corporation. From a monitoring standpoint, inside and outside counsel have relative advantages: the outside counsel has independence, while the inside counsel has knowledge.

Over the last 30 years, the legal profession has to a considerable degree followed the business model of the accounting profession. In particular, law copied accounting in adopting a strategy of multi-branch firms that have increasingly become international in scope.[8] The shock of intensified competition hit both the legal and accounting professions at about the same time, beginning in the mid-1970s. In the case of the accounting profession, antitrust regulators forced changes, compelling the profession to drop professional ethics rules against competitive bidding and direct solicitation of business. In contrast, the bar never sought to discourage competition (possibly because it was never as concentrated as the accounting profession), and it quickly accepted new practices, such as 'beauty contests' at which rival firms presented themselves for the client's evaluation.

Law firms similarly followed accounting firms in consolidating through mergers in order to realize economies of scope and scale. A series of changes—the growth of multi-branch firms, law firm mergers, the lateral mobility of partners, revised 'eat-what-you-kill' compensation practices, and the portability of clients—all appeared together as more or less interconnected developments that collectively spurred competition within the legal profession. Indeed, only the Enron scandal halted another development that had begun and was gathering momentum: the rise of multi-disciplinary professional firms that practiced law along with other professions, such as accounting or consulting.[9]

The development that most encouraged competition among law firms, however, was the rise of the in-house general counsel to a new status as a general manager of legal services. Originally, the motivation was simply economic; these new, in-house managers of legal services were hired to control rapidly rising legal costs and did so by increasingly insisting on competitive bidding by law firms. But in-house general managers quickly realized that to ensure their unrivaled hegemony as the primary legal advisers to management, it was useful to spread business around multiple firms and prevent the ascendancy of a single dominant law firm. As a result, for the outside professional, the corporate client came to be viewed as the inside general counsel, who hired and set the compensation of all outside attorneys.

Increased competition can undercut professional values. Within the legal market, two destabilizing changes that threaten professional values came in sequence. First, the rise of the general counsel compelled outside attorneys to redefine their role as more that of transactional specialists and less that of 'wise counselors.' Second, as law firms became increasingly populated with specialists who served numerous clients on a shorter term or one-shot basis, the lateral mobility of the specialist partner increased. The specialist partner was less locked within a complex web of relationships that existed to serve a predominant client and more an independent actor with his or her own professional reputation. This new lateral mobility of 'star' partners forced law firms to shift to more short-term, 'eat-what-you-kill' compensation formulas for all partners, lest they lose high-billing partners. This shift in turn increased the pressure on all partners to maximize their billings. All these developments both increased the leverage of the corporate client over the attorney, and also increasingly marginalized the partner who may have preferred to lead a mixed career of public and private service—the 'lawyer statesmen' of mid-20th century America.

Ironically, just as law (much like accounting) became more of a business and less of a profession in the last decades of the 20th century, the idea that the lawyer owed gatekeeping responsibilities to investors was first seriously raised in a series of unprecedented regulatory actions that began in the 1970s. First the SEC and then federal banking regulators brought actions against prominent law firms, charging them essentially with abandoning the interests of investors in their desire to serve management.[10] In response, the bar closed ranks and amended its own legal ethics rules to minimize the limited prospect that attorneys could take public-regarding actions at the expense of their clients. Until Enron and related scandals changed the political climate, the bar had successfully frustrated the SEC's reform initiatives. Much like the accounting profession, the bar protected its own autonomy and resisted the imposition of gatekeeping responsibilities. But, much as did the accounting profession, the legal profession lost some (although probably less) of its cherished autonomy with the passage of the Sarbanes-Oxley Act.

This chapter starts by reviewing this history in Section A, beginning with the Progressive Era's formulation of an alternative legal ethic—the Republican lawyer—and then tracing its gradual eclipse over subsequent decades until legal ethics came to say little more by way of admonition than that the lawyer should not commit crimes or assist clients known to be planning them. But tracing this history does not answer the broader question: to what degree can the corporate lawyer under the changed economic and organizational circumstances of the 21st century function as a gatekeeper? To what obligations, if any, can such a lawyer realistically be asked to be faithful? This issue has long polarized the legal profession, with the organized bar and academic lawyers taking radically different positions. Within the bar, the dominant view has long been that legal ethics commands lawyers to engage in zealous advocacy on behalf of their clients' positions and permits them to take any action up to the point where such behavior becomes unlawful. Thus, the lawyer may pursue any lawful goal of the client, however socially or morally unappealing, and may raise any non-frivolous legal claim or assert any permissible procedural defense on its behalf. Predictably, this position shocks legal ethics professors and public interest practitioners, who have articulated the polar counter-view, which is traceable back to Louis Brandeis, that 'the lawyer should take such actions as, considering the relevant circumstances of the particular case, seems likely to promote justice.'[11]

Few have attempted to stake out any intermediate position. But the idea that the corporate lawyer today can act on the basis of a personal vision of the public interest, pursuing it, more or less, as Louis Brandeis arguably did nearly a century ago, seems increasingly untenable. Put bluntly, the social and economic circumstances that placed Brandeis in a position where he could be both professionally independent and counsel broadly 'for the situation', have probably gone with the wind. Moreover, even if the corporate attorney did act in accordance with a personal vision of 'the public interest,' the empirical evidence suggests that he or she would view that public interest in about the same way as the corporate client does.[12] Section B of this chapter will therefore turn to the organizational changes that have redefined legal practice in order to ask what responsibilities can realistically be placed on inside and outside counsel. Later, this book will propose a narrower, more functionally specific definition of the normative role that can realistically be mandated for the corporate lawyer. By training and by professional orientation, the lawyer can be expected to insist upon accurate and full disclosure of material information. Based on this foundation, the independent lawyer could be asked to monitor the corporation's disclosures in a functionally similar fashion to the manner in which the independent auditor monitors the corporation's financial performance. To be sure, attorneys are not auditors, and this proposed gatekeeper role is not intended as an exhaustive or exclusive statement of legal ethics. Rather, the idea of the independent attorney as a gatekeeper over the disclosure process represents a context-specific set of norms, capable of feasible implementation, that lie midway between the all-or-nothing positions of the bar and academia.

From the Progressive Era to the Present: An Abbreviated History

The American bar began to specialize by the mid-19th century. The initial driving force was the growth of the railroads. Railroads retained the elite of the bar on long-term retainers, and, under the normal ethical rules regarding conflicts of interest, those attorneys could not represent the numerous plaintiffs who wished to sue railroads. The 19th century railroad lawyer was a generalist—acting as an advocate in court, a lobbyist before the legislature, and an adviser to management. But as the century wore on, specializations developed. Railroads had an insatiable need for capital, which they typically raised in debt offerings (because the equity market was not yet well developed). The corporate lawyer arose as a specialist who designed and implemented these offerings. Corporate control was also frequently at issue. When the Robber Barons warred over a railroad's control (as Commodore Vanderbilt and Jay Gould fought bitterly over the Erie in the 1880s), it was corporate lawyers who devised the tactical stratagems that gave the victory to Gould.[13] Later, when the Sherman Anti-Trust Act and the industry's own desires for consolidation produced an unprecedented merger wave in the 1890s, corporate lawyers engineered the complex and recurrent reorganizations and/or mergers that created the great trusts and later U.S. Steel, General Electric, and a host of other industrial giants. Investment bankers, such as J. P. Morgan, may have conceived and brokered these transactions, but the embryonic New York law firms that later grew to dominate the corporate legal market were usually their engineers.

The Progressive Era's Aspirations

As a political movement largely fueled by public revulsion at the excesses of the Robber Barons, the Progressive Era naturally focused on the relationship between corporations and their counsel. In 1905, at the height of Progressive Era optimism and energy, the American Bar Association was persuaded to draft a national model ethics code. That project culminated in 1908 in the ABA's Canons of Ethics, which shaped legal ethics in the United States for at least the next half-century.[14] The impetus to undertake this project seems to have come both from a speech delivered before the ABA in 1905 by President Theodore Roosevelt, in which he characteristically castigated corporate lawyers for assisting their clients in evading regulation, and from the fact that the American Medical Association had adopted its own code of professional ethics in 1903.[15] If doctors could draft a code of ethics, lawyers did not want to appear any less modern or professional.

In the drafting process, one ethical issue became the center of attention and debate: the so-called 'duty to do justice' obligation. Nineteenth century treatise writers on legal ethics perceived a self-evident duty, grounded on religious principles, for the lawyer to do justice. A number of states had adopted 'lawyers oaths', which required a lawyer to swear that:

I will counsel and maintain such actions, proceedings, and defenses only, as appear to me legal and just, except in the defense of a person charged with a public offense.[16]

Some members of the ABA Committee similarly wanted such a provision in the ABA's Canons in order to express the lawyer's ethical accountability for the justice of the causes they filed on behalf of clients. Translated into our vocabulary, these members wanted even the litigator to be a gatekeeper, filing only actions in which he believed his client was 'justly entitled to some measure of relief.'[17] Opposing their position on the Committee were the positivists—hard-boiled practitioners who did not accept the duty-to-do-justice premise, but saw lawyers more as value-neutral technicians.

Not surprisingly, the ABA Committee compromised, including in Canon 30 only a significantly altered and watered down version of the obligation to appraise the merits of the client's action. Canon 30 asserted that a lawyer's

appearance in Court should be deemed equivalent to an assertion on his honor that in his opinion his client's case is one proper for judicial determination.[18]

What did 'proper for judicial determination' mean? In reality, it meant that the traditional form of the lawyer's oath could be retained, but with its substance largely drained. Despite the temper of the times and the widely felt need for some moralistic statement from the bar, the positivists triumphed in committee by deleting any meaningful requirement that the attorney play gatekeeper before filing an action.

But as in most compromises, there was something for both sides. Canon 32 of the ABA's 1908 Canons stated:

No client, corporate or individual, however powerful, nor any cause, civic or political, however important, is entitled to receive, nor should any lawyer render, any service or advice involving disloyalty to the law, whose ministers we are, ... or deception or betrayal of the public .... The lawyer ... advances the honor of his profession and the best interests of his client when he renders service or gives advice tending to impress upon the client ... exact compliance with the strictest principles of moral law ....[19]

This language certainly contained sufficient references to attorneys as 'ministers' of law, duty bound to demand 'exact compliance with the strictest principles of moral law' to satisfy the moralists, and it expressed enough skepticism of 'corporate' and 'powerful' clients to demonstrate the bar's independence from the corporate behemoths of the day. But, Canon 32 was essentially unenforceable because no objectively measurable standard was expressed. The ABA Committee drafting Canon 32 was neither cynical nor disingenuous, but only deeply conflicted and unable to take meaningful action. Still, Canon 32's proscription of any 'deception or betrayal of the public,' even if too amorphous a norm to be enforced, may be the first explicit recognition by the ABA of any gatekeeper-like obligation to third party non-clients.

So what happened to Canon 32 and indeed the ABA's Canons of Ethics? Here, it is necessary to skip ahead in our history, but the answer frames much of the dilemma in relying on ethical standards to regulate attorneys. The ABA's 1908 Canons of Ethics were widely adopted; indeed, within well less than a decade, 31 of the then 45 star bar associations had adopted it.[20] Inevitably (and fairly quickly), courts came to use the Canons as a basis for disciplining attorneys. Predictably, the ABA reacted to the increasing enforceability of the Canons by amending them – in 1927, 1933 and 1937.[21] By the 1960s, the ABA had decided that the Canons were out of date. Their aspirational language had proved too unconfineable and invited litigation against attorneys. Thus, in 1969, the ABA adopted the Code of Professional Responsibility, which was divided into three sections: Canons, Ethical Considerations, and Disciplinary Rules. While the first two sections were aspirational in character, only the third was mandatory. In effect, professional ethics were separated from minimum rules, and the practical lawyer could concentrate only on the latter, leaving the former for academics and a few stray ethicists.

The Code was also widely adopted, but it provoked recurrent controversies and was repeatedly amended between 1969 and 1977.[22] Within only a few years, the ABA resolved to abandon the tripartite division of the Code and start over. This effort produced the ABA Model Rules of Professional Conduct in 1981. The Model Rules abandoned any reference to 'ethical considerations' and were set forth in the traditional Restatement format of 'black letter' minimum standards. Gradually but inexorably, the bar had drained the ethical content from its 'professional' rules. Aspirational statements had proved troubling because there was always the risk that courts might actually enforce them, and 'black letter' rules could more easily be distinguished, evaded or, if necessary, amended. While the proponents of these changes were well meaning and even idealistic, the bar was only comfortable with precise rules, not softer-edged norms. A comparison here is unavoidable: over roughly the same period, accountants in the United States revised generally accepted accounting principles to move from a principle-based system to a rule-based system. The threat of litigation was an even more palpable motivator in their case.

The adoption of the Model Rules has not ended controversy or calls for still more amendments, but it did finally purge all traces of the loftier sentiments that lurked in the 1908 Canons. In this process, as will be seen later, any suggestion of the attorney having gatekeeping responsibilities was eliminated—at least for a time.

Nonetheless, during the Progressive Era—at least for a brief moment—the attorney was seen as a gatekeeper. For the clearest statement of this view, one must look not to the ABA, but to that iconic representative of Progressivism, Louis Brandeis. In his 1914 speech, 'The Opportunity of the Law,' Brandeis explains why in his view the prestige of the bar had fallen and concluded:

Instead of holding a position of independence, between the wealthy and the people, prepared to curb the excesses of either, lawyers have, to a large extent, allowed themselves to become adjuncts of great corporations and have neglected to use their powers for the protection of the people....[23]

The core or 'Republican' idea here was that the attorney has a public role, which positions the attorney midway 'between the wealthy and the public,' in order to serve as the guardian of liberty and the values of legalism.[24] Consistent with Canon 32, such a public guardian was obligated to counsel respect for the law, including its broader purposes, and could not simply advise a course of technical evasion.

While Brandeis's vision of law as a public career never took root in any ABA or state bar pronouncement, it probably did influence a generation of lawyers, who rose to power and prominence after World War I. Among these were many corporate and business lawyers who came to hold public office: Henry Stimson, Elihu Root, Dean Acheson, Grenville Clark, John J. McCloy and Adolf Berle.[25]

While the Brandeisian ideal faded during the laissez-faire 1920s, the New Deal revived the ideal, and hundreds of lawyers rushed to Washington imbued by it. Many were young corporate lawyers, who helped write the federal securities laws and staffed the SEC. Some later migrated to Washington and New York law firms, where they spent the remainder of their careers representing clients against the SEC. A few may have lived up to the Brandeisian ideal, but more probably represented their clients and fought the SEC with the same adversarial intensity as lawyers who had no SEC experience or Brandeisian ambitions.

The Bar and the SEC: The History of a Troubled Relationship

The enactment of the federal securities laws initiated a less conspicuous development that profoundly changed the functional activity of corporate lawyers. The first of the federal securities statutes, the Securities Act of 1933, imposed strict liability on any issuer that made a material misstatement or omission in the disclosure document—known as a 'registration statement'—that that Act required the issuer to file with the SEC and disseminate to the market in order to sell securities to the public. In addition, underwriters, accountants, and officers and directors of the issuer were also made liable, but they received an affirmative defense under which they would escape liability, notwithstanding a material misstatement or omission in the issuer's registration statement, if they conducted 'a reasonable investigation' and had 'reasonable grounds to believe' in the accuracy of the statements made.[26] In effect, the 1933 Act's strategy was to focus on the gatekeepers and other persons associated with the issuer and compel them to conduct an adequate investigation of the issuer—or face liability alongside it. This obligation to conduct a 'reasonable investigation' was largely delegated by underwriters and directors to their corporate lawyers.

As a result, after 1933, both the lawyers for the issuer (who also represented the directors who wished to rely on this defense) and the lawyers for the underwriters saw a common need to investigate all statements made in draft registration statements—in order to establish a 'due diligence' defense. Due diligence became the mainstay of securities practice. In this respect, the Securities Act of 1933 had much the same impact on the bar as the British Company Act amendments in the mid-19th century (which mandated an annual audit) had on the accounting profession earlier. In both cases, the legislation stimulated demand for the professional's services and converted the professional into at least a quasi-public gatekeeper.

In principle, lawyers could have conducted their due diligence inquiries mainly for their cosmetic value. During some 'bubbly periods' in the market—for example, in the late 1960s—the rush to bring offerings to the market may have overtaken the need to perform adequate due diligence, and merely cosmetic efforts may have been made. Still, on an overall basis, corporate lawyers did internalize this norm. Young lawyers learned their trade performing due diligence on large offerings, and the natural competitiveness of lawyers made the process genuinely investigative. Well-known stories have entered the folklore of Wall Street about frauds discovered during due diligence investigations.[27]

Courts also demonstrated that they could distinguish serious efforts at due diligence from purely cosmetic efforts. In 1968, a federal district court in the Southern District of New York issued a landmark decision in *Escott v. BarChris Construction Co.*[28] that laid down what became the defining standards for the judicial evaluation of due diligence. Criticizing the registration statement before it as a 'scissors and paste-pot job,' whose contents had been largely borrowed from earlier prospectuses, the court made clear that a lawyer could not simply rely in this context on the client's statements, but should, at the very least, conduct 'a check of matters easily verifiable.'[29] This mandatory 'check' did not involve an audit, but did require that the attorney 'test the information by examining the original written record.' On this basis, the attorney could not summarize contracts or transactions in the registration statement without first reviewing the actual documents. Although the court did permit attorneys and their clients to rely on the auditor with regard to the financial statements, statements made elsewhere in the registration statement required the attorney to find factual support in documentary evidence if the due diligence defense was to be established.

Particularly as securities class action developed in the 1970s and thereafter, securities attorneys were compelled to investigate their own clients and, unlike the advocate, could not accept their oral assertions at face value. Nor did the bar shrink from this task. Due diligence efforts became more serious and formalized after the *BarChris* decision. To be sure, the bar had little reason to resist, because due diligence activities represented a Full Employment Act for law firms doing public offerings and probably accounted for most of the billable hours in a typical public offering. Due diligence work was also the training ground for young associates, where they could prove their attention to detail by finding discrepancies between the draft registration statement and the actual documents.

In fairness, the securities bar did more than simply exploit the economic potential of the due diligence defense. Rather, the securities bar accepted due diligence as a normative concept, doing so in a manner that clearly distinguished them from litigators. An excellent expression of this view was given in 1974 by A. A. Sommer, a long-time leader of the securities bar and at the time an SEC Commissioner. In a speech entitled 'The Emerging Responsibilities of the Securities Lawyer,'[30] he distinguished the ethics of securities practice from that of legal practice generally:

I would suggest that in securities matters (other than those where advocacy is clearly proper) the attorney will have to function in a manner more akin to that of auditor than to that of the attorney. This means several things. It means that he will have to exercise a measure of independence that is perhaps uncomfortable if he is also the close counselor of management in other matters, often including business decisions. It means he will have to be acutely cognizant of his responsibility to the public who engage in securities transactions that would never have come about were it not for his professional presence. It means that he will have to adopt the healthy skepticism toward the representation of management which a good auditor must adopt. It means that he will have to do the same thing the auditor does when confronted with an intransigent client—resign.

The elements in Sommer's definition of the securities lawyer's ethical responsibilities overlap with our definition of a gatekeeper:

(i) independence from the client;
(ii) professional skepticism of the client's representations;

(iii) a duty to the public investor who relies on the lawyer; and

(iv) a duty to resign when the integrity of the attorney's work would otherwise be compromised.

It is simply impossible to imagine the litigator recognizing the same obligations. The criminal defense attorney could not, for example, express skepticism about his client's alibi defense. Even though he may doubt it and may advise his client not to testify, the litigator's ethical obligation was still to zealously assert any colorable defense and point out any deficiency in the prosecution's evidence that corroborated it. Nor would the litigator worry, as Sommer's does in the above quotation, about the attorney's 'responsibility to the public' or other third parties. Finally, Sommer's analogy of the securities attorney to the auditor is unthinkable in the case of the litigator.

Sommer's views were strongly stated, but were neither idiosyncratic nor unique to him. Although other securities lawyers might have swallowed hard at his analogy between attorneys and auditors, the corporate and securities bar did accept by this point that they had an ethical obligation to tell an accurate story, which they had duly investigated, in preparing registration statements and other SEC filings.[31] In short, by at least the 1970s, the securities lawyer and the litigator had come to accept different professional norms.

The next step in this story involves a possibly surprising reversal in direction, one that must be understood as part of a broader political reaction to overregulation. Full-scale due diligence of the kind envisioned by *BarChris* was both costly and time-consuming. The elaborate registration procedures used by the SEC also slowed down offerings, and thus could deny issuers the ability to exploit what they at least perceived as attractive 'market windows.' As a result, in the early 1980s, in a deregulatory climate that differed from the 1930s as night from day, the SEC decided to expedite the offering process in two critical respects. First, it permitted established issuers to use a streamlined prospectus that simply listed previously filed 1934 Act reports (i.e. Form 10-Ks and Form 10-Qs), which were thereby deemed to have been 'incorporated by reference.' Known as 'integrated disclosure,' this approach meant that a registration statement did not have to be drafted from scratch; rather, the issuer could prepare it in as little as a day by listing and updating its previously filed 1934 Act filings. Second, the SEC permitted issuers to register securities 'for the shelf'—that is, for future sale over a two-year period. Thus, the issuer could access the market virtually at any time because it would always be 'registered.'

Each of these deregulatory reforms had a different practical impact, but in combination they significantly undermined the then prevailing system in which lawyers functioned in practice as gatekeepers by performing due diligence in connection with securities offerings.[32] Integrated disclosure meant that registrations statements could be prepared, filed, and declared effective by the SEC in a very brief period, typically consisting of less than a week—a time frame that simply did not permit significant 'due diligence' to be performed. Shelf registration had even more sweeping implications: securities could be registered for sale for up to two years later, and no further legal work by the attorneys would be strictly necessary (although some would typically be quickly performed). Thus, only a compressed time frame existed in which attorneys could realistically perform a gatekeeping role. Although issuers and underwriters were not required to exploit this new freedom to do shelf offerings or to skip serious due diligence efforts, competitive pressures pushed underwriters to agree to match the fastest time schedule that any rival offered. As a result, underwriters essentially accepted the prospect of increased Section 11 liability (because of reduced due diligence efforts) as a cost of doing business. Only in the case of the initial public offering and some other offerings that were ineligible for shelf registration did full scale due diligence persist.

In retrospect, a reasonable debate seems possible about whether the benefits of expedited offerings and shelf registration exceeded their costs. The benefits consisted of significantly reduced transaction costs to issuers and underwriters and immediate access to the market, but investors may have borne the less visible costs associated with the undetected frauds that reached the market because of the de facto elimination of the securities lawyer as a gatekeeper. In fairness, one cannot present the SEC's adoption of integrated disclosure and shelf registration as simply a product of the deregulatory Reagan Revolution that swept through Washington in the early 1980s. In fact, the first movements by the SEC in this direction came during the late Carter Administration, and the bar, itself, had long pushed for deregulation. One cannot pretend to know either whether investment bankers, armed with securities counsel performing elaborate due diligence, would have spotted the frauds at Enron and WorldCom. Indeed, given the 'bubbly' climate of the late 1990s, considerable skepticism is justified about how effective or eager private agents would have been in halting transactions that the market was eager to consummate.[33]

Nonetheless, the role of the attorney as a gatekeeper was significantly eclipsed, or at least downsized, by deregulation at the SEC in the 1980s. In this light, the practical issue for the future is not whether the SEC was right or wrong (as the changes are today irreversible), but whether an alternative institutional design is feasible that could re-introduce due diligence by securities attorneys without forcing a significant delay in the access of issuers to the capital markets.[34]

Ironically, at the same time as the SEC's Division of Corporation Finance was deregulating the offering process, the SEC's Enforcement Division first began to insist that lawyers were gatekeepers. The late 1960s and early 1970s had witnessed a mini-bubble in the equity markets, and in its wake courts responded by placing higher burdens on defendants (as the *BarChris* decision in 1968 certainly did). The SEC similarly was moved to greater activism,[35] which quickly provoked a major confrontation with the bar. In 1972, the SEC filed a complaint against both National Student Marketing Corporation (NSMC) and its outside counsel, the prestigious New York law firm of White & Case. NSMC was the 1970s paradigm case of accounting manipulation—a symbol of how to use acquisitions as a substitute for earnings. Exploiting the long controversial 'pooling of interests' accounting convention, NSMC systematically made numerous acquisitions of smaller companies, particularly towards the end of each year (and often afterwards as well). It then included the year-to-date revenues and earnings of these acquired companies in its own income statement, thereby achieving constantly increasing earnings (at least so long as it could find an adequate number of merger candidates). Ultimately, its founder and chief executive, Cortes W. Randall, was sentenced to prison, and NSMC's accounting chicanery—which the accounting critic Abraham Briloff had incisively dubbed 'dirty pooling'—was defended by none.

The startling development in the case was the SEC's decision to name the lawyers on both sides of one of NSMC's merger transactions as defendants, for having assisted their respective managements in closing the transaction without providing full disclosure to shareholders. The specific transaction on which the SEC chose to focus was a merger by means of which NSMC acquired a much smaller corporation, Interstate National Coporation (INC), in return for NSMC stock, which was issued at an exchange ratio highly favorable to INC's shareholders. A precondition to this merger was that NSMC's public accountants deliver a 'comfort letter' to INC, containing certain representations about NSMC's current earnings. When the accountants refused to deliver a clean opinion, the law firms for both sides conferred with their clients and decided to proceed, waiving this condition.[36] Although INC's lawyers orally obtained approval for this waiver from a majority of the INC board (who in turn held a majority of INC's stock), the SEC asserted that the lawyers for both sides had violated Rule 10b-5 by failing to halt the transaction in order to resolicit shareholders (whose approval had been obtained based on a proxy solicitation that now appeared to be materially incomplete). As a practical matter, the attorneys had the power to stop the closing in its tracks because the merger was conditioned on their delivery of their own closing opinions, which in the SEC's view they could not deliver. From the law firms' perspective, their clients had only made a decision to waive a closing condition in order to effect a merger both sides still considered attractive. Conversely, the SEC argued that lawyers had knowingly deprived the shareholders of material information showing the deal to be suspicious.[37]

With the issues so defined, the SEC and the bar faced each other in a stark confrontation, each side incensed at the other. The SEC asserted that even if the directors had insisted on going forward, the lawyers were obligated to resign, informing shareholders, and (at least according to the SEC's original position) notifying the SEC about the non-disclosures. The bar replied that lawyers did not make business decisions for their clients and certainly did not report them to the SEC. The role of the bar in its own eyes was to protect the client from the state, not serve as a policeman for the state.

In fact, the SEC may well have had the better argument in terms of the existing rules of legal ethics. Under the ABA's own Canons of Ethics, which traced directly back to the 1908 Canons discussed earlier, a lawyer who discovered fraud or deception by his client was under an obligation to

endeavor to rectify it; at first by advising his client, and if his client refuses to forego the advantage thus unjustly gained, he should promptly inform the injured person or his counsel, so that they may take appropriate steps.[38]

To read these rules as inapplicable, the bar had to argue that the rules on rectification of fraud were subordinate to the rules on client confidentiality—a strained interpretation that was far from self-evident.

By the time the SEC's action came to trial, White & Case had quietly settled,[39] but the federal district court found that INC's own lawyers (who seemed much the less culpable of the two firms) had indeed aided and abetted a securities fraud in violation of Rule 10b-5. The Court ruled:

Upon receipt of the unsigned comfort letter, it became clear that the merger had been approved by the Interstate shareholders on the basis of materially misleading information. In view of the obvious materiality of the information, especially to attorneys learned in securities law, the attorneys' responsibilities to their corporate client required them to take steps to ensure that the information would be disclosed to the shareholders. However, it is unnecessary to determine the precise extent of their obligations here, since it is undisputed that they took no steps whatsoever to delay the closing pending disclosure to and resolicitation of the Interstate shareholders. But, at the very least, they were required to speak out at the closing concerning the obvious materiality of the information and the concomitant requirement that the merger not be closed until the adjustments were disclosed and approval of the merger was again obtained from the Interstate shareholders. Their silence was not only a breach of this duty to speak, but in addition lent the appearance of legitimacy to the closing.[40]

The decision ducked the question of whether attorneys had any obligation to notify the SEC, finding it unnecessary to go beyond their more obvious obligation to insist upon postponement and a revised proxy solicitation of shareholders. Emphatic as its language was, the Court declined, however, to enjoin the lawyers, finding it unlikely that they would otherwise repeat their violation.[41]

The SEC may have won the battle, but the war was soon to be fought on a far broader front. Faced with the fact that legal ethics seemingly required the lawyer take action to rectify a client fraud, the bar simply changed the rule. In 1974, the ABA rewrote Disciplinary Rule 7–102(B)(1) so that lawyers could not disclose client fraud, even when the client refused to comply.[42] This took some 'chutzpah', because it effectively asserted that a professional rule could overcome the SEC's theory of the lawyer's obligations under the federal securities laws.[43] A year later in 1975, while the *NSMC* case was still awaiting decision, the ABA adopted and broadly circulated a 'Statement of Policy Regarding Responsibilities and Liabilities of Lawyers in Advising With Respect to the Compliance by Clients with Laws Administered by the Securities and Exchange Commission.'[44] Questioning the SEC's legal authority for its position in the *NSMC* case, it concluded:

[A]ny principle of law which, except as permitted or required by the [Model Code of Professional Responsibility], permits or obligates a lawyer to disclose to the S.E.C. otherwise confidential information should be established only by statute after full and careful consideration of the public interests involved and should be resisted unless clearly mandated by law.[45]

Lest the *NSMC* court miss its point, the ABA added in its final paragraph that it would be particularly unfortunate if some lawyers were deterred from performing their duties to their clients by an 'erroneous position of the S.E.C. or a questionable lower court decision.'[46]

The SEC was also unwilling to back down—at least more than a half step. In 1979, it followed up on the *NSMC* case by commencing an even more controversial in-house administrative proceeding against two experienced securities lawyers at a major New York City firm. These lawyers were accused not of assisting a fraud, but of failing to prevent one—by not taking appropriate affirmative action to control their corporate client where they were aware that the client had begun to issue false disclosures to the market (but without their direct assistance).[47] That client, National Telephone Company, was on the brink of insolvency, and its creditors had negotiated an agreement with it under which, unless its financial condition improved, it would wind down its business, entering a state of suspended animation that the parties called the 'lease maintenance plan,' that allowed it to conduct no active business. Nonetheless, despite its deteriorating condition, National Telephone continued to issue optimistic press releases, which were drafted by its overconfident chief executive. Although the two outside attorneys expressed dissatisfaction with these press releases, they initially took no action. Eventually, National Telephone's financial condition worsened to the point that it was required to enter the 'lease maintenance plan' and wind down its business. The two lawyers strongly advised the chief executive to disclose this fact, but he refused. When he later asked them to draft a legal opinion to National Telephone's creditors, advising them that the lease maintenance mode had not been triggered, they refused and expressed their shock at his improper request. But they did nothing else and did not advise the board of the company's status.

On this basis, the SEC's staff charged the two lawyers with unethical conduct under what is today Rule 102(e) of the SEC's Rules of Practice, which limits the ability of both attorneys and accountants to practice before the Commission. In effect, the SEC staff's position was that passivity in the face of fraud constituted unethical conduct. The Administrative Law Judge agreed with the staff, sustained its charges, and barred the two attorneys from appearing before the Commission for one year and nine months, respectively.

On appeal, the Commission was faced with a problem of some delicacy. Unlike the attorneys in *National Student Marketing*, the two defendants—Carter and Johnson—had resisted their client and had counseled law compliance. But they had neither blown the whistle nor gone to the company's board of directors. Accordingly, when it heard the appeal of the ALJ's ruling, the Commission sought to strike a compromise. It agreed that attorneys in the position of Carter and Johnson could not remain passive, but it reversed the ALJ's decision, because the ethical obligations of corporate lawyers had 'not been so firmly and unambiguously established' to give fair notice to the bar.[48]

To make those responsibilities clear, the Commission articulated a standard to govern a lawyer's conduct in such situations. One sentence in this opinion captured its critical norm:

When a lawyer with significant responsibilities in the effectuation of a company's compliance with the disclosure requirements of the federal securities laws becomes aware that his client is engaged in substantial and continuing failure to satisfy those disclosure requirements, his continued participation violates professional standards unless he takes prompt steps to end the client's non-compliance.[49]

Obviously, the *Carter & Johnson* opinion was the Commission's effort to fashion a Solomonic compromise, one softer and less sweeping than its initial position in *National Student Marketing Corp*. As the above quotation shows, the new norm was to apply only to 'lawyers with significant responsibilities in the effectuation of a company's compliance with the disclosure requirements of the federal securities laws'; thus, at most, it made the securities lawyer a gatekeeper, but not the patent lawyer or real estate specialist who arguably would not have recognized a securities law violation. More importantly, the *Carter & Johnson* standard was triggered only by the client's 'substantial and continuing' violation, not a one-shot disclosure failure. Indeed, on this narrowed basis, the law firm for Interstate National Corporation (INC) in *National Student Marketing* might have legitimately claimed that it had not aided and abetted a securities law violation.

Even if the lawyer fell within the foregoing standard because he had 'significant responsibilities' and the violation was a 'substantial and continuing' one, the lawyer's obligations were not onerous under *Carter & Johnson*. Such an attorney was instructed to take 'more affirmative steps ... to avoid the inference that he had been co-opted willingly or unwillingly into the scheme of nondisclosure.'[50] The attorney could go to the board or resign or possibly take other steps, but no longer was the Commission insisting that he had to report the violation to the SEC.[51]

Although the Commission had neatly sidestepped any judicial test of its power by reversing the ALJ's sanctions and had offered an olive branch to the bar in the form of a softer standard, the bar was not appeased. The bar knew that *Carter & Johnson* had been issued by the 'old' SEC under its Democratic chairman, Harold Williams, in early 1981, just days before a new Republican SEC chairman appointed by newly elected President Ronald Reagan was to replace Chairman Williams. That new Commission, under Chairman John Shad, showed no inclination to implement *Carter & Johnson* with proposed rules.[52] Not only was the decision's name rarely spoken, but in 1982 the Commission's general counsel delivered a conciliatory speech in which he predicted that the Commission would normally limit its discipline of attorneys to instances where the conduct also violated established ethical rules of state bar organizations.[53] In 1988, the Commission, itself, formally ratified this policy, stating that the Commission had 'not sought to develop or apply independent standards of professional conduct ... [and] generally refrains from using its administrative forum to conduct *de novo* determinations of the professional obligations of attorneys.'[54] In effect, while the bar had not defeated the SEC in court, it had outlasted the SEC politically.[55]

The SEC has not subsequently brought an enforcement action against an attorney under Rule 102(e), except in cases where the attorney has been criminally convicted. But it has attempted to outflank its compromise with the bar by exploiting other statutory sections of the federal securities laws to reach an attorney whom it believed responsible for misleading disclosures. Again, however, the bar closed ranks and fought the SEC to a standstill. In 1987, the SEC brought a proceeding under Section 15(c)(4) of the Securities Exchange Act of 1934 against George C. Kern, Jr., a prominent 'mergers and acquisitions' partner with Sullivan & Cromwell.[56] That little-used Section had been amended in 1984 to reach any person who 'was the cause' of a violation of the provisions of that Act that require continuous disclosures by publicly-held companies. The SEC's theory was that Kern, as the lawyer principally responsible for Allied Stores' SEC filings, had 'caused' it to fail to properly amend its disclosures to reveal material facts about its negotiation with a white knight as it sought to evade a hostile tender offer by Campeau Corporation. In 1988, the Administrative Law Judge sustained the SEC's position on the merits, but ruled that because Allied Stores no longer existed as a public company (Campeau having eventually won the takeover battle), he lacked jurisdiction to grant any relief against Kern. Rather than letting the case die, the Commission decided on its own motion to review this ruling, but, under pressure, delayed any decision for three years until 1991. Then, a Commission with a very different composition from the Commission that had earlier accepted the appeal decided to affirm the ALJ's ruling finding no jurisdiction.[57] Over the interim, the ABA had issued a public report concluding that the SEC was misusing its authority under Section 15(c)(4).[58]

In between this near constant sparring with the SEC, the ABA also took steps to reduce the prospect that lawyers could voluntarily disclose client fraud. In the late 1970s, the ABA created the Kutak Commission to redraft its model rules of legal ethics, which largely dated back to the ABA's 1908 Canons of Ethics. Many expected the new and reform-minded Committee to soften the ABA's hard-line position taken in 1974, when the ABA had hurriedly rewritten Disciplinary Rule 7–102(B)(1) while the *NSMC* case was pending. In fact, the Kutak Commission did suggest a sensible compromise: that lawyers could disclose client fraud (in their own discretion) when their services had been used to perpetrate the fraud.[59] But the ABA would not tolerate even this much of a symbolic concession. Instead, it wrote Model Rule of Professional Conduct 1.6 ('Confidentiality of Information') more narrowly, to permit a lawyer to disclose client confidences only to the extent necessary 'to prevent the client from committing a criminal act that the lawyer believes is likely to result in imminent death or substantial bodily harm.'[60] This exception clearly did not apply to securities and financial frauds.

Later, an important escape clause was added to the comments of Rule 1.6 to permit a withdrawing attorney to disaffirm or withdraw an opinion or other document issued during the representation.[61] Although this provision arguably permitted a form of 'noisy withdrawal,' that was not its intent. Rather, its purpose was solely defensive: to protect the attorney from civil liability under state law to third parties claiming that they had reasonably relied upon the attorney's opinion.[62] Client confidentiality was thus not an absolute value; it could yield to the attorney's need to protect himself and to his desire to warn other attorneys, but not to a need to protect persons injured by his clients during the course of his representation. So viewed, the attorney was anything but a gatekeeper.

The Attack of the Banking Regulators

If the bar was able consistently throughout this era to fight off the SEC's attempts to impose even modest gatekeeping responsibilities on it, the bar proved unprepared for the sudden and uncompromising assault that it faced in the early 1990s from the banking regulators. The difference in the regulators' intensity probably lies in the magnitude of the crisis (and this may also explain the SEC's greater success post-Enron). Between 1980 and 1991, 1,073 savings and loan institutions failed, costing the government approximately $119 billion.[63] Of these the most significant failure – both in size and symbolism – was that of Charles Keating's Lincoln Savings and Loan, which cost the federal government over $2 billion.[64] In response, on March 1, 1992, the Office of Thrift Supervision (OTS) filed a $275 million enforcement action against the law firm of Kaye, Scholer, Fierman, Hays & Handler (Kaye, Scholer), which was the principal law firm representing Lincoln Savings and Loan.

Kaye, Scholer was by no means alone. Between 1989 and 1992, the government recovered $1.7 billion from claims against professional advisers associated with failed thrifts, mainly accountants and attorneys.[65] All told, the government brought over 90 civil or administrative actions against the law firms that represented failed thrifts.[66] But Kaye, Scholer was the symbolic case in which the government unleashed new weapons that brought the firm to a screeching halt[67] and unveiled a considerably broader theory of attorney liability than the SEC had ever advanced.

Essentially, the OTS asserted three different types of claims against Kaye, Scholer:

(i) that it had knowingly misrepresented facts to the Federal Home Loan Banking Board ("FHLBB");

(ii) that it had breached its professional duties to its client by failing, for example, to give competent advice, and

(iii) that it had made factual representations to the FHLBB that revealed less than all the material information known to Kaye, Scholer.

Only this third category of claims was controversial, because it seemed to contemplate that, at least in dealing with regulatory authorities, the attorney must act as a fully candid intermediary who was obligated to disclose all material information known to it. For example, under the settlement order that resolved the action, Kaye, Scholer was barred from acting 'as counsel for an insured depositary institution concerning a matter in which a Kaye, Scholer attorney knows that one or more of the institution's officers or employees is ... violating any applicable federal banking statute or regulation, including by attempting to evade any such statutes or regulations by elevating form over substance.'[68] Similarly, Kaye, Scholer was required to disclose all material facts relating to a banking matter, even those that it considered irrelevant, if it knew that the banking agency might consider the same facts relevant under its different view of the law.[69]

Behind these provisions lay a broad theory of professional responsibility, most fully articulated by the OTS's general counsel, Harris Weinstein, under which attorneys with regulatory responsibilities were required 'to practice the whole law' and avoid 'loophole lawyering.'[70] Put simply, this theory of professional responsibility seems to contemplate a duty to volunteer facts to an opposing party (at least when the opposing party was a regulator) that the client would prefer remain confidential. Because such a duty was clearly in conflict with the attorney's traditional duty of confidentiality, the bar literally howled in protest.[71]

An ABA task force criticized the banking regulators' interpretations of lawyers' ethical obligations and urged them to submit 'novel or non-traditional interpretations of professional codes' to the ABA or state bars 'for authoritative rulings' before acting on their interpretations.[72]

But it was to no avail. The OTS had no willingness to leave attorney regulation to the private bar and, in the wake of the S & L debacle, it had been given *in terrorem* weapons by Congress to coerce law firms into submission.

The OTS's success may have also spurred the SEC to new activism at about this same time. In late 1992, the SEC discovered that Salomon Brothers had submitted false and/or fraudulent bids in numerous auctions of government securities. On learning of these actions by a mid-level employee, Salomon's general counsel advised senior management that such conduct was likely to be criminal and should be reported. Salomon's CEO, however, did nothing (indeed, he stalled)—until the scandal came to light. Although the SEC and banking regulators barred Salomon's chief executive officer for life from any further supervisory role in the industry,[73] their actions with respect to the general counsel were subtler. Officially, they did nothing, but the general counsel resigned, and the SEC indicated in its release that an attorney in his position had only three options: (1) go to the board; (2) resign, or (3) disclose the wrongdoing to the appropriate regulatory authority.[74] In substance, this was the *Carter & Johnson* standard brought back from its apparent grave.

Still, although the assault of the banking regulators did show the bar that they were vulnerable, the SEC was not armed with similar weapons of mass destruction. It could not freeze law firms' assets on its own motion, and the Salomon Brothers settlement was largely driven by the defendant's need to escape criminal prosecution and disbarment from future government securities auctions. More importantly, the SEC's ability to deter law firms was even more undercut in 1994 when the Supreme Court decided in the *Central Bank of Denver*[75] case that Rule 10b-5 provided no cause of action against those who aided and abetted a securities fraud. The SEC won back some of what it lost a year later when the Private Securities Litigation Reform Act of 1995 (the PSLRA) authorized the Commission (but not private parties) to sue persons who knowingly aided a fraud. But this compromise required the SEC to accept the PSLRA, which significantly constrained private securities litigation, and even this restoration of SEC authority over aiders and abetters required the SEC to prove that the aider had acted 'knowingly' (whereas previously it had been sufficient to allege that a secondary participant had 'recklessly' aided the primary violator).[76]

Unchanged by this legislative compromise was *Central Bank*'s preclusive impact on private litigation against secondary participants in alleged securities frauds. In this respect, the legal profession remained far more insulated than the accounting profession, which still faced primary liability for its certification of the issuer's financial statements (because such a public certification was an explicit statement that gave accountants primary, rather than simply secondary, liability). In retrospect, the Savings and Loan crisis taught the bar that it could suffer significant losses if sued by the government, but on the whole it had escaped significant exposure in private litigation.

Enron and the Sarbanes-Oxley Act

Uniquely, the legal profession was blind-sided by the impact of the Enron, WorldCom and associated scandals. Accountants in contrast had been fighting off attempts to restrict their conflicts of interest for some time and were experienced (and largely successful) participants in the Washington lobbying process. The bar was not. Although it had stood off the SEC throughout the 1980s, it had not faced, except briefly during the S&L crisis, any real prospect that its self-regulatory status would be challenged.

When that challenge came, however, it came from a surprising direction and developed an irresistible momentum—ironically because of the SEC's own admission of its limited jurisdiction. Following Enron's collapse, Professor Richard Painter, a law professor specializing in both legal ethics and securities regulation, organized a group of law professors that wrote a letter to SEC Chairman Harvey Pitt, asking the SEC to promulgate a rule that essentially codified the *Carter & Johnson* case.[77] That letter, dated 7 March, 2002, arrived at the SEC well before any effort had begun in Congress to draft legislation dealing with attorneys. Within a month, Professor Painter's letter was answered by David Becker, the then General Counsel of the SEC, who essentially replied that the Commission lacked authority to prescribe the ethical responsibilities of attorneys and implied that only Congress could take such action.[78] Ironically, but for this relatively quick and candid response, the matter would probably have gone no further. But the SEC's confession to its lack of authority to enforce its *Carter & Johnson* decision (after years of attempting to assert such an authority) invited Congress, which was searching for post-Enron reforms to enact, to take action.

Three Senators with unique professional backgrounds agreed to cosponsor what became Section 307 of the Sarbanes-Oxley Act. Senator

John Edwards (D–North Carolina) was a highly successful trial lawyer (who perhaps had a political need to show that he could be tough on lawyers); Senator Michael Enzi (R–Wyoming) was the Senate's lone accountant; and Senator Jon Corzine (D–New Jersey) was the former chief executive of Goldman, Sachs & Co., an investment banking firm. Together, they introduced Section 307 as a floor amendment late in the legislative consideration of Sarbanes-Oxley. Senator Enzi, the accountant and lone Republican co-sponsor, reviewed the recent corporate scandals and dryly told the Senate:

[O]ne of the thoughts that occurred to me was that probably in almost every transaction there was a lawyer who drew up the documents involved in that procedure.[79]

Senator Corzine followed him and added:

In fact, in our corporate world today—and I can verify this by my own experiences—executives and accountants work day to day with lawyers. They give them advice on almost each and every transaction. This means when executives and accountants have been engaged in wrongdoing, there have been some other folks at the scene of the crime—and generally they are lawyers.[80]

These comments succinctly captured the mood of the public and explained why Section 307 sailed through the Senate. If the Enron and WorldCom scandals justified public regulation of accountants and federal restrictions on corporate governance, the legal profession could not escape regulation as well. No one believed lawyers were untarnished by the recent scandals.

The ABA was caught flat-footed. Unlike the accountants, the legal profession did not have a well-organized lobbying arm in Washington. But even if it had, by the time Senator Edwards made his floor amendment in July of 2001, the momentum for reform was probably unstoppable. The bar hoped to resist the legislation in the House, but opposition there, which initially was strong, collapsed, and the House simply agreed to pass the Senate bill in its entirety to avoid the politically damaging appearance (in an election year) of foot-dragging.

Section 307 was, itself, a model of simplicity. It instructed the SEC to prescribe 'minimum standards of professional conduct for attorneys' who appeared or practiced before the SEC and further specified that these rules must require attorneys representing public companies 'to report evidence of a material violation of securities laws or breach of fiduciary duty or similar violation by the company or any agent thereof' to the corporation's chief legal officer or chief executive. If these officers did not take appropriate action, Section 307 finally mandated that the SEC's rules require the attorney to report the evidence to the corporation's audit committee, its independent directors, or the board as a whole. In a nutshell, this was only what the *Carter & Johnson* decision had said a decade before in more equivocal terms.[81]

The SEC moved quickly to draft rules implementing Section 307, but now the bar had an opportunity to regroup and comment. When the final rules emerged in early 2003,[82] the simple idea of reporting material violations up the ladder no longer seemed simple. The trigger for this reporting obligation was set forth in an elaborate definition of 'material violation,' which defined that term to mean:

credible evidence, based upon which it would be unreasonable, under the circumstances, for a prudent and competent attorney not to conclude that it is reasonably likely that a material violation has occurred, is ongoing, or is about to occur.[83]

Awkward as this widely criticized double negative formulation was, it at least attempted to adopt an objective standard that was less demanding than the 'actual knowledge' standard long used by the ABA's Model Rules of Professional Conduct, while still requiring more than gossip, hearsay, or innuendo. Nonetheless, it remains open to question how effectively this standard can be applied in real world settings. Given the complexity and ambiguity in this phrasing, it is also likely that attorneys reluctant to comply can rationalize that they have not received sufficiently credible evidence of a crime or fraud to require 'up the ladder' reporting by them. Predictably, the creative legal mind can find a host of reasons why it would not be 'unreasonable' to stop short of concluding that a crime had likely occurred.

Once an attorney reports a material violation to the corporation's chief legal officer or chief executive pursuant to this rule, the attorney is under a continuing obligation to go further up the ladder to the audit committee or the full board of directors, *unless* the attorney receives an 'appropriate response within a reasonable time.'[84] This is the critical provision that forces information up to the corporation's audit committee or board. But the SEC's rules give the term 'appropriate response' a particularly complex definition that includes a broad escape clause that may undercut this 'up the ladder' reporting obligation. Specifically, if the corporation retains a second attorney to review the evidence reported by the first attorney, and if this second attorney advises that a 'colorable defense' can be asserted, then this advice from the second attorney constitutes an 'appropriate response.'[85] At this point, everything stops—unless the first attorney is brave or fearless enough to consider the second attorney's opinion unreasonable. The practical result may be to encourage opinion-shopping, because if the corporation's chief legal officer can find a second attorney to opine that there is a 'colorable defense,' everyone is off the hook.[86]

Still, even if its standards are murky and the scope of its escape clauses is overly broad, the Commission's new rule will likely have impact. Attorneys who 'appear' or 'practice' before the Commission are now converted into policemen who, at least sometimes, must report internally evidence of a 'material violation.' To this extent, a watershed has been crossed. Prior to the enactment of Section 307, the attorney was basically only obligated to avoid knowingly assisting the client in criminal or fraudulent conduct. Now, the attorney must report such evidence upward. To the extent that risk-averse clients consult with attorneys whenever they recognize a legal risk, a great deal of corporate misbehavior becomes known to attorneys, and much of it will be subject to up-the-ladder reporting.[87]

In terms of the scope of the attorney's gatekeeping responsibilities, the duties so placed on the attorney by Section 307 are far more modest than those imposed on the auditor. The auditor must report to the corporation's investors and has potential liability to them under state and federal law if it malpractices or misstates or omits material information. In addition, Section 10A of the Securities Exchange Act of 1934 requires the auditor to inform the board (and ultimately the SEC if the board does not act) when it discovers a material violation of law.[88] In muted contrast, attorneys need make no public statement; they are protected by considerably broader escape clauses surrounding their duty to report up the ladder, and they probably incur no liability to investors under the federal securities laws even if they breach a duty imposed by Section 307.[89]

When the Commission proposed its 'up-the-ladder' reporting in late 2001, it also proposed a far more controversial rule requiring a 'noisy withdrawal' by an outside attorney when the attorney fails to receive an appropriate response to the attorney's report of a material violation, and in addition, the attorney believes that the material violation is either ongoing or about to occur.[90] This rule would have corresponded closely to the duty placed on the auditor by Section 10A of the Securities Exchange Act of 1934. Arguably, a noisy withdrawal by the attorney who becomes aware of a fraud had been recognized by the ABA as an appropriate response since the time of the *O.P.M.* case. In response to the *O.P.M.* case, a comment had been added to ABA Model Rule 1.6, to the effect that an attorney or law firm could disaffirm or withdraw a prior opinion or representation and not thereby mislead the incoming firm that was replacing it.[91] But, the critical difference is that the SEC's proposed rule would have made mandatory what the ABA only made permissible.[92]

While the bar accepted 'up-the-ladder' reporting with relatively little opposition, it formed a solid phalanx to oppose any form of mandatory 'noisy withdrawal.' Its chief argument is that any such obligation to blow the whistle would dry up the flow of information to the attorney and thereby result in less communication between counsel and client, with the likely result that attorneys would be unable to counsel law compliance. Arguably, the attorney subject to such a duty might therefore prevent fewer law violations than under existing rules.[93] This is neither a frivolous argument nor one that is easily resolved empirically. Considerable reason exists to be skeptical of the claim that such a rule would 'dry up' client communications to the attorney, but for the moment, the relevant point is that this argument, coupled with the bar's adamant opposition, caused the SEC once more to back off a proposal for regulating legal ethics. Since the SEC issued a revised version of its proposed 'noisy withdrawal' rule in February 2003, it has taken no further action on noisy withdrawal, nor is action believed to be likely.

In fairness, the bar has not reacted to Enron and the associated scandals by stonewalling all reforms of the legal profession. Instead, it has drawn the line between permissive ethics and mandatory duties. In response to Enron, the ABA formed a Task Force on Corporate Responsibility to examine 'systemic issues relating to corporate responsibility arising out of the unexpected and traumatic bankruptcy of Enron and other Enron-like situations which have shaken confidence in the effectiveness of the governance and disclosure systems applicable to public companies in the United States.'[94] That Task Force made a number of constructive recommendations and did succeed in modifying the ABA's restrictions on client confidentiality along approximately the same lines as the Kutak Commission had recommended in the early 1980s. Under the latest version of Model Rule 1.6, approved by the ABA in 2003 based in part on the recommendation of this Task Force, a lawyer may reveal information relating to the representation of a client that would otherwise be privileged if the lawyer reasonably believes it necessary to prevent 'a crime or fraud that is reasonably certain to result in substantial injury to the financial interests or property of another and in furtherance of which the client has used or is using the lawyer's services.'[95] Similarly, revelation of client information is permitted if reasonably believed necessary to 'prevent, mitigate or rectify substantial injury to the financial interest or property of another' that has resulted or 'is reasonably certain to result' from 'a crime or fraud in furtherance of which the client has used the lawyer's services.'[96] This change represents a basic reversal of the ABA position taken in the mid-1970s in response to the SEC's position in the *National Student Marketing* case.[97]

But the ABA has not changed its position on mandatory notification or 'noisy withdrawal.' Instead, it stopped well short of the SEC's new rules in several respects. First, although it did marginally tighten Model Rule 1.13 so that it is now presumptively necessary for the attorney to report up the ladder to higher authorities in the corporation when the attorney discovers a material violation of law, it did not use the objective standard formulated by the SEC under Section 307 of Sarbanes-Oxley. Instead, under Model Rule 1.13, as amended, the attorney is only under an obligation to report 'up the ladder' if the attorney 'knows' of such misconduct, and Model Rule 1.13 defines 'knows' to mean 'actual knowledge of the facts in question.' This is in contrast to the SEC's earlier discussed standard which focuses on the receipt of 'credible evidence' that would alert the reasonably competent and prudent attorney.[98] This deviation is important because the ABA's standards apply to all attorneys, while the SEC's rules apply only to attorneys appearing or practicing before it.

Second, the ABA's Model Rules recognize a broad and ambiguous escape clause under which the attorney need not report up the ladder if the 'lawyer reasonably believes that it is not in the best interest of the organization to do so.'[99] What this means in practice is anyone's guess.

Finally, Model Rule 1.13 permits the attorney to make a 'noisy withdrawal' and reveal information relating to the representation 'but only if and to the extent the lawyer reasonably believes necessary to prevent substantial injury to the corporation.'[100] This is a permissive standard, and few attorneys can be expected to blow the whistle voluntarily on their client.

Because the ABA's Model Rules (and the similar rules of the vast majority of the states) now permit an attorney to make an ethical decision to blow the whistle on a client, but never require the attorney to do so, the legal profession's code of ethics seems strangely incomplete. In a critical area, it essentially says: 'Do whatever you want! Use your own ethical judgment, because we can offer no guidance.' In fairness, the counter-argument is that any stronger rule would do more harm than good by causing clients not to divulge sensitive information to their counsel. How realistic is this claim that client communications would dry up? Here, two balancing observations must be made that may offset each other in their implications.

First, to the extent that the corporate employee or agent may not confide in the corporation's counsel because the attorney may 'blow the whistle' on him, this disincentive already exists, and the proposed 'noisy withdrawal' rule would not affect it more than marginally. The corporate counsel represents the firm, not the employee or agent. Thus, such counsel is duty-bound to tell the firm if misconduct by a corporate employee comes to the attorney's attention that threatens serious injury to the interests of the corporation. Sarbanes-Oxley mandates this, but even prior to its enactment, an experienced attorney would probably tell the firm's general counsel if the attorney believed that an employee or officer's conduct was violating the law in a manner that threatened injury to the firm. For the attorney, this was simply self-protection.

Today, however, a new dimension has been added. When any serious scandal comes to light, the corporation is likely to be compelled to conduct an internal investigation, which usually will be handled by an independent law firm with which the corporation has no recent relationship. Both the SEC, and increasingly U.S. Attorneys, are likely to demand such a response. Further, they will insist that the results of this report be turned over to them and that the corporation waive the attorney–client privilege. Caught between the rock and the hard place, the corporation has little choice. As a result, any reasonably intelligent corporate employee or agent should recognize today that whatever damaging material information he or she tells counsel is likely to go to the chief legal officer, and possibly the board, at least if it discloses credible evidence of a crime or fraud. Moreover, the corporation has every incentive to waive its privilege and effectively turn the employee in to save its own hide.

Accordingly, because 'up the ladder' reporting and the likelihood that the corporation's privilege will be waived in any major crisis already threaten the corporate employee involved in wrongdoing, the additional threat imposed by this new duty to make a 'noisy withdrawal' seems marginal at best. As a practical matter, the corporate employee is protected from identification to the government and from the release of privileged communications only in those very few cases where the board is willing to stonewall. Ironically, the bar's vociferous argument that any duty to withdraw and disclose cuts off the flow of information to counsel is probably better applied to the SEC's 'up the ladder' reporting rule that the bar did not resist. In short, if communications to the attorney were likely to 'dry up,' they should have done so by now.

On the other hand, some skepticism is also necessary about the practical impact of a mandatory 'noisy withdrawal' rule. Will it actually be obeyed? Here, some relevant data exists with regard to the behavior of accountants under Section 10A of the Securities Exchange Act of 1934. Since 1995, that Section has required accountants to report to the SEC material violations of law that they discover in their audits if the corporate client refuses to rectify or prevent the violation. What has happened under Section 10A? 'Very little' is the short answer.

According to a General Accounting Office Study, over the 7½-year interval between January 1, 1996 and May 15, 2003, accounting firms reported material violations of law to the SEC in only 29 instances.[101] Given a population of roughly 12,000 to 14,000 publicly-held companies over this volatile time period, this figure of 29, which comes to approximately four reports a year, suggests a low rate of compliance for auditors. Would lawyers behave differently? Possibly, lawyers are more law compliant. But, conversely, their own legal culture is even more resistant to 'blowing the whistle' than that of auditing (where public disclosure has always been the fundamental duty).

In short, it is rash to predict that the imposition of a 'noisy withdrawal' rule by the SEC would 'dry up' confidential communications to counsel, but it is also rash to predict that such a rule, if adopted, would be obeyed or would elicit much information. Outright defiance seems unlikely, but rationalization is a skill that lawyers have honed to a fine edge. For the attorney, 'blowing the whistle' on the client is perceived as career suicide, and mass suicide should rarely be assumed or predicted.

Organizational Dynamics: What Happened to the Attorney as 'Wise Counselor'?

To evaluate the degree to which the corporate attorney can play a gatekeeping role, it is necessary to understand that the corporate attorney's role has not been static, but has evolved markedly over recent years. This section will examine those changes first from the perspective of in-house counsel and then from that of outside counsel.

The Rise of In-House Counsel

The conventional wisdom explains the decline of the independent professional by pointing to the growth of the in-house legal departments. As these have grown, it is argued, outside counsel has become more of a transactional specialist, forced to bid for work in competitive contests and lacking any continuing relationship with the client. The actual evidence is somewhat more complicated. Between 1970 and 1980, the decade when the trend began, the number of in-house counsel jumped by 40 percent.[102] But in-house counsel have remained a fairly constant percentage of the total bar's size. As of 2002, there were some 65,000 in-house counsel in the United States.[103] Viewed, however, in percentage terms, in-house counsel have represented about 10 percent of the bar since 1960.[104]

The change in the position and leverage of the outside counsel is real, but it is not based on any explosion in the size of in-house legal departments. Rather, until well into the 1970s, the relationship between a large public corporation and a large law firm was one of bilateral monopoly. The corporation relied on one principal supplier of legal services,[105] while the law firm received so much of its revenues from its largest client that it too was dependent on the relationship. Economically, neither was truly independent of the other.

During the 1970s, the rise of mergers and acquisitions and an early boom in underwritings showed law firms that transactional business was far more profitable than pedestrian corporate housekeeping work. Associate salaries soared in this era, and so in response did billing rates. While corporations confronting a hostile takeover would pay any price for the best, most skilled practitioner who could save them (much as a millionaire facing brain surgery would want the best surgeon without regard to price), other corporations with more mundane problems saw legal costs skyrocketing and needed to economize. Corporations thus faced a classic 'make or buy' decision, as they had in many other areas. They responded to this choice by deciding to 'make'—that is, by expanding in-house staffs to handle recurring transactions. Corroborating this explanation is the fact that, even today, most in-house counsel tend to be generalists, who identify their specialization as 'general corporate transactions.'[106] Outside counsel rationally priced themselves out of the market for general corporate practice, because transactional practice was much more profitable.

The participant in this drama who gained the most from this transition was the in-house general counsel, who now became as much a general manager of legal services as an actual counselor to management. For his or her own self-interested reasons, the general counsel typically did not want competition from outside counsel. He or she wanted to be the primary conduit of legal advice to management and hence sought to discourage any long-term, continuing relationship between senior management and outside counsel. As much for this reason as to encourage price competition, the in-house counsel moved legal business around, thereby assuring his or her own monopolistic position as the supplier of legal advice to senior management. What shifted then was not the relative number of inside versus outside counsel, but the balance of power between them.

This transition was an extremely self-conscious one. The American Corporate Counsel Association was formed in early 1982 as the trade association and institutional representative for 'the corporate counsel perspective.'[107] Within bar associations, in-house counsel fought for (and obtained) proportional representation on prestigious bar committees. As legal departments expanded, the prestige level of the in-house general counsel also rose, in part fueled by prominent personalities attracted out of private practice to head such offices and in part by the high compensation that such positions began to carry. Because corporations could use stock options to compensate in-house general counsel, their incomes approached or surpassed those of the most highly compensated partners in private practice.

Nevertheless, the in-house movement did not mean that corporations significantly reduced their use of outside counsel. According to a recent census by the American Corporate Counsel Association (ACCA), approximately 40 percent of the budget of the average corporation's legal department was spent on outside legal fees (with litigation-related fees slightly exceeding non-litigation counsel services).[108] But clearly outside counsel reported to inside counsel.[109] This shift appears to have produced no resistance from outside counsel, who were happy to deem the in-house general counsel as their client. Indeed, outside counsel may have found it easier to report to a fellow professional, rather than a lay client. If inside counsel did feed outside counsel stylized versions of the facts, with difficult details left out (as some critics have asserted), outside counsel appear to have accepted this docilely. After all, it made their life easier.

Who does inside counsel report to? In a majority of the cases (61.4%), the ACCA census found that the in-house general counsel reports to the CEO of the corporation.[110] But this implies that in nearly 40 percent of the cases, in-house general counsel does not have direct access to the senior-most executive of the corporation.[111] In at least a significant portion of the cases then, there may be no 'wise counselor' with any direct access to the CEO.

A larger problem in this shift of power to the inside counsel is the fragmentation of work and responsibility that can result from a managerial system in which no one exercises overall oversight.[112] Some general counsel conceive of their role as primarily that of a businessman—in effect, a purchasing agent for legal services who does not himself or herself take substantive legal positions. Interestingly, Enron's general counsel has been reported to have been very much an exemplar of this non-substantive, managerial style.[113] This low-profile approach may be politically prudent because it allows the in-house counsel to evade responsibility and survive for the long-run, but it produces fragmentation. At its worst (and Enron may have exemplified this), each division consults its own outside lawyers, and their legal advice does not reach the top in a consistent or undistorted fashion. Also, because different divisions may have conflicting interests (or interests that conflict with those of the corporation as a whole), such fragmentation ensures that the broader interests of the corporation may go unrepresented.

More typically, inside counsel does monitor outside counsel and remains involved in the substantive legal assessment. But in so doing, inside counsel today typically defines the legal problem for outside counsel and structures outside counsel's relationship with the organization. Potentially, the result is that outside counsel has only a tunnel vision of the corporation's overall legal problems and may not see broader patterns.

Academic critics have long argued that inside counsel's control over the relationship precludes the outside counsel from being proactive, causing him to define the client's problems too narrowly and frame his or her response in an equally formalistic and narrow fashion.[114] These reformers want outside counsel to define their role more expansively— in effect to practice what Harris Weinstein once called 'holistic law.'[115]

Among the practical problems with this ethical prescription is that it exists in considerable tension with traditional legal ethics. The ABA's Model Rules of Professional Conduct mandate that '[a] lawyer shall abide by a client's decision regarding the objectives of representation.'[116] If the organization as client wants to use outside counsel in a narrow fashion, asking them only technical questions and structuring the relationship so that outside counsel is neither invited nor equipped to provide 'holistic' advice, the organization would seem entitled to do so. By no means is this to say that such a constrained relationship is advisable, but lawyers may not dictate the terms of their relationship with their clients. Reformers acknowledge this tension, but try to avoid its implication that lawyers are client-serving professionals by stressing the lawyer's professional duty to investigate and re-define the scope of the problem.[117] However, even if this answer works on an intellectual level, there is no evidence that lawyers will respond actively to any invitation to define their role expansively. For the reasons next discussed, absent external legal changes (such as legislation or SEC rules), the current equilibrium under which inside counsel defines outside counsel's role seems likely to persist, even if the rules of legal ethics were amended to permit or require outside counsel to do more.

Outside Counsel

For at least a generation, the bar has defended its role in representing corporations by arguing that the practitioners in the large private firm uniquely possess the professional independence that enables them to counsel law compliance and play the role of the 'wise counselor.' The implicit claim here is that the outside lawyer functions as a de facto gatekeeper. While the overall truth of this proposition is increasingly debatable, some early social scientific research did tend to confirm it.[118]

The world of private practice has changed significantly over the last twenty odd years. The rise of inside counsel has already been reviewed, but it has been accompanied by an equally significant change: the decline in law firm stability as 'star' attorneys increasingly practice in a free agent market.[119] Lateral mobility has made the legal market more competitive, for individual partners as well as for clients.

What caused this change? No simple answer suffices,[120] but a number of factors bear some responsibility:

(i) the growth and branching of traditional firms into nationwide networks, which growth required that they make lateral acquisitions in order to open new branch offices;

(ii) sudden changes in firm compensation practices, which left some partners dissatisfied and eager to move;

(iii) the tendency for some very specialized attorneys to have a more 'mobile' practice which they could take with them to another firm;

(iv) the growth of litigation revenues as a percentage of overall law firm revenues (because litigated cases tend to be portable with the senior litigator involved);

(v) the publication of partnership compensation information by the legal press, which awoke competitive jealousies and caused successful partners to seek positions in higher paying firms; and

(vi) the refusal of courts to enforce anti-compete clauses that once locked partners to their firms.[121]

More important, however, is the impact of this new mobility (and the associated portability of clients) on law firms. Here, much commentary has emphasized that lateral mobility was destructive of firm culture, principally by forcing firms to alter their compensation practices to reward the partner who brings in business over those more skilled at the craft.[122] A less conspicuous impact may have been an erosion in the willingness of the large firm to support, protect and shelter the partner whose ethical sensitivities cause him or her to lose a client. Under the 'eat what you kill' compensation formulas towards which law firms gravitated in order to hold onto their most mobile partners, the 'ethical' partner is automatically disciplined by reduced compensation if he or she loses business.

The net result may be to induce the outside counsel to become a more aggressive advisor. Definitive proof of this hypothesis that corporations are demanding more aggressive legal advice is lacking, but anecdotal evidence is everywhere.[123] In today's more competitive market, corporate clients 'want a champion, not a chaperone.'[124] The careful, ethical counsel—even one who falls well short of the Brandeisian activist—may be perceived by the corporate client as passive or insufficiently aggressive. And the one certainty is that an inside counsel will be looking over outside counsel's shoulder and possibly seeking second opinions from other counsel who would happily represent the corporation differently.

Despite this change in market conditions, academic criticism of the bar has remained unchanged. Academic critics have long insisted that outside counsel must define their role more expansively and proactively. Their premise is that if outside counsel were required by legal ethics to ascertain and consider the corporation's broader interests, such counsel would become again the 'wise counselor,' admonishing the corporation as client to comply with the spirit of the law. This is, of course, the Brandeisian ethic. Noble as this prescription may be, is it realistic in the light of market conditions?

The limited empirical evidence suggests that the standard academic prescription is unlikely to have much impact. Like a commencement address, it will be politely applauded—and largely ignored. Based on extensive survey research, Professor Robert Nelson has concluded that lawyers in large firms undergo a socialization process that leads them to 'strongly identify' with their corporate clients' interests.[125] As a consequence, his pessimistic assessment is that:

It is highly unlikely, therefore, that lawyers in large firms will act as an independent voice that checks the self-interest of clients.[126]

Nelson also found a trend for increased passivity on the part of outside counsel, which he attributed to an 'increasingly competitive market.'[127] Indeed, not only were outside counsel unlikely to resist the client, but their own political and ethical views were so closely aligned with those of their clients that 'given an unconstrained power to change the law, the majority would change the law to suit the interests of their clients....'[128] The premise that outside 'lawyers struggle with clients over fundamental questions about the common good,' Nelson concluded, 'is simply wrong.'[129]

The Brandeisian model has at least two critical elements. First, it posits that the outside counsel is an independent adviser who must consider and respond to the entire social context surrounding the corporation. Second, it asks the attorney to balance the client's desires against the public interest. As a moral exhortation, this is fine, but, as a policy prescription, it looks increasingly empty. Factors other than increased competition make the Brandeisian model seem remote and endangered. These factors also suggest that the world in which Brandeis rose has gone with the wind and cannot be recreated. Brandeis after all practiced in a small law office that he had founded and dominated. Since then, the increasing complexity of the law and the need for specialization has compelled firms to increase their size and scale. As a result, it is doubtful that a Brandeis could compete effectively today in a small boutique firm or that he could practice in the same independent fashion in the far more bureaucratic setting of today's multi-branch 'mega' law firm. Brandeis also practiced a unique blend of law and social science, offering an amalgam of law, economics and sociology to his corporate clients.[130] Yet, his ability to do so reflected the immaturity of the social sciences in his time. Today, the corporation seeking social scientific advice will find a rich array of consulting firms eager to offer their services. If it ever was, law is no longer regarded as the queen of the social sciences, and few practicing lawyers today would feel comfortable offering the broad advice that Brandeis did. Nor would they likely be listened to.

By no means is it here asserted that there will never again arise an independent lawyer/statesman of the Brandeisian mould. Nor is it denied that lawyers do possess ethical discretion and should inquire, explore, and redefine the problems on which they are asked to work. But, as a policy prescription, these are weak reeds on which to rely.[131] Because legal ethics at its core views the attorney as a client-serving professional who is not permitted to dominate the relationship (and because market conditions make it unlikely that lawyers could do so today), legal ethics does not hold out a practical remedy for gatekeeper failure. One must therefore look beyond legal ethics and the moral exhortations it provides to find a realistic means to empower the attorney as gatekeeper.

Evaluation

Two conclusions stand out from the foregoing tour. First, much like the accounting profession, the legal profession has fought zealously to protect its own autonomy, successfully resisting the SEC prior to Sarbanes-Oxley and encountering only a temporary setback at the hands of the banking regulators. Even more than in the case of the accounting profession, private self-regulation within the legal profession has been conspicuous mainly by its absence.[132] No disciplinary action appears yet to have been taken by the bar against lawyers involved in corporate or securities scandals unless they were first convicted of a crime. In contrast, accountants at least implemented a highly structured procedure (e.g. peer review) to assure the quality of their services.

Second, much like the accounting profession, the corporate lawyer has lost leverage vis-à-vis its corporate clients. Where once the public corporation believed it needed a stable, long-term relationship with a single law firm, it now has acquired a professional manager of legal services in the in-house general counsel, who can expertly play the market. Monogamy has thus given way to polygamy, as the corporation flirts with many outside counsel. This produces both improved price competition and, more relevantly, reduced discretion for the outside counsel. Changes in the legal marketplace also imply that the outside professional has reduced autonomy, because firm stability has eroded and less shelter probably exists within the firm for the independent professional who resists the client.

If that is the basic diagnosis, what then is a sensible prescription? Undoubtedly, some recent reforms, including most notably the SEC's 'up-the-ladder' reporting rules, should have a desirable impact. But the SEC's rule is written in sufficiently awkward prose that rationalization and evasion by lawyers who do not wish to report upward becomes predictable. Nor do the SEC's rules make the attorney into a true gatekeeper. For example, no obligation is placed on the attorney by the SEC's rule to make inquiry or diligently search for law violations, and the ABA's Model Rule is triggered only by an 'actual knowledge' standard.[133]

What more should be done? For decades, prominent legal ethicists have called for the corporate attorney to behave as a Brandeisian activist. Academics with tenure are notoriously demanding of practitioners struggling to survive in competitive markets. But the overlooked problem with their prescription is its implementation. Ethical norms lack any meaningful mechanism for their enforcement, and bar associations are not about to take action against attorneys for failing to consider the public interest. Finally, even if corporate lawyers were to consider their own view of the public interest, Professor Nelson has convincingly shown us that their view largely matches that of their corporate clients.[134]

A more realistic approach to the problem of inducing reluctant corporate lawyers to assume greater gatekeeping responsibilities begins by asking three questions: (1) 'What has basically gone wrong?'; (2) 'What law compliance functions do corporate lawyers already perform?'; and (3) 'How can the law build on the norms that they have internalized?'

What has gone wrong?   The draftsmen of Section 307 believed that law-yers were present at the 'scene of the crime', assisting others in planning financial fraud. Perhaps, this has happened, but the greater danger is that lawyers were nowhere near the scene of the crime, thereby enabling others to orchestrate the fraud. Given Section 307's 'up-the-ladder' reporting obligation, the best law compliance strategy is to ensure that lawyers know more about their client's activities. Here, the real problem is the fragmentation of legal services so that no lawyer has an integrated view of the client's operations. Fragmentation keeps lawyers ignorant and so undermines their law compliance potential.

What law compliance role can lawyers best perform?   The outside cor-porate attorney is already trained, accultured, and committed to the craft of 'due diligence'. The corporate lawyer knows how to investigate the facts and test the adequacy of disclosures and, far more than the auditor, is an expert on the central question of materiality. Due dili-gence was traditionally limited to primary offerings of securities; this was a result of the Securities Act of 1933, which gave an affirmative defense of due diligence precisely in order to encourage gatekeepers to monitor management.[135] The significance of this incentive was largely undercut, however, by the SEC's integrated disclosure system, adopted in the early 1980s,[136] which permitted companies to simply incorpo-rate by reference their previously filed annual and quarterly disclosure documents.[137]

How can the law build on what lawyers do well?   If the SEC were to require that the issuer's annual and quarterly corporate disclosure documents had to be reviewed and certified by an 'independent' attor-ney, who would be required to opine that, after reasonable inquiry, he believed such disclosures not to be materially misleading, the result would be to re-introduce the outside counsel into the disclosure pro-cess, effectively mandating such counsel's use as a gatekeeper.

The specifics of this proposal will be deferred to Chapter 10, but the contemplated required certification is less novel than it first appears. As will be argued later, even in the private market today, attorneys for the corporation in securities underwritings do give functionally simi-lar representations to the certification described above, as a matter of course. However, today they give them only to private parties, not to the SEC or public investors. Thus, the immediate goal is to generalize what the private market does in the limited context of primary offer-ings, extending it to the SEC's continuous disclosure system in order to require the corporation's disclosures to be regularly reviewed in depth by independent outside counsel. Viewed more broadly, this is a response to both the problem of fragmentation and the need to empower the law-yer as a gatekeeper. Such a certification requirement seeks to shift power and discretion back to the outside counsel. Functionally, this strategy is similar to that of the British Companies Act in the 1840s, which required the corporation to conduct a statutory audit—and thereby created an assured market for the then embryonic auditing profession.

In overview, this approach is the antithesis of the Brandeisian model. It does not ask the attorney to represent the public interest, but only to perform a task that is at the center of the attorney's professional competence. Rather than constrain the attorney, this proposal gives the attorney increased authority and leverage. Its starting point is to ask what counsel already does well and then seek to enlarge these activities into a fuller, more formalized gatekeeping responsibility.

Endnotes

1. The classic statement of this view was delivered by Lord Brougham in the 1821 trial of Queen Caroline for adultery, when he asserted:

   An advocate, in the discharge of his duty, knows but one person in all the world, and that person is his client. To save that client by all means and expedients, and at all hazards and costs to other persons, and, among them, to himself, is his first and only duty; and in performing this duty he must not regard the alarm, the torments, the destruction which he may bring upon others. (See 2 The Trial of Queen Caroline 8 (J. Nightingale ed., London, Albion Press 1821), quoted in Charles Fried, Right and Wrong 177 (1978)).

   See Model Code of Professional Responsibility EC7-1 (1981) ('The duty of a lawyer, both to his client and to the legal system, is to represent his client zealously within the bounds of the law ....'). These ethical norms, developed largely in the context of criminal litigation, co-exist uneasily at best with the world of corporate representation. Nonetheless, the bar favors the status quo and is reluctant to qualify these norms. Respected bar leaders continue to claim that the norm of zealous advocacy should control in the corporate context and is inconsistent with any real gate-keeping role for the attorney. See Evan Davis, *The Meaning of Profes-sional Independence*, 103 Colum. L. Rev. 1281 (2003). On the other hand, the SEC has argued, since at least 1973, that '[v]ery little of a securities lawyer's work is adversary in character,' and hence different standards should apply. See *Emmanuel Fields*, Securities Act. Rel. No. 5404 (18 June, 1973), CCH Fed. Sec. L. Rep. Para. 79, 407 at 88, 175 n 20.

2. This too is changing, and the law on attorney liability for misleading statements in securities filings is in flux. See *In re Enron Corp. Secs., Derivative & ERISA Litig.*, 235 F. Supp. 2d 549 (S.D. Tex. 2002) (holding that attorneys who prepare and review disclosure filings can be sued as 'makers' of the statement). Whether this decision will be followed by other courts is at present highly uncertain.

3. This was a leading conclusion in Erwin Smigel's classic study of Wall Street lawyers of the early 1960s. See Erwin Smigel, The Wall Street Lawyer 6 ('Lawyers often use their positions as advisors to guide their clients into what they believe to be proper and moral legal positions.') (1964). Smigel also found that the Wall Street firms that he studied were successful in protecting their partners' professional independence. Ibid. at 354. His conclusions are consistent with my own experience in one of the most respected Wall Street firms as an associate in the 1970s. Professor Robert Gordon has suggested that this self-image of the 'wise counselor' guided many of the statesmen/advisers of the post-World War II era. See Robert Gordon, Symposium: *Crisis in Confidence: Corporate Governance and Professional Ethics Post-Enron*, 35 Conn. L. Rev. 1185, 1208–1211 (2003).

4. Robert Nelson's research for the American Bar Foundation has found little difference between the independence of large firm lawyers and in-house counsel. Both, he asserts, tend to identify with the interests of their clients. See Robert Nelson, Partners With Power: Social Transformations of the Large Law firm (1988). See text and notes at nn 125 to 129 below.

5. Beginning in the 1960s, observers have regularly reported that large firm independence did protect professional ethics by insulating the partner from pressure. See J. Carlin, Lawyers Ethics (1969); Erwin Smigel, n 3 above, at 354.

6. These statistics have been assembled by Professor Marc Galanter of the University of Wisconsin Law School. See Marc Galanter, *'Old And In the Way': The Coming Demographic Transformation of the Legal Profession and Its Implications for the Provision of Legal Services*, 1999 Wis. L. Rev. 1081, 1090 (1999).

7. In 1975, in a well-known study, Heinz and Laumann found that 53% of the total effort expended by the Chicago bar was devoted to corporate clients. See John P. Heinz & Edward O. Laumann, Chicago Lawyers: The Social Structure of the Bar (1982) at 42. When they performed the same survey again twenty years later in 1995, they found that the size of the Chicago bar had roughly doubled, but the proportion of total efforts devoted to corporate clients had risen to 61%. See John P. Heinz et al., *The Changing Character of Lawyers' Work: Chicago in 1975 and 1995*, 32 L. & Soc'y Rev. 751, 765 (1998). Although this is a study of only one city, it indicates that the growth in the bar's size in that city is largely explained by the increased demand for legal services from corporate clients.

8. For in-depth discussions of the changes in the structure and economics of the large law firm, see Ronald J. Gilson and Robert H. Mnookin, *Sharing*

Among Human Capitalists: An Economic Inquiry into the Corporate Law Firm and How Partners Split Profits, 37 Stan. L. Rev. 313 (1985); Ronald J. Gilson, *The Devolution of the Legal Profession: A Demand Side Perspective*, 49 Md. L. Rev. 869 (1990).

9. As of 2000, the rise of professional firms that would serve as 'one-stop shopping centers for clients,' offering legal, audit, tax, information consulting, and financial planning services, seemed likely, and accounting firms in particular were gearing up to merge law firms into themselves (and had already done so in Europe). Several state bar associations amended their rules to encourage 'multi-disciplinary practice' (or MDP in the vernacular of the era). In the wake of Enron, however, enthusiasm waned, and the SEC took stops to prevent the practice of law and accounting within the same firm. For an overview, see Robert A. Prentice, *The SEC and MDP: The Implications of the Self-Serving Bias for Independent Auditing*, 61 Ohio St. L. J. 1597 (2000).

10. See text and notes at nn 32 to 70 below.

11. See William H. Simon, The Practice of Justice: A Theory of Lawyers' Ethics (1998) at 9 and 138. Professor William Simon has been the most outspoken and articulate proponent of this view. But others within academia clearly share it. See David Luban, Lawyers and Justice: An Ethical Study (1988); David B. Wilkins, *Legal Realism for Lawyers*, 104 Harv. L. Rev. 468 (1990); Robert W. Gordon, *The Independence of Lawyers*, 68 B.U.L. Rev. 1 (1988).

12. This is the conclusion that Robert Nelson of the American Bar Foundation has reached after detailed surveys. See Nelson, n 4. See text and notes at nn 125 to 129 below.

13. The epic battle between Jay Gould and Commodore Vanderbilt over the Erie Railroad eventually turned into a corrupt auction as both sides bribed judges and the New York legislature. For the standard account, see John Steele Gordon, The Scarlett Woman of Wall Street (1988). While Jay Gould was a man viewed as a rogue by his contemporaries, he was able to hire the best-known and most respected lawyers of his day on Wall Street: David Dudley Field, Samuel J. Tilden, and Thomas Shearman (founder of Shearman & Sterling). See Maury Klein, The Life and Legend of Jay Gould (1986) at 81–86. The predecessor firm to Cravath, Swaine & Moore also represented Daniel Drew, a confederate of Jay Gould in the Erie affair. The collective legal assistance of these firms was critical to Gould as they essentially found an arcane technique to outflank legal restrictions on stock issuances and thus to dilute the massive purchases that Vanderbilt made of Erie stock.

14. Technically, the ABA's Committee on Code of Professional Ethics produced the 1908 Canons of Ethics. For an overview of this process, on which the chapter relies, see Susan D. Carle, *Lawyers' Duty to Do Justice: A New Look at the History of the 1908 Canons*, 24 Law & Soc. Inquiry 1 (1999).

15. See Carle, n 14 above, at 7.

16. Ibid. at 16–17. Professor Carle finds that some eighteen states, mainly mid-western and southern, then mandated such an oath. Ibid. at 17.

17. Ibid. at 18 (discussing the position of Thomas Hamlin Hubbard, a New York corporate lawyer and a founder of a major New York law firm bearing his name).

18. Ibid. at 29. The lawyers' oath was also retained but modified to read: 'I will not counsel or maintain any suit or proceeding which shall appear to me to be unjust, nor any defense except such as I believe to be honestly debatable under the law of the land.' Ibid. at 30. At most, this language would seem to restrict the attorney from filing a frivolous or harassing action—conduct that today could be a grounds for civil sanctions under Rule 11 of the Federal Rules of Civil Procedure.

19. See Gordon, n 3 above, at 1208.

20. See Benjamin Barton, *The ABA, The Rules and Professionalism: The Mechanics of Self-Defeat and a Call for a Return to the Ethical, Moral, and Practical Approach of the Canons*, 83 N.C.L. Rev. 411, 430–431 (2005).

21. Ibid. at 432–433.

22. Ibid. at 437.

23. See Robert Gordon, *The Independence of Lawyers*, 68 B.U.L. Rev. 1, 2 (1988) (quoting speech), Brandeis went on to criticize what he termed the erroneous assumption 'that the rule of ethics to be applied to a lawyer's advocacy is the same where he acts for private interests against the public, as it is in litigation between private individuals.' Ibid.

24. For a fuller analysis of Brandeis's speech and its historical context, see ibid. at 14–15.

25. A balancing observation is here necessary: deeply conservative lawyers, such as John Foster Dulles, also engaged in repeated public service, probably without considering Brandeis to be their mentor.

26. See Section 11(b)(3) of the Securities Act of 1933. 15 U.S.C. §77(k)(b)(3).

27. For example, the failure of Penn Central, which was at the time the largest bankruptcy in U.S. history, followed shortly on the heels of lawyers at Sullivan & Cromwell advising their underwriter client, Goldman Sachs & Co., that Penn Central's financial statements were unreliable.

28. 283 F. Supp. 643 (S.D.N.Y. 1968). For other decisions following *BarChris* that found defendants not to have established their due diligence defense, see *Feit v. Leasco Data Processing Equip. Corp.*, 332 F. Supp. 544 (S.D.N.Y. 1971); *Sanders v. John Nuveen & Co., Inc.*, 619 F. 2d 1222 (7th Cir. 1980), *cert. denied*, 450 U.S. 1005 (1981) (finding due diligence defense not satisfied under Section 12(a)(2)).

29. 283 F. Supp. at 690.

30. See A. A. Sommer, Jr., 'The Emerging Responsibilities of the Securities Lawyer,' Address to the Banking Corporation & Business Law Section, N. Y. State Bar Ass'n, (Jan. 24, 1974), reprinted in [1973–4 Transfer Binder] Fed. Sec. L. Rep. Para. 79, 631 at pp 83, 686–690.

31. Even prior to Sommer's speech, Marshall Small, a prominent securities attorney and later the presiding partner at Morrison & Foerster, wrote an influential article recognizing the securities attorney's distinctive obligation to investigate and disclose facts and concluded that the securities attorney 'will usually have the same objective as the independent certified public accountant in insuring that full disclosure is made.' See Marshall Small, *An Attorney's Responsibilities Under the Federal and State Securities Laws: Private Counselor or Public Servant?*, 61 Cal. L. Rev. 1189, 1235 (1973).

32. This was widely noted and debated at the time. See Merritt Fox, *Shelf Registration, Integrated Disclosure, and Underwriter Due Diligence: An Economic Analysis*, 70 Va. L. Rev. 1005 (1984). The SEC argued that issuers could do advance 'due diligence' by appointing a firm as counsel to future underwriters at the time it filed periodic reports under the 1934 Act. But in the 20 years since the SEC adopted integrated disclosure and shelf registration, few, if any, issuers have attempted this theoretically available technique.

33. Indeed, full scale due diligence continues to be required and performed in the case of initial public offerings, and this safeguard did not preclude numerous issuers with flawed books and even more flawed business plans from reaching the market. Of course many of the 'Internet' IPOs of this era disclosed their frighteningly long-shot prospects in full detail, and thus did provide full disclosure.

34. This issue will be the subject of Ch. 10.

35. Although the most important lawsuit brought by the SEC was its complaint in the National Student Marketing case (See Complaint, *SEC v. National Student Marketing Corp.*, 457 F. Supp. 682 (D.D.C. 1978), reprinted in [1971–2 Transfer Binder] Fed. Sec. L. Rep. Para. 93, 360 at p 91, 913 (D.D.C. Feb. 3, 1972), this was not the only instance of SEC activism that worried the bar. In *SEC v. Spectrum Ltd.*, 489 F. 2d 535, 542 (2d Cir. 1973), the Second Circuit held at the SEC's urging that a lawyer who negligently prepared an erroneous opinion used to sell securities could be enjoined from future violations of the securities laws. Later, the Supreme Court would hold that an allegation of scienter was necessary in a suit under Rule 10b-5.

36. See *SEC v. National Student Marketing Corp.*, 457 F. Supp. 682, 687–699 (D.D.C. 1978).

37. The SEC was probably also concerned that the 'insider' INC shareholders who had learned the truth would bail out and sell their NSMC shares, letting the minority hold the overvalued stock.

38. See Canons of Professional Ethics, Canon 41 (1968). In other jurisdictions, the ABA's Model Code of Professional Responsibility, written in 1969, was then in force, but it similarly commanded that a lawyer 'who receives information clearly establishing that … [h]is client has, in the course of the representation, perpetrated a fraud upon a person …

shall promptly call upon his client to rectify the same, and if the client refuses or is unable to do so, he shall reveal the fraud to the affected person ....' See Model Code of Professional Responsibility, Disciplinary Rule 7–102(B)(1) (1969).

39. The partner at White & Case who principally represented NSMC accepted a temporary suspension from practice before the SEC, and the firm itself contributed to a $2.6 million settlement of a private class action. Both the CEO of NSMC and its outside audit partner at Peat, Marwick were criminally convicted of securities fraud.

40. 457 F. Supp. 682, 713.

41. The court characterized the violations as 'part of an isolated incident, unlikely to recur and insufficient to warrant an injunction.' Ibid. at 716.

42. See ABA Model Code of Professional Responsibility DR-7–102(B)(1) (1974) (restricting disclosure to victim requirement 'when the information is protected as a privileged communication.'). For overviews, see Geoffrey C. Hazard, Jr., *Rectification of Client Fraud: Death and Revival of a Professional Norm*, 33 Emory L. J. 271 (1984); Junius Hoffman, *On Learning of a Corporate Client's Crime or Fraud*, 33 Bus. Law. 1389, 1406–1409 (1978) (discussing broader efforts by ABA and state bars to limit the obligations of lawyers by passing narrower ethics rules or issuing interpretive opinions).

43. In fact, however, only a minority of the states, probably around 14, adopted this revised rule. See Hazard, n 42 above, at 294 n 38.

44. 31 Bus. Law. 543 (1975).

45. Ibid. at 544–545.

46. Ibid. at 545.

47. See *In re Carter & Johnson* [1981 Transfer Binder], Fed. Sec. L. Rep. (CCH), Para. 82, 847 (March 25, 1981). See also Securities Exchange Act Release No. 17597 (March 25, 1981).

48. Ibid. at p 84, 170.

49. Ibid. at p 84, 172.

50. Ibid.

51. The Commission summarized its requirements by stating: 'What is required, in short, is some prompt action that leads to the conclusion that the lawyer is engaged in efforts to correct the underlying problem, rather than having capitulated to the desires of a strong-willed, but misguided client.' Ibid.

52. The SEC did publish a release in September 1981 soliciting public comments on its decision in *Carter & Johnson* and 'as to whether that interpretation should be expanded or modified.' See Securities Act Release No. 33–6344 (Sept. 21, 1981). The Commission did not, however, follow up on this release, but rather let it die a quiet death.

53. See Edward Greene, 'Lawyer Disciplinary Proceedings Before the Securities and Exchange Commission,' 14 Sec. Reg. L. Rep. 168 (1982).

54. See Sec. Exch. Act Rel. No. 25893; see also Goelzer and Wyderko, *Rule 2(e): Securities and Exchange Commission Discipline of Professionals*, 85 Nw. U.L. Rev. 652 (1991).
55. The scope of the SEC's authority under Rule 2(e) was challenged by the bar in cases involving accountants. See *Checkosky v. SEC*, 23 F. 3d. 452 (D.C. Cir. 1994) ("Checkosky I") and *Checkosky v. SEC*. 139 F. 3d 221 (D.C. Cir. 1998). In these cases, the D.C. Circuit criticized the SEC for attempting to deem negligence to constitute 'improper professional conduct.' Eventually, the Commission amended what is now Rule 102 to expressly cover negligence in the case of accountants, and Section 602 of the Sarbanes-Oxley Act codified this result.
56. See George C. Kern, Jr., (Allied Stores Corp.), Admin. Proc. file No. 3–6869 (March 21, 1988) (Opinion by Chief Administrative Law Judge Blair), 1988–9 Fed. Sec. L. Rep. (CCH) Para. 84, 342 (1988).
57. See George C. Kern, Jr., 50 SEC 596 (1991).
58. See Report of the ABA's Section of Business Law Task Force on SEC Section 15(c)(4) Proceedings, 46 Bus. Law. 253 (1990).
59. For a description of the Kutak Commission and its debates, see Hazard, n 42 above, at 296–304.
60. ABA Model Rules of Professional Conduct Rule 1.6 gave the attorney one other justification for disclosure of client information: self-defense. Under Model Rule 1.6(b)(1), the attorney could use such information to 'establish a claim or defense on behalf of the lawyer ....'
61. This comment states that Rule 1.6 does not prevent a lawyer from withdrawing or disaffirming an opinion. It was apparently intended to address the problem of an ongoing fraud in which the lawyer's work had been used. Thus, it was intended more to protect the lawyers than injured victims. See Hazard et al., The Law and Ethics of Lawyering at 62–103 (3d edn 1989).
62. The comment to Rule 1.6 was probably motivated by the bar's reaction to the OPM scandal, which broke in 1982. There, a law firm learned that its principal client (OPM) had been fraudulently pledging the same collateral to secure multiple loans. (OPM stood for 'Other Peoples' Money', suggesting how brazen the scam was). The law firm resigned, but kept quiet about the fraud (in part because New York law had followed the ABA's 1974 revision of the rules on confidentiality to bar notification to victims). In particular, the law firm did not inform incoming counsel. This failure to alert incoming counsel offended the bar's notion of fair play among attorneys and led to a revision in the form of a new comment to Rule 1.6. Under this Comment to Model Rule 1.6, one law firm could signal another that fraud was afoot by withdrawing or disaffirming its prior opinions, but it could not communicate the same facts in more intelligible terms to investors. See Susan P. Koniak, *When the Hurlyburly's Done: The Bar's Struggle With the SEC*, 103 Colum. L. Rev. 1236, 1262–1264 (2003).

63. See U.S. Gen. Accounting Office, Report to Congressional Committees, Bank and Thrift Regulation: Improvements Needed in Examination Quality and Regulatory Structure (1993) at 8.

64. For an overview of this scandal and the government's response, see Howell E. Jackson, *Reflections on Kaye, Scholer: Enlisting Lawyers to Improve the Regulation of Financial Institutions*, 66 S. Cal. L. Rev. 1019 (1993); Nancy Amoury Combs, *Understanding Kaye, Scholer: The Autonomous Citizen, the Managed Subject and the Role of the Lawyer*, 82 Calif. L. Rev. 663 (1994).

65. See Jackson, n 64 above, at 1023 n 12.

66. See Harris Weinstein, *Attorney Liability in the Savings and Loan Crisis*, 1993 U. Ill. L. Rev. 53, n 124.

67. The OTS issued a temporary cease and desist order freezing the firm's assets and the personal assets of three Kaye, Scholer partners; this freeze could effectively have prevented the firm from paying its staff. Six days after the OTS filed its Notice of Charges, Kaye, Scholer settled the case for $41 million. See Combs, n 64 above, at 664.

68. See Peter M. Fishbein, OTS AP No. 92–24, para. 15(c) ('Settlement Order') (quoted in Combs, n 56 above, at 682).

69. Ibid. at para. 12(d).

70. See Harris Weinstein, 'Issues of Professional Responsibility Arising From the Savings and Loan Failure, Remarks Before the University of Michigan Law School' (March 24, 1992), in Emerging Issues in the 'New' Business of Banking (PLI Commercial Law & Practice Course Handbook Series No. A-637) (1992), 405, 415.

71. See e.g. Lawrence Fox, *OTS v. Kaye, Scholer: An Assault on the Citadel*, 48 Bus. Law. 1521 (1993). This author was among those who expressed doubt about the OTS's tactics. See John C. Coffee, Jr., 'Due Process for Kaye, Scholer?,' *Legal Times*, March 16, 1992 at 22. Egregious as its conduct was; I continue to believe that the use of the freeze order against Kaye, Scholer was unjustified.

72. See Ted Schweyer, *Foreword: Legal Process Scholarship and Regulation of Lawyers*, 65 Fordham L. Rev. 33, 58 n 124.

73. See *In re Gutfreund*, Securities Exchange Act Release No. 34–31554, [1992 Transfer Binder] Fed. Sec. L. Rep. (CCH) Para. 85, 067 (Dec. 3, 1992).

74. Ibid. at pp 83, 608. See also, James Doty, *Regulatory Expectations Regarding the Conduct of Attorneys in the Enforcement of the Federal Securities Laws: Recent Development and Lessons for the Future*, 48 Bus. Law. 1543 (1993).

75. *Central Bank of Denver v. First Interstate Bank of Denver*, 511 U.S. 164, 169 (1994).

76. The PSLRA added Section 20(e) to the Securities Exchange Act of 1934, which authorized the SEC to sue 'any person that knowingly provides substantial assistance to another person in violation of a provision of this title ....' See 15 U.S.C. §78t(e).

77. See Letter from Richard Painter and Several Professors of Securities Regulation and/or Professional Responsibility of Noted Law Schools to Harvey L. Pitt (March 7, 2002). It bore the caption 'Expressing Concern About the Role of Professionals in the Enron Matter and Other Frauds on Investors.' For Professor Painter's own explanation of his role and intent in the enactment of Section 307, see Symposium, *The Evolving Legal and Ethical Role of the Corporate Attorney After the Sarbanes-Oxley Act of 2002*, 52 Am. U.L. Rev. 613 (2003). There, he explains that he had served on the Ethics Committee of the Association of the Bar of the City of New York and had cast the lone dissenting vote against a statement by that committee condemning the OTS's freeze order against Kaye, Scholer. Ibid. at 615–616.

78. Letter from David Becker, General Counsel, U.S. Securities and Exchange Commission to Richard Painter and others, dated March 28, 2002.

79. See 148 Cong. Rec. S 6554 (daily ed. July 10, 2002).

80. Ibid. at S 6556.

81. Under *Carter & Johnson*, it was arguable that the attorney could simply resign from representing the corporation in the questionable transaction (and possibly be retained again in the future).

82. See Securities Act Release No. 33–8185 (February 6, 2003) ('Implementation of Standards of Professional Conduct for Attorneys').

83. See 17 C.F.R. 205.2(e).

84. See 17 C.F.R. 205(3)(b)(3).

85. See 17 C.F.R. 205(2)(b).

86. In fairness, this 'colorable defense' escape hatch does require that a report be made to the board or a committee thereof, so that the evidence will be reported up the ladder. Still, the board or committee will principally hear the second attorney's conclusions. As explained in Release 33–8185, the term 'colorable defense' does not require a conclusion that the defense is meritorious, but only that it is 'non-frivolous.'

87. Some comparative studies suggest that lawyers are more likely to take ethical and similar rules of professional conduct seriously than other professionals. See Susan P. Shapiro, *Bushwhacking the Ethical High Road: Conflicts of Interest in the Practice of Law and Real Life*, Law and Social Inquiry 87 (2003) (contrasting responses of several professions to conflicts of interest and finding that law firms internalize far more elaborate and meaningful procedures to address these issues).

88. See 15 U.S.C. §78jA

89. Part 205.7 provides that there is no private right of action against any attorney or law firm for compliance or non-compliance with the Commission's 'up-the-ladder' reporting rule and vests exclusive authority to enforce it in the Commission. See 17 C.F.R. 205.7.

90. For the Commission's latest statement of this proposal, see Securities Act Release No. 33–8186 (February 6, 2003). Under proposed 17 C.F.R.

205.3(d)(1), which is unlikely to be adopted, an attorney is required to withdraw from representing the issuer, give written notice of this withdrawal to the Commission, 'indicating that the withdrawal was based on professional considerations,' and disaffirm any opinion, document or representation 'that the attorney reasonably believes is or may be materially false or misleading.'

91. See text at n 62.

92. Under the SEC's proposal, the attorney would be under this duty only if there was not an 'appropriate response,' the 'material violation is ongoing or about to occur,' and the violation 'is likely to result in substantial injury to the financial interest or property of the issuer or of investors.' See proposed 17 C.F.R. Part 205.3(d)(1).

93. By the same token, however, this argument equally applies to 'up-the-ladder' reporting. The executive, employee or agent who knows that an attorney will report his misconduct to the chief legal officer and/or the board also faces a disincentive to free communication with his attorney. At some point, this argument proves too much. The real question is where that point is located.

94. See Report of the American Bar Association Task Force on Corporate Responsibility, 59 Bus. Law. 145, 145–6 (2003).

95. See Model Rule 1.6(b)(2) (adopted by the ABA House of Delegates, August 2003).

96. See Model Rule 1.6(b)(3).

97. Of course, the ABA's position was followed by only a small minority of the states, and hence this change actually reverses the law nowhere (because the ABA Model Rules are not binding on any state) and will eventually produce changes in probably only a few states.

98. See text and at n 83 above.

99. See ABA Model Rule 1.13(b). In a comment, Model Rule 1.13 explains that a failure to report upward might be justified if the violation were an innocent one that would not be repeated. This narrow an exclusion could have been dealt with in the commentary and certainly did not require the broad language in the text of Rule 1.13 that permits an attorney to fail to report upward if the attorney 'reasonably believes' that it is not in the corporation's best interests for the attorney to do so.

100. See ABA Model Rule 1.13(c). Under this Model Rule, the attorney can reveal information even if Model Rule 1.6 does not authorize such disclosure. However, Model Rule 1.13(c) focuses only on an injury to the corporation, while Model Rule 1.6(b) more broadly deems injuries to investors to also justify disclosure.

101. See U.S. Gen. Accounting Office, Securities Exchange Act: Review of Reporting Under Section 10A, at 1 (Sept. 3, 2003).

102. See Robert Rosen, *Symposium: The Growth of Large Law Firms and Its Effect on the Legal Profession and Legal Education: The Inside Counsel*

Movement, Professional Judgment and Organizational Representation, 64 Ind. L. J. 479, 482 n 7 (1989).

103. Susan Hackett, *Inside Out: An Examination of Demographic Trends in the In-House Profession*, 44 Ariz. L. Rev. 609, 610 (2002).

104. Ibid. at 610–611; Rosen, n 102 above, at 482 n 7 (finding a small decline to 9.7% in 1985).

105. Why did the public corporation tend to rely on a single outside law firm? The best known theory is that offered by Professor Gilson. He stresses 'informational asymmetries,' namely that the corporation could not on its own assess the relative quality of counsel and so relied on a single firm in whom it had confidence to select counsel for it (either by training its own or finding outside specialists). Once the corporation had, however, hired an in-house counsel of high prestige, this person could perform that same function at lower cost. See Gilson, n 8 above.

106. See Hackett, n 103 above, at 611 (finding over 40% of in-house counsel to fall into this category with the only other sizable categories being intellectual property (12.9%) and employment law (5.9%)). Thus, roughly 60% of in-house counsel fall into one of these three categories.

107. See Rosen, n 102 above, at 497 n 74.

108. See Hackett, n 103 above, at 613.

109. Since at least the 1980s, inside counsel have not only hired outside counsel, but also organized their work and structured their reporting relationship with the client organization. See J. Randolph Ayre, Corporate Legal Departments: Strategies for the 1980s, 138, 146 (1984); see also R. Nelson, n 4 above, at 58.

110. See Hackett, n 103 above, at 612.

111. In 15.5% of the cases, the general counsel reported to the president; and in 7%, the general counsel reported to the chief financial officer. Ibid. In-house general counsel appear to resent and resist reporting to an officer other than the chief executive, and in particular resist reporting to the chief financial officer (which is a common European pattern). Ibid.

112. For a detailed consideration of this fragmentation problem, see Robert E. Rosen, *Problem-Setting and Serving the Organizational Client: Legal Diagnosis and Professional Independence*, 56 U. Miami L. Rev. 179 (2001).

113. According to one account, James Derrick, Jr., Enron's general counsel, was a 'hands off manager' who 'doesn't even know the names of his counsel.' See David Hechler, 'Enron's legal staff battered, confused,' National Law Journal, February 4, 2002 at A-1. Other commentators have reported that Derrick 'had no means of controlling or supervising all of the legal advice that the company was receiving, because the different divisions all had their own lawyers and outside firms.' See Gordon, n 3 above, at 1193.

114. For representative statements of this critique, see Rosen, n 102 above. This position dates back at least to William Simon, *Ideology of*

Advocacy: Procedural Justice and Professional Ethics, 1978 Wis. L. Rev. 29 (1978); see also, Robert Gordon, nn 3 and 23 above.

115. See text and note at n 70 above.

116. See ABA Model Rules of Professional Conduct Rule 1.2 (2001). The comments to this rule further provide that 'the client has ultimate authority to determine the purposes to be served by the representation.' See ABA Model Rules of Professional Conduct Rule 1.2 comment ('Scope of Representation').

117. See Rosen, n 102 above, at 212.

118. See text and notes at nn 3 and 5 above.

119. For an overview and assessment of these developments, see Milton Regan Jr., *Law Firms, Competition Penalties and the Values of Professionalism*, 13 Geo. J. Legal Ethics 1 (1999).

120. All that is clear is that the lateral mobility of partners was once rare and is now a pervasive fact. See, e.g. Hillman, *Law Firms and Their Partners: The Law and Ethics of Grabbing and Leaving*, 67 Tex. L. Rev. 1, 2 (1988).

121. Professor Regan points to a series of court decisions, beginning in the late 1980s, that have invalidated anti-competition clauses in partnership agreements. See Regan, n 119, at 15–18 (citing, in particular, *Cohen v. Lord, Day & Lord*, 550 N.E. 2d 410 (N.Y. 1989)).

122. For such an argument, see S. S. Samuelson and L. J. Jaffe, *A Statistical Analysis of Law Firm Profitability*, 70 B.U.L. Rev. 185, 191 (1990).

123. One much cited example was the decision of Lincoln Savings to replace the Jones, Day firm with the supposedly more aggressive Kaye, Scholer firm. See Regan, n 119 above, at 65. As discussed earlier, Kaye, Scholer's representation of Lincoln Savings resulted in a major enforcement proceeding brought against Kaye, Scholer by the OTS. See text and notes at 64 to 70 above.

124. See Gilson, n 8 above, at 909.

125. See Nelson, n 4 above, at 5.

126. Ibid.

127. Ibid. at 263 (noting that in such a market, outside counsel 'are less likely than ever to play a mediating role with respect to client demands.').

128. Ibid. at 247.

129. Ibid. at 258. Nelson researched the rate at which outside counsel refused an assignment or potential work for ethical reasons and found it to be very low. Specifically, he found that attorneys in large law firms resigned because they were unable to convince the client to follow their advice in only about 2% of the relevant instances. Ibid. at 254. This, of course, does not deny that outside counsel may still give more independent advice than inside counsel or that such counsel may resist senior management more resolutely.

130. For a description of how Brandeis served his clients, see P. Sturm, Louis D. Brandeis: Justice for the People 96–102 (1984). Some historians

also believe that Brandeis's sharp criticisms of the organized bar were a product of his marginalized status as an outsider, as a still deep seated anti-semitism excluded him from membership in the major Boston firms of his day. See M. Urofsky, A Mind of His Own: Brandeis and American Reform (1971). This too has largely passed. But, as a consequence, a Brandeis within a major institutional firm might have been a far softer, quieter voice.

131. It may be thought that in expressing skepticism about the efficacy of legal ethics as a policy lever I am ignoring Holmes's distinction between the 'good man' and the 'bad man' under which the 'good man' obeys ethical commands while the 'bad man' does so only if there is a sufficient deterrent threat. See Holmes, 'The Path of the Law' in O.W. Holmes, Collected Legal Papers, 169–171 (1921). But that is not my point. Even the 'good man' will not interpret the Brandeisian edict to consider the public interest in the manner that the academic activists intend. As Professor Nelson has shown, the corporate attorney identifies with his client's interests and perspective.

132. An abundant literature has catalogued the self-regarding tendencies of private regulation within the bar and the absence of meaningful enforcement or disciplinary systems. For overviews, see Deborah L. Rhode, In the Interests of Justice: Reforming the Legal Profession (2000) at 19–20, 158–161 (criticizing the narrow, reactive character of disciplinary enforcement, inadequate funding, and weak sanctions). For other recent criticisms, see Ted Schneyer, *Professional Discipline for Law Firms?*, 77 Cornell L. Rev. 1 (1991) (arguing that a major failure of bar discipline is that it applies only to the individual lawyer and not the law firm); David B. Wilkins, *Who Should Regulate Lawyers?*, 105 Harv. L. Rev. 799 (1992); Manuel Ramos, *Legal Malpractice: Reforming Lawyers and Law Professors*, 70 Tul. L. Rev. 2583, 2591–2599 (1996); Leslie C. Levin, *The Emperors' Clothes and Other Tales About the Standards for Imposing Lawyers Discipline Sanctions*, 48 Am. U. L. Rev. 1 (1998). Even the ABA has criticized itself. In the 1970s, the ABA's Special Committee on Evaluation of Disciplinary Enforcement called the state of lawyer discipline 'scandalous.' See Levin, at 1 above. But little has changed.

133. See text at nn 98 to 99 above.

134. See text at nn 125 to 129 above.

135. See 15 U.S.C. §77k(b)(3); see also text and notes at nn 26 to 29 above.

136. See text and notes at nn 31 to 34 above.

137. The SEC requires a public corporation to file a Form 10-K within 75 days after the close of its fiscal year and a Form 10-Q, shortly after the close of each of the first three quarters.

7

Securities Analysts

Introduction

For the capital markets, securities analysts are the critical gatekeepers, who both test and interpret corporate disclosures—and then extrapolate from them, making their own predictions as to the corporation's future prospects. In contrast to other gatekeeping professions, analysts are distinctive in the following respects.

1 Underdeveloped Standards   Securities analysts are the youngest profession serving investors, dating back only to the 1920s. They also are the smallest profession, with only a fraction of the members of the law or accounting professions.[1] As a result, their institutional structure and governing norms are more fluid and transitional. While accountants can resort to an elaborate inventory of 'generally accepted accounting principles,' no similar set of criteria or methodology applies to the analyst projecting a firm's future earnings.

2 Limited Regulation   Unlike lawyers or accountants, securities analysts are not licensed by the state. Only those analysts employed by a broker-dealer are subject to NYSE or NASD regulation, which has historically been modest.[2] Much like accounting early in its development, the absence of entry regulation denies analysts the professional credential that a licensed lawyer or a certified public accountant possesses. Not surprisingly, the profession has followed the model of accounting and worked hard to develop a similar professional credential (the title 'Chartered Financial Analyst' is awarded by its principal trade association, the CFA Institute, to candidates who pass a detailed and rigorous examination). Nonetheless, passing such an exam is not a precondition to entry into the profession, but only a professional merit badge.

Securities analysts have also largely escaped litigation. They are generally exempt from the Investment Advisers Act of 1940, are protected by the doctrine of 'loss causation' from liability in securities class actions,[3] and have also been granted a substantial degree of immunity from insider trading by the Supreme Court in recognition of their watchdog role.[4] For the immediate future, the litigation risk faced by securities analysts is only a faint shadow of the risk faced today by auditors.

3 Competition Through Duplication   Although there is competition (to varying degrees) in all markets for gatekeeping services, the competitors do not normally duplicate each other's services. Thus, two auditors do not audit the same corporation; nor do two law firms prepare rival drafts of registration statements. But a large public corporation might be followed by twenty or more securities analysts, each making its own report, rating the security and predicting the company's future earnings. Analysts are not unique in this regard (as debt ratings agencies also cover the same companies), but in no other profession can the gatekeeper's relative success be as easily measured by comparing the analyst's prediction to the corporation's ultimate performance. In turn, this seeming ease of accountability breeds a tendency towards herding, with most analysts sticking close to consensus predictions.[5]

4 The Necessity of Subsidization   Securities analysts are not directly paid by the investors that rely on their advice. Instead, research departments within large broker-dealer firms depend upon subsidies from other departments of the same firm that find it useful from a marketing standpoint to have 'star' analysts employed by their firm. Throughout the 1990s, investment banking principally subsidized analyst research, but, prior to that, the brokerage division of the integrated broker-dealer firm picked up the cost of research out of the brokerage commissions that the analyst's research generated, primarily from institutional investors. Obviously, this system of indirect payment for research creates conflicts of interest,[6] but the existence of conflicts does not truly distinguish law or accounting. Prior to Sarbanes-Oxley, auditors were also paid and hired by the corporate managements that they monitored, and lawyers are still so compensated. Although Sarbanes-Oxley addressed that problem by assigning control over auditor compensation to the audit committee, no comparable solution seems possible for analysts.

More importantly, recent reforms instituted by the NASD and NYSE that seek to erect a stronger Chinese Wall between investment banking and research in order to protect analyst independence have created a still largely unrecognized public policy dilemma. By reducing employer ability to pressure the analyst, these reforms have unintentionally also reduced the firm's willingness to subsidize the analyst. The ironic cost of reform is that today a far smaller percentage of public companies are followed by analysts.[7] To this degree, enhanced independence has come at the price of diminished market transparency. From a public policy perspective, this suggests that optimal reform must not only protect analyst independence, but find a means of subsidizing them that does not bias their research.

Today, the 'small' and 'mid cap' markets (and even many firms of greater size) now trade without effective analyst supervision. This implies not only a loss of transparency, but a greater exposure of these companies to fraud and manipulation. Ultimately, while no one would mandate full employment for analysts, a good case exists for some form of subsidy to provide minimal oversight. The real issue is how to provide a subsidy that does not corrupt. Essentially, this requires severing the link between payment of the subsidy and control over analyst discretion.[8]

5 A Profession or a Conspiracy of Snake-Oil Salesmen?   The case for subsidization can be disputed. While the professional status of auditors or attorneys is not seriously disputed, the status of at least the sell-side analyst is. Many believe that no matter what prophylactic rules are implemented to insure the analyst's independence, the analyst will remain a salesman with an incorrigible bias towards optimism.[9] Even the 'independent' analyst has roughly the same biases and tendency towards excessive optimism as the analyst employed by the large underwriter.[10] Yet, a growing body of evidence also suggests that the securities analyst is a critical actor in ensuring market efficiency and that the level of analyst coverage affects firm value. At present, greater independence does not necessarily translate into greater accuracy. Optimal reform then requires a subsidy, but one that motivates the analyst towards increased accuracy.

A Snapshot of the Industry

Securities analysts tend to be employed in one of three capacities:

1 the majority are employed on the 'buy-side'—that is, by institutional investors and chiefly by mutual funds—where they engage in private proprietary research for their employers;

2 most of the remainder are employed on the 'sell side,' working for large broker–dealer firms that also provide investment banking services to corporations; and

3 the balance—a small but growing minority—work for 'independent,' sell-side firms, typically broker–dealers that do not provide investment banking services.[11]

By one recent estimate, 60 percent of all analysts are on the buy-side, 30 percent work for integrated firms on the sell-side, and 10 percent work for independent firms.[12] Membership data for the principal industry group—the CFA Institute—shows 65,700 worldwide members in 2003.[13] If we estimate that half of these are employed in North America, this leaves us with a total of almost 33,000 North American analysts—of which 30 percent (or almost 10,000) are probably employed on the sell-side. In all likelihood, this population has further declined since 2001, as numerous analysts have either been terminated, moved to the buy-side, or left the industry. But, rough as this estimate is, it indicates that we are dealing with a relatively small population—one dwarfed, for example, by the over one million lawyers practicing in the United States today.

Small as this population may be, it is also well-paid and influential. One recent estimate places the compensation of a sell-side analyst with five years experience at between $400,000 and $500,000, and top analyst salaries are in the $2.5 million range (this is down from even higher salaries that star analysts commanded in the late 1990s).[14] No accountant and very few partners in Wall Street law firms earn similar compensation.

Not surprisingly, at these salaries, entry into the profession is highly competitive. In fiscal 2004, almost 110,000 persons enrolled to take the six-hour Chartered Financial Analyst exam administered by the CFA Institute.[15] To qualify as a CFA, an applicant must have three years of relevant experience in the financial industry, take a three-part exam, and pay over $2,000 in fees.[16] Currently, there are some 57,512 active Chartered Financial Analysts worldwide, of whom about 18 percent work in equity securities analysis.[17] Although a CFA credential is not required to be an analyst, it appears to be becoming standard, at least for the younger generation of analysts.

What does the sell-side analyst do? Typically, he or she will specialize in a single industry (e.g. banking, telecommunications, or automobiles) and concentrate on a limited number of stocks (usually ten to fifteen).[18] The analyst will prepare detailed research reports on these stocks, which will involve not only analysis of the company's published financial information but meetings with management and industry sources (including customers and suppliers). These reports were in the past available only to clients of the analyst's brokerage firm, but increasingly they are distributed through research resale firms. Also, analyst earnings estimates on a firm are gathered and collectively reported by Thomson First Call on its website.

The buy-side analyst in contrast will perform proprietary research for his or her employer (typically a mutual fund or hedge fund, but possibly an insurance company or pension fund), which research will be private and not disseminated beyond the client. Typically, buy-side analysts will cover more companies,[19] in part because they can rely on sell-side research, and their research will be more focused on immediate investment decisions (as opposed to industry or macro-economic trends).

Independent analysts may or may not work for a broker-dealer. For example, Sanford Bernstein & Co. is probably the best-known independent research firm and does operate as a broker-dealer, but other firms may publish an investment newsletter or directly sell proprietary research to institutional clients and possibly individual investors.[20]

Not all companies are covered by an analyst. While it is usually estimated that there are between 14,000 to 15,000 publicly traded companies in the U.S. today, fewer than 6,000 are regularly covered by even a single analyst.[21] Even within this 6,000 figure, less than half of these companies are covered by two analysts, meaning that a single analyst's opinion may be decisive. Recently, there has been a marked decline in the number of public companies that securities analysts cover, which decline seems directly attributable to the reduced profitability of research to broker-dealer firms. Reuters Research, which tracks over 4,000 public companies, has reported that some 666 of these firms now have no analyst covering them, up from only 85 just two years earlier.[22] An even safer generalization is that the majority of the 'small cap' market is today not covered by any securities analyst.[23] In response to this shortfall in analyst coverage, smaller companies have taken to hiring an analyst (usually a 'freelance' analyst not employed by any firm) to cover them, thereby raising a new issue surrounding analyst independence.

Conflicts of Interest

It has escaped no one's attention that analysts are subject to conflict of interests, but the range and character of these conflicts seldom receives adequate attention. Identifying the range of analyst conflicts is important, because recent reforms respond to some, but not all, of these conflicts. Essentially, analyst conflicts can be grouped under six headings.

1 Personal Conflicts   Conceivably, analysts may rationally issue or maintain a favorable rating on a stock because they own it. Indeed, companies long recognized and exploited this conflict by giving or selling key analysts their stock prior to their IPO. A 2001 SEC study found that nearly one-third of the analysts surveyed had made pre-IPO investments in a company that they later covered after the IPO.[24] This same study also found that broker-dealer monitoring of 'the private equity investments of employees, including analysts, was poor'[25] and that broker dealers were generally 'unable to identify all of their employees' investments in companies that the firm took public.'[26]

Perhaps even more surprising, evidence was uncovered in the wake of the Internet bubble's collapse that analysts had frequently traded in a manner inconsistent with their public recommendations—for example, selling securities that they were contemporaneously recommending as a 'buy.'[27] Such behavior suggests that the analyst's own rating or recommendation was disbelieved by the analyst, implying again that pressure from the issuer may be driving analyst ratings. Some firms, but clearly a minority, responded to these disclosures by prohibiting their own analysts from buying stock in companies that they cover.[28] The rules of the principal self-regulatory organizations still do little to control these conflicts.[29] The SEC has, however, adopted Regulation AC, which requires analysts to certify that they truly agree with their own stock recommendations.[30] Definitional as this may sound, the rule was sensibly intended to empower the analyst so that analysts could better resist pressure from their employer. But, even if veiled, that pressure remains so long as the analyst does not generate direct revenue for the firm.

2 Brokerage Commission Conflicts   Analysts are more likely to generate brokerage commissions for their employer by positive recommendations (i.e. 'buys') than by negative recommendations (i.e. 'sells'). This is because any investor can potentially buy on a 'buy' recommendation, while only those owning the stock (or willing to take the risky step of selling short) can profit from a 'sell' recommendation. Hence, the audience for 'buy' recommendations is much broader and likely to produce more commissions. Also, if sell recommendations are strongly phrased, they may 'spook' the market, causing small investors to flee the market and invest in other assets, and leaving institutional clients of the brokerage firm holding large stakes that they cannot easily liquidate. Hence, institutional investors, as much as the issuer, tend to disfavor public 'sell' recommendations by analysts.

3 Investment Banking Conflicts   Since brokerage commissions were subjected to competition in 1975, the profit center of the contemporary large broker-dealer firm has shifted to investment banking, and away from brokerage. During the 1990s, broker-dealers competed to land investment banking clients (both for underwritings and merger and acquisition transactions) by hiring the 'star' analysts who could most influence the client's market valuation.

Much evidence has shown that analyst ratings are very sensitive to the identity of the firm's investment banking clients. Analysts at underwriting firms appear to inflate their estimate of firm clients,[31] and higher investment banking fees correlate with more positive predictions.[32] Not only does the quantitative evidence strongly suggest that analysts inflate their ratings of firm clients, but from time to time documentary evidence has surfaced from within broker dealers corroborating that firm policy was not to make 'negative comments' about clients. In 1992, the Wall Street Journal obtained and published a memorandum signed by the managing director of corporate finance at Morgan Stanley in which he bluntly instructed all firm employees that:

Our objective is ... to adopt a policy fully understood by the entire firm, including the Research Department, that we do not make negative or controversial comments about our clients as a matter of sound business practice.[33]

This conflict not only affects the analyst employed by the lead underwriter to the company, but also other analysts at other underwriting firms that want this lucrative business and that therefore may be even more prepared to inflate their research opinions in order to curry favor and win a role as a co-managing underwriter.

4 Issuer Access Conflicts   Even when the issuer is not a client, the analyst still has a further reason to soft-pedal criticism and inflate evaluations: the analyst needs to maintain access to the issuer in order to perform his or her job. Issuers traditionally released information about themselves to 'friendly' analysts in advance of public disclosure. Such 'selective disclosure' is now forbidden by the SEC's Regulation FD, which was adopted, after much controversy, in 2000, but companies still may stonewall an analyst they consider hostile, cutting such an analyst off from telephone conference calls and refusing to answer his or her questions. This fear of retaliation and lost access leaves open the question of whether 'sell-side' analyst research can ever be fully objective.

5 Investor Conflicts   To the extent that an analyst is not subsidized by investment banking revenues, then the analyst is dependent upon brokerage commissions. Such commissions are disproportionately paid by institutional investors, who characteristically hold substantial long positions in stocks, which they cannot liquidate easily. As a result, institutional investors are often displeased when an analyst issues a 'sell' recommendation, particularly when it comes as a surprise, because they are essentially locked-in to their positions and cannot sell them off before public investors react and cause a sharp price decline. Although these clients want unbiased research, themselves, they prefer to receive it privately and do not like public 'sell' recommendations that can panic the retail investor.[34] This explanation that institutional investors resist 'sell' recommendations accounts for the fact that even 'independent' firms, such as Sanford Bernstein & Co., which does virtually no investment banking business, still have the same (or higher) 'buy' to 'sell' ratios characterizing their recommendations as do brokerage firms that handle a substantial volume of underwritings.[35]

6 Herding As a Conflict   Multiple reasons can explain why independent analysts who sense a problem with a corporation may fail to sound the alarm. Enron supplies a good illustration because, as late as October 2001, just two months before Enron's bankruptcy, 16 out of the 17 analysts covering Enron maintained 'buy' or 'strong buy' recommendations on its stock.[36] Yet, much publicly available information already suggested that Enron was overpriced and could not maintain its prior rate of growth.[37]

Assuming that not all those analysts were conflicted in any of the foregoing senses, why would they be slow to respond? For the past decade, economists have had an explanation for why few analysts dissent from the consensus prediction. Money managers and analysts, they argue, fear making an individual mistake far more than a collective mistake, because they are in competition with each other and are evaluated principally on their relative performance.[38] Hence, analysts and money managers tend to herd, fearing to deviate far from the consensus prediction. If the consensus prediction is wrong, they suffer little injury vis-à-vis their colleagues who made similar predictions. Of course, if the analyst correctly predicts a downturn in a firm's earnings or stock price, he or she will attract favorable attention. But, even in this case, a problem remains: if the analyst prematurely predicts a downturn and the market does not drop promptly, investors who relied on his or her judgment may lose money and are not appeased by the fact that the analyst is eventually proved correct.

The empirical evidence supports this hypothesis that career concerns motivate securities analysts to stick close to consensus earnings forecasts—and in particular to avoid downward deviations. According to this research, accuracy does not improve analysts' career prospects as much as do predictions that err systematically on the side of optimism.[39] The policy implications of this research are discouraging, because it implies that even if traditional economic conflicts could be purged, the sell-side analyst would still not behave as the independent gatekeeper that reformers desire. Careerist concerns would still be likely to bias objectivity.

History: The Rise of the Analyst

The earliest precursors to the modern securities analyst were probably financial journalists. From the mid-19th century, the New York newspapers featured reporters and columns that specialized in finance.[40] Both Edward T. Jones and Charles H. Dow, the co-founders of Dow Jones & Company, were originally financial journalists whose specialty was the analysis of railroad financial statements.[41] The analysts of this era principally focused on bonds and other debt instruments, particularly railroad bonds, because railroads published more financial information than other companies.[42] Bonds were also what individual investors chiefly held, and institutional investors had not yet arisen. Indeed, it was not until 1928 that the total value of publicly traded equity exceeded that of outstanding debt.[43]

In 1916, the New York Society of Financial Statisticians was founded under the leadership of a New York University professor.[44] As the public became more interested in common stocks during the 1920s, other societies were founded in Chicago in 1925, San Francisco in 1929, Los Angeles in 1931, Toronto in 1936, and then—seemingly belatedly—in 1937 in New York with the founding of the New York Society of Security Analysts.[45] By 1947, a sufficient number of local societies existed for a national network to be formed, and representatives of eleven analyst societies voted in that year to form the National Federation of Financial Analyst Societies, which held its first annual convention in New York in 1948.[46] By the end of the 1950s, the National Federation had agreed on a long-term strategy to increase its professional recognition: the creation of a special professional credential, the Chartered Financial Analyst, which would be awarded only after a detailed examination. To this end, the Institute for Chartered Financial Analysts (ICFA) was incorporated in 1962, and awarded its first certificates in 1963. Obviously, this was a strategy that closely tracked the AICPA's successful marketing of CPA certification almost a half century earlier.

For this strategy to succeed and for a professional credential to have value, there first had to be a professional discipline to practice. The foundations of the new profession had been laid by the publication in the 1920s of Arthur Stone Dewing's The Financial Policy Of Corporations (1926) and Edgar Lawrence Smith's Common Stocks As Long-Term Investments (1925). Then, in 1934, the soon-to-be bible of the new field appeared: Benjamin Graham and David Dodd's 'Security Analysis', which codified the basic techniques and methodology of fundamental valuation analysis.[47] Graham and Dodd essentially shifted the focus of equity security analysis from dividends to earnings and instructed the analyst that the first task was to determine a company's true operating earnings. Just as Patton and Littleton's 1940 accounting text (with its focus on the matching principle) had supplied the doctrinal foundation for the 'golden age' of accounting,[48] Graham and Dodd furnished the intellectual construct that energized the rise of securities analysis as a profession. Instantly, it furnished both a methodology and an orthodoxy. Ben Graham, unquestionably the intellectual mentor of the profession, appears also to have been the first to propose professional certification, suggesting the title, 'Qualified Securities Analyst' as early as 1942.[49]

Although the elements were in place for the rise of the profession as of the late 1920s, a combination of events—the 1929 Crash, the Depression, and then World War II—slowed its growth. The membership rolls of the New York Society of Security Analysts, long the largest society, reveal this, showing a modest initial growth, and then acceleration during the 1960s and early 1970s. Founded with 66 members in 1937, the NYSSA grew to 450 in 1943, 1,200 in 1947, 2,320 in 1957, 4,146 in 1967, and 5,124 in 1977. But then, membership stopped growing from 1975 to 1977, fell from 1978 to 1980, and did not surpass the 1977 peak level until 1991.[50] What happened? In 1975, Congress ended the practice of fixed brokerage commission rates, prohibiting the stock exchanges from setting minimum rates and exposing brokerage commissions to competition.[51] Of course, commissions fell, swiftly declining 57 percent for institutional investors and 20 percent for individual investors.[52] For the brokerage industry as a whole, however, the change was beneficial, as, to their surprise, broker-dealer profitability increased with higher trading volume.[53] But for securities analysts, the change produced a crisis, because ending fixed brokerage rates necessarily implied an 'unbundling' of research and brokerage. Discount brokers quickly sprang up, offering cheap brokerage services without research, and research publications and consultants offered research (for a fee) that was not associated with any brokerage service.

How could competitive brokerage rates be good for the brokerage industry but bad for securities analysts? Under the old system of fixed brokerage commissions, brokerage rates were effectively inflated by an industry cartel, but newly powerful institutional investors had forced brokers to compete by demanding free research. That is, the institutions responded to fixed and inflated non-competitive rates by directing their brokerage business to broker-dealers who also provided them free research from sophisticated analysts. This response forced brokerage firms to compete on a basis other than price, and they hired analysts as the means by which they fought for the institutional market. Many of the analysts of this era worked for smaller 'boutique' brokerage firms (the first was probably Donaldson, Lufkin & Jenerette) that essentially survived on institutional brokerage and 'soft dollars' from larger broker-dealers who passed on their research to their clients.

When 'May Day' (the date on which the Congressional prohibition of fixed commissions took effect) came in 1975, the resulting 'unbundling' of research and brokerage enabled institutions to choose between lower brokerage rates or higher rates plus free research. Enough of them chose the former to cause a reduction in 'sell-side' research staffs. Although the standard account of this period usually explains that it became more difficult to compensate analysts out of progressively thinner and thinner commissions, this view misses the real transition. Brokerage firm revenues actually rose because of May Day, so broker-dealers could have afforded to subsidize sell-side analysts if there had been sufficient market demand for their services. In fact, institutional demand for research did not decline, but the market redefined what it wanted. As a result of May Day, institutional investors faced a classic 'make or buy' decision. Many institutions, particularly mutual funds, chose to 'make' by bringing securities research in-house, hiring analysts as employees on their own research staffs. Interestingly, this movement roughly paralleled the contemporaneous growth of in-house counsel at large corporations. In both cases, the user of the professional service opted to develop an in-house capacity, partly to escape inflated rates and partly to give it greater control over the provision of the service. In the case of institutional investors, the in-house option offered special advantages. By moving research in-house, institutions ensured (a) that research was kept private and proprietary, whereas purchased research from 'sell-side' analysts might have been given to others first; and (b) that research would be objective (or at least less tainted by sell-side analyst conflicts).

Yet, even if the 'buy-side' of the market increasingly relied on in-house proprietary research, 'sell-side' research still moved the market, because public investors had come to depend on it. One study in the mid-1990s found that the issuance of a new 'buy' recommendation by a sell-side analyst (either as the result of an upgrade from a lower category, or on the initiation of coverage by the analyst) produced on average a 3 percent stock price increase over the three-day period following the recommendation's issuance. In contrast, a new 'sell' recommendation—already an infrequent event—yielded a 4.7 percent decrease over the same period.[54] Whatever the new recommendation—'buy' or 'sell'—a substantial increase in the trading volume of the stock followed, thereby increasing brokerage commissions.[55]

Given the emphatic market impact of 'sell-side' analyst research, the next development now seems predictable in retrospect. Sell-side analysts needed a new external source to subsidize research at brokerage firms, and one external source had a strong interest in encouraging favorable research: the corporations who were rated by the analyst. The rational interests of both produced what can be viewed as a Faustian bargain: corporations would happily—if indirectly—pay high compensation to analysts in return for the analysts' sacrifice of their objectivity. To broker this arrangement, both sides relied upon the investment banking division of the large broker-dealer firm to subsidize and monitor analyst research. If sell-side analyst research increased or supported the issuer's stock price, the issuer would find a way to compensate the broker-dealer, which in turn would reward the analyst. Because senior personnel in investment banking firms already received the majority of their compensation in a year-end bonus, it fitted this pattern to reward research analysts through a similar year-end bonus for their service to firm's underwriting clients.[56]

Another transition also can be dated to this time. In the 1960s, when the analyst population boomed, broker-dealers were supported by brokerage revenues. For example in 1967, commission revenue accounted for 57 percent of Merrill Lynch's revenues, and investment banking contributed less than one-tenth that amount.[57] Thereafter, commission revenue as a percentage of the industry's aggregate revenues declined from a high of 55 percent in 1973 to 36 percent in 1980.[58] By the 1990s, investment banking accounted for the vast majority of the revenues of the large integrated broker-dealer.[59] Also during the 1990s, a series of consolidating major mergers brought most large retail brokerage firms under the control of a larger investment banking firm (for example, Morgan Stanley acquired Dean Witter; Smith Barney was absorbed into Salomon and Citigroup, etc.). As a result, only a handful of large broker-dealer firms continued to specialize in brokerage without also underwriting securities. Yet, even these brokerage firms that did not underwrite securities could still be subjected to reprisals if one of their analysts criticized an issuer.[60]

The importance of the 'star' analyst to the firm's investment bankers needs a special explanation because it changed during the 1990s. Although investment banks compete actively for underwriting clients, this competition was not based on price (indeed, most underwriters have long charged the same standard 7 percent to 7.5 percent underwriting discount for underwriting an IPO).[61] Other things being equal, corporate clients tended to select the underwriter who employed the leading analyst in their industry, expecting that the analyst would support their stock's price with favorable recommendations. This expectation was strongest in the case of IPO clients. Typically, IPOs are marketed to institutional investors through the institution of the 'road show'—a series of meetings around the country at which the issuer and its 'star' analyst answer questions, often predicting future earnings. Often the analyst would predict the new issuer's likely earnings for the forthcoming year, and the sophisticated institutions at the roadshow would understand that such a prediction had been precleared with the underwriter. While such efforts by the analyst helped 'build the book' for the offering, the analyst was even more valuable to the management and any controlling shareholders of the IPO issuer. Almost invariably, these persons are contractually restricted in the stock they can sell, both in and after the offering; the standard provision, insisted upon by the underwriters, is a six month 'lockup' to ensure that the insiders would not appear to be 'bailing out' in the offering or its immediate aftermarket. As a result, because they cannot sell at the time of the offering, these insiders logically focused less on the IPO price than on the likely price of their stock at the expiration of their lockups.

The one person who could most affect this aftermarket price was the 'star' analyst in their underwriter's research department. Often, the competition among underwriters for an IPO involved a 'bakeoff'—a series of meetings between the issuer and the contending underwriters at which each would bring their 'star' analyst in the field to explain how he or she could support its stock price. Sometimes, the analyst might intimate that he or she would deliver what the industry called a 'booster shot'—a favorable research report just before the expiration of the lockup period. Those insiders desiring to sell (as they usually did desire in order to diversify their new wealth that their IPO had created on paper) needed this timely support because they feared that short sellers might otherwise exploit the end of the lockup period to make concentrated sales, thereby depressing their stock price. In short, high among the analyst's services was the protection of the issuer's management and insiders from a 'bear raid' by short sellers at a vulnerable moment.

In any event, as the media in the 1990s made the names of 'star' securities analysts almost as well known as those of rock stars (albeit for the same ephemeral period), the analyst's value to the client rose, and underwriters naturally began to compete to hire 'star' analysts in order to win underwriting clients. Analysts who were the beneficiaries of this competition saw their salaries soar in the 1990s past those of the other professions and enter the realm of NBA free agents.

Even though they were princes of the stock market culture of the 1990s, analysts remained vulnerable. All analysts feared that a negative rating or report would elicit retaliation in the form of a denial of access by the subject company. Because most analysts specialized in a particular industry and covered a relatively small number of stocks, a decision by any major firm in that industry to cease communicating with the analyst significantly disabled the analyst. The disfavored analyst could expect to be cut off from the regular flow of selective disclosures by which the company tipped other analysts ahead of any public announcement as to changes in its earnings outlook or other developments. In truth, these selective disclosures may have been precisely what many institutional investors (most notably, the mutual funds) chiefly wanted from the analyst—namely, material non-public information provided from the issuer to the analyst, and relayed to the institutions before any public announcement was made. So long as the analyst was the key intermediary in this process of selective disclosure, the analyst's value to the institutions was obvious, even if the analyst's objectivity was deeply compromised.

Although the ability of analysts to relay material non-public information in this fashion to institutional investors may have looked like an obvious example of insider trading, the case law had largely exempted the analyst. This special dispensation was the product of the highly favorable light in which the analyst was then viewed. In 1983, the Supreme Court in *Dirks v. SEC*[62] deliberately redefined the law of insider trading to protect the analyst who relayed material information from the issuer to institutional investors, giving the analyst a virtual immunity from insider trading liability so long as the analyst did not receive a 'pecuniary benefit' from its tippees.

Why did the Court throw such a broad blanket of immunity over the analyst? In *Dirks*, the Supreme Court confronted a vivid set of facts that convinced it that the securities analyst played a critical watchdog role, which in turn necessitated that it receive greater legal protection. Raymond Dirks, a well-known analyst specializing in the insurance industry and working for a broker-dealer firm, received information from a whistle-blower—Ronald Secrist, a former officer of Equity Funding of America, a corporation that principally sold life insurance and mutual funds—that the assets of Equity Funding Corporation had been vastly overstated. Equity Funding was in fact insolvent, meaning that its insurance policies on which many middle-class families were relying for protection or retirement income were largely worthless. Secrist further told Dirks that he had informed regulatory authorities, but could not get them to take him seriously. Deciding to investigate Secrist's charges, Dirks flew to Los Angeles and interviewed a variety of corporate employees. While many denied the fraud, Dirks was able to corroborate its essential details. He passed on this information on a contemporaneous basis to the Wall Street Journal, which he urged to expose the fraud, but the Journal was unwilling to believe that so massive a fraud had escaped detection or to take the risk of liability for libel. Dirks also informed his institutional clients of his investigation and its findings, and, late in his investigation, Dirks also communicated his findings to the SEC's regional office in Los Angeles. Although the regulatory authorities responded slowly to Dirk's findings, the market characteristically reacted much more quickly. During Dirk's two week investigation in Los Angeles, Dirks' clients began to sell—and the market price of Equity Funding fell from $26 per share to less than $15. This price fall plus associated market rumors led the NYSE to halt trading in the stock. At this point, the Wall Street Journal at last published a front page story based on the information Dirks had given it—and the jig was up for Equity Funding. The California insurance regulators moved in and shut Equity Funding down as insolvent.

To most observers, Ray Dirks was the hero of this story. His investigation had uncovered an extraordinary fraud in which the senior management of a public life insurance company were literally counterfeiting bogus insurance policies to fool their auditors into believing they were solvent. Ultimately, Dirks brought down Equity Funding, more or less at the same moment that two Washington Post reporters—Robert Woodward and Carl Bernstein—exposed the essential facts about the Watergate scandal and similarly brought down the Nixon Administration. Seemingly, Dirks deserved the securities analyst's equivalent of the Pulitzer Prize. Yet, if most thought that Dirks had performed a public service, the SEC did not. Instead, it charged him with aiding and abetting a violation of Rule 10b-5 because he had passed material non-public information obtained from a corporate insider to his clients.

The SEC's decision to charge Ray Dirks proved an epochal blunder for the Commission. Although it won its case before an administrative law judge and the lower federal court, the Supreme Court reversed the SEC's decision and, in the process, rewrote the law of insider trading to protect analysts in Dirks' position. Noting (perhaps over-optimistically) that '[i]t is commonplace for analysts to "ferret out and analyze information," '[63] the Court held that insider trading required a prerequisite breach of fiduciary duty. Because Secrist had revealed information to Dirks for a valid purpose (i.e. to halt a fraud), Dirks was effectively free, it found, to use and exploit this information. Dirk's obligations, the Court decided, were entirely derivative of the insider's (i.e. Secrist's) obligations; therefore, if the insider (i.e. Secrist) had breached no duty, then his tippee (i.e. Dirks) could also not violate the law.

Broad as this rule was, the Court took it one important step further: to protect the analyst, it said, courts must 'focus on objective criteria, i.e. whether the insider receives a direct or indirect personal benefit from the disclosure, such as a pecuniary gain or a reputational benefit that will translate into future earnings.'[64] This was extremely protective, because analysts never paid money or other personal benefits to the corporate officer who tipped them as to future earnings or other material developments. In effect, the Court went well beyond crafting a fact-specific exemption for the analyst/investigator who uncovers a fraud. Instead it broadly immunized all analysts who receive selective disclosures—at least unless, on some rare set of facts, the analyst agreed to provide a pecuniary or reputational benefit in return for the information.

Predictably, the result was to legitimize selective disclosure by issuers to analysts. Once legitimized, the practice of selective disclosure both increased the corporation's control over the analyst and the analyst's value to institutional investors. Even an analyst of indifferent ability could be useful to institutions if he or she served as the conduit by which the institutions received corporate earnings predictions that had not yet been publicly released. Perversely, however, analysts of high ability and real independence suffered a diminution in their value because such analysts' access to the issuer might suffer as a result of their independence. Other things being equal, the corporation could be expected to reward its most loyal analysts with priority access to non-public information. To institutional investors, priority in time meant everything, because new information becomes stale quickly in fast-moving markets. Whether correct or overwritten (and the debate has long continued), the *Dirks* decision enhanced the importance of access to the issuer, and thus increased the issuer's leverage over the analyst as gatekeeper.

Dirks viewed the security analyst as a hero—a private attorney general who detected fraud and held corporate management accountable. Exaggerated as this view might have been, it helped define the analyst's image in the public's mind, and that public image soared during the 1990s. To the public, who saw analysts lionized on CNN and CNBC and in the print media, analysts possessed an uncanny ability to predict winners, identify new trends in technology, and set target prices for stocks that quickly became self-fulfilling prophecies. When Henry Blodget in 1998 predicted that Amazon.com's stock, then trading at $243 per share, would trade at $400 per share within 12 months, and when Amazon.com's stock price exceeded $400 per share within three weeks thereafter,[65] Blodget's fame was assured, and his 'rock star'-like celebrity status contributed significantly to the short-term deification of securities analysts as modern prophets. Symptomatically, in the wake of his success, Blodget moved from CIBC Oppenheimer, a small brokerage firm, to Merrill Lynch to head its Internet research group, where he replaced Merrill's prior Internet analyst, who had dared to express doubts about the long-term profitability of Internet.com companies.

If the public investor came to idolize the analyst during the 1980s, institutional investors remained more skeptical, placing more trust in independent analysts than in 'sell-side' analysts associated with underwriting firms.[66] Nonetheless, because public investors did rely on analysts, they were affected by a striking shift in analyst behavior during the 1990s. A survey by Thomson Financial/First Call found that the ratio of 'buy' recommendations to 'sell' recommendations shifted from 6-to-1 in 1991 to nearly 100-to-1 by 2000.[67] A later, fuller study by academic financial economists gives a fuller picture of the transition from just 1996 to 2000:[68]

Table 7.1   *Analyst stock recommendations, 1996–2000*

	No. of recommendations	No. of companies	Strong Buy/ buy	Hold	Sell/strong sell
1996	22,409	5,480	65.2%	31.3%	3.5%
1997	29,647	6,390	66.4%	30.1%	3.5%
1998	42,321	6,783	66.4%	30.1%	3.5%
1999	43,248	6,806	70.1%	27.1%	2.8%
2000	41,965	6,666	72.1%	26.3%	1.6%

This period (1996 to 2000) is the heart of the 'bubble era,' and by its end in 2000, 98.4 percent of analyst recommendations were either 'buys' or 'holds,' with only 1.6 percent being 'sells' or 'strong sells.' Equally important, over this period the number of analyst recommendations nearly doubled (from 22,409 in 1996 to 43,248 in 1999), raising questions about whether analysts were over-extending themselves. Because the total population of analysts could not have grown that significantly between 1996 and 1999, the nearly 100 percent increase from some 22,000 odd analyst recommendations in 1996 to over 43,000 reports in 1999 implies that analysts were spending less time per report, seemingly cranking them out on an assembly line basis. Although the bias towards optimism has attracted most of the commentary and criticism, this sudden increase in the number of recommendations may be just as revealing, because it suggests that this increase in output exceeded the industry's ability to effectively monitor. NASD rules require that an NASD 'member must have a reasonable basis for the recommendation...'.[69] The one-year increase in analyst recommendations from 29,647 in 1997 to 42,321 in 1998 alone suggests that member firms would have been hard-pressed to determine that a reasonable basis existed for this vastly greater number of recommendations—at least without substantially increasing the industry resources devoted to the supervision of analysts.

But there is an even stranger side to this story. Recent research has found that analyst recommendations at the end of the bubble were perverse: stocks rated as 'buys' in 2000–2001 not only underperformed the market, but also underperformed the relatively few stocks given a sell recommendation.[70] This was a complete reversal of the prior pattern. Earlier research had shown that stocks that were the recipients of consensus 'buy' recommendations outperformed the market, while stocks with 'sell' recommendations underperformed the market.[71] Yet, in 2000 and 2001, the performance of these two portfolios reversed, and the most recommended stocks earned a market-adjusted return of negative 7 percent in 2000 and 2001, while the market-adjusted return on the 'sell' stocks was a very healthy 17.6 percent in 2000 and a still desirable 9.3 percent in 2001.[72] At this point, the inherent value of securities research begins to seem suspect.

One other change over the 1990s merits special attention. By studying the advancement of securities analysts within firms and among firms, two social scientists sought to identify the criterion that most determined career advancement among analysts. Their answer: relative optimism.[73] A bias towards optimism outranked even overall accuracy in determining career advancement as an analyst.[74] Although accuracy did matter, they found both that a tendency to be more optimistic than the consensus of analysts was critical and that the importance of a bias towards optimism increased in the 1990s.[75] Finally, they found that such a bias was most important in the case of analysts who covered stocks underwritten by their own firms.[76] Their conclusion was blunt: 'Wall Street lost any self-discipline to produce accurate research during the recent stock market mania.'[77]

But the 'research' was still valuable to institutions because it led the market. At their worst, analysts in this era were not so much professionals as legally immune purveyors of inside information, moving such data from issuers to institutions.

The Regulatory Reaction

The collapse of the Internet.com bubble in the Spring of 2000 swiftly brought an angry reaction from the public and financial journalists, who all noted that the famed analysts of the era had maintained their 'buy' recommendations on stocks while they lost 80 percent or more of their value. Particularly in the case of the most famous analysts, nothing seemed to shake their confidence in stocks whose prices were in free fall.

Following the bubble's collapse in 2000, the first significant SEC action affecting analysts was not directly aimed at analyst reform, but may have accomplished this indirectly. That action came in the Fall of 2000 when the SEC adopted Regulation FD, which banned selective disclosure by issuers to analysts (and others). Adopted after a contentious battle with Wall Street, it was a major achievement of SEC Chairman Arthur Levitt's tenure, but it was not based on any perception that analysts were biased. Rather, it was principally based on an ethical distaste for selective disclosure (and possibly the political perception that average retail investors profoundly disliked issuers tipping institutions, who then unloaded overvalued stocks onto them). Nonetheless, the impact of Regulation FD on analysts was profound, but complex. In terms of their relationship with issuers, Regulation FD strengthened analyst independence because issuers were no longer free to cut off skeptical analysts from the flow of non-public material information. By halting that flow, Regulation FD placed all analysts on a relatively level playing field. If the issuer could no longer tip favored analysts with a preview of next quarter's earnings, the issuer could also no longer threaten independent analysts with a denial of access to the same information (or at least the issuer's threat was less chilling).

In terms of the analyst's relationship with the broker-dealer firm that employed the analyst, however, Regulation FD probably reduced the analyst's value to the firm. No longer was the analyst the key intermediary who moved material non-public information from the issuer to eager institutional investors. The institutions now had even more reason to rely on in-house buy-side analysts and less reason to reward sell-side analysts with brokerage commissions. Indeed, Regulation FD may well have reduced the accuracy of sell-side analyst's forecasts, because ironically the more conflicted the analyst, the greater the likelihood of its receiving highly accurate information from sources inside the issuer.[78] In sum, the impact of Regulation FD probably was to increase analyst independence and objectivity, but to reduce the analyst's value to the analyst's principal audience, the institutional market.

As a profession, securities analysts had long been sheltered from litigation and SEC enforcement by a variety of protective doctrines (including, of course, *Dirks*'s protective rule on insider trading). The first true fissure in that wall of protection came in 2001 when a Merrill Lynch investor filed an arbitration claim against Henry Blodget and Merrill Lynch, alleging that Blodget's strong recommendation of a high tech Internet company had been the result of conflicts of interest and Blodget's desire to increase his own compensation by supporting Merrill Lynch's investment banking division.[79] While Merrill Lynch denied the charge, it settled the case for a seemingly generous $400,000, suggesting to many that it did not want to disclose documents or attract further publicity on this topic.

Among those whose curiosity was piqued by this settlement was New York State Attorney General Eliot Spitzer. Because Blodget and Merrill Lynch were based in New York, he had jurisdiction, and he opened an investigation in the summer of 2001, which principally focused on the stocks covered by Blodget's Internet research team.[80] After an intensive review of Merrill Lynch's internal emails, Spitzer's staff found clearcut evidence that Merrill Lynch's enthusiastic public support of a number of Internet stocks was often contradicted by contemporaneous email correspondence among Merrill Lynch staffers showing that the analysts' actual evaluation of the same stocks was highly negative.[81] For example, Blodgett, himself, described stocks highly rated by Merrill Lynch as 'a disaster ... there really is no floor to this stock' or 'a piece of junk.'[82] Spitzer's staff assembled a simple chart showing stocks with a high Merrill Lynch rating and contemporaneous internal email comments describing it as a 'piece of crap' or 'piece of junk' or worse.[83]

More generally, Spitzer charged that not only had Merrill Lynch deceived the public about its true evaluations, but it failed to disclose that its own policy was not to issue 'sell' or 'reduce' ratings (which were the bottom two tiers of its five-tier rating system).[84] Also, it had failed to acknowledge that:

Merrill Lynch's ratings were tarnished by an undisclosed conflict of interest: the research analysts were acting as quasi-investment bankers for companies at issue, often initiating, continuing, and/or manipulating research coverage for the purpose of attracting and keeping investment banking clients, thereby producing misleading ratings that were neither objective nor independent, as they purported to be.[85]

While the existence of these and similar conflicts surrounding sell-side analysts were well understood by more sophisticated investors, retail investors seemed largely ignorant of them and responded to Spitzer's disclosures with outrage. Ultimately, Spitzer's staff succeeded in painting a devastating portrait of analysts who knew they were misrepresenting the truth and were in some cases feeling guilty about doing so. Perhaps the most dramatic statement uncovered by the Spitzer team was an email by one analyst to Blodget protesting a favorable (i.e. 'accumulate') rating, which ended with the following warning to Blodget:

… i don't think that's the right thing to do. We are losing people money and i don't like it. John and mary smith are losing their retirement because we don't want Todd [the CEO of the client] to be mad at us.[86]

When Spitzer filed his action in April 2002, his vivid allegations had the impact of a bombshell. Although many had suspected that the Chinese Wall between analysts and investment banking had leaks, he documented a clear pattern of analysts seeking to satisfy investment banking and issuer demands for favorable ratings (and expressing clear signs of distress about their own involvement in a thoroughly conflicted process). Recognizing its exposed position, Merrill Lynch quickly entered into a $100 million settlement with Spitzer on May 21, 2002, roughly one month after the Attorney General's action was filed.[87]

But this was just the start. Following the Merrill Lynch settlement, Spitzer turned to the other major underwriting firms, and he was quickly joined in this investigation by the SEC, the NASD, the NYSE, and other state regulators—all of whom were now eager to jump on his bandwagon. After protracted negotiations, ten major underwriting firms entered into a 'Global Settlement' with Spitzer and the other regulators in April 2003.[88] Once again, the regulators' complaint chiefly alleged that each of the ten firms had 'engaged in acts and practices that created or maintained inappropriate influence by investment banking over research analysts, thereby imposing conflicts of interest on research analysts that the firms failed to manage in an adequate or appropriate manner.'[89]

This Global Settlement levied a collective penalty on the ten firms of $1.3875 billion.[90] That was the easy part. The more difficult question was what reforms would curb the conflict of interest problems that had been uncovered. Here, the basic strategy underlying the global settlement was two-fold: (1) the defendants would separate and insulate their research departments, thereby protecting them from the now presumptively sinister influence of investment bankers; and (2) they would provide independent research to their clients along with their own research reports.[91] The first approach can be described as a 'Reinforced Chinese Wall' strategy, while the second approach sought to subsidize independent research.

The first approach was implemented by elaborate rule-making that sought to free securities analysts from the supervision and control of investment banking personnel. To this end, the NASD and NYSE adopted rules that barred investment banking personnel from:

(i) having any influence or control over the compensation of securities analysts;[92]

(ii) reviewing any pending research report (or even discussing it with the analyst);[93]

(iii) tying analyst compensation to 'specific' investment banking business;[94] or

(iv) influencing company-specific analyst coverage decisions (such as whether to initiate or terminate coverage of a company).[95]

Instead, the new rules required that analyst compensation be determined based on elaborately prescribed criteria that excluded any consideration of service or contribution to the investment banking division.[96] To reduce the pressure on them, analysts, in turn, were prohibited from participating in 'bakeoffs' (or other efforts to solicit investment banking business)[97] and 'roadshows' (or other marketing efforts for an investment banking transaction),[98] and firms were forbidden to offer favorable research or a rating in return for business or compensation.[99] Also intended as a means of reducing pressure on analysts, a new SEC regulation—Regulation AC—required broker dealers to include in any research report a certification by the individual analyst that the views stated in the report stated his or her own personal view.[100] Finally, the global settlement mandated that the budget of the research division (and the allocation of its expenses) be determined 'without input from Investment Banking and without regard to specific revenues or results derived from Investment Banking, though revenues and results of the firm as a whole may be considered."[101]

This last provision about the research division's budget brings us to the crux of the matter. While it is possible (although not easy) to divorce research from investment banking, the more perplexing question is: who will subsidize research? Excluding investment banking from any participation in the determination of the research division's budget or analyst compensation does not mean that other divisions (or senior management) will willingly subsidize research. Rationally, they will instead focus on the analysts' contribution to firm profitability, which may be modest. Although brokerage commissions may be enhanced by analyst research, brokerage commissions are only a fraction of investment banking revenues.[102] Hence, only a proportionately smaller subsidy could be expected from the brokerage side of the integrated firm.

By some estimates, a significant research department has an annual cost of over $500 million, and only investment banking can earn returns sufficient to justify such an investment. If the firm cannot earn a return on research that matches its overall return on capital, it became predictable that the firm will reduce its investment in securities research, cutting back both on analyst compensation and employment. In this light, the post-Spitzer reforms are probably desirable, and will likely curtail some of the more egregious abuses and instances of retaliation against analysts, but they still fall well short of assuring analyst independence. Even with a Maginot Line of Chinese Wall proportions, analysts will understand that their compensation ultimately depends principally on their utility to investment banking.

Given these problems, the second strategy underlying the global settlement—subsidizing independent research—was a necessary complement. Indeed, the most innovative provision in the Spitzer settlement with Merrill Lynch, which was later copied in the Global Settlement, was its requirement that Merrill Lynch provide research advice to its customers from independent analysts. Specifically, the Global Settlement mandated that, for a five-year period, each defendant investment bank was required to offer independent research reports (paid for by it) paralleling the research done by its in-house analysts.[103] The independent analysts were to be selected by an independent consultant appointed (with the approval of the regulators) for each defendant.[104] Although each defendant was required to notify customers of the availability of this research on their account statements and on the first page of research reports, no mandatory obligation was imposed to transmit the independent reports along with the firm's own reports.[105] Rather, the customer had to request the independent research report, and this provision may partly explain the tepid response that followed.

Viewed in the abstract, the mandatory requirement of independent research seemed a brilliant stroke—the perfectly designed answer to the problem of tainted research because it both cured the conflict and preserved the subsidy. Essentially, it redirected each defendant broker-dealer's subsidy for research from its in-house analysts to external 'independent' analysts. The subsidy became not voluntary, but obligatory. In response, most investment banks reduced their employment of in-house analysts, but the substitution of independent analysts for conflicted in-house employees should have been exactly what reformers would have wanted. In theory, the reform cut the Gordian Knot that had long stalemated reform by severing the link between the provision of the subsidy and control over the analyst. That, at least, was the theory.

Unfortunately, the early evidence suggests, however, that the independent research mandated by the Global Settlement has had less impact than anticipated. Individual investors in particular have ignored the websites on which the independent research reports commissioned by the ten underwriting firms participating in the Global Settlement are posted.[106] Several of the independent consultants monitoring each firm under the settlement have also acknowledged that usage by individual investors has been well less than anticipated.[107]

Why? One reason may be that investors only want the opinions of securities analysts who carry name recognition—in effect, the 'stars' of the particular industry. Most of the independent analysts hired under the settlement fall well short of that level of 'brand name' reputation. Another reason may be that retail investors would read and give weight to unknown analysts if they were provided with their views, but are unaware of their rights to request such research (or are simply unmotivated to make the necessary request). Finally, there is the possibility that investors consider these independent analysts to be equally conflicted.

Indeed, considerable evidence does suggest that even independent analysts have their own bias towards optimism. Although early research in this field found that the 'buy' recommendations of analysts employed by independent brokers outperformed those of brokers affiliated with underwriters,[108] more recent work has found 'independent' research to be no less optimistic and somewhat less accurate than research conducted within large broker-dealers. For example, one study divided securities analysts into three categories— investment banks, brokerage firms (with no investment banking activity), and independent research firms—and found that 'analysts at large investment banks are less optimistic, more timely and more accurate in their forecasts than analysts at other institutions.'[109] An even more recent 2004 study of 7,400 analyst recommendations relating to recent IPOs finds little difference in the market reaction to recommendations by independent analysts versus analysts affiliated with investment banks.[110]

Even after the Global Settlement, this pattern has persisted. In 2004, the first year after the Global Settlement, Thomson Financial, which compiles research ratings into aggregate tables, found that 'independent' analysts had a higher level of optimism than in-house analysts. Specifically, the independent analysts had a slightly higher percentage of 'buy' ratings (47.4% compared to 43.7% for in-house analysts) and a slightly lower percentage of 'sell' ratings (8.9% compared to 9.1% for in-house analysts).[111] Paradoxical as this sounds, it at least shows that the premise that greater analyst independence implies greater objectivity may not be as irrefutable as reformers thought.

Why are 'independent' analysts more optimistic than analysts working within conflict-laden investment banking firms? The most logical interpretation is that the independent firm depends for its revenues on the buy-side, and the buy-side dislikes public 'sell' recommendations because they may panic retail investors and cause a massive sell-off of a stock in which the buy-side institution holds a large and illiquid position. Also, investment banks are required by the Global Settlement to disclose their percentage of 'sell' ratings and so may pressure their analysts to issue some minimum percentage of 'sell' ratings. Finally, the independent analyst may sometimes be more vulnerable to threats of retaliation from issuers than the sell-side analyst. A company does not lightly exclude Merrill Lynch's analyst from its phone conferences (even if the analyst gave it a negative rating), but it has less to fear from an independent analyst who downgraded it. This may explain why even the best known of the independent research firms has a more lopsided 'buy' to 'sell' ratio than did the major underwriting firms.[112]

Nonetheless, independent research clearly has a future. In 2004, roughly 14 percent of all stock ratings issued by Thomson Financial were issued by independents, up from only 4 percent in 2002—an increase of over 300 percent in two years.[113] What explains this? Prior to the adoption of Regulation FD in 2000, analysts working at investment banks had a systematic advantage over independent analysts: they could be lawfully tipped material information by corporation officials, who often gave them such information in return for inflated ratings. It was an unholy bargain, but it left the market facing an uncertain tradeoff: analysts at investment banks typically had both more bias but better information than analysts at independent firms. Today, however, the superior access of the analysts at the investment banking firm has been ended (largely anyway) by Regulation FD. As a result, the analyst at the large investment bank may still be subject to greater bias, but no longer has necessarily superior informational advantages.

Where then are we left? Today, it increasingly appears that the independent analyst can compete, but the system of mandated independent research required by the Global Settlement has generated little excitement. Because this mandated research is very costly and yet is seemingly ignored by most investors, few expect this subsidy to be renewed after the five-year term of the Global Settlement expires. But, as next discussed, there is a possibility that the private market can find less costly and more effective ways to subsidize independent research.

After the Scandals: The Contemporary Context

At the height of the 'bubble,' 'buy' recommendations vastly exceeded 'sell' recommendations, and the latter fell to a miniscule 1.6 percent of the total of all recommendations.[114] Today, this has changed. As of mid-2003, one survey of the recommendations of the top ten brokerage firms found that 16.5 percent of all recommendations were 'sells,' 35.9 percent were buys, and 47.9 percent were 'holds.'[115] While a bias towards optimism still remains, it is far less pronounced.

What caused this change? In part, it was the impact of the Global Settlement. But, even more likely, it was the natural consequence of a market crash in 2001–2002 that made investors leary of excessive optimism by analysts and that placed the entire profession under a cloud. The New York Attorney General's revelations only confirmed investors' doubts.

The Global Settlement and the market crash have heavily impacted industry employment. In their wake, there has been significant reduction both in the size of sell-side research departments and in the number of companies covered by their analysts.[116] While some analysts were laid off, even more migrated to the 'buy' side. As a consequence, of the roughly 14,000 publicly-traded companies in the U.S., fewer than 6,000 are today covered by even a single analyst (and less than half of these 6,000 are covered by two or more analysts).[117] Because large market cap companies generate trading and thus brokerage commissions, they continue to be followed by analysts, and the reduction in coverage has chiefly affected the middle-to-small cap world of Nasdaq, where far fewer companies are today covered by a full-time analyst. Thus, on the policy level, if one believes that securities research has value, the goal of reform cannot be simply to make analysts 'independent.' Rather, some form of subsidy must be devised that succeeds in extending analyst coverage over most of the market—without compromising analyst objectivity. 'Perfect' independence would come at too high a price if it necessarily resulted in an equity market that was only thinly covered.

Already, in response to this cutback by research departments, new and problematic relationships are developing between analysts and small companies. Unable to gain coverage from shrunken research departments, a number of Nasdaq companies have taken to hiring freelance analysts to write research reports on them for a fee paid by the company.[118] Although such 'issuer-paid' research hardly sounds 'independent,' the companies hiring analysts justify these payments by pointing to the fact that auditors are also compensated by the corporations that they audit. Bad as the practice of company-paid research may look, the alternative may arguably be worse: no research and an increasingly opaque Nasdaq market.

Given this seemingly stark choice, The CFA Institute, the analysts' trade organization, and the National Investor Relations Institute, a trade organization of corporate investor relations officers, jointly drafted 'best practices' guidelines in 2004 that sought to legitimize 'issuer-paid' practice.[119] Essentially, the guidelines require disclosure of the fact and amount of the payment, recommend that payment to the analyst be in cash (not in stock or options), and seek to keep the substance of the report unreviewed by the subject corporation until after its release.[120] Of course, this resolution hardly cures the conflict. The freelance analyst who receives a modest payment for such a report naturally hopes to receive future business and know that a negative review may deny it that chance.

What then is the answer? One real possibility is a new development called 'intermediated research.' Several new organizations have very recently appeared that are seeking to play a 'marriage broker' role under which the issuer pays them a fee for research and they select the 'independent' securities analyst to perform the research.[121] Such a system of 'intermediated research' has clear advantages over 'issuer paid' research. First, if properly administered, such a system could break the linkage between an issuer subsidy and issuer control over the analyst. Second, under this system, analysts at brokerage firms receive a direct payment (from the marriage broker) to their division for their research, thus creating a profit center and ending the need in principle for other divisions of the brokerage firm to subsidize the analyst. Third, if the intermediary picking the analyst does so on the basis of relative accuracy, the independent analyst at last is given a strong incentive to enhance accuracy—one that now appears to be strangely lacking.

Such a system of 'intermediated research' can work if—and only if—the 'marriage broker' selecting the analyst can play a 'gatekeeper role'; that is, it must accumulate reputational capital and convince the market that the analysts it selects will be objective and independent (or at least more so than other sell-side analysts). It is premature to predict whether these new entrants will succeed or whether various regulatory problems can be overcome.[122] But 'intermediated research' does represent a conceptually attractive new institutional design—one which once again depends on creating a role for a reliable gatekeeper.

Viewed in the abstract, the challenge is how to structure a gatekeeper intermediary so that it can fund research without corrupting it. That topic of institutional redesign will be analyzed in more detail in Chapter 10. But at this point, it is important to understand how the two key problems just discussed interrelate: (1) the lack of transparency in the 'small cap' market because of the inadequate incentives for firms to subsidize research and (2) the persistent problem of analyst retaliation. One recent study finds the 'buy-to-sell' ratio to be considerably higher in case of 'large cap' companies than 'small cap' companies. In the case of 'large cap' stocks, the current buy-to-sell ratio is 48 percent to 8 percent, or 6 to 1; but in the case of 'small cap' stocks, it appears to be 36 percent to 15 percent, or 2.4 to 1.[123] This seems anomalous, because historically smaller firms experienced greater growth and were once the 'darlings' of the bubble era. The most logical explanation for this pattern is that larger firms can more easily threaten retaliation. Small cap firms generate so little stock trading (and hence brokerage commissions) that investment banks do not want to expend funds researching them. Hence, the smaller firm must virtually beg for research and cannot threaten to retaliate against the analyst. But the larger firm can. Although the large cap firm can no longer selectively tip favored analysts (at least not without violating the SEC's Regulation FD), it can exclude unfavored analysts from conference calls and can refuse to attend their conferences. As a result, research in the case of the 'large cap' market tends to be more optimistic (i.e. there is a higher buy-to-sell ratio). Paradoxically, the 'large cap' market should be more efficiently priced and thus should offer fewer bargains (or 'strong buys'). Hence, this evidence that the 'buy-to-sell' ratio is higher in their case, corroborates this hypothesis that larger issuers can more easily retaliate against the analyst.

The bottom line then is that for the securities analyst to perform as an honest gatekeeper, two linked problems must be solved that have persisted, even after the Global Settlement purged the more obvious conflicts of interest: (1) analysts must be protected from retaliation, including pressures from the buy-side and issuers, and not just from pressures within the investment banking firm (which is the only context that Sarbanes-Oxley addresses); and (2) a means must be found by which to subsidize research in the case of the smaller cap market without that subsidy distorting the research.

Endnotes

1. The total membership of the Association for Investment Management and Research (AIMR), the principal trade organization for securities analysts (now called 'The CFA Institute'), was reported to be 65,700 as of August 2003, of which roughly half were employed in North America. See AIMR Annual Report 2003 at p 26. Another relevant statistic is that there are currently 57,512 active Chartered Financial Analysts licensed by AIMR world-wide, and probably half of these are in the United States. See Ieva Augstums, 'Analysts Who Pass Tests Reap Multiple Rewards,' Dallas Morning News, July 18, 2004 at 11J.

2. 'Research analysts' employed by NASD or NYSE members must be registered with the NASD and NYSE and must pass a qualification examination and comply with a continuing education requirement. See NASD Rules 1050 and 1120, and NYSE Rules 344 and 345A.

3. See *Lentell v. Merrill Lynch & Co. Inc.*, 396 F. 3d 161 (2d Cir. 2005) (affirming dismissal of securities class action against Henry Blodgett and Merrill Lynch for allegedly biased and fraudulent research reports). This dismissal was principally on the ground that plaintiffs had failed to plead loss causation, which will be a substantial barrier in most other cases as well. But see, *Demarco v. Lehman Bros.*, 222 F.R.D. 243 (S.D.N.Y. 2004) (upholding a similar class action against a motion to dismiss).

4. See text and notes at nn 62 to 65 below.

5. See text and notes at nn 37 to 39 below.

6. One measure of the intensity of the conflicts surrounding analyst research is that between May 2000 and February 2001, the Nasdaq index fell by over one-third, but analyst 'sell' recommendations 'held steady at ... 0%.' See Barbara Moses, 'Research Analysts Under Fire,' in ALI-ABA Broker-Dealer Regulation Course of Study (10–11 Jan 2002), quoted in Jill Fisch and Hillary Sale, *The Securities Analyst as Agent: Rethinking the Regulation of Analysts*, 88 Iowa L. Rev. 1035, 1035 (2003). There have been various computations of the 'buy' to 'sell' recommendation ratio during the 1990s, but all suggest an extreme bias towards optimism. See text and notes at nn 67 to 70 below.

7. One estimate, made in mid-2004, is that research departments at broker-dealer firms, have reduced their coverage of public corporations by over 20 percent since the Global Settlement. See Ann Davis, 'Wall Street, Companies It Covers, Agree on Honesty Policy,' Wall Street Journal, March 11, 2004 at C-1, 6.

8. Others have also made this point. See Stephen Choi and Jill Fisch, *How To Fix Wall Street: A Voucher Financing Proposal for Wall Street*, 113 Yale L. J. 269 (2003) (recommending a voucher based system for the funding of analyst research).

9. For a well-argued statement of this view, see John L. Orcutt, *Investor Skepticism v. Investor Confidence: Why the New Research Analyst Reforms Will Harm Investors*, 81 Denv. U.L. Rev. 1 (2003).

10. See Daniel Bradley, Bradford Jordan and Jay Ritter, Analyst Behavior Following IPOs: The 'Bubble Period' Evidence, (Working Paper, October 29, 2004). This paper studied 7,400 analyst recommendations in the year following an IPO for IPOs conducted in 1999–2000. It found little difference in the market reaction to recommendations from affiliated and unaffiliated analysts and hypothesizes that unaffiliated analysts may have the greater conflict because they are seeking to 'curry favor' to attract underwriting business.

11. The term 'independent' as applied to analysts can mean different things to different people. It can include large brokerage firms that lack any investment banking capacity (for example, A. G. Edwards, Edward Jones, or Prudential), or it can mean purely independent research firms, such as Sanford C. Bernstein & Co., Argus Research, or Standard and Poor's. Even in this last category, conflicts can be hypothesized, as for example Sanford Bernstein is owned by Alliance Capital, a money manager, which is in turn controlled by AXA Financial, an insurance company.

12. See Jeffrey C. Hocke, Security Analysis on Wall Street: A Comprehensive Guide to Today's Valuation Methods, at 19 (1998). Since 1998, it is likely that there has been further migration from the 'sell-side' to the 'buy-side' and independent research firms.

13. See 1 above.

14. See Susanne Craig and Ken Brown, 'Though Pay is Down, Elite Stock Analysts Are Hot Commodity,' Wall Street Journal, March 29, 2004 at C1 (citing estimates of compensation expert, Allen Johnson). In 2001, Henry Blodget's compensation topped $8 million, and Jack Grubman's compensation was roughly $20 million a year over his last four years at Citigroup. Ibid. Other sources have placed Grubman's annual compensation as high as $25 million. See Charles Gasparino, 'The Soaring 90s: Behind the Investing Giants and Stocks that Marked a Decade,' Wall Street Journal, Dec. 13, 1999, at C1.

15. See 'CFA a prized certification as Wall Street boosts hiring,' Miami Daily Business Review, July 14, 2004, vol. 79; No. 3; p 5. This level

was up 15 percent from the number enrolling in 2000 before the stock market nosedived. The passing rate on the exam (for all three parts) was 49 percent in 2003. Ibid.

16. Ibid.
17. See statistics cited at n 1 above.
18. For this estimate, see John L. Orcutt, n 9 above, at 8.
19. Orcutt estimates that 'buy-side' analysts cover 30–40 companies. Ibid. at 9.
20. Examples of such research groups are the Gartner Group or Forrester Research.
21. Orcutt, n 9 above, at 12.
22. See Roben Farzad, 'Back to Basics: A Year and a Half After Eliot Spitzer Tried to Clean Up Wall Street Research, The Jury is Still Out on Whether Honest Research Can Pay,' Boston Globe, August 8, 2004 at D1.
23. One estimate provided by Thomson/First Call is that nearly 60 percent of all publicly-traded companies in the U.S. receive no analyst coverage and that overall analyst coverage is down by 35 percent since 2001. See 'Reuters Says Investrend Research Affiliate Fundamental Research Scores With Investors', Financial Wire, July 19, 2004.
24. See Rachel Witmer McTague, 'Unger Says Securities Firms Complied Poorly With Rules Relating to Analysts' Investments,' 33 Sec. Reg & Law 1136, 1138 (August 6, 2001). See also Orcutt n 9 above, at 23.
25. McTague, n 24 above.
26. Ibid.
27. See Jessica Sommar, 'Red-Faced SEC Targets Two-Faced Analysts,' *New York Post*, May 24, 2002 at 41.
28. Merrill Lynch is the leading, but not the only, example. See 'New Merrill Lynch Policy Prohibits Analysts From Buying Shares in Companies They Cover,' *Securities Law Daily*, July 11, 2001.
29. The NYSE requires disclosure of financial positions held by a firm and its analysts in the securities of a recommended issuer, but is satisfied with a broad, conditional boilerplate disclosure that 'the firm and its employees may own securities of a recommended issuer.' See NYSE Rule 472. The NASD requires disclosure of ownership of options, but not common shares. See NASD Rule 2210.
30. In 2003, in response to disclosures suggesting that analysts were trading against their own recommendations and sometimes even receiving direct compensation from issuers for their recommendations, the SEC adopted a new regulation—Regulation Analyst Certification (Regulation AC)—which requires brokers, dealers and certain affiliated personnel to include in research reports a certification by the analyst that the views expressed by the analyst reflected his or her own personal view. See Securities Act Release 33–8193 (Feb. 27, 2003).
31. See Roni Michaely & Kent L. Womack, *Conflict of Interest and the Credibility of Underwriter Analyst Recommendations*, 12 Rev. Fin. Stud. 653 (1999);

Hsiou Wei Lin & Maureen McNichols, *Underwriter Analysts' Earnings Forecasts and Investment Recommendations*, 25 J. Acct. & Econ. 101 (1998).

32. For a review of multiple studies, see Fisch and Sale, n 6 above, at 1048–1049.

33. See 'The Rohrbach Memo: "No Negative Comments,"' Wall Street Journal, July 14, 1992, at A-6. The memorandum went on to insist that this 'no negative comment' rule be incorporated into the firm's Research Compliance Manual.

34. See Bradley, Jordan and Ritter, n 10 above, at 6 (noting that 'firms, such as Sanford Berstein, where little investment banking business is done, still are faced with an important conflict. Institutional investors who are long in a stock … want that analyst to publicly have a "buy" recommendation').

35. As of October 2002, Sanford C. Bernstein & Co., the best known independent research firm, had a 'sell' or 'strong sell' recommendation on only 5.4 percent of the stocks it rated, which was below the 8.1 percent sell and strong percentage for all brokerage firms. See Choi and Fisch, n 8 above, at 284–285.

36. See 'The Collapse of Enron: The Role Analysts Played and the Conflicts They Face: Hearings Before the Senate Committee on Governmental Affairs', 107th Congress, 2d Sess. (Feb. 27, 2002) (prepared testimony of Frank Torres, Legislative Counsel, Consumers' Union). The seventeenth analyst had a 'hold' rating on Enron, and none were suggesting that the stock should be sold. Ibid.

37. See Paul Healy & Krishna Palepu, *The Fall of Enron*, J. Econ. Persp., Spring 2003, at 3 (noting that Enron's stock price was trading at 70 times earnings and six times its book value and seemed overpriced by all standard criteria).

38. The term 'herding' was coined in a 1990 article. See David S. Scharfstein & Jeremy Stein, *Herd Behavior and Investment*, 80 Am. Econ. Rev. 465 (1990).

39. See Harrison Hong et al., *Security Analysts' Career Concerns and the Herding of Earnings Forecasts*, 31 Rand J. Econ. 121, 122–123 (2000); see also Ivo Welch, *Herding Among Security Analysts*, 58 J. Fin. Econ. 369 (2000); Harrison Hong & Jeffrey Kubik, *Analyzing the Analysts: Career Concerns and Biased Earnings Forecasts*, 58 J. Fin. 313, 345 (2003) (optimism more important than accuracy).

40. See AIMR, From Practice to Profession: A History of the Financial Analysts Federation and the Investment Profession (1997) at 8–9.

41. Ibid. at 9–10.

42. Ibid. at 10–11.

43. Ibid. at 9.

44. Ibid. at 7.

45. Ibid. at 7 to 15.

46. Ibid. at 25 and 27–36. Within a year, the name of the organization was changed to the Financial Analysts Federation, which later became the

Association for Investment Management and Research (AIMR) and, ultimately (or at least currently), the CFA Institute.

47. Benjamin Graham and David Dodd, Security Analysis: Principles and Technique (4th edn 1962).

48. See W. A. Patton and A. C. Littleton, An Introduction to Corporate Accounting Standards (1940).

49. See AIMR, n 40 above, at 17 and 41–42.

50. Ibid. at 22, 24.

51. The Securities Act Amendments of 1975 effected this result by adding Section 6(e) to the Securities Exchange Act of 1934, which prohibited an exchange from imposing fixed or minimum brokerage rates on its members. This provision was adopted only after a long and bitter fight between the SEC and the NYSE, which had predicted a parade of horrors if fixed brokerage commissions were ended. See Joel Seligman, The Transformation of Wall Street: A History of the Securities and Exchange Commission and Modern Corporate Finance (3rd ed 2003) at 480–486.

52. Ibid. at 484.

53. Ibid. at 484 to 485. Between 1974 and 1980, aggregate share volume on national securities exchanges more than tripled, and NYSE brokers, which had lost money in 1973 and barely broken even in 1974, became highly profitable for the remainder of the decade. Ibid. at 485.

54. See Kent L. Womack, *Do Brokerage Analysts' Recommendations Have Investment Value?*, 51 J. Fin. 137 (1966).

55. Ibid. at 138.

56. See Orcutt, n 9 above, at 21.

57. See Benjamin Mark Cole, The Pied Pipers of Wall Street: How Analysts Sell You Down the River, 50 (2001).

58. See Seligman, n 51 above, at 485. Much of this revenue shift was the result of new sources of income: options, commodities, money market funds, etc.

59. For example, in 1999, *Institutional Investor* reported that the underwriting revenues of the major firms came to $24.6 billion, while their brokerage revenues amounted to only $9.5 billion. See Carolyn Sargent, 'The 2000 All-American Research Team,' *Institutional Investor*, October 2000, at 72.

60. Benjamin Cole gives the example of NationsBank, which instructed its trust officer not to trade securities through Kidder Peabody, which had issued a sell rating on NationsBank. See Cole, n 57 above, at 81. Thus, even non-clients of the investment banking division of the firm could still cost the firm business in response to a negative report.

61. For some time, the standard underwriting discount in an IPO has been 7%, possibly with some reduction in larger offerings. Underwriters do not, however, compete for deals by offering a lesser discount. See

In re Pub. Offering Fee Antitrust Litig., 2001 U.S. Dist. LEXIS 1380 (S.D.N.Y. February 14, 2001) at *9 (noting that 95% of IPOs between $20 million and $80 million between 1995 and 1997 had a 7% underwriting discount).

62. 463 U.S. 646 (1983).
63. 463 U.S. at 658.
64. Ibid. at 663.
65. See John L. Orcutt, n 9 above, at 26 n 134.
66. See R. Michaely & K. Womack, n 31 above, at 653.
67. See 'Analyzing the Analysts: Are Investors Getting Unbiased Research from Wall Street?: Hearings Before the House Subcomm. on Capital Markets, Insurance, and Government Sponsored Enterprises,' 107th Cong. (June 14, 2001) (opening statement of Congressman Paul E. Kanjorski, Ranking Democratic Member).
68. See Brad Barber, Reuven Lehavy, Maureen McNichols, and Brett Trueman, *Reassessing the Returns to Analysts' Stock Recommendations*, Financial Analysts Journal, Mar./Apr. 2003, 88, at 90. In 2001, the percentages changed again, with 'buy' recommendations falling to 62.1 percent and 'sell' recommendations rising to 3.6 percent, but by this point the bubble had already burst and public attitudes were changing.
69. NASD Rule 2170(d)(2)(B)(i) ('[I]n making a recommendation ... a member must have a reasonable basis for the recommendation.')
70. See Barber, Lehavy, McNichols, and Trueman, n 68 above, at 89.
71. See B. Barber, R. Lehavy, M. McNichols and B. Trueman, *Can Investors Profit from the Prophets? Consensus Analyst Recommendations and Stock Returns*, 56 J. Fin. 531 (2001). Much research has found that analysts tend to err heavily on the side of optimism, overestimating future earnings. See Vijay Kumar Chopra, *Why So Much Error in Analysts' Earnings Forecasts?*, Fin. Analysts J., Nov./Dec. 1998 at 35. Not surprisingly, early research concluded that one could not outperform the market based on analyst research. See Dennis E. Logue & Donald L. Tuttle, *Brokerage House Investment Advice*, 8 Fin. Rev. 38 (1973). This is precisely what efficient market theory would predict, because sell-side research predictions are publicly available and the efficient market incorporates all publicly available information into price. But beginning in the mid-1990s, researchers began to find otherwise: analyst recommendations did affect the future value of the stock and stocks favored by the consensus of analysts thereafter outperformed the market. See Kent L. Womack, *Do Brokerage Analysts' Recommendations Have Investment Value?*, 51 J. Fin. 137 (1996).
72. See Barber, Lehavy, McNichols and Trueman, n 68 above, at 89.
73. Harrison Hong & Jeffrey Kubik, *Analysing the Analysts: Career Concerns and Biased Earnings Forecasts*, 58 J. Fin. 313 (2003).
74. Ibid. at 345.

75. Ibid. at 342 and 346 (finding that between 1996 and 2002, such a bias protected an analyst from downward movement in the profession and that accuracy mattered less during this period).

76. Ibid. at 341.

77. Ibid. at 345–346.

78. Some recent research actually suggests that analysts at firms that had underwriting relationships with the issuer were more accurate forecasters of the firm's future earnings. See Jonathan Clarke, Ajay Khorana, Ajay Patel, and Panambur Raghavendra Rau, *Analyst Behavior at Independent Research Firms, Brokerages, and Investment Banks: Conflicts of Interest or Better Information?* (Working Paper 2004, available on SSRN at Ibid=562181). The simplest explanation for their superior ability to forecast earnings is that they received material nonpublic information.

79. Charles Gasparino, 'Deals & Deal Makers: All Star Analyst Faces Arbitration After Internet Pick Hits the Skids,' Wall Street Journal, 2 March, 2001, at C-18.

80. See Affidavit of Eric Dinallo, Assistant Attorney General of the State of New York, in Support of the Application for an Order Pursuant to New York General Business Law, s 354, (hereinafter, 'Dinallo Affidavit'), at 2.

81. See Dinallo Affidavit at pp 10–13.

82. Ibid. at 11–12.

83. Ibid. at 13. The most repeated comment was to compare the highly rated security with excrement.

84. Ibid. at 3.

85. Ibid.

86. Ibid. at 26.

87. Merrill Lynch neither admitted nor denied the specific charges made against it, but it did issue a public apology to its clients 'for the inappropriate communications brought to light by the New York State Attorney General's investigation.' See Agreement Between the Attorney General of the State of New York and Merrill Lynch, Pierce, Fenner & Smith, Inc. (May 21, 2002) at Exhibit B.

88. The ten firms were (in alphabetical order): Bear Stearns & Co. Inc.; Citigroup Capital Markets Inc. (which had assumed Salomon Smith Barney within it); Credit Suisse First Boston LLC; Goldman, Sachs & Co.; J.P. Morgan Securities, Inc.; Lehman Brothers, Inc.; Merrill Lynch Pierce Fenner & Smith, Inc.; Morgan Stanley & Co., Inc.; UBS Warburg LLC; and U.S. Bancorp Piper Jaffray Inc. Later, Deutsche Bank and Thomas Weisel Partners also joined the settlement in 2004, paying penalties, respectively, of $87.5 million and $12.5 million. See 'Two Firms Pay $100 Million to Settle with the SEC,' *New York Times*, 27 August, 2004, at C-5.

89. See Joint Press Release, Securities and Exchange Commission, New York Attorney General's Office, North American Securities Administrators

Association, National Association of Securities Dealers and New York Stock Exchange, 'Ten of Nation's Top Investment firms Settle Enforcement Actions Involving Conflicts of Interest Between Research and Investment Banking' (April 28, 2003); see also Orcutt, n 9 above, at 32–33.

90. Of this amount, $487.5 million constituted penalties; $387.5 million was paid as disgorgement for investors; $432.5 million was earmarked for independent research; and $80 million was allocated to investor education. See Press Release, n 89 above.

91. In addition to these two strategies, the Global Settlement, and the new NASD and NYSE rules, have also increased disclosure requirements, for example, by mandating that broker-dealers disclose the percentage breakdown of their 'buy,' 'hold' and 'sell' recommendations. See NASD Rule 2711(h)(5); NYSE Rule 472(k). No debate exists as to the desirability of enhanced disclosure.

92. See NASD Rule 2711(b)(1); NYSE Rule 472(b)(1). There is a 'small firm' exception to these rules.

93. See NASD Rule 2711(b)(2); NYSE Rule 472(b)(2).

94. See NASD Rule 2711(d)(1); NYSE Rule 472 (h)(1).

95. This provision is in Section 1.7 to Addendum A to the Final Judgment that embodied the Global Settlement. See *SEC v. Bear Stearns & Co.*, No. 03 Civ. 2937 (S.D.N.Y. 28 April, 2003), available at http://www.sec.gov/litigation/litreleases/judgment18109.htm (hereinafter, 'Final Judgment').

96. See NASD Rule 2711(d)(2); NYSE Rule 472(h)(2).

97. See NASD Rule 2711(c)(4); NYSE Rule 472(b)(5).

98. This provision is in Section I.11.a, b to Addendum A to the Final Judgment. Thus, it applies only to the defendants in the global settlement and not to other underwriters.

99. See NASD Rule 2711(e); NYSE Rule 472(g)(1). Related rules also forbid retaliation by the firm against analysts for unfavorable or negative research or ratings. See NASD Rule 2711(j); NYSE 472(g)(2).

100. See Securities Act Release 33–8193 (Feb. 27, 2003).

101. See Section 1.3 to Addendum A to the Final Judgment.

102. In 1999, the ratio of investment banking revenues to brokerage revenues among major firms was $24.6 billion to $9.5 billion or almost 2.6 to 1. See text and note at n 61 above.

103. See Section III.1 to Addendum A to Final Judgment. The Global Settlement also required each participating investment bank to hire at least three independent analysts.

104. Ibid. at Section III.2, III.3, and III.5.

105. Ibid. at Section III.1(c), III.1(g) and III.4.

106. See Judith Burns, ' "Independent" Stock Research Hasn't Been Must-See,' Wall Street Journal, November 26, 2005 at 13–3. For example, the independent research website maintained by Credit Suisse First Boston has had 10,000 'hits,' but only 110 were from retail customers—suggesting that a firm's brokers may consult this

research, but not retail investors. Similarly, Lehman Brothers' found that less than 1 percent of the hits to its website were for independent research.

107. Ibid. (quoting Lehman Brothers' independent consultant that 'usage by the expected prime beneficiaries, individual investors' was less than anticipated).

108. See Roni Michaely & Kent Womack, *Conflict of Interest and the Credibility of Underwriter Analyst Recommendations*, 12 The Rev. of Fin. Stud. 653 (1999) (IPO stocks recommended by an unaffiliated analyst increase on average 4.4 percent, while stocks recommended by an analyst working for the lead underwriter increase on average only 2.7%). This same pattern was also found to prevail in 'follow-on' equity offerings. See Hsiou-wei Lin & Maureen F. McNichols, *Underwriting Relationships, Analysts' Earnings Forecasts and Investment Recommendations*, 25 J. Acct. & Econ. 101 (1998).

109. See Clarke, Khorana, Patel and Rau, n 78, at 24. Their conclusion may slightly overstate what their data showed. They did find that analysts at independent research firms issued a smaller percentage of Buy and Strong Buy recommendations and that market reactions to upgrades and downgrades were more pronounced in the case of such independent analysts. Ibid.

110. See Bradley, Jordan and Ritter, n 10.

111. See Karen Richardson, Peter McKay and Serena Ng, 'Street Sleuth: Desperately Seeking Research,' Wall Street Journal, September 19, 2005 at C-1.

112. In October 2002, Sanford C. Bernstein & Co., the best known of the independent research houses, had 'sell' or 'strong sell' recommendations on just 5.4 percent of the stocks it rated, which compared with an 8.1 percent 'sell' and 'strong sell' percentage for all firms. See Choi and Fisch, n 8, at 284–285.

113. See Richardson, McKay and Ng, n 111 above, at C-1.

114. See text and notes at nn 68 to 69.

115. See 'Settlement fuels extra "sell" advice,' *Chicago Tribune*, 18 May, 2003 at C-9. Not only are fewer companies covered, but the individual analyst may also be required to cover more companies—and thus engage in a less intense and more cursory style of research. In short, there are hard-to-quantify effects, both in terms of the amount of research and the quality of research.

116. One estimate in mid-2004 was that research departments have reduced their coverage of corporations by over 20 percent since the Global Settlement. See Ann Davis, 'Wall Street, Companies It Covers, Agree on Honesty Policy,' Wall Street Journal, March 11, 2004 at C-1, C-6.

117. See text and notes at nn 22 to 23 above.

118. This practice of 'issuer-paid' research appears to have accelerated since the global settlement, both because Wall Street research departments

have cut back on coverage and because laid-off analysts are eager to prepare research reports on a freelance basis. See Davis, n 7, at C-6.

119. Ibid. These 'best practices' guidelines do not have the force of law and have not been approved (or disapproved) by the SEC or the NASD.

120. However, their guidelines do permit a factual review by the issuer, and only a slippery slope separates such a review from an analyst/issuer negotiation over the rating and recommendation.

121. Two leading examples are the National Research Exchange ('NRE'), formed in 2005 by the former CEO and chief operating officer of Nasdaq, and the Independent Research Exchange, formed somewhat later in 2005 as a joint venture between Nasdaq and Reuters. The NRE has a more ambitious agenda, because it also requires the issuer to agree to a code of conduct under which it will not retaliate or exclude analysts who publish unfavorable research. This author is a director of NRE.

122. 'Intermediated research' faces major obstacles in gaining acceptance from the regulators. Under the Global Settlement, the SEC, NASD and other regulators have prohibited the participating underwriters from receiving 'issuer paid' compensation on behalf of their analysts. At present, these regulators have been unwilling to recognize that 'intermediated research' is different from 'issuer paid' research. As a result, analysts who wish to be hired by the independent consultants under the global settlement cannot receive revenue from the 'marriage broker' for research. Although the regulators could certainly specify criteria for recognizing 'intermediated research,' this across-the-board refusal to recognize that 'intermediated research' is different from 'issuer paid' research seems myopic. Although still evolving, 'intermediated research' seems more part of the answer than part of the problem.

123. This computation, based on 2004 data, was performed by Investars, a research firm that has assisted Attorney General Spitzer in investigating securities rating data. It found that the ten underwriting firms participating in the 2003 Global Settlement collectively had the above 6:1 ratio in the case of 'large cap stocks' (defined as companies with a market cap of over \$8.5 billion), but only 2.4 to 1 in the case of small cap issuers (defined as companies with a market cap of under \$1.5 billion). This disparity may be even more pronounced in the case of smaller brokerage firms.

8

The Ratings Agencies

Introduction

Ratings are a fact of life in modern society where non-specialists want complex information distilled by experts into easy-to-use symbols and rankings. Even outside the financial sector, ratings are a major commercial activity: U.S. News and World Report finds it highly profitable to rank colleges and universities; Underwriters Laboratories has tested and rated consumer appliances for safety since the early 20th century.[1] Often, these ratings are highly subjective (such as Michelin's restaurant ratings, Robert Parker's wine ratings, or Siskel and Ebert's movie reviews); other times, the rankings are based on the collective preferences of a substantial number of raters (e.g. Hollywood's Oscars or Zagat's restaurant ratings). Informational intermediaries supply ratings to the markets for such information, based either on (a) their superior access to information or expertise in its analysis, or (b) their ability to predict the market's own taste or preferences through the collective judgment of the many raters that they use.

Within the financial sector, numerous ratings services exist. Morningstar Inc. uses a 'star' rating system of from one to five stars to rate mutual funds.[2] Security analysts rank companies within an industry, which assessments are collected and publicly aggregated by Thomson First Call. Analysts are themselves rated each year by several services, with the best-known survey being Institutional Investor magazine's 'Annual All-America Team.'[3]

Unique among ratings organizations, however, are the credit-rating agencies. Their clout is legendary. New York Times columnist Thomas L. Friedman overstated only marginally when he declared:

There are two superpowers in the world today in my opinion. There's the United States and there's Moody's Bond Rating Service. The United States can destroy you by dropping bombs, and Moody's can destroy you by downgrading your bonds. And believe me, it's not clear sometimes who's more powerful.[4]

Since at least 1909 (when Moody's first published its bond ratings), credit-rating agencies have provided extremely standardized and condensed information about the creditworthiness of bonds, distilled into an alphabetical symbol. This condensation of highly nuanced information into a single symbol makes ratings easily comprehensible to even the dullest user and enables markets to respond quickly and, more or less, uniformly to changes in ratings (e.g. upgrades or downgrades). Although rating terminology varies somewhat with each agency, the ratings agencies in common rate long-term debt from AAA (the highest category) down to D, with ratings below BBB-being deemed 'non-investment grade'—a characterization that carries serious legal consequences because it will likely restrict the ability of many institutional investors to buy or hold such a debt security.[5] Even within the universe of investment-grade securities, a rating downgrade or upgrade is likely to dramatically affect the issuer's cost of capital.

The market for credit ratings is distinctive from other markets for information in three critical respects.

1 Concentration   Even the market for auditing services (dominated as it is by the Big Four) looks open and competitive in comparison to the market for credit ratings. Since early in the 20th century, credit ratings have been dominated by a duopoly—Moody's Investors Services, Inc. (Moody's) and Standard & Poor's Ratings Services (Standard & Poor's). Each is highly profitable, earning a consistently high rate of return that seems incompatible with a competitive market.[6] Only recently has a third firm—Fitch Investor Service, Inc.—been able to develop a toehold in some specialized submarkets.[7] One recent estimate placed Standard & Poor's market share in 2001 at 41 percent; Moody's at 38 percent; and Fitch at 14 percent.[8] But this may understate the dominance of Moody's and S & P in the U.S. market, because Fitch is most active in some highly specialized and international markets.

This level of concentration suggests that high natural barriers exist to entry into this market. Logic suggests that there should be a significant barrier, because reputational capital cannot be acquired overnight. Indeed, some view Moody's and S & P as the functional equivalents of the Educational Testing Service, which designs and administers the SATs and similar tests used by college admissions officers and which never has received significant competition—in short, a natural monopoly.[9] Still, an alternative theory may better explain the modern domination of the Moody's and S & P duopoly: as will be seen, the SEC has erected a high barrier that has discouraged entry into this market for at least 30 years. It has done so by entitling selected ratings agencies (but only a few) to confer de facto dispensations to issuers from various regulatory requirements if the issuer receives a high or 'investment grade' rating from the ratings agency. While the SEC understandably fears fly-by-night credit-rating agencies and a race to the bottom, its attempt to exclude new entrants has arguably resulted in a government-created duopoly—one that may be more an artificial than a natural monopoly. Much depends on whether one views credit-rating agencies as enjoying a natural or an artificial monopoly; indeed, policy prescriptions logically flow from this starting point.

From a public policy perspective, this lack of competition is important, not for the traditional reason that it permits the oligopolists to charge inflated prices to their customers (here, corporate and municipal debt issuers), but for a different reason: it permits these nominal competitors to shirk, engaging in less effort and research than if there were true active competition. Indeed, the principal recent criticism of credit-rating agencies has been that they have been reactive, rather than proactive, belatedly responding to negative information that has been publicly released, but seldom anticipating any serious decline.[10] Surveys show that participants in this market consider ratings changes to be sluggish, often inaccurate, and seldom made to 'favor the interests of investors.'[11]

Enron and WorldCom both illustrate this sluggish response, as the two major agencies downgraded each corporation to below investment grade status only a few days to a few weeks, respectively, before each declared bankruptcy. This pattern in which a ratings downgrade resembles more an obituary than a prophecy again suggests the absence of real competition. Rationally, the nominal competitors may prefer to enjoy the quiet life and not invest in the personnel or monitoring necessary to detect financial decline before it becomes public knowledge.

If some evidence fits this profile, other evidence suggests that the credit-ratings agencies are highly sensitive to the danger of reputational damage and have aggressively sought to preserve their reputational capital. In fact, the credit-rating agencies have in recent years significantly expanded their ratings personnel, in part to detect credit deterioration.[12] Moreover, even if Moody's and Standard & Poor's share a duopoly in the United States market, they compete aggressively in the global market, where they face numerous competitors and where their position is not nearly as entrenched. Finally, before one concludes that credit-rating agencies have shirked, one must recognize that the scope of operations of a major credit-rating agency vastly exceeds that of the typical securities research department of a brokerage firm (which at most covers a few thousand stocks). In contrast, in 2003, Moody's monitored over 85,000 corporate and governmental issuers.[13] Hence, constant updating of debt ratings on outstanding debt securities may not be as feasible in this larger context.

Nonetheless, after all these points are acknowledged, considerable evidence does support the charge that the principal credit-rating agencies typically respond slowly to signs of financial danger. The reasons for their sluggish pace are complex (for example, the agency may often fear that if it downgrades an issuer's credit, this downgrade will, itself, cause bankruptcy because of the 'trigger' clauses common in many bond indentures that turn a downgrade below investment grade status into an event of default). But this slow response pattern underscores the questionable social policy inherent in the SEC's long-standing refusal to open up this market to competition. Logically, active competition among credit raters should lead to a quicker response to the signs of credit deterioration.

2 *Conflicts of Interest*   Michelin and Zagat sell their restaurant ratings to the retail customers who buy their guides; Institutional Investor and U.S. News and World Report profit from their rankings through increased revenues from subscribers and advertisers. Even securities analysts do not generally accept direct payment for their ratings from the issuers that they rate. But credit-rating agencies do. Approximately 90 to 95 percent of the credit-rating agencies' annual revenues comes from issuer fees.[14] Obviously, this heavy dependence on issuer fees gives rise to a fundamental conflict that logically could lead to ratings inflation.

Still, credit-rating agencies have long policied this conflict by adopting a number of policies that minimize the incentive to go easy on one's paying clients. For example, the fees paid by the issuer to the agency are usually fixed at two to three basis points of the amount of the bond offering, thereby precluding any low-visibility exchange of above-market fees for inflated ratings.[15] In addition, the market, itself, imposes further important restraints. Issuers do not seek the rating of only one agency, but typically feel compelled to seek the ratings of both Moody's and Standard & Poor's.[16] Because of this well-established norm that two ratings are necessary, issuers cannot play one agency against the other, and the principal two credit-rating agencies probably feel little, if any, pressure to inflate ratings for a client for a fear that it will instead hire their rival. Although this nearly uniform practice eliminates the danger of a race to the bottom, it also reduces active competition between the principal two agencies and instead allows them to enjoy the advantages of the quiet life. Finally, the credit analysts who are employed by the principal credit rating agencies rate many issuers and do not receive incentive-based compensation. Hence, they are less subject to 'client capture' than are the audit partners of a major accounting firm who often serve (and are thus dependent upon) only a single client.[17]

Even if the conflicts inherent in having the issuer pay for its rating have been adequately monitored to date, this issue remains open for the future. Much like accounting firms, the credit-rating agencies began to receive significant additional revenue from issuers for ancillary or consulting services beginning in the 1990s.[18] With such revenues comes the possibility that the issuer can increase or decrease its fees to the extent that it is satisfied or dissatisfied with its rating.

3 The Role of the Rater: Reputational Intermediary or Dispensation Giver   In a simple world, the role of ratings is simply to provide information. But the real world is more complex. Although creditors and trading partners certainly need information about the creditworthiness of prospective borrowers and counterparties, ratings may do much more than simply provide information. Sometimes, ratings create value for their customers and users. For example, the value of the Michelin 'three star' rating may be to convey a cachet to both the restaurant owner and its customers that they could not gain in the absence of such a ranking. Alternatively, a rating may protect the manufacturer of the rated product from tort liability (this was a major reason why Underwriter Laboratories' ratings of consumer appliances became popular). Or, a rating may immunize from liability the fiduciaries who make investment decisions if an investment later sours (this was an early impact of the 'investment grade' rating given by credit-rating agencies). In these cases, the informational role of ratings may become secondary to their legal impact, which is to insulate users from liability and reduce their regulatory costs.

Another key feature of the debt-rating agency is its ability to assure the confidential communication of sensitive information. To minimize its cost of capital, the debt issuer has an incentive to disclose information that shows the superior quality of its debt securities. It can do this by (a) disseminating information to the world at large; or (b) sharing confidential information that may be proprietary and non-public with a third party (the credit-rating agency) who can evaluate and verify its disclosures without revealing non-public information to the world (or, most importantly, to the firm's competitors).[19] From this perspective, bond ratings are a signal that spares above-average quality issuers from having either to bear inefficiently the cost of 'average quality pricing'[20] or to disclose proprietary information that they wished to keep non-public. Partly for this reason, credit-ratings agencies are exempted from Regulation FD, which bars selective disclosure.[21] Thus, issuers can disclose information and forecasts in confidence to credit-ratings agencies, but they cannot selectively disclose the same information to securities analysts. From this perspective, the issuer uses the reputational intermediary to send a credible signal that its securities are of above average quality in order that it can pay a below average interest rate. This technique works, of course, only if the intermediary has sufficient reputational capital to be trusted by investors.

Although the foregoing 'reputational intermediary' model has long been the dominant view of the credit-rating process, it is being contested by an alternative model of the role played by such agencies. This alternative model focuses on the regulatory consequences of ratings and the non-informational needs of both investors and issuers. These non-informational benefits of a credit rating enable the rating agency to confer a 'regulatory license' on its customers either because: (a) a rating enables issuers to escape costly regulatory burdens or prohibitions to which they would otherwise be subject;[22] or (b) portfolio managers and institutional investors gain legal protection by virtue of such a credit-rating, because it insulates them from potential claims that they breached their fiduciary duties to investors in buying or holding the security (if the investment later sours or defaults).

The core idea behind this alternative 'regulatory license' model is that regulation imposes costs which a favorable rating can reduce. To the extent that a rating reduces the issuer's costs or the costs of financial intermediaries, then rating agencies can sell 'regulatory licenses' to enable such persons to avoid these costs. Such sales of regulatory licenses need not be based on trust or reliance on the rating agency (as the 'reputational intermediary' model assumes), but only on the short-term cost savings realizable. As a result, the rating agency has less need to invest in or protect its reputational capital—at least so long as it does not jeopardize its ability to issue regulatory licenses.

A prerequisite to the 'regulatory license' model's applicability is that the Government vary the level of regulation based on the credit rating applicable to the securities being sold. In the early days of credit ratings, regulators did not do this, and indeed they paid little attention to them. But this began to change in the 1930s. The first regulator to take notice of credit ratings was the Federal Reserve System, which, beginning in 1930, implemented a system for evaluating a bank's entire portfolio based on the credit ratings on the bonds in that portfolio.[23] In 1931, the United States Treasury Department accepted credit ratings as the best measure of the quality of a national bank's bond portfolio.[24] Specifically, bonds below a specified investment grade were required to be written down on the balance sheet of a national bank, but bonds with a higher rating could be carried at cost. New Deal banking legislation later limited the ability of national banks to buy bonds that did not comply with criteria promulgated by the Comptroller of the Currency,[25] and in 1936 the Comptroller required that bonds purchased by national banks be rated as of investment grade 'by not less than two ratings manuals.'[26] At a stroke, this regulatory action arguably granted Moody's and Standard & Poor's a license to coin money, because banks had to use both of them, thereby reducing their need to compete. State banking regulators soon adopted similar rules. As a result, banks needed ratings on their bonds, not for information or investment decision-making, but to satisfy regulators.

The next major use of credit ratings by regulators came in 1973, when the SEC revised Rule 15c3–1, its 'net capital' rule for broker dealers, to explicitly incorporate credit ratings—but only those ratings promulgated by what it defined as 'Nationally Recognized Statistical Ratings Organizations' (or NRSROs).[27] Much like earlier federal banking regulation, the SEC's 'net capital' rule required mandatory write-downs (or 'haircuts' in the parlance) on the broker's balance sheet for securities that it owned, which were deemed risky or speculative. Rather than elaborately define the various levels of risk and the criteria that determined them, the SEC instead found it much simpler (and probably more accurate) to rely on the credit ratings on the debt securities held by the broker-dealers. By mandating that the higher the credit rating, the less the writedown that the broker-dealer had to place on the bond, Rule 15c3–1 strongly encouraged broker-dealers to invest in rated bonds.

Still, the SEC realized that if it stopped at this point and only required a credit rating from some recognized rater, new raters would come out of the woodwork overnight. Fearing the proverbial 'race to the bottom', the SEC decided to recognize only the credit ratings issued by the major credit-rating agencies that pre-existed its new rule. To this end, it defined the term 'Nationally Recognized Statistical Ratings Organizations' (or NRSROs) so as deliberately to exclude start-ups and fly-by-night small firms that lacked reputational capital. Only credit-rating agencies that had long been recognized were permitted to give the now required ratings. But in so doing, the SEC effectively gave Moody's and Standard & Poor's a monopoly on the issuance of 'regulatory licenses' to broker-dealers.

Once the concept of NRSRO became established, it was quickly adopted for a variety of other regulatory purposes. For example, in the early 1980s, the SEC began to regulate the new field of money market funds, and it modified Rule 2a-7 under the Investment Company Act of 1940.[28] That rule limited money market funds to investments in 'Eligible Securities,' which term was defined to mean securities given a high rating by at least two NRSROs (or by the only NRSRO that rated the security). In 1991, the SEC further revised this rule to provide essentially that a money market fund could invest no more than five percent of its assets in unrated commercial paper (and no more than one percent in any single unrated issuer of commercial paper).[29] Because money market funds invested heavily in commercial paper, they were forced to redirect their investments to the commercial paper of issuers who had NRSRO ratings—thereby reinforcing the duopoly of Moody's and Standard & Poor's.

Not only were institutional investors forced to use NRSRO agencies, but issuers were as well. In the early 1980s, the SEC introduced an important deregulatory system known as 'shelf-registration,' which permitted qualified corporate issuers to register significant amounts of securities in advance of any specific contemplated offering.[30] This liberalization conferred speed and significant cost savings on those issuers who qualified for shelf registration, because it gave these issuers control over the timing of their public securities offerings. No longer did they have to wait out an uncertain period until the SEC declared the registration statement covering their securities 'effective.' Eligibility to use shelf registration was limited by the SEC to issuers of high-quality debt. In determining what debt securities qualified for shelf registration, the SEC predictably followed the course of least resistance and made eligible any issuer that had obtained an 'investment grade' credit rating from an NRSRO credit-rating agency.

The insurance industry has similarly piggybacked on the NRSRO concept. The National Association of Insurance Commissioners (NAIC) maintains a Securities Valuation Office (SVO), which monitors the financial condition of insurers, principally by reviewing the credit quality of their investments.[31] The NAIC relies heavily on NRSRO credit ratings and thus effectively penalizes insurance companies that invest in low-rated or—even worse—unrated debt.[32]

Small wonder then that NRSRO designation has become critical. Whatever the category of institutional investor—federal or state bank, mutual fund, broker-dealer, or insurance company—its capital structure is understandably regulated to assure financial solvency. But across a broad range of contexts, state and federal regulators have found it simpler to delegate the task of risk assessment to the NRSRO credit-rating agencies. Moreover, on the global level, international bank regulators appear have followed this same well-traveled path at least part way, as the new Basle Accords for regulating bank solvency place considerable weight on the credit ratings applicable to each bank's investments.[33] Potentially, credit-rating agencies may thus acquire a worldwide license to reduce the regulatory costs of banks.

Obviously, this common policy made it very attractive to become an NRSRO agency. Over the years, a number of small and start-up credit-rating agencies have applied to the SEC for admission to this exclusive club, but only a few gained admission. Unsuccessful applicants described the process as ensnaring them in a 'Catch-22' dilemma: they could not get the NRSRO designation until they were 'nationally recognized,' and they could not become 'nationally recognized' until they received the NRSRO designation that gave legal effect to their ratings.[34] One unsuccessful applicant for NRSRO status reported that throughout its failed effort it was contacted only twice by the SEC: once in 1992 to acknowledge receipt of its application, and again in 2000 to reject it.[35] Lace Financial has been seeking to gain admission for 13 years, and Egan-Jones Ratings Co. since 1998.[36]

All told, the SEC did grant NRSRO status to four applicants between 1980 and 2000—only to see each of them quickly acquired by the original three NRSROs.[37] As a result, in 2003 when the Sarbanes-Oxley Act required the SEC to report to Congress on the responsibility of credit-rating agencies for Enron and similar financial debacles, the SEC had to face the hard truth that only the original three NRSROs remained.[38] Faced with growing criticism from both academics and practitioners about its parsimonious attitude toward recognizing NRSROs, the SEC responded by granting NRSRO status later in 2003 to Dominion Bond Rating Service Ltd., a Canadian firm,[39] and in 2005, it has indicated that it will also recognize A. M. Best Co., a specialized rater of insurance firms. But little else has changed: the level of concentration in the credit-agency market continues to imply oligopoly.

Did the SEC cause this de facto oligopoly in the credit-rating market? Or, was it inevitable? On this issue, even the U.S. Government has divided. In 1997, when the SEC proposed a more formalized rule to govern the recognition of NRSROs, the U.S. Department of Justice objected to the SEC's proposed rule, because it continued to rely on the NRSRO designation.[40] In Justice's view, the SEC's proposed requirement that a credit-rating agency must have achieved 'national recognition' before its ratings would qualify to trigger any of the exemptions under the SEC's rules created a 'nearly insurmountable barrier to new entry into the market for NRSRO services.'[41] In the face of this and other criticism, the SEC never adopted its proposed rule—but it still persisted in using the same informal practice that put primary emphasis on 'national recognition.'

Probably the most telling evidence that the extremely concentrated character of the credit-rating market in the United States is not the product of a natural monopoly is the existence, outside the United States, of as many as 130 to 150 rating agencies, all currently operating.[42] That a sufficient demand exists in the world market for credit information to support this large a number of producers undermines the claim that a natural monopoly exists. One reason for this diversity of firms is that they may cater to different investor needs. For example, one team of researchers has recently concluded that non-NRSRO credit research primarily seeks to inform the valuation process, while the ratings of NRSRO credit agencies are almost exclusively focused on the risk of future default.[43] Similarly, the persistence of a 'two ratings' norm, both domestically and internationally, indicates that users want more than simply a 'regulatory license.' After all, an issuer seeking only a 'regulatory license' would be content with a single rating; thus, only the 'reputational intermediary' model can account for this insistence on two ratings by credit information users.

In any event, the key policy question is whether the government should keep the barriers to entry into this market high in order to preclude fly-by-night credit raters or instead open up the field to competition by relaxing the criteria for an NRSRO designation. This issue turns on what one thinks competition would produce.

History: The Rise and Record of Credit-Rating Agencies

Historically, the modern credit-rating agency can be traced back to earlier mercantile credit agencies that principally served suppliers and other business and trade creditors. The earliest of these in the United States, The Mercantile Agency, was formed in 1841, following a market crash in 1837 that had shown businessmen the need for better credit information.[44] Other firms followed in its wake, including R. G. Dun and Company, which was organized in 1859 to promote the Dun rating book, which contained some 20,000 listings.[45] Eventually, Dun merged with its leading competitor to form Dun and Bradstreet, Inc., long the dominant mercantile credit firm, which until 2001 owned Moody's. These early firms corresponded with merchants and business people to acquire opinions about the reputations and standing of business owners across the country.[46] Such information may have been anecdotal and speculative, but merchants eagerly bought these services because it was the best information available.

In 1860, Henry Varnum Poor published the first edition of his History of Railroads and Canals of the United States. Unlike the mercantile credit agencies, he focused on the leading issuers of debt securities: railroads and canals. His business model was also different: to sell data to purchasers of his book, thereby making his information public, rather than advising commercial clients on a confidential basis. In due course, competitors arose, and one of these, the Standard Statistics Bureau was formed in 1906, also to publish financial data that had previously been unavailable or confidential. Eventually, in 1941, Poor's Publishing Company and the Standard Statistics Bureau merged to form Standard & Poor's Corporation, which in 1966 was in turn acquired by the McGraw-Hill Companies, Inc., also a major publisher specializing in business publications.[47]

During the late 19th century, these two industries—the mercantile credit agencies and the debt manual publishers—co-existed, never quite converging, each serving a different client base. The next major innovation came from a relative outsider, John Moody, who first published his Moody's Manual of Industrial and Miscellaneous Securities in 1900. Although Moody's firm failed during the stock market crash in 1907, John Moody returned to Wall Street in 1909 with a new and improved product: Moody's Analysis of Railroad Investments. First published in that year, this volume not only collected data, but also analyzed railroad securities, using a consistent methodology, and then condensed that analysis into a single rating symbol. Such letter grades had earlier been used by the mercantile agencies, but they had not been previously applied to outstanding debt securities.[48]

Simplicity sold, and Moody's rating system was an instant hit with investors. Moody quickly expanded his scope of operations to include industrial corporations in 1913 and municipal bonds in 1914. By 1924, Moody's ratings were available with respect to nearly every publicly traded bond in the U.S. bond market.

Success attracted competition, and soon Standard Statistics and later Poor's Publishing, the two precursors of S & P, also began to give debt ratings to corporate bonds. By 1940, Standard Statistics also was rating municipal bonds. The third significant entrant into this market, The Fitch Publishing Company, began publishing ratings in 1924.[49] Only one other significant entrant, Duff and Phelps Credit Rating Co., entered this field, and it confined itself to public utility companies from 1932 until 1982 (when it expanded its coverage to include other public companies). Never a significant player in the broader public markets, Duff and Phelps eventually merged into Fitch. Ultimately, Fitch became the buyer of last resort for several new entrants that tried and failed to crack the Moody's/S & P duopoly.[50]

Despite these failures, it is difficult to believe that there were high barriers to entry into the credit-rating market during the first half of the 20th century. Over this period, the paucity of competitors may have been more the product of the common perception that the market was simply too small to justify the start-up costs incident to covering the large universe of publicly-held bonds. In their early years, the bond rating agencies drew their revenue exclusively from subscribers, not from issuers. Not only did issuers not pay them, but some resisted the rating process regarding it as an 'intrusion.' Ultimately, however, resistance proved futile. In response to a low rating, the issuer had no practical recourse other than to cooperate and provide additional data to the rating agency in the hopes that it would lead the agency to upgrade its rating.

The reliance placed on bond ratings varied with the client. During the 1920s, large banks, having their own internal credit analysts, seem to have made only marginal use of them, but smaller banks and trust companies depended on them.[51] In part, this was because judicial decisions, dating back to 1897, had protected trustees and other fiduciaries who had purchased bonds recommended by established bond manuals, such as Poor's Manual.[52] These cases essentially found that fiduciaries who consulted the recognized bond manuals (Poor's or Moody's) and purchased investment-grade, non-speculative securities were not liable to their beneficiaries for a lack of due care if the bonds later defaulted. As a result, to trustees and other fiduciaries, ratings not only carried valuable information, but they also conveyed a degree of immunity. By the 1920s, trust indentures sometimes explicitly limited the trustees' investment discretion so that they could only purchase bonds rated as of 'investment grade.'

Traders also came to value ratings, because they began to observe that any change in a rating implied a subsequent price change in the value of the bond rated.[53] In effect, even if the rating agency lacked any non-public information, its upgrade or downgrade became a self-fulfilling prophecy which traders could not ignore in a market where little public information existed.

The value and prestige associated with a high bond rating probably peaked in the 1930s, when an escalating series of bond defaults during the Depression forced investment managers to become preoccupied with the risk of default. In contrast, during the 1940s and 1950s, this pattern reversed itself. The economy prospered, bond defaults decreased, and overall bond volatility also declined. Correspondingly, however, as volatility declined, the utility of bond ratings to investment managers also fell. In consequence, the bond-rating agencies experienced a period of contraction during the post-war era.

Although bond volatility increased again during the 1970s, the relevance of bond ratings had by now come under attack. Institutional investors and other buy-side investors grew exponentially in size during the 1970s, and, as they did so, they began to internalize their own credit analysis staff. These staff typically produced more sophisticated research than a simple bond rating. Academic studies also challenged whether bond ratings (and particularly changes in bond ratings) provided new information of material value. One such study, covering corporate bond rating changes between 1950 and 1972, concluded that such changes merely reflected information that had already been incorporated into the stock market prices of the same issuers.[54] Indeed, it found a lag time of approximately one and a-half years between the public release of the information and the rating change. So viewed, the ratings provided by the credit-rating agencies had little informational value (and were purchased mainly for the legal protection they gave banks and trustees).

What explains this quick reversal between the high prestige of bond ratings in the 1920s and 1930s and their reduced prestige in the 1970s? The most plausible explanation is that the passage of the federal securities laws in the 1930s greatly deepened the informational resources available to the market about the creditworthiness of bonds. By the 1970s, the credit analyst at a bank, insurance company or other institutional investor had available to him or her the same information that in the 1920s had been made available only privately to the credit-rating agency. As a result, the agency's rating largely duplicated what a more sophisticated market already knew. Not surprisingly then, rating agencies during the 1960s and 1970s entered a period of austerity and experienced little growth.

In response to this contraction, the ratings agencies in the 1970s collectively changed their basic business model. Instead of relying exclusively on revenue from subscribers (as they had in the past), they began to charge issuers for rating their debt securities. Although this change gave rise to an obvious conflict of interest problem, it made sound economic sense, because it solved the 'free rider' problem that the industry had long faced. Information (including ratings) has the character of a public good; inevitably, information leaks from the subscriber who has paid for it to others who have not. The inability to tax these latter 'free riders' implies that the bond rating agency cannot compel all who benefited from its services to pay for the value conferred on them. But, by requiring the issuer to pay for its rating, the industry could effectively tax all users of its ratings, because the issuer could pass on the cost of the rating to the bond purchasers in the form of a slightly lower interest rate. Thus, the free rider was at last taxed its fair share of the rating agency's cost.

This transition did, however, force the bond rating industry to face the claim that increased public regulation and oversight were necessary in view of these new conflicts of interest. In response, the industry made two valid points: (1) because its members typically charged fees based on a formula (for example, two or three hundreds of a percent of the debt issue rated), they had little incentive to inflate their fees for so modest an amount (at least when their reputational capital was also at stake); and (2) because most issuers faced great pressure from investors to obtain ratings from both Moody's and S & P, there was little likelihood of any race to the bottom under which one competitor would inflate its rating in return for a higher fee. That is, if the market wanted the ratings of both firms, neither would be excluded if the other underbid it.

These two arguments remain generally valid, but they still overlook some conflict problems that have in fact arisen. For example, on very large debt offerings, even a two-or three-basis point fee can be significant and thus the rating agency might be tempted to inflate its rating (at least if it feared being excluded from the ratings process).[55] Another problematic practice that developed was the use of unsolicited ratings. Critics have charged that Moody's used the practice of giving unsolicited ratings to issuers to coerce them into hiring it.[56] That is, if Moody's gave a deliberately low rating to an issuer that had not hired it, that issuer might reconsider its decision to forego a Moody's rating—particularly if it sensed that by hiring Moody's, it would obtain a higher rating. Much criticized for this policy, Moody's has largely retreated from this practice and now gives unsolicited ratings only in the case of high-yield junk bonds.[57] This suggests that, for all their oligopolistic power, credit-rating agencies do remain sensitive to any loss of reputational capital.

While credit-rating agencies stagnated or contracted in the 1960s and 1970s, they rebounded dramatically in the 1980s and 1990s, doubling and tripling their staff over this period. A major reason for this expansion was the growth of structured finance. These new transactions—basically asset securitizations—were ratings driven; that is, their architects aimed to achieve a high rating for the special purpose entity created to issue the debt. As a practical matter, such transactions did not go forward unless the desired high rating was achieved.[58] Because they were complex transactions, the ratings agencies' fees on them were also typically higher.

The idea that these transactions require a specified rating before they can be accomplished (i.e. that they are 'ratings-driven') has offended some critics who see this as a sign that the ratings are contrived.[59] But the real, underlying issue here is the accuracy of these ratings. Critics point to a series of well-known crises in which the rating agencies failed to predict insolvency, beginning with the bankruptcy of Penn Central in 1970, and extending to the insolvency of Orange County in the 1980s, the Asian financial crisis that crested in 1997, and finally the Enron, WorldCom and related bankruptcies in 2001–2002. In response to this criticism, the industry asserts that few investment-grade rated bonds ever default: Moody's in fact has not experienced such a default since Johns Manville, a single A-rated company, filed for bankruptcy in 1982, and S & P has had only one such default on its investment grade debt over the same period (in 1989).[60] But this response will satisfy only the truly naïve, because it ignores the tendency (as in Enron) for ratings agencies to downgrade an issuer's debt to below investment-grade status only days before a default occurs. It is as if a doctor claimed that none of his patients had ever died, without disclosing that he usually resigned when they became seriously ill. Default statistics are thus as cooked as Enron's books.

A better measure of ratings accuracy may be ratings' stability. Here, Standard & Poor's asserts, based on an analysis of 9,169 companies whose debt it has rated, that its ratings are highly stable. For example, all its A-rated companies at the beginning of a given year have a 87.94 percent likelihood of maintaining that same rating at year's end.[61] Again, however, a methodological problem lurks here. That ratings are stable may be the problem, not the answer, in a volatile world. The standard criticism of rating agencies is that rating changes tend to lag well behind public disclosures that indicate credit deterioration. If so, demonstrating that ratings are stable does not demonstrate that they are accurate or timely.

As an alternative, some critics argue that the better measure of relative creditworthiness is credit spreads, not credit ratings.[62] In particular, Professor Frank Partnoy argues that NRSRO rating requirements in federal banking and securities regulation should be junked, and instead creditworthiness tests should be framed in terms of credit spreads. But, while provocative, his trenchant views have not yet attracted any consensus of support, and many academics believe that investment grade ratings for corporate securities remain reliable.[63] The question of whether other measures can outperform ratings has only a marginal relevance to the public policy debate, because literally no one has suggested that ratings agencies should be prohibited from publishing ratings. Still, if other measures of risk, such as credit spreads, work better than the credit agencies' subjective ratings, that probably is a reason to drop or relax the NRSRO requirement and encourage greater competition. In any event, the critical public policy question is: What government-initiated reforms might produce more timely updating of credit ratings? What levers can the government pull?

Scenarios for Reform: What Might Work?

Essentially, four basic policy options seem plausible:

(i) public policy could rely on increased competition (and thus the SEC could either abandon or liberalize its now highly exclusive NRSRO designation);

(ii) public policy could seek to impose greater liability on the credit-rating agencies, hoping thereby to cause them to update their ratings more quickly in the face of new information;

(iii) the SEC could treat the credit-rating agencies as a regulated industry, imposing higher training and monitoring standards and, itself, disciplining poor performance, much as it does in the case of broker-dealers; or

(iv) the SEC could seek to restore the original principal–agent relationship that once existed by requiring rating agencies to be paid by the users of their information, not the issuer corporations who today pay them.

The third option of close administrative regulation makes sense if one believes that the dominant ratings agencies possess a natural monopoly and so should be supervised like public utilities. Conversely, if one doubts that rating agencies are a natural monopoly, the first option of enhanced competition logically should be preferred. The second option of increased liability could be used in combination with any of these other options, but will be the hardest to implement (because it requires either legislation or new judicial decisions).

Each of these options merits a brief review:

1 Can the Principal–Agent Relationship Be Restored?   The fourth option of restoring a principal–agent relationship is particularly promising, but faces a basic problem in terms of its economic feasibility. Although public policy could seek to restore credit-rating agencies to their former position as the agents of their subscribers (for example, by prohibiting credit-rating agencies from receiving fees from the issuers of the securities that they rate), such a policy may be confounded by the free-rider problem and the rapid flow of information. The credit-rating agency is different from the security analyst precisely to the extent that the credit-rating agency condenses its information into a ratings symbol—that is, AAA to DDD. This condensed information can instantly be leaked in the age of the Internet to non-paying users by any subscriber. Thus, only a fraction of the users of this information might pay for it, and the producer of this information would not be able to capture its full value because of the non-excludability of non-paying users. Arguably, this might be why the major rating agencies came in time to charge the issuer, not the consumer.

This objection is not, however, as compelling as it first appears. Some non-NRSRO rating agencies (most notably Egan Jones Rating Company) do charge their subscribers (and not the issuer). Perhaps as a result, they appear to change their ratings twice as frequently as the typical NRSRO agency,[64] thereby satisfying the constituency that pays them with more timely ratings. Still, Egan Jones does not attempt to meet with or consult the issuer or receive access to its non-public information (as it is permitted by law to do). This may be because it cannot undertake a costly investigation based on the modest fees it receives.

Even if the Egan Jones business model were revised so that it did consult with the issuer, its incentive would still be to keep its research and ratings confidential and proprietary, informing only its subscribers of ratings changes. But such a policy essentially permits its subscribers to profit from material, non-public information. Thus, to the extent that the ratings agency receives non-public information from the issuer in the course of its credit review and passes that information along only to its subscribers (rather than the public generally), this system can be viewed as institutionalizing a de facto system of selective disclosure. As a result, some (possibly including the SEC) may prefer to let the issuer pay for its rating, thereby collectivizing its cost among its shareholders, but then require immediate public disclosure by the issuer of the rating.

2 Can Competition Improve Rating Agency Performance?　Here, two distinct questions must be evaluated: (1) Will competition produce a 'race to the bottom,' as low-cost, substandard rating agencies enter the field in order to sell cheap 'regulatory licenses'; and (2) Can new competitors break into the market and raise the overall level of performance?

The first scenario of a race to the bottom has obviously long troubled the SEC. Some evidence does support it. Less established competitors, such as Fitch, have at times been perceived as more generous in their ratings than S & P or Moody's.[65] Logically, a new competitor needs to offer something, either a price concession or a more attractive rating, to induce an issuer to drop one of its established raters and turn to it. Not surprisingly, one empirical study has found that Fitch on average gave higher ratings than did its two larger, more established rivals.[66] But even if this tendency for ratings inflation exists, it does not follow that inflated ratings are taken seriously by the market. Rather, the norm that issuers must secure two ratings seems a protection mandated by the market to guard against the danger of ratings inflation.

The market for credit ratings is also a uniquely sophisticated market, because the vast majority of corporate debt securities are held by institutional investors that have their own credit analysts and probably as a result place only partial reliance on the agency's rating. But, if so, why is there then a demand for inflated ratings if the market does not believe them? One answer takes us back to the concept of the 'regulatory license': the issuer wants the inflated rating less for its impact on the market than for its ability to reduce its regulatory costs. The market protects itself from inflated ratings by insisting on the two-ratings norm, thus restricting the issuer's ability to purchase its ratings from less than independent raters. But the issuer may still have an incentive to 'buy' an investment grade rating from a lower-quality rater in order to achieve some specific regulatory goal or immunity. In this light, the NRSRO system creates an incentive to hire a lax ratings agency, which incentive in turn leads the SEC to keep the pool of NRSRO raters very small. That this problem is circular seems to have escaped the SEC's attention.

Another perspective on the 'race to the bottom' scenario emerges from research that suggests that new raters appear in the market not to sell inflated ratings, but to meet other unmet investor needs. From this perspective, non-NRSRO agencies do different things than NRSRO agencies. For example, a recent study of Moody's Investor Services versus a non-NRSRO credit-rating agency (Egan-Jones Ratings Company) found that the younger non-NRSRO agency (Egan-Jones) was more timely in its ratings and that its ratings more closely paralleled market changes.[67] Typically, the non-NRSRO agency would lead Moody's in its ratings changes by up to six months, but it was less accurate in predicting bond defaults. Essentially, it appears to be servicing customers who wanted more timely information than Moody's was giving them.

On this basis, the dangers from encouraging competition seem modest and worth the risk. If the SEC were to relax the eligibility criteria for its NRSRO designation, some small firms might well enter the market in order to sell 'regulatory licenses,' and some ratings inflation might occur. But major institutional investors seem likely to pay little attention to lesser known ratings agencies (or might only consult them to determine current valuations). More importantly, the SEC has an obvious solution available to it for dealing with this danger of regulatory licenses: that is, to admit only those new entrants to NRSRO status who earn their revenues from subscribers, not issuers. Such firms have little incentive to issue lax ratings because they profit only by convincing subscribers of their independence and integrity.

If new competition able to challenge the duopoly of Moody's and Standard & Poor's ever appears, it will be likely to surface not as an across-the-board challenge to their dominance, but through localized challenges in industries where the new entrant already enjoys a reputation for greater expertise. For example, A. M. Best Co. has long rated the insurance industry in terms of the ability of insurers to meet insurance claims. Thus, it was positioned to rate the bonds of insurance companies, a field that it has now entered aggressively.[68] Other investment advisory firms or firms of independent securities analysts might also have special expertise with regard to, say, bank stocks or public utilities. Hence, the most plausible scenario for increased competition is not the overnight appearance of a major new competitor, but rather creeping competition around the edges, as new entrants compete for a specialized segment of the market (as Fitch, itself, has successfully done). That such firms have not in fact entered the credit-rating field may reflect their estimate of the low profit potential, not the high barriers to entry. Nonetheless, the SEC should be especially prepared to relax its NRSRO barrier and admit firms like Egan Jones, even if they lack 'national recognition,' where they have expertise in some specialized area.

The factor that may be keeping some existing highly specialized firms out of a lucrative market is that they use highly paid, highly-educated employees, while the credit-rating agencies have long paid their credit analysts only a fraction of what securities analysts and young investment bankers make.[69] Thus, these potential entrants may be higher cost competitors who would have to charge more than Moody's and S & P to provide the same service (although they might provide it in greater depth). To be sure, other new entrants might have lower costs and could seek to compete by offering lower prices or a cheaper product, but such lower-cost entrants would do little to improve overall industry performance.

If there is a consensus to the contemporary criticism of the credit-rating industry, it is that the established firms have made only a limited effort to update credit ratings in the light of new information (while the newer firms do better). Constant monitoring of issuers is expensive, and the costs so incurred will not necessarily be recouped from the issuer (which today pays the ratings agency only when it issues debt). Because the major ratings agencies have learned that they may wait years between debt issuances, they probably economize on the potentially unreimbursed costs of ongoing monitoring and ratings changes. Precisely because it is costly to follow current developments at thousands of companies, one cannot expect that new entrants with smaller capitalizations and budgets will seek to compete on an across-the-board basis. What they will do, however, is focus on the needs of the constituency that pays them, and if they are paid by their subscribers, not the issuer, they will provide more timely ratings changes.

From this perspective, the SEC should admit new ratings agencies into the hallowed halls of NRSROdom, particularly new entrants willing to commit more capital and invest more heavily in ongoing monitoring than the existing credit-rating agencies have been willing to do so. Ratings agencies paid by subscribers seem likely to be quicker and more timely in meeting the needs of subscribers, but they may be unable to make more than a toe-hold entrance into a limited sector of the ratings market. Today, the SEC's NRSRO policy probably discourages even such a piecemeal entry.

3 Can Litigation Induce Reform?   If credit-rating agencies move slowly to update their ratings, in effect following the market, rather than leading it, one potential answer is to increase the deterrent threat facing them. Today, the ratings agencies enjoy a virtual immunity from private litigation. This may seem surprising because, after all, bonds and publicly-traded notes are 'securities,' and statements made by any person 'in connection with the purchase or sale of a security' are potentially within the reach of SEC Rule 10b-5.[70] Thus, a particular rating (or its upgrade or downgrade) could constitute a material misstatement and be actionable under Rule 10b-5; similarly, the failure to update ratings in light of new information could be a material omission. Of course, these misstatements and omissions would be actionable only if the ratings agency acted with scienter, but under current law 'recklessness'—meaning a conscious recognition that a statement might be false or an indifference to its truth or accuracy—suffices to satisfy the scienter standard under Rule 10b-5.

Nonetheless, the reported cases, while few in number, have been extraordinarily protective of ratings agencies (far more so than the judicial decisions on security analysts). One judicial response has been to deem credit-agency ratings to be mere opinions and therefore protected speech under the First Amendment.[71] An alternative approach has been to protect the ratings agency by finding the plaintiff's reliance on the agency's rating to have been 'unreasonable.'[72] This latter approach is particularly ironic because for over a century institutional investors have been found by courts to have satisfied their due diligence obligation as fiduciaries when they relied on 'investment grade' ratings from the ratings agencies. Yet, when investors attempt to sue over an allegedly flawed rating, they are told that their reliance on the rating was 'unreasonable.' At the least, judicial treatment of credit ratings has been inconsistent.

The relevance of a meaningful litigation remedy seems obvious. The standard critique of the dominant ratings agencies is that they have not made a sufficient investment in research and tend to slight ongoing research after initially assigning a rating.[73] Even the agencies, themselves, concede that 'they do not purport to go beyond what company officials tell them.'[74] Senator Joseph Lieberman contended that S & P's analysts had not even read Enron's proxy statement.[75] Holding ratings agencies to the same anti-fraud standard that securities analysts and auditors are held to would arguably motivate them to research more thoroughly and update more regularly.

Still, there is a potential downside to holding ratings agencies to a more liberal standard of liability. First, the price of their services would increase, as they would be forced to invest more heavily in ongoing monitoring. Second, they might begin to exhibit a self-protective conservative bias in their ratings. That is, the more conservative the rating, the less the litigation risk. Third, at some point, the market could collapse. In the case of the rating agencies, the disproportion between the fee from the client/issuer and the astronomic potential liability to investors is even greater than in the case of the auditor. In contrast to the auditor who today may charge a fee in the tens of millions for auditing a large, public corporation, the credit-rating agency's fee is typically only two or three basis points of the amount of the debt issuance.

Realistically, however, a number of factors suggest that credit-rating agencies will not face astronomic liabilities for a flawed rating, even if its issuer/client becomes insolvent. First, as a result of the Private Securities Litigation Reform Act of 1995 (the PSLRA), securities law defendants typically face only proportionate liability, not joint and several liability. This means that the total investor losses found by the court to have been caused by a securities fraud must be allocated among all defendants in terms of their relative culpability. In the case of a credit-rating agency, even if it were found to have committed securities fraud, its proportionate share of the total liability would most likely be modest in percentage terms, because it typically will be far less culpable than its issuer/client. Second, the PSLRA further shelters credit-rating agencies from liability by mandating special pleading rules that require the plaintiff at the outset of its case to plead 'with particularity' facts giving rise to a 'strong inference of fraud.' Without such pleadings, the plaintiff cannot obtain discovery against the defendant. In practice, this rule means that few actions are generally brought against secondary defendants (such as a rating agency) because the plaintiff faces a 'Catch 22'-like dilemma: it is unable to plead fraud with respect to a secondary defendant without first obtaining substantial discovery from it, and it cannot get that discovery until it first pleads fraud with particularity. In truth, these pleading rules may be the principal reason why, even in major credit disasters, little liability has been imposed on the rating agencies.[76]

What then could be done on the practical level to create an adequate deterrent threat without risking market failure? One possibility would be for the SEC to promulgate a 'safe harbor' rule that would define the nature of the review that the rating-agency should make on an on-going basis. Such a rule might require, for example, a periodic review of all public SEC filings by the issuer, and direct contacts with the issuer, before the ratings agency published a rating; further contacts and investigation would be necessary if the credit-rating agency maintained the rating for longer than a specified period. Procedurally, such a safe harbor rule would provide that compliance with these due diligence standards immunized the credit-rating agency from any claim that its rating was fraudulent (at least for purposes of the federal securities laws), but in substance the rule would imply (without itself creating liability) that a failure to comply with these standards could amount to 'reckless' conduct that was actionable under Rule 10b-5. The practical impact of such a rule would be to advise courts that a credit-rating agency that grossly failed to investigate an issuer (or that left its rating recklessly outstanding without periodic review) could be liable under Rule 10b-5.

4 SEC Monitoring: What Can It Achieve?   The SEC actively monitors broker-dealers and investment advisers and specifies a variety of standards with which they must constantly comply. Should they do the same for credit-ratings agencies? A critical difference is that broker-dealers and investment advisers manage 'other peoples' money,' while credit-rating agencies do not. In addition, broker-dealer firms are fiduciaries to a retail clientele, which likely contains the proverbial 'widows and orphans', but credit-ratings agencies serve an almost exclusively institutional clientele. Further, in contrast to auditing firms, credit-rating agencies have less serious conflicts of interest and generally have not awarded comparable incentive compensation or stock options.[77] Hence, the credit-rating analyst faces less pressure than the securities analyst to upgrade its opinion in order to please the client and also has less incentive than the auditor to do so. Put more simply, credit-rating agencies cover thousands of corporate clients, none of whom pay fees approaching the same order of magnitude as the annual multi-million dollar fee paid by Enron to Arthur Andersen. Nor is any credit-rating analyst tied to a single major client the way an audit partner of an accounting firm often is.[78] In short, the SEC has less reason to worry about the independence of the credit analyst than that of either the auditor or the securities analyst.

But if the SEC has less reason to worry about independence, it has as much or more reason to worry about rating-agency performance. This is because the major competitors today operate on a low-cost business model that arguably is designed to protect them from new entrants and increased competition. Arguably, because the major credit-ratings agencies are today all registered investment advisers, the SEC may have authority to require a higher level of performance. How should it seek to improve performance? In 2003, the SEC published a concept release in which it proposed possible approaches for closer regulation in the light of criticism of the rating agencies for their failure to detect approaching corporate insolvencies.[79] Specifically, it asked whether it should condition NRSRO recognition 'on a rating agency developing and implementing procedures reasonably designed to ensure credible, reliable and current ratings?'[80] It suggested that each NRSRO could be required to 'ensure that a similar analysis is conducted for similar companies and that current information is used in the rating agency's analysis.' In addition, it pondered whether it should 'establish minimum due diligence procedures for ratings agencies.'[81] Other questions posed by the SEC for public comment included (a) whether it should limit the number of companies assigned to an analyst;[82] (b) whether it should adopt 'minimum standards for the training and qualifications of credit analysts';[83] and (c) whether it should supervise 'the extent of contacts with the management of issuers (including access to senior level management of issuers).'[84]

Incorporating these criteria into the process for recognizing NRSROs would address the recent lackluster performance of credit-rating agencies in failing to detect financial deterioration at rated companies, but it would also involve the Commission deeply and intrusively in the business practices of rating agencies. It will not be simple for the Commission to develop 'minimum due diligence' procedures for ratings agencies or any profession. In so doing, it might also raise the barriers to entry for potential new entrants. In this light, encouraging rating agencies to obtain their fees from subscribers, rather than issuers, may do more than governmental monitoring to make agencies responsive to the needs of investors.

Sensible compromises are also possible. One such proposal, advanced by Fidelity and the Investment Company Institute, would be to make the NRSRO designation periodically renewable, much as broadcast licenses are periodically renewed.[85] This would permit liberalization of the recognition criteria for NRSROs in order to encourage new entrants, but also condition recognition on a periodic backward look to weed out those firms that had failed or proven to be fly-by-night operators selling 'regulatory licenses.' At such a periodic review, regulators could also look at the accuracy of the issuer's ratings, thereby focusing on outputs, rather than inputs.[86]

Another route to this same end could be the creation of a 'self-regulatory organization' (or SRO) for credit-rating agencies, much like the NASD or the PCAOB. This would allow the industry to propose self-regulatory standards; but today this approach is compromised by the unavoidable fact that the industry is an oligopoly.

Summary

All these approaches offer some promise: increased competition could work to bring in some specialized competitors with greater expertise who would be willing to make a greater investment in monitoring their chosen segment of the market; an enhanced litigation remedy should encourage greater due diligence and investment in research. SEC standards could also work—modestly and marginally at least—to require greater investment and to allow the Commission to review actual performance periodically. At present, it appears that the SEC will soon receive new legislative authority to regulate credit-ratings agencies.[87] But what it will do with that authority remains a mystery. Finally, the Commission could encourage the growth of subscriber-funded ratings agencies by offering them easier admission to the coveted NRSRO-status. This option probably makes the greatest sense, because it is difficult to understand why subscriber-funded ratings agencies would lead the race to the bottom that the SEC evidently fears. Their market lies instead in convincing their subscribers that they can provide more timely information.

Endnotes

1. Underwriters Laboratories, Inc. was organized in 1901 by a group of insurance companies to test and generate reliable information about the risks associated with tested products. Underwriters Laboratories applied its label to approved products, and by the 1920s, consumers had learned to appreciate this label as a signal of safety, thereby giving products with this label a marketing advantage. By the 1990s, Underwriters Laboratories had grown to the point that it employed over 3,900 people and applied its distinctive logo to over six billion new products a year. Although Underwriters Laboratories arose and grew as a private body that pledged its reputational capital, it has become—much like credit-rating agencies —entangled in government regulation, as the Occupational Safety and Health Administration (OSHA) recognizes it as an authorized independent testing and certifying organization for a number of OSHA procedures. See Frank Partnoy, *The Siskel and Ebert of Financial Markets?: Two Thumbs Down for the Credit-Rating Agencies*, 77 Wash. U.L.Q. 619, 685–687 (hereinafter, 'Partnoy'). As Professor Partnoy has incisively suggested, recognized rating agencies in any field predictably become relied upon by government agencies, which piggyback on their ratings and thereby enable the rating agency to sell a form of regulatory immunity that he terms a 'regulatory license.'

2. Moringstar Inc. uses a one to five 'star' ranking to rate the approximately 8,000 U.S. mutual funds. As of the late 1990s, approximately 100 five star rankings had been awarded. See Charles Gasparino, 'Mutual Funds Show Managers the Money,' Wall Street Journal March 7, 1997 at C1.

3. Institutional Investor conducted its 33rd annual survey of sell-side analysts in 2004, asking money managers to rank securities analysts by industry. See 'Lehman analysts rated best; survey asks money managers to list favorites,' Houston Chronicle, October 15, 2004 at 2. It is well understood that a high ranking in this survey translates into a high bonus for the manager, and investment banking firms compete to do well in this survey, just as movie studios compete to win Oscars.

4. See Partnoy at 620. Mr Friedman made this statement in 1996 in an interview on 'The News Hour' with Jim Lehrer.

5. The major agencies vary slightly in their terminology. While Standard & Poor's and Fitch use capital letters—e.g. AAA, BBB and so forth— Moody's uses Aaa, Baa and so on. The first two also use '+', no gradation, or '−', to show further refinements, while Moody's may add a 1, 2, or 3 numerical rating to its letter grade (i.e. 'Baa1'). See Staff of Senate Comm. on Governmental Affairs, 107th Cong., 'Financial Oversight of Enron: The SEC and Private-Sector Watchdogs,' S. PRT. No. 107–75 (Comm. Print 2002) (hereinafter "Watchdogs"). The credit-rating agencies also use slightly different terminology for shorter-term debt.

6. Professor Partnoy estimates that Standard & Poor's had an operating margin of 29 percent in 1999, and Moody's was in his judgment similarly

profitable. See Partnoy at 654. Others have estimated that Moody's rate of return was even higher. Because Standard and Poor's is owned by a larger company (McGraw-Hill Companies, Inc.), precise calculation of its profits is not possible. Moody's was similarly owned for many years by Dun & Bradstreet, but was spun off as a public company in 2000. Since then, its profit margins have been estimated as being as high as 50 percent and its return on assets at over 40 percent. See Claire Hill, *Regulating the Ratings Agencies*, 82 Wash. U.L.Q. 43, 52 (2004) (hereinafter, 'Hill'). Professor Hill also notes that after Moody's was spun off by Dun & Bradstreet in 2000, its market capitalization quickly rose to $6 billion. Ibid. at 48.

7. Fitch is owned by a French conglomerate, FIMALAC, and is the successor to several smaller agencies that were compelled to merge in order to survive, including Fitch, IBCA, Duff & Phelps, and Thomson Bank-Watch. See Hill at 47. During the 1990s, Fitch dominated the market for ratings of mortgage-backed securities. See Partnoy at 675.

8. See Aline Van Duyn, 'Big Three Learn Lessons from Enron,' *Financial Times* (London) May 27, 2002 at 4.

9. This analogy to the SATs was first suggested by NYU Economist Lawrence White (who nonetheless appears to think greater competition is possible). See 'Rating the Ratings Agencies: The State of Transparency and Competition: Hearing Before the Capital Markets Subcommittee of the House Financial Services Committee,' 108 Congress (2003) at 150 (testimony of Lawrence White). Actually competitive alternatives have recently emerged even for the SATs.

10. See Hill at 65; Partnoy at 655 to 664. The essence of this claim is that ratings simply reflect negative information that is already publicly available. Hence, even if ratings correlate closely with bond default rates, correlation does not necessarily imply causation. Surveys of financial professionals reveal that a high percentage of them doubt that changes in ratings are timely; that is, they believe that rating-agency decisions to upgrade or downgrade debt are less informed than their original ratings decisions. See Hill at 65 n 110 (citing surveys).

11. A 2002 survey by the Association for Financial Professionals found that only 40 percent of professionals who worked for companies with rated debt believed changes in ratings to be 'timely;' only 29 percent found ratings to be accurate, and only 22 percent believed that ratings 'favored the interests of investors.' See William H. Beaver, Catherine Shakespeare and Mark Soliman 'Differential Properties in the Ratings of Certified vs. Non-Certified Bond Ratings Agencies,' (SSRN Working Paper, September 2004) (SSRN *Ibid* = 596626) at p 7.

12. The number of credit-rating agency employees grew by more than ten-fold between 1985 and 1995 and has further increased by over 50 percent over the last decade. In 1980, for example, the S & P Industrials group employed only 30 professionals; in 1985, it employed 40, but by

1995 it had 800 analysts and a total staff 1,200. See Partnoy at 649. As of late 2004, S & P employed over 1,250 ratings analysts worldwide. See www.standardandpoors.com/Aboutus. Much of this growth reflects the international expansion of the credit-rating agencies, and also their new profitability, which has risen dramatically with the growth of structured finance.

13. In 2003, Moody's provided credit ratings and analysis on 85,000 corporate and governmental securities, 73,000 public finance obligations, 4,300 corporate relationships, and 100 sovereign nations, all totaling over $30 trillion of debt. See Claire Hill, *Rating Agencies Behaving Badly: The Case of Enron*, 35 Conn. L. Rev. 1145, 1146 n 8 (2003).

14. See Partnoy at 652; relying on more recent 2003 data, Professor Hill places the figure at 90 percent in the case of Moody's. See Hill at 50.

15. Ibid. (noting that S & P charged 2.5 basis points per issue and Moody's charged $10,000 to $25,000, depending on the issue's size). In more complex deals, however, fees of $90,000 have become common, and thus greater reason for bias exists in this context. See House, Rating the Raters, Institutional Investor Oct. 1995 (Int'l Edition) at 53.

16. The evidence is clear that the market reacts more favorably to debt with Moody's and S & P's ratings than it reacts to debt with only one of these two ratings. See Hill at 66; see also Richard Cantor and Frank Packer, 'Multiple Ratings and Credit Standards: Differences of Opinion in the Credit Rating Industry' in 12 Federal Reserve Bank of New York Staff Reports (1996).

17. See Beaver, Shakespeare and Soliman, n 11 above, at 7.

18. See Securities and Exchange Commission, Report on The Role and Function of Credit Rating Agencies in the Operation of the Securities Markets (January 2003) at 23–24.

19. See Partnoy at 631–633.

20. The debt-rating agency is in this sense a solution to the classic 'market for lemons' problem. In principle, given the prospect of fraud and default, an issuer will be forced to pay the interest rate applicable to the average quality issuer unless it can credibly signal its superior credit to the market. The gatekeeper in effect decides if the signal is credible. For an explanation of the 'market for lemons,' see George A. Akerlof, *The Market For Lemons: Qualitative Uncertainty and the Market Mechanism*, 84 Q.J. Econ. 488 (1970). Such a market and inefficient average cost pricing typically arise when the individual competitor cannot credibly distinguish its product from the herd of similar products.

21. See 17 C.F.R. 243.100 (b)(2) (exempting from Regulation FD 'an entity whose primary business is the issuance of credit ratings, provided the information is disclosed for the purpose of developing a credit rating and the entity's ratings are publicly available;').

22. The fullest and best account of this 'regulatory license' model has been provided by Professor Frank Partnoy. See Partnoy at 681–703.

23. See Partnoy at 686–7.
24. Ibid. at 687. The Comptroller of the Currency ruled in 1931 that bonds rated BBB or higher could be carried at cost, but lower rated bonds had to be written down on the bank's balance sheet.
25. Ibid. at 688. Section 308 of the National Banking Act of 1935 limited national banks to purchasing only securities that satisfied the definition of 'investment securities' promulgated by the Comptroller of the Currency.
26. Partnoy at 688 (summarizing Comptroller of the Currency's regulations).
27. See Sec. Exch. Act. Rel. No. 34–10,525 (Nov. 29, 1973). Rule 15c3-1 remains in force to this date. See 17 C.F.R. 240.15c3-1.
28. Rule 2a-7 exempts money market funds from the requirement, applicable to most mutual funds, that they mark to market on a daily basis the value of portfolio securities, provided that the money market fund observe certain risk-limiting conditions. See 17 CFR 270. 2a-7.
29. See Securities Act Release No. 33–6882 (Feb. 20, 1991) (defining 'second tier' commercial paper in terms of NRSRO ratings).
30. The adoption of Rule 415, which authorized shelf-registration for large public corporations, provoked a major confrontation between the SEC and the investment banking community that did not want the increased competition for underwriting business that the new faster rule encouraged. The Commission, itself, divided over this rule. See Securities Act Release No. 6491 (November 17, 1983) (adopting Rule 415).
31. State insurance regulators created the NAIC in 1871, and the Committee on Valuation of Securities, the forerunner of the SVO, was formed within it in 1907. See Partnoy at 700.
32. Ibid. at 701.
33. The Basle Committee on Banking Supervision promulgates 'voluntary' global standards governing the adequacy of capital for international banks. Its regulatory approach relies in part on credit ratings in preference to heavier-handed regulation. For a criticism of this approach, see Frank Partnoy, *Why Markets Crash and What the Law Can Do About It*, 61 U.P.H.L. Rev. 741, 788–82 (2000).
34. See Leslie Wayne, 'Credit Raters Get Scrutiny and Possibly a Competitor,' *New York Times*, Apr. 23, 2002, at C1 (describing unsuccessful experience of Egan-Jones Ratings).
35. See Hill, at 55 n 61 (discussing application by LACE Financial for NRSRO status); see also Jenny Wiggins, 'A Chance to Step Into the Light: Credit Rating Agencies: The Failure of S & P and Moody's to Detect Problems at Enron Has Spurred Regulators to Consider Opening Up the Market,' *Financial Times*, Dec. 9, 2002, 2002 WL 103396934.
36. See Robert Schroeder, 'Credit Ratings Agencies Could Face More Regulation,' CBS MarketWatch, September 14, 2004.
37. The four successful applicants were Duff and Phelps, Inc. (in 1982); McCarthy Crisanti & Maffei, Inc. (in 1983), IBCA Limited (in 1990), and Thomson Bank Watch, Inc. (in 1999). See U.S. Securities and Exchange

Commission, Report on the Role and Function of Credit Rating Agencies in the Operation of the Securities Markets (Jan. 2003) at p 9. (hereinafter, 'SEC Report on Role and Function of Credit Rating Agencies').

38. Ibid.
39. See Kathleen Day, 'SEC Backs 4th Credit Agency,' *Washington Post*, February 25, 2003, at E2.
40. See SEC Report on Role and Function of Credit Rating Agencies at 37.
41. *Ibid.*
42. Ibid. The Basle Committee on Banking Supervision estimated that some 130 rating agencies were active worldwide in 1999, and an official of the U.K.'s financial Services Authority placed the number at 150 in 2002. Ibid. New York University Professor Lawrence J. White, an economic expert on banking, places the number of active ratings agencies in the world-wide market somewhat lower at between 35 to 40 (plus Moody's and S & P). See Lawrence J. White, 'The Credit Rating Industry: An Industrial Organization Analysis' 7–8 (2001) (available on SSRN).
43. See Beaver, Shakespeare and Soliman, n 11 above, at 27. The non-NRSRO agency (Egan Jones) was found to be much more timely in its ratings changes and more responsive to the needs of investors (who after all paid its fees), whereas the NRSRO agency (Moody's) performed more of a 'quasi-regulatory function' and had a more 'conservative bias,' but did better predict bond defaults.
44. See Richard Cantor & Frank Packer, The Credit Rating Industry, Federal Reserve Board N.Y.Q. Rev. 1 (Summer–Fall 1994); see also Partnoy at 636–637.
45. Cantor & Packer at 1–2; Partnoy at 637 n 74.
46. See J. Wilson Newman, 'Dun & Bradstreet: For the Promotion and Protection of Trade,' in 'Reputation: Studies in the Voluntary Elicitation of Good Conduct' 85, 86 (Daniel Klein ed., 1997).
47. Much of this information is set forth on Standard & Poor's website. (See www.standardandpoors.com).
48. Most of these facts are set forth on Moody's website. (See www.moodys.com/aboutmoody's).
49. See Partnoy at 639.
50. See Hill at 47 (see also www.fitchratings.com/corporate/aboutfitch).
51. See Partnoy at 644.
52. For the early decisions, see *In re Bartol*, 38 A. 527 (Pa. 1897); *In re Detre's Estate*, 117 A. 54 (Pa. 1922). This line of cases continues to this date. See *Glennie v. Abitibi-Price Corp.*, 912 F. Supp. 993 (W.D. Mich. 1996) (finding that fiduciary exercised due diligence where it consulted Moody's and S&P's ratings and found that their ratings remained 'investment grade,' despite the fact that the issuer had encountered a variety of financial problems that had been publicized).
53. See Partnoy at 644–645.

54. See George Pinches & J. Clay Singleton, *The Adjustment of Stock Prices to Bond Rating Changes*, 33 J. Fin. 29 (1978); see also Frank J. Reilly & Michael Joehnk, *The Association Between Market-Dominated Risk Measures for Bonds and Bond Ratings*, 31 J. Fin. 1387 (1976).

55. For example, on a very large offering of $1 billion in debt, two basis points comes to $200,000. Also, higher fees may be charged for complex offerings, such as asset securitization transactions. This is, of course, exactly the profile of some Enron offerings.

56. See 'Credit-Rating Agencies. AAArgh!', *Economist*, Apr. 6, 1996 at 80; see also Frank A. Bottini, Jr., *An Examination of the Current Status of Rating Agencies and Proposals for Limited Oversight of Such Agencies*, 30 San Diego L. Rev. 579, 598–600 (1993); 'Now It's Moody's Turn for a Review,' Bus. Wk., April 8, 1996 at 116.

57. See Hill, *Regulating the Rating Agencies*, n 6 above, at 52.

58. Ibid. at 49.

59. See Partnoy at 664–670. For a rebuttal, see Hill, *Regulating the Ratings Agencies*, n 6 above, at 49–50.

60. See Steven L. Schwarcz, *Private Ordering of Public Markets: The Ratings Agency Paradox*, 2002 U.Ill. L. Rev. 1, 13–14.

61. Ibid. at 14.

62. See Partnoy at 704–707.

63. See Charles Adams et al., International Capital Markets Developments, Prospects, and Key Policy Issues at 137–139, 203 (International Monetary Fund survey, Sept. 1999). The agencies' ratings on sovereign and municipal debt were, however, found to be less reliable.

64. See Beaver, Shakespeare and Soliman, n 11 above, at 3 (finding that Egan Jones changes its ratings twice as frequently as Moody's).

65. Professor Hill notes that the 'perception' long existed that Fitch 'was in the business only of giving inflated ratings to a company after Moody's or Standard & Poor's refused to give an issuer the rating it desired.' Hill at 51–52.

66. See Richard Cantor and Frank Packer, *Multiple Ratings and Credit Standards: Differences of Opinion in the Credit Rating Industry*, in 12 Federal Reserve Bank of New York Staff Reports 3, 27 (1996).

67. See Beavers, Shakespeare and Soliman, n 11 above, at 3, 27. Egan Jones was found to make twice as many ratings changes as Moody's. Ibid. at 3.

68. Press reports suggest that A. M. Best Co. will be the next firm to receive the coveted NRSRO designation. See Alec Klein, 'SEC Prepares to Change Rules for Credit Raters,' *Washington Post*, February 25, 2005 at E-2.

69. See Partnoy at 72; Hill at 72. Hill agrees that rating-agency personnel 'may not be as sophisticated, or … as highly motivated, as the (mostly institutional) investors supposedly being informed by the ratings' (Ibid.), but argues that such personnel 'need not be exceedingly skilled to provide' valuable information. Ibid. at 73. That comment, however, misses the point that we may want the ratings agency to dig deeper and uncover the information that they missed in Enron and other cases.

70. The general standard is that a public statement, such as a press release, that will forseeably impact the market will be deemed to have been made 'in connection with a purchase or sale of a security' (which language appears both in Rule 10b-5 and Section 10b of the Securities Exchange Act of 1934) and so can violate Rule 10b-5 if made with the requisite intent. Thus, for purposes of the reach of Rule 10b-5, a credit rating is not conceptually different from a securities analyst's 'buy' recommendation or an auditor's opinion that the issuer's financial statements comply with GAAP.

71. See, e.g. *Jefferson County Sch. Dist. v. Moody's Investor Services, Inc.*, 988 F. Supp. 2d 1341, 1348 (D. Colo. 1997), aff'd, 175 F.3d 848 (11th Cir. 1999); *Compuware Corp. v. Moody's Investors Servs.*, 324 F. Supp. 2d 860 (E.D. Mich. 2004) (Moody's qualified for reporter's privilege under New York statute). These two cases involved, however, actions by the issuer brought against the rating agency where the issuer claimed that the agency had given it too low a rating. The more relevant litigation remedy is that available to the investor who relies upon an 'investment grade' rating, and this is the context in which Rule 10b-5 applies. Some commentators have argued that there should be no or little liability in this context. See Gregory Husisian, *What Standard of Care Should Govern the World's Shortest Editorials?: An Analysis of Bond Rating Agency Liability*, 75 Cornell L. Rev. 411 (1996). But this view of ratings as editorials (or as political speech) seems increasingly dated.

72. See *Quinn v. McGraw Hill*, 168 F.3d 331 (7th Cir. 1999).

73. See Hill at 81.

74. Ibid. at 79.

75. Ibid. at 70–1.

76. Following its bankruptcy in 1995, Orange County sued many of its advisers and underwriters for professional negligence, breach of contract, and breach of fiduciary duty. Overall, it recovered $860.7 million from all of them, but only $140,000 from S & P, which was sued by Orange County on each of these theories. See Partnoy at 641 n 97 and 710–711.

77. See Hill at 91–92.

78. Typically, a credit-ratings analyst covers up to 35 companies. See Frank Partnoy, 'The Paradox of Credit Ratings' in Ratings, Rating Agencies and the Global Financial System at 72 (Richard M. Levich, et al., eds., 2002). Credit analyst compensation, which is modest in comparison to the other gatekeeping professions, also does not seem dependent on the fees paid by any individual client, particularly because such fees are generally fixed by a formula. See Hill at 76.

79. See Securities Act Release 33-8236 (June 12, 2003).

80. Ibid. at Question 13. 68 FR35258 at 35261.

81. Ibid.

82. Ibid. at Question 17.

83. Ibid. at Question 16.
84. Ibid. at Question 14.
85. See Hill at 88. Professor Hill notes, however, that the threat not to renew a broadcast license has never been credible. Hence the threat not to renew a Moody's or a S & P would seem similarly hollow.
86. This has been a criticism long made by Professor Lawrence J. White of New York University: i.e. that regulators unwisely focus on 'inputs,' rather than 'outputs'—i.e. the rating agency's actual record as a predictor. See Hill at 86.
87. The SEC has been concerned about its statutory authority to regulate credit-rating agencies and may have been done little for this reason. See Deborah Solomon, 'SEC Says It Can't Police Credit-Ratings Firms', Wall Street Journal, February 25, 2005 at C-4. Legislation appears likely to pass congress in 2006 that would give the SEC enhanced authority to regulate credit-rating agencies and might require the SEC to drop its NRSRO designation. Whether the SEC would then move aggressively to register new entrants into this field remains, however, an open question. See Jennifer Hughes, 'Credit Ratings Groups Come Under Attack,' *The Financial Times*, March 8, 2006, p.45

Part III

The Search For Reform

9

What Went Wrong?

The Story So Far

The 1990s witnessed a number of major transitions affecting gatekeepers. The deterrent threat posed by both public and private enforcement weakened, as the result of Supreme Court decisions and the passage of the Private Securities Litigation Reform Act of 1995. Concomitantly, changes in executive compensation, plus the expectations of an overly exuberant market, gave corporate managers a greatly enhanced interest in maximizing short-term earnings. At the same time, the major accounting firms were seeking to redefine themselves as diversified financial consultants, using auditing as the portal of entry to the client through which they could cross-sell other, more lucrative services. Investors meanwhile had been lulled into a euphoric passivity by an extended stock market bubble, and they expected earnings to rise hyperbolically. All these circumstances combined to explain why gatekeepers acquiesced in a variety of financial irregularities.

However, this still leaves a major puzzle: even if legal protections had eroded, why wasn't the gatekeeper's interest in preserving its reputational capital sufficient to protect investors? Every gatekeeper asserts that its reputational capital is critical to it, and from a rational actor perspective, it should be. But their collective behavior during the 1990s seemingly belies this claim. Few took serious precautions to protect their reputations (and many relaxed controls that had previously been in place). Thus, the central mystery becomes: Why did gatekeepers risk, or even willingly sacrifice, reputational capital that they had diligently amassed over decades?

Tentative answers to this question are best grouped under three broad headings: (1) Competitive Environment; (2) Conflicts of Interest; and (3) The Market for Reputational Capital.

Competitive Environment

The starkest, most basic fact about the four gatekeepers just examined is that two of their gatekeeping markets—law and securities research—are characterized by active competition, while the other two—auditing and credit-rating services—are not. Not surprisingly, the markets that are the least competitive are those in which the role of reputational capital looms the largest. Auditors and credit-rating agencies need to possess significant reputational capital in order for investors to perceive them as resolute and unlikely to defer to corporate managements. Their reputations must be at risk in order to assure investors that any economic gain that the corporate client could confer on the gatekeeper for acquiescing would be exceeded by the cost of long-term reputational loss. As a result, the need for pre-existing reputational capital creates a major barrier to entry that precludes new entrants and probably explains, at least in part, the concentrated character of these markets.

The impact of competition on gatekeepers is more debatable. A trade-off seems likely. If the gatekeeper enjoys a near monopoly, it can better resist pressure from the client. For example, few corporations can credibly threaten Moody's or Standard & Poor's, which share a near monopoly and need not compete intensely because of the 'two ratings' norm. But the gatekeeper's willingness to resist pressure will still depend on whether it also faces either exposure to litigation from investors or the potential loss of its reputational capital. The other side of this trade-off is that, in a truly monopolistic market, the gatekeeper has little reason to invest in new technology or controls—or, more simply, to improve its product or service. Instead, organizational slack becomes likely (as some believe has occurred in the contemporary credit-rating agency market).

Competition should spur the gatekeeper to improve its product or service, but it may also leave the gatekeeper more vulnerable to client pressure. The legal profession seemingly provides the clearest example: a law firm that is less aggressive and combative, or less willing to bless transactions that come close to the line, will probably lose clients to fiercer competitors. But, unlike auditors and credit-rating agencies, corporate attorneys are only part-time gatekeepers. At best, they have only weak incentives to play a gatekeeping role, and they are probably more prized for their ability to outmaneuver regulators, exploit loopholes, and generally economize on regulatory costs. Certainly, this is what their corporate employers expect, and if investors have a different preference or expectation, the attorney will more likely conform to the corporate client's expectations than to the investor's.

Thus, misbehavior by attorneys does not provide a counter-example to the reputational capital model because their reputations rest on a different foundation. Law firms probably also compete more on the basis of price and quality of service than on the basis of their reputation for integrity. This is why new start-up firms can (and do) enter the market and compete successfully. Also, because the corporate client's general counsel is the actual purchaser of legal services and can conduct a sophisticated search, law firms can prosper even though their identities are unknown to the general public. In contrast, corporations hiring independent auditors are necessarily more concerned with reassuring investors and so need to find an auditor with an instantly recognizable identity. To sum up, although a highly competitive market may inhibit law firms from playing a gatekeeping role, this was probably only a secondary factor. The larger problem involves the weakness of the incentives motivating the corporate attorney to play a gatekeeping role in the first place.

Securities analysts present a more intriguing case because, despite active competition and clear sensitivity to reputational concerns, they still did not resist pressures during the 1990s to inflate their recommendations. Interestingly, the performance of securities analysts and credit-rating agencies differed sharply during the 1990s, with analysts seemingly being far more acquiescent to issuers than the rating agencies. Why? Although both perform functionally similar services, their two markets are polar opposites, with securities analysts, unlike the ratings agencies, inhabiting a highly competitive market. The implication may then be that competition fosters acquiescence.

Why are the two markets—credit rating and securities research—so different when their services are so similar? The answer may lie in whose reputation is at stake. Typically, the individual securities analyst advances based on his or her own personal reputation, while in contrast investors never even learn the identity of the credit analyst who conducts Moody's or S & P's assessment of an issuer. Investors want a creative vision from the securities analyst, but only a standardized (and highly condensed) comparative rating from the credit-rating agency. In addition, only an institution—and not an individual—can generate comparative rankings on thousands of issuers prepared on a consistent basis. Arguably, creativity tends to be personal, and thus securities research spawns a market with many competitors and low barriers to entry. In contrast, investors want something very different in the case of credit ratings: namely, a consistent methodology that is objectively and evenly applied to all rated firms, which requirement necessitates that an institution, not an individual, be the rater. Given this need for greater scope and scale, it is not surprising that the market for credit ratings is more concentrated and the barriers to entry are higher.

In any event, the relevant policy issue is not why some markets are competitive and others not, but rather whether encouraging competition would enhance or erode gatekeeper influence and reliability. Arguably, competition could do more harm than good. The credit-rating agencies, which have historically faced little or no competition, appear to have remained largely uncaptured by their corporate clients—even if they were slow to respond to new information. Thus, the SEC has long feared that new entrants into this market would produce a 'race to the bottom' that lowered standards.[1] In contrast, securities analysts during the 1990s probably were the most 'captured' gatekeepers, despite intense competition. The case of attorneys also reinforces this generalization, as increased competition in the market for corporate legal service appears to have coincided with the arguable decline of the lawyer/statesman.

There is another side to this story, however. Enhanced competition could well increase auditor independence and incline firms to resist the demands of a client more resolutely. Why? Today, in a highly concentrated market, the Big Four can all assume that both their firm and their rivals will take a certain number of reputational 'hits'—that is, all will be predictably involved in some messy scandals. Because it is a cost of doing business, no firm with a substantial market share can expect to remain unscathed. Although spectacular failures (such as Arthur Andersen's collapse during the Enron implosion) will attract attention and destroy a firm's reputational capital, investors cannot meaningfully discriminate among shades of gray. Thus, they cannot distinguish Ernst & Young from a Deloitte. Each has had its share of embarrassing moments, and investor memory may be short. As a result, reputations become noisy, and investors can only recognize the outliers. This absence of reputational competition may be just what these firms want because it enhances their discretionary ability to cooperate with corporate managements, knowing that none of their rivals will seek to embarrass them or distinguish themselves. In short, competitors in a concentrated market can collude in a variety of implicit ways. Deciding not to compete over reputation could be a very rational strategy.

Suppose instead though, that the market for auditing services had a dozen or more large auditing firms, each logistically capable of providing global services to a large corporate client. In a market that was less concentrated, not all firms would face the inevitability of audit failures and consequent reputational injury, and a few firms might distinguish themselves for being 'tougher' on the client. Such a stance might not please all, or even most, large corporate clients, but it would be attractive to clients seeking to bond themselves with investors. Interestingly, Arthur Andersen adopted such a profile from its earliest days through at least the 1950s, during which period its leaders repeatedly criticized generally accepted accounting principles for being too soft and permissive.[2] At that time, the accounting industry was less concentrated, and Andersen was a relatively young and smaller firm. During this era, the stock market was far less frothy than during the 1990s, with the result that investors may have been more interested in the auditor's reputation. Andersen's strategy seemed to work, and given similar circumstances, it might work again for others in the future. But Andersen abandoned this policy once it became more lucrative to expand one's business with existing clients through consulting than to attract new auditing clients. Thus, competition will work to induce desired behavior only to the extent that some firms want to compete based on their reputations. This is not inevitable.

Enhancing competition can also work as a reform strategy only if the costs of entry into the market are not prohibitive. Today, the auditing market has become global, and the new entrant seeking to provide global auditing services to major corporations faces much higher minimum capital requirements incident to attaining global scale. Yet, in 2003 and 2004 alone, over 10 percent of all publicly-held corporations changed their auditors, and in this process, the Big Four lost a net total of over 400 corporate clients.[3] In most cases, these clients were dropped by the Big Four, which has concluded that the risk–return ratio on smaller clients makes them undesirable to retain. However, whatever the reason, smaller auditing firms are picking up clients, and increased competition is becoming a reality.

The impact of enhanced competition on securities analysts and credit-rating agencies is more speculative. The market for securities research is already highly competitive. The real problem is that the analyst generates little or no direct revenue, and recent reforms have restricted the indirect revenues (i.e. underwriting income) that securities research once generated. As a result, broker-dealers have cut back on research coverage and have reduced incentives to invest in research. Although analyst research still does attract brokerage commissions, securities research is likely to remain a 'loss leader' for most broker-dealer firms, in which they will make only modest investments. Only if securities research were to generate ascertainable revenues and became a profit center for broker-dealers would a strategy of encouraging competition likely work within this market. As will be discussed in the next chapter, this is a realistic possibility.

Credit-rating agencies present an even more debatable case. Although the Moody's/S & P duopoly cannot be accused of acquiescing to client pressure, it has also not invested in providing the market with updated, current credit information, preferring instead to enjoy the quiet life. Competition is thus desirable, but new entrants face major barriers. Conceivably, competition could be encouraged either from (a) specialized firms that already possess expertise with respect to a particular industry (for example, insurance or banking, where such expert firms clearly exist), or (b) professional services firms that enjoy high reputational capital. For example, if a PricewaterhouseCoopers began to offer credit-rating services for non-audit clients, investors would be likely to consider their ratings credible—on the assumption that such a firm would take considerable safeguards to avoid reputational injury.

The principal credit-rating agencies have long behaved as 'quasi-regulatory' bodies, content to receive high rents and disinclined to provide more timely monitoring of their issuer clients. This reluctance is partly a consequence of their source of revenues. Because the rating agency bills the issuer/client on an upfront basis, the rating agency has less incentive to invest in continuing research after it has been paid. Much as with securities research, rating agencies need to be incentivized (or threatened) into making a greater investment in ongoing research. But the typical new entrant will have far less capital to invest than the two established oligarchs, Moody's and S & P. Hence, the new entrant who may most affect their behavior is the new entrant who is paid by its subscribers, not by issuers, because it will be more likely to provide timely updates to satisfy its subscribers (and thus will challenge the dominant, but slow-moving, oligarchs).

To sum up, although competition is not a panacea, it can motivate firms to invest in their reputational capital. Unfortunately, as in the market for legal services, competition may also tend to erode professional values. It is thus, by itself, less than a complete solution.

Conflicts of Interest

Across all markets for gatekeeping services, much evidence suggests that gatekeepers lost leverage vis-à-vis their clients over recent decades. The clearest example is the legal marketplace. Although it is debatable whether the arguably mythical lawyer/statesmen ever truly existed in significant numbers, corporate reliance on a single outside attorney— one who exercises judgment as well as expertise—has clearly decreased in response to the rise of the in-house general counsel.

Within the auditing marketplace, an academic debate continues as to whether the desire to cross-market more lucrative consulting services compromised auditor independence during the 1990s. The participant observers have largely reported that the climate within auditing firms changed over this period as auditors were retrained to become salesmen and cross-sell consulting services. But here a seeming paradox arises, because most of the regression studies do not confirm this hypothesis. Rather, these studies find in general that a high ratio of non-audit services to audit services did not correlate with a higher probability of a financial statement restatement or with greater earnings management.[4] The premise of these studies is that if clients who rewarded their auditors with substantial consulting services did not experience a higher rate of restatements, then the hypothesis that the rise of consulting services compromised auditing is refuted. Numerous financial economists have expressed this conclusion.

But this mode of reasoning misses a key point. In a highly concentrated industry, the major auditing firms all wanted to attract lucrative consulting income from their clients, even if they had not yet achieved that goal. Each knew more or less what its rivals were doing. During the 1990s, each changed its business model in order to use auditing as a portal of entry through which they could market consulting services to audit clients, because consulting revenues, unlike auditing revenues, could grow exponentially. Thus, even if the auditor was currently receiving little consulting income from a particular client, it might still be as deferential to that client as it was to another audit client from which it was receiving substantial consulting income—so long as the prospect of future consulting income existed. Once the audit partner was converted into a salesman and compensated on his ability to market non-audit services, both current consulting income and the potential for such income gave rise to nearly equivalent conflicts. As a result, regression studies showing little difference in the behavior of corporations, based on the amount of consulting revenues that they paid their auditors, prove little.

At most, the fact that corporate clients with a high ratio of non-audit services to audit services from their auditor did not experience a higher rate of restatements suggests that such corporations were not consciously using non-audit services as an inducement (or 'bribe') to secure auditor acquiescence. But this does not change the fact that the audit firm had an across-the-board incentive to acquiesce. Once they changed their internal compensation systems, they altered the behavior of their own audit partners. The sharp and pervasive rise in accounting restatements in the late 1990s provides the strongest evidence that the behavior of auditors did change and that they did increasingly acquiesce in dubious accounting policies. Although the regression studies may show that the major audit firms did not distinguish among clients based on the relative amount of consulting revenues received, these studies cannot refute that the behavior of these firms (and the profession) changed.

Fundamentally, the business model changed for the major audit firms during the 1990s. Previously, audit firms marketed by seeking new clients, but during the 1990s they came to recognize that the greatest profit potential lay in marketing new services to existing clients. Stealing a client from a rival firm was hard, but marketing new services to an existing client was easy and very lucrative. Once this premise was accepted at senior management levels, it followed that the audit partner should be compensated as much as a salesman as an auditor. At this point, the audit partner became conflicted—and not just in the case of the client that rewarded it with consulting services. Indeed, the last · thing that the auditor would want now was a reputation for unbending toughness, because that would hurt it with all its clients.

The impact of conflicts of interest is even clearer in the case of securities analysts. The 1990s saw an extraordinary growth in IPO and underwriting activity, which created strong incentives for broker-dealers to organize their research departments as marketing agents for their underwriting clients. The only debate here is whether this caused real social harm. Again, as in the case of auditors, the empirical studies show conflicting results. Some studies find that the market discounted the recommendations of 'conflicted' analysts employed by the corporation's underwriters, but other studies do not.[5] But once again, these studies attempt to answer the wrong question. That wrong question is whether the market considered analysts working for the issuer's underwriter to be more conflicted than analysts working for other broker-dealers. In fact, all broker-dealer firms were conflicted. Not only were firms that did underwriting conflicted by the need to appease their underwriting clients, but so were firms that either wanted to be underwriters or, even in the absence of any such interest, still wanted to please the institutional investors who were their largest brokerage clients. Both the corporate client and the institutional client disliked 'sell' recommendations that were publicly communicated. Finally, all corporate issuers, including even non-clients, possessed a formidable weapon by which to threaten or punish analysts who published negative research: they could cut such analysts off from the further flow of selective disclosures, thereby virtually driving such an analyst out of the market.[6] All these forces combined to distort research and make the analyst more a salesman than a gatekeeper.

Alone among the gatekeepers, the major credit-rating agencies were not 'captured' by their clients during the 1990s. This was both because they approached the status of a natural monopoly and because they had the least dependence on individual large clients. But, from a public policy perspective, the absence of capture does not define success. As gatekeepers, the credit-rating agencies did not monitor clients closely after the point of their initial rating. Thereafter, rating downgrades generally followed the market, rather than led it.

The Market for Reputational Capital

In theory, gatekeepers should not risk the reputational capital built up over decades to maximize the earnings from a single client. For example, even in the case of Arthur Andersen, which saw Enron as a $100 million a year potential client, the firm's total earnings in its last year exceeded $9 billion. Hence, because in the absence of the Enron (and later WorldCom) fiascos, Andersen would probably still be alive today, its deference to Enron's dubious demands looks irrational in hindsight. But its experience and other failures show that somewhere a fallacy underlies the logical premise that 'rational' gatekeepers would always protect their reputational capital.

Several different hypotheses can be advanced to explain this failure. Obviously, one explanation is that litigation risk declined, and with that decline came a reduced risk of reputational injury because litigation attracts publicity and produces reputational damage. Although this may account for much of the change in the 1990s, restatements and market declines will cause reputational damage, even in the absence of lawsuits. Hence, other independent explanations need to be considered to explain the apparent willingness of professional firms to risk, or even sacrifice, reputational capital.

An Inability to Monitor Agents   While it was irrational for Arthur Andersen to defer as it did to Enron, it was not irrational for the audit partners at Arthur Andersen handling the Enron account to do so. Their career interests were arguably more closely aligned with their corporate client than with their audit firm. This explanation is simple but incomplete. Why didn't the audit firm take better precautions to control its agents? 'Agent capture' is a problem in internal control that a sophisticated accounting firm should have anticipated. Arguably, if Andersen had truly wished to curtail audit partners from identifying excessively with the client's interests, Andersen could have adopted more prophylactic measures (such as a limit on consulting income from an audit client or a mandatory rotation policy under which the audit partner would rotate every two or three years). Extreme as such measures may seem (clients would obviously not like the constant replacement of their audit partners), auditing firms could have minimized the risks associated with this conflict of interest.

Because controlling conflicts of interest is costly, however, some level of agency costs had to be accepted. Yet, Andersen was distinctive in allowing the local audit partner to make sensitive decisions that other firms required this partner to pass up to the home office. Andersen's failure to use more aggressive measures to protect its agents from client capture suggests that it placed the need to market its services above the need to protect its integrity. Given the climate of the 1990s, this was not a surprising choice.

Reputational Schizophrenia   Protecting its reputational capital is not the only goal that a professional firm has in terms of marketing its image. Law firms present a special case. Uniquely, the law firm may wish to promote inconsistent images of itself to different persons. To the corporate general counsel, it is the tough, relentless advocate, the hard-driving negotiator and the skillful planner who is able to exploit whatever loopholes the law offers. To investors and the public generally, it is the wise statesmen with an impeccable reputation for integrity whose opinions can be relied upon. These competing self-definitions can blur, or the law firm may vacillate between them, playing sometimes the advocate and sometimes the gatekeeper. The underlying policy point here is that it may be necessary to insist that a law firm choose a single role that it is to play for the corporate client, and this may restrict the law firm's ability to provide inconsistent services.

Similarly, audit firms may wish to market themselves as resolute and principled to investors, but as flexible and problem-solving to clients. The gatekeeper must then be forced to tell a consistent story.

Regulatory Licenses?   Another explanation for gatekeeper failure is that gatekeepers saw more profit in selling 'regulatory licenses,' than in protecting their reputational capital. This theory applies with some plausibility to the credit-rating agencies where the SEC has uniquely privileged those rating agencies that have gained the SEC's elusive NRSRO rating. The NRSRO designation enables these firms to reduce their clients' regulatory costs significantly, and this license, not credible information, is arguably what they market. This theory seems a little cynical even in the case of ratings agencies, but, outside this narrow context, it is clearly overextended. Some would apply this theory to auditors as well. Their view is that the federal securities laws similarly gave a regulatory license to auditors by mandating an independent audit for publicly traded companies.[7] But this interpretation overstates the 'regulatory license' theory's logic. Legislation that mandates an audit may increase a public corporation's regulatory costs, but it does not enable a gatekeeper to reduce those regulatory costs in return for its fee (as the NRSRO designation does). Federal law that mandates use of a gatekeeper may create a market that would not have otherwise existed, but it does not enable the gatekeeper to sell immunity from otherwise applicable regulatory requirements.

Implicit Collusion?   In a concentrated market, the competitors can decide the bases on which they will compete. Actual collusion is not necessary, as implicit signals can be exchanged. Over the last twenty-odd years, auditing firms have not actively competed in terms of relative integrity or commitment to accurate financial reporting. At least, none challenges its rivals on this score. Not only would such a competition invite destructive retaliation from their rivals, but the competitors knew that this was an ineffective strategy by which to win clients. Cooperation and flexibility won clients. Senior managers and clients wanted auditors who would assist them in maximizing the firm's stock price by using any accounting principle or convention not clearly prohibited. Although reputational injury and litigation risk always placed some limitations on what the auditor could accept, both of these constraints were relaxed significantly during the 1990s. Even price competition became less important, as auditors found it more profitable to develop their existing client base, treat auditing as a virtual 'loss leader,' and exploit the opportunities for more lucrative consulting income. They had found that competition over existing clients resulted, more often than not, in a near zero-sum game in which the auditor won one client only to lose another. Accordingly, they chose to focus more on exploiting the opportunities for cross-selling non-audit services to audit clients than on stealing clients from rivals.

One aspect of this preference for reduced levels of competition was the closed-ranks solidarity shown by the accounting industry throughout the 2001–2002 corporate scandals. To be sure, a similar solidarity may also characterize other professions. After all, doctors do not describe their rivals to the press as 'quacks'; nor do lawyers typically denounce their adversaries in public as 'shysters' or 'ambulance-chasers.' But as others have noted,[8] throughout the intense criticism that the accounting profession attracted during and after the collapse of Enron and the passage of the Sarbanes-Oxley Act, the principal audit firms and their partners remained steadfastly silent. No accounting professional in private practice called for reform of the profession. This was in marked contrast to the often public and nasty debates within the more competitive securities brokerage industry.

Post-Enron, as the litigation risks have risen and as the possibility of crippling reputational injury is much more evident, the major audit firms have taken action to unload their riskiest clients, usually passing them along to smaller audit firms not in the Big Four. But prior to Enron and the new reforms, such resignations were rare. Clients were too valuable to be surrendered, because, even if their audit fees were modest and static, the non-audit fees from such clients could be projected to grow exponentially.

In contrast to the closed ranks solidarity of the auditors, a very different pattern characterized the market for securities research. That analysts often disagree about individual companies is not surprising (in part because some analysts work for firms that have client relationships with the subject corporation and others do not). But it is instructive to observe that brokerage firms responded very differently to the adverse publicity that focused on them, beginning with New York Attorney General Eliot Spitzer's investigation of Merrill Lynch's securities analysts. In response, some major firms quickly and voluntarily adopted strict new conflict of interest policies (for example, Merrill Lynch prohibited its analysts from covering stocks that they personally owned), but others did not. Other firms (most notably, Charles Schwab & Co.) aggressively and publicly criticized their rivals in widely televised commercials attacking their conflicts of interest.[9] This level of combat occurs only in a truly competitive market (the brokerage industry has long been fiercely competitive), and it contrasts sharply with the solidarity shown by the nominal rivals in the accounting industry.

Noisy Reputations   Another reason that audit firms did not take more aggressive steps to protect their reputational capital prior to Enron may be that they realized their reputations had largely blurred and investors could not distinguish clearly among them. Once, a decade or so earlier, a clear hierarchy was discernible within the accounting industry, with Price Waterhouse and Arthur Andersen being regarded as the 'Tiffany' firms within the profession. But then came a wave of mergers among accounting firms, and reputations blurred, as firms with the best reputations often acquired firms with mediocre reputations.

In overview, that these mergers occurred shows that senior management at the acquiring firms believed size and scale were more important to their future than prestige. As audit firms grew to a global scale in the 1980s, a wave of consolidating mergers followed, which often combined high status audit firms with less aristocratic competitors. Reputational capital was in this sense deliberately diluted in order to gain scale and clients in an increasingly global marketplace.

This willingness to accept dilution of their firm's reputational capital expressed itself in other ways as well. Some empirical evidence suggests that a high level of non-audit fees at a particular audit client alarmed investors and made them question the reliability of the corporation's earnings.[10] Although these studies did not necessarily prove that auditor independence was in fact impaired, they did indicate that apparent conflicts attributable to a high level of non-audit fees caused the market to discount the corporation's earnings. In effect, investors questioned the auditor's independence and thus reduced the stock price. Despite this reaction, prior to Enron, investor anxieties do not appear to have slowed auditors in their race to maximize consulting revenues from audit clients. Even placing a ceiling on such consulting revenues was too high a price to pay for protecting their reputational capital.

The Impact of the Bubble Any comprehensive explanation of the apparent willingness of auditors to risk their reputational capital must factor in the impact of the market bubble that began in the mid-1990s and continued to early 2000. Arguably, a market bubble made investors less concerned with backward-looking financial information and more focused on forward-looking disclosures. Under this view, the gatekeepers' reputations were less noisy than irrelevant. If investors had lost their natural skepticism because of a decade of constantly increasing earnings and stock prices, then investors might have become no more concerned about the identity and reputation of their auditor than are the tenants of a skyscraper about the identity of their elevator inspector. Like elevator failure, audit failure was discounted as a trivial risk. But if these risks seemed remote, then issuers would also come to perceive that the costs of rigorous gatekeeping exceeded their benefits. More generally, during the 1990s, investors may have come to rely more on securities analysts than on auditors.

To the extent that this scenario has validity, auditors may have sensed that investors in an exuberant market were becoming indifferent to the auditor's relative professional reputation. Arguably, the corporate client merely needed some minimally reputable auditor to certify its financial statements in order to satisfy the SEC. Although auditors were necessary for legal reasons, they did not create value for their clients, and hence they had reduced leverage. From this perspective, if your client places little value on your services, your best strategy for holding a lucrative client is to become very compliant. To be sure, this theory may seem over broad and too cynical as applied to all clients, but it could easily apply to some.

The common denominator to all these accounts is that reputational capital can be risked or sacrificed, either because its value had declined in a market that viewed the gatekeeper as an old-fashioned, non-essential service provider or because the gatekeeper could not profit from its 'excess' reputational capital. By the end of the 1990s, the auditor arguably needed only to have a qualifying level of reputational capital, and it could not justify expending resources to protect any 'excess' level of such capital, particularly if it interfered with its ability to market other more lucrative services. Indeed, the rational manager disposes of 'excess' assets (and certainly invests little in protecting them). Although there is no evidence that accounting firms deliberately liquidated their 'excess' reputational capital, there is considerable evidence that they ceased to protect it zealously.

The Post-Scandal Markets

In the wake of scandals and the reforms of the Sarbanes-Oxley Act, much has changed. As noted earlier, auditors are shedding their riskier clients and observing (for the time at least) a norm imposed by institutional investors that non-audit revenues from any audit client must stay below its audit revenues. Conflicts of interest are thus reduced, and, in any event, litigation risk is also perceived as higher in the post-Enron environment. Securities analysts have similarly changed their behavior, and while optimism still dominates pessimism in their recommendations, the percentage of 'sell' recommendations is now substantial. But there has been a cost to reform: employment and coverage within the field of securities research has declined markedly. The dilemma underlying these reforms is that securities research is today more independent but also less prevalent.

Against this backdrop, it is now time to move from description to prescription and consider what reforms might work.

Endnotes

1. As discussed in Ch. 7, this attitude seems myopic. Particularly if new entrants into this market were dependent upon subscribers for their revenues, they could lead a race to the top.

2. Leonard Spacek, the managing partner of Arthur Andersen & Co. who took over as the firm's leader in 1947 on the death of Arthur Andersen, its founder, was known within the profession as the profession's conscience. He not only preached the need for high integrity but organized Andersen around a strong system of internal controls and second partner review, and he was outspoken in his criticism of some generally accepted accounting principles as too lax. Many of his contemporaries at other firms disliked his lecturing of the profession, which they saw as marketing, but at the time it seems to have attracted business for Andersen. See Christine Earley, Kate Odabashian and Michael Willenborg, *Enron, the*

Demise of Andersen and the Ethical Climate of Accounting, 35 Conn. L. Rev. 1013, 1028 (2003); Previts & Merino at 310–311.

3. See Ch. 4 at [n 282]. In 2004, the Big Four resigned from 210 public companies; in 2003, from 152; in 2002, from 78. By dropping higher risk clients, the Big Four is opening the door to real competition. See Lynnley Browning, 'Sorry, the Auditor Said, But We Want a Divorce,' *New York Times*, February 6, 2005, s 3, p 5. Most of these changes were, of course, because the Big Four has decided to drop smaller, higher-risk clients, but the result is still to make the market less concentrated.

4. These studies now amount to a considerable literature. For representative examples, see Mark Defond, Kannan Raghunadan, and K. B. Subramanyam, 'Do Non-Audit Services Impair Auditor Independence? Evidence from Going Concern Audit Opinions' (SSRN. com/abstract=297747) (January 2002); Hollis Ashbaugh-Skalfe, Ryan Lafond, and Brian Mayhew, 'Do Non-Audit Services Compromise Auditor Independence? Further Evidence' (SSRN.com/abstract=305720) (February 2003); Kannan Raghunandan, William Read, and Scott Whisenant, 'Are Non-Audit Fees Associated with Restated Financial Statements?' (SSRN.com/abstract=394844) (April 2003); Caitlin M. Ruddock, Sarah J. Taylor, Stephen L. Taylor, 'Non-Audit Services and Earnings Conservatism: Is Auditor Independence Impaired?' (SSRN. com/abstract=303343) (April 2004). Not all these studies agree. Some do find earnings management to become more likely when a high level of non-audit fees are paid to the auditor. See Carol Callaway Dee, Avalen Lulseged, and Tanya S. Nowlin, 'Earnings Quality and Auditor Independence: An Examination Using Non-Audit Fee Data' (SSRN. com/abstract=304185) (January 2002).

5. Compare Daniel Bradley, Bradford Johnson and Jay Ritter, 'Analyst Behavior Following IPOs: The "Bubble Period"' (Working Paper, October 2004) (studying 7,400 analyst recommendations and finding little evidence that the market discounted the views of affiliated analysts in comparison to unaffiliated analysts) with Xia Chen, 'Analyst Affiliation, Ranking and the Market Reaction to Stock Recommendations for IPOs' (Working Paper, October 2004) (studying 7,354 stock recommendations relating to 1,666 IPOs in 1996–2000 and finding such a market discount for the positive recommendations of analysts employed by a lead or co-lead underwriter).

6. This conflict has been at least partially mitigated by the adoption of Regulation FD in late 2000, which prohibits selective disclosure to analysts.

7. See Sean O'Connor, *Be Careful What You Wish For: How Accountants and Congress Created the Problem of Auditor Independence*, 46 B.C. L. Rev. 741 (2004).

8. See William W. Bratton, *Rules, Principles, and the Accounting Crisis in the United States*, 5 European Business Organization Law Review, 7, 27 (2004).

9. In 2002, Charles Schwab ran a series of satirically barbed TV commercials in which hypothetical sales managers at rival brokerage firms pushed their brokers and analysts to deceive their clients by saying 'Let's put some lipstick on this pig.' See Neil Weinberg, 'Holier than Whom?: Lipstick on the Schwab Pig,' Forbes, June 2003 at p 71. Perhaps because Charles Schwab was not an underwriter, it was freer to attack the conflicts that tainted the research of its rivals.

10. See J. R. Francis and B. Ke, 'Disclosure of Fees Paid to Auditors and the Market Valuation of Earnings Surprises' (working paper on SSRN at id=487463) (high non-audit fees leads to a 17% reduction on average in the market valuation of quarterly earnings surprises).

10

What Should Work? (and How to Get There)

Surveying the Options

The preceding chapter has concluded that gatekeepers will not always seek to protect their reputational capital. Circumstances can arise in which it is rational to risk that capital. Particularly in concentrated markets, the rational gatekeeper may recognize that it does not need an unblemished record, but only one not significantly worse than its rivals. Indeed, if its rivals have tarnished records, while it instead resembles Snow White, it arguably has made an excessive investment in reputational capital on which it will realize little return. Finally, to the extent that the gatekeeper is hired by corporate managers to reassure its shareholders or investors, a reputation for unbending intransigence may alienate corporate managers, even if it pleases investors—thereby producing an uncertain trade-off. In short, there is no natural equilibrium. Professional firms market themselves on an ad hoc and shifting basis, always conscious of what their principal competitors are doing and that they need to please both corporate managers and investors.

How then can the law encourage them to improve their performance? Here, serious analysis of how to reform gatekeepers has been conspicuous mainly by its absence. Only with the Sarbanes-Oxley Act in 2002 has any real effort been made to address the conflicts to which gatekeepers are subject. But Sarbanes-Oxley's approach was basically to prohibit specified conflicts of interest. This may well be justified, but it faces the regulator with a Sisyphean task. Prohibit one conflict and an alternative one springs up in its place. The regulator's task thus becomes unending, and the regulator is always playing 'catch up,' one step behind its quarry. Ultimately, the result is a maze of rules and at best limited success.

The basic inventory of policy options is limited and can be briefly surveyed.

Litigation   Exposing gatekeepers to a higher threat of litigation would logically make them more attentive to the interests of investors. As earlier discussed, considerable reason exists to believe that the decline in the deterrent threat of civil litigation in the 1990s at least partially explains the shortfall in gatekeeper performance. Nonetheless, this was the one approach that the Sarbanes-Oxley Act—an eclectic mixture of many reforms—did not pursue (probably because it was too politically controversial). Yet, even if litigation remedies should be enhanced, it is difficult to believe that they provide the principal or best means by which to reform gatekeepers. Gatekeepers are professionals. So also are doctors. By analogy, few would seriously argue that the best way to improve medical care in the United States was to increase the threat of malpractice litigation against doctors.

Obvious problems arise if we pursue reform by relying primarily on litigation. First, corporate and securities litigation tends to be driven by the plaintiff's attorney, who may be at least as conflicted and compromised an agent of investors as any gatekeeper. Second, the market for gatekeeping services could fail, as professionals could leave a particular market for related fields.[1] For example, it is not unimaginable that accounting firms could give up auditing public companies because of the threat of litigation. Auditors now face potentially astronomic liabilities in the United States, and a single litigation (such as an Enron, WorldCom, or Parmalat class action), if it were litigated to judgment, could drive any of the Big Four into insolvency.

This does not mean that litigation reforms are infeasible. A case can be made for a stricter standard of liability coupled with a possible ceiling on liability to preclude insolvency based on a single failure.[2] This topic will be returned to in the final chapter, but for the moment the tentative conclusion is only that litigation offers no 'magic bullet' solution. Moreover, the key American innovations that make private litigation an effective deterrent—for example, the class action, the contingent fee, and the 'American rule' against fee shifting—are controversial and most likely cannot be transported to other legal regimes outside the United States.

Disclosure   This is the classic answer of corporate law to conflicts of interest. The premise is that if the agent were forced to disclose his or her conflicts of interest, the agent would shun them to avoid the embarrassment incident to disclosure. The problem is that recent empirical research suggests that this premise may be wrong. Social psychologists find that disclosure of conflicts may instead have a perverse effect. It may cause the party to whom the disclosure is made to let down its guard and assume that those making full disclosure of their conflicts will for that very reason deal with them fairly.[3] Worse yet, the conflicted party making the disclosure apparently feels that, having disclosed, it can now pursue its own interests aggressively. In short, the recipients of biased advice will not adequately discount it, but those making the disclosure may thereby feel 'morally licensed' to act in their own self-interest (and possibly increase the level of bias in their advice). For example, informing shareholders that the auditor is conflicted because of other work it is performing for the company at the behest of management may only cause the shareholder to assume that the auditor will overcompensate to avoid favoritism or bias, which assumption could be entirely incorrect. In any event, shareholders cannot respond to this information in any meaningful fashion, other than by taking the extreme step of selling their shares.

Peer Review   This is often the preferred mechanism for controlling the performance of professionals. In some settings (for example, the university or medicine), it may work well, as tenure review arguably weeds out the weaker performers. But, as already emphasized in earlier chapters, the critical fact about many markets for gatekeeping services is their extreme concentration. With only four major auditing firms and two major credit-rating agencies, one cannot generally expect competitors to review each other's performance objectively or without fear of retaliation. Indeed, peer review was the practice that failed most egregiously in the case of the auditing profession, where all the major firms could expect that the competitor they reviewed today might review them in turn tomorrow. In such a world, norms of reciprocity swiftly develop (e.g. 'You be soft on me, and I will be soft on you'), thereby undercutting the effectiveness of this strategy.

Restoring a Principal–Agent Relationship   Now we come to the most promising reform. The striking fact about most contemporary markets for gatekeeping services is that the gatekeepers are hired and compensated, not by the investors that they serve, but by corporate managers they are to monitor. Except in very special circumstances, corporate officers hire the attorneys, investment bankers, and other consultants who in turn advise shareholders. Obviously, this raises the prospect that the advice and opinions so given may be biased in favor of management. Watchdogs hired by those they are to watch typically turn into pets, not guardians.

What can be done about this? Piecemeal reforms can seek to restrict conflicts of interest or to enhance the litigation threat to deter disloyal behavior by gatekeepers. Thus, Sarbanes-Oxley Act bars auditing firms from engaging in certain types of consulting services for auditing clients. But such reforms are always incomplete as well as costly, and new evasions are invented more or less as quickly as older ones are prohibited.

In this light, the simplest, cleanest way to cut through this Gordian Knot may be to re-establish a direct principal–agent relationship between investors and their gatekeepers. If feasible, this is the elegant solution to the problem of gatekeeper capture because it would mean that investors (and not corporate officers) would hire, fire and compensate the gatekeeper. As noted in the earlier chapters on each profession, such relationships did once exist. For example, securities analysts were originally compensated out of brokerage commissions paid by shareholders. Until the mid-1970s, the credit-rating agencies marketed their ratings to investors who subscribed to their services, and the rating agencies were not paid by the corporate issuer. Originally, in 19th century Britain, shareholders hired their own auditor. In each case, these practices changed so that corporate managers came—directly or indirectly—to choose and compensate the gatekeeper.

But attempting to establish such a direct principal–agent relationship in a manner that makes gatekeepers directly responsible to investors is easier said than done. After all, the principal reason that gatekeepers turned to corporations to support them was that investors would only do so parsimoniously. Later, this chapter will examine the feasibility of such an approach in the case of five gatekeepers: (1) the auditor, (2) the securities analyst, (3) the credit-rating agency, (4) the corporate attorney, and (5) the investment banker. The basic premise is that if a strong shareholder group, or some functional substitute, could be created to serve as the principal, that principal could pick for itself loyal and qualified gatekeepers. Ideally, a strong principal can find its own agents, and the law would not need to regulate the process closely. But, as will be seen, the problem of creating a principal overlaps with problems in subsidizing the gatekeeper. Ultimately, it may be feasible to create a stronger principal, but direct shareholder selection of the gatekeeper appears to be a reform that is more illusory than practical.

Two Case Studies

Before surveying the problems with this approach, it is worth examining two recent regulatory experiments in which attempts have been made to introduce new gatekeepers. In the U.S., the experiment seems to be working, and its apparent success may lie in the fact that a very conflicted agent of investors now reports to a stronger principal. In the U.K., the experiment is at a much earlier stage, but a flaw seems apparent: the new gatekeeper does not report to a principal with strong incentives to discipline its agent.

The Lead Plaintiff

In class action litigation alleging corporate or securities law violations, the plaintiff's attorney serves as the agent of investors, representing them collectively in cases where it would not be feasible economically for them to sue individually. But because shareholders are dispersed and under-informed, the plaintiff's attorney lacks any strong principal and may act opportunistically to pursue its own interests. For example, the plaintiff's attorney may subordinate its client's interest in receiving a large recovery to its own interest in receiving a large fee award (which the defendants can rationally offer it in exchange for a 'cheap' settlement).[4] In 1995, Congress sought to reform securities class actions by enacting the Private Securities Litigation Reform Act of 1995 (the PSLRA). Congress believed that class action securities litigation was too often a 'lawyer-driven' phenomenon that maximized the interests of the plaintiff's counsel more than those of the shareholders that the attorney represented. Typically, plaintiff's attorneys would use the same small shareholder over and over in successive class actions, and the relationship resembled one in which the lawyer was the puppeteer; and the small shareholder, the puppet. Many believed that these small shareholders took on the role of class representative not because of any interest in the litigation (as their individual recovery would have been trivial), but because of under-the-table payments to them by the plaintiff's attorney.[5] As a result, the small shareholder serving as class representative would remain passive and not object, even if the settlement were inadequate and the proposed fee award excessive.

From our perspective focused on the principal–agent relationship, this relationship can be seen as a 'pseudo-principal–agent relationship.' In reality, the attorney hired the shareholder/client, not the reverse. Congress responded to this problem in the PSLRA by adopting a suggestion proposed by two law professors.[6] The law professors' proposal was to give control of the securities class action not to the first plaintiff to file an action nor to the class counsel elected by all plaintiffs who filed an action (both of which practices had been followed in many federal courts), but rather to the shareholder with the largest stake in the action—namely, the shareholder who appeared to have suffered the greatest losses. In effect, the party with the largest stake in the action was made the presumptive principal to monitor and select the attorney to represent the class. At a stroke, this reform established a true principal–agent relationship, and such a plaintiff–called the 'lead plaintiff' by the PSLRA—was authorized to take control of the action and generally supervise the litigation. Effectively, this gave large institutional investors the power to select the class action attorney.

What happened? The evidence is mixed, but it seems to show that when large public pension funds replaced the small shareholder as the 'lead plaintiff,' recoveries to the class went up.[7] In short, a stronger principal seems to have produced superior performance by the agent. While conflicts did not disappear,[8] the creation of a strong principal to monitor the agent cost little and appears to have produced quantifiable benefits. Optimists can read this evidence to imply that if stronger principals were created in a variety of related contexts where gatekeepers serve investors, results would also improve in these contexts.

Nomads

Established in 1995, the Alternative Investment Market (AIM) has been the London Stock Exchange's answer to Nasdaq—a market intended to attract young, emerging entrepreneurial firms on a worldwide basis. To date, it has been highly successful, attracting over 1,800 listings as of mid-2005, many from Israel and Canada, where new issuers would formerly have listed on Nasdaq.[9] AIM's principal attraction has been its lack of regulation and low cost. Although companies listed on the London Stock Exchange (LSE) are subject to the regulation of the UK Listing Authority, which is part of the Financial Services Authority (FSA) (Britain's SEC), regulatory oversight of companies listed on AIM has instead been delegated to private bodies, known as 'Nomads.' Nomads—or 'nominated advisors'—are financial service firms, typically investment banks, but also accounting and even law firms. Nomads must be approved by the LSE, and as of mid-2005, there were some 75 such firms registered with it, including major American investment banks, such as Merrill Lynch, Morgan Stanley and Goldman Sachs.[10]

The basic premise underlying AIM is that an intimate advisory relationship with an experienced professional could substitute for close regulation. Thus, AIM is willing to list shell corporations with no trading history, no public shareholders, no financial results, and few assets—if they have secured the services of a Nomad. The Nomad is required by the LSE's rules to confirm to the LSE that the directors of the AIM-listed company have received satisfactory advice and guidance as to compliance with AIM's rules, that the applicant's securities are 'appropriate to be admitted,' and that the nominated advisor is and will be available at all times to advise and guide the directors as to their compliance obligations.[11]

Potentially, the Nomad is a powerful gatekeeper, because if it were to resign, the listed company could not remain on AIM (unless it immediately found another Nomad). But the Nomad's obligations are remarkably vague, in part because AIM's compliance rules are remarkably thin. The Nomad's position is further undercut by the usual problem of conflicts of interest. Most Nomads are underwriters who logically view the listed company (which often has not yet done an initial public offering) as a potential client. Thus, the underwriter's desire to take the client public may conflict with its chaperone-like responsibilities as a Nomad. Further, because it is hired by a corporation that often has no, or few, public shareholders, there is no adequate principal to monitor it.

In overview, Nomads probably present the limiting example of reliance on a gatekeeper. Effectively, they have been given the power to block an initial listing or to revoke an ongoing one. But they have neither clearly defined duties nor a strong principal. Proponents of the system believe that they can serve as an effective interface between the institutional investors who dominate the AIM market and its start-up companies. Time will tell, and problems have already surfaced. Mining, oil drilling, and exploration companies have flocked to AIM to list and raise capital, and their stocks are naturally volatile and vulnerable to manipulation. Some Nomads also appear to have largely delegated their advisory functions to law firms hired by the Nomad to prepare advisory memos.

Flawed as the system seems, the more interesting question is whether it could be made to work. If the Nomad were appointed by the exchange, instead of hired by the to-be-listed company, the gatekeeper would at least have a stronger principal. Although the LSE presumably has a healthy concern for its own reputation, it still is not the ideal principal with a strong economic stake in the gatekeeper's performance. Alternatively, the Nomad could be appointed at the time of the stock flotation on AIM by the institutional investors who purchase in the offering. Although this selection process might be controlled by the issuer's management, liability rules could supplement this process and furnish a powerful disincentive for cozy issuer/Nomad relationships. For example, if the Nomad were made automatically liable for some portion (say 20%) of the investors' losses attributable to securities fraud, it would then have an incentive to monitor its issuer more closely.[12] The bottom line here is that the use of an investment banking firm (or some other financial services firm) as a gatekeeper for start-up companies is promising, but the conflicts of interest need to be mitigated and a stronger principal created (or some deterrent threat generated).

The Feasibility of Stronger Principal—Agent Relationships

The idea of restoring strong principal–agent relationships is certainly attractive. Sometimes, it may work, but as the following tour will suggest, it also encounters numerous problems.

The Auditor

In principle, shareholders, rather than management or an audit committee, could select the corporation's auditor. This may have worked well in mid-19th century Great Britain, when such a practice was mandated by legislation. But it is far less feasible once the shareholders have become dispersed. As a practical matter, dispersed shareholders, holding small stakes in numerous corporations, could not feasibly negotiate with multiple auditors over how they would perform audits at thousands of corporations or as to what other relationships the auditor could have with these corporations or their managements. This constraint is not necessarily fatal to the proposal. Potentially, shareholders could insist on one set of model terms (which could conceivably be designed by a proxy adviser, such as Institutional Shareholder Services (ISS)), but this approach invites rigidity and simply invents a new agent—the proxy adviser—to monitor the auditor's contract. Moreover, in most circumstances, the shareholders are likely to be rationally apathetic about the choice of auditor. Hence, they would most likely defer to any recommendation made by management—until a crisis developed. Finally, shareholder choice is greatly limited by the highly concentrated nature of the market for auditing services. Because the 'Big Four' possess market power vis-à-vis the shareholders of any single firm, the major audit firms might simply refuse to negotiate or accept any limitations on their discretion. For all these reasons, shareholder selection of the auditor does not seem a promising reform.

So what answers are left? Some have suggested random assignment of auditors—for example, choosing auditors by means of a lottery.[13] But this still leaves the auditor without a strong principal to monitor it and prevent its capture by the issuer's management. And if the lottery were limited to the Big Four (plus a few other firms), none would face any competitive pressure to change. Even if the frequent rotation of auditors might be desirable in some settings, one cannot expect, in an oligopolistic market with only four major firms, that lotteries, or the rapid rotation of auditors in general, will accomplish much. More likely, it would only produce a revolving door (and increased expense) with no real change in the behavior of the major audit firms.

Thus, the search for a strong principal to monitor the auditor must look elsewhere than to shareholders. One provocative proposal that has attracted considerable attention has been made by an accounting professor: insurance companies could monitor the auditor. Under this proposal, originally advanced by New York University accounting professor Joshua Ronen,[14] public companies would, with the approval of their shareholders, purchase 'financial statement insurance,' insuring their shareholders from market loss in the event that fraud or irregularity was later discovered in the financial statements so insured. The insurer selling this insurance would only sell it to the issuer after first conducting a rigorous audit. Thus, the insurer would hire the auditor to protect it, and at least in theory the insurer would have the incentive to monitor its agent closely. Moreover, because insurers would sell policies to many companies, they would need to hire auditors on a large scale basis and hence would possess the negotiating leverage to insure the auditor's independence and freedom from conflicts. At a stroke, a strong principal is created.

The proposal is both ingenious and flawed. On the one hand, it does seemingly solve the problem of auditor capture. The auditor would realize that its client was the insurer and would have no reason to defer to the corporation's management. But, on the other hand, how closely would the insurer monitor? Potentially, it could charge high enough premiums from the corporation to cover its losses, even if it perceived a high risk of fraud.[15] Thus, it might have little incentive to monitor. Indeed, many believe that insurers have generally failed to monitor in the 'D&O' insurance market where the corporation buys liability insurance for its directors and officers, because again the insurer can increase its premiums to cover any likely loss.[16] Although the proponents of the financial statement insurance proposal believe that disclosure of the premium and the policy's terms would alert shareholders to the company's level of risk, these disclosures provide only very noisy information, which shareholders might find it difficult to digest and decode for dissimilar companies. Worse yet, insured shareholders might no longer care about the riskiness of their corporation's accounting practices, thereby eliminating internal pressure for reform. In short, a moral hazard problem arises. If insurers could protect themselves with high premiums and if shareholders could rely on their insurance, the net result might be that no one would truly monitor the auditor.

An even greater problem, however, concerns the incentives of the insurer to conceal fraud once it has sold the insurance. Even a rigorous audit might miss evidence of fraud or irregularities, which may only come to light at a later time. And when this evidence did eventually come to light, after the issuance of the policy, the insurer would then be liable and so would have every reason to discourage the auditor at this point from pursuing indications suggesting fraud or irregularity. Indeed, an insurance company that has guaranteed the issuer's financial statements does not want problems coming to light *post hoc*; its incentives to suppress signs of fraud at this point are the same as the issuer's. As a result, the financial statement insurance model works on a one-time only basis, but not if the insurer covers multiple accounting periods during which previously missed problems begin to surface. Once the insurer discovers signs of trouble, its rational goal would be to suppress this information and sell no more insurance to the issuer, letting some other insurer cover risks that it now knows are high. But escape may not be easy, because the insurer's decision to drop the issuer as a client would be a clear signal to the market of potential problems. Hence, the issuer might become locked in and would seek to conceal information over even an extended period in order to avoid a market decline and resulting investor claims against it. Put simply, no one wants a fraud discovered on their watch, and no one has stronger incentives to resist discovery than an insurer who would be strictly liable.

In this light, it is instructive to compare the incentives of such an insurer as monitor, with those of the typical audit committee. If directors on an audit committee are informed by their auditor of irregularities or a material weakness in internal controls, their obvious incentives are to correct the problem, because their principal liability is for passivity in the face of a known risk.[17] If they take corrective action, however, they are likely to escape liability, even if the corporation does incur a loss. Hence, directors have relatively good incentives to investigate and uncover the fraud. In contrast, the insurer has stronger incentives to investigate at the outset before it sells insurance, but much less afterwards once it fears becoming liable on the fraud's discovery.

In this light, Sarbanes-Oxley may well have gotten it right. That is, it assigned responsibility for monitoring the auditor to a new principal: the independent audit committee. Such a committee may not have the economic leverage or depth of knowledge of a major insurer, but it has better continuing incentives. At least so long as its directors face some risk of liability, they have little incentive to conceal. The bottom line then is that, in the case of the auditor, an ideal principal is not easily identified, and the audit committee may be the best available.

The Securities Analyst

In the case of the analyst, the possibility of creating a stronger principal may be more feasible. Originally, securities analysts were compensated by investors out of brokerage commissions. Thus, they were the agents of investors and they profited to the extent that they satisfied their clients. But that today is ancient history. In part, commissions shrank as the result of increased competition and the end of fixed brokerage commissions. By the 1990s, securities analysts as a group were being largely subsidized by the underwriting divisions of their investment banking firms. That too has now ended with the Global Settlement between the securities regulators (led by New York Attorney General Eliot Spitzer) and the major underwriting houses.[18]

Ironically, the Global Settlement has spawned its own crisis for this profession because it has made Wall Street firms less willing to subsidize securities research. To be sure, the former subsidy from the underwriting side of the investment bank tended to distort research by inducing the analyst to issue favorable 'buy' ratings on the stocks and of IPO and other firm clients. But this system did support analysts who, at least in the case of non-clients, remained free to write their own objective opinions. Yet, if investment banks can no longer influence research in their clients' interests, they have less reason to subsidize it. Securities research does not pay for itself, and thus the cost of Global Settlements' reforms are non-trivial. The overall impact of the Global Settlement is that Wall Street is today less conflicted but also less transparent.

This is best understood by focusing on the decline in the number of public corporations covered by analysts. Investment Dealers Digest, a leading industry publication, reports that only 55 percent of all publicly traded corporations are now covered by even a single analyst.[19] This statistic actually understates the problem, because historically a public company was only deemed adequately covered if at least four analysts followed it regularly. Between January 2002 and March 2005, 691 public companies lost all analyst coverage.[20] The vast majority of these 'orphaned' companies have a market capitalization of under $1 billion, but above that level many major companies are today covered by only one or two analysts. In response, many smaller companies are beginning to commission their own research by directly compensating an analyst—a practice that certainly creates a strong principal, but hardly an independent one.

Viewed in the light, the public policy dilemma is that if we insist that the securities analyst be compensated only out of brokerage commissions, sell-side research could adequately cover only a modest portion of the market, leaving smaller companies to trade largely in the dark. Ideally, then, public policy must have a dual objective: (1) to create a strong principal to monitor the analyst as agent, and (2) to find an adequate subsidy for securities research.

Academics have proposed one possible answer to this problem. Professors Stephen Choi and Jill Fisch have advanced an ingenious voucher financing proposal under which the issuer would distribute vouchers to its shareholders, who could use them to purchase securities research from the analyst of their choice, with the analyst redeeming the voucher for cash from the issuer.[21] This proposal does have the clear virtue of creating a subsidy that the issuer cannot control. Hence, analysts are subsidized without their research being biased by the subsidy. But this proposal faces other problems, both practical ones of implementation and more fundamental ones of structure and strategy. The complexity of distributing vouchers to millions of shareholders on a continuing basis obviously presents serious problems of implementation. But even more importantly, their proposal does not create a strong principal to monitor the analyst as agent. Small individual shareholders would remain weak and dispersed. Thus, even if they exercised their right to receive vouchers with which to purchase research, they might use their vouchers to purchase either stale research that a major underwriting firm had already revealed to its preferred clients, or biased research that the firm produced to promote the interest of its corporate client because of its ties to the issuer. To be sure, institutional investors could protect themselves from this danger, because they are more sophisticated and have closer ties to analysts. But in their case a different problem arises. Institutions might find ways to use vouchers to fund their own 'buy side' research. That is, they might require an analyst they paid with vouchers to keep his or her research and opinions confidential, with the result that no new research reached the public market.[22] Thus, market transparency might not improve.

So what is the answer? Properly defined, the problem here is one of creating a subsidy without biasing the resulting research. Potentially, this is a problem that the market may be able to solve on its own. Adequate securities coverage is, after all, in the interest of all market participants. If so, the best proxy for the market may be the securities exchanges. Consider then this alternative, which can be structured either as a regulatory proposal or as a private ordering solution: each exchange would appoint and compensate one (or more) analysts for each company listed on it that lacked a defined minimum level of analyst coverage. The selection of the analyst would be based on objective criteria, such as, for example, the most accurate prediction of the issuer's prior earnings. The contract between the exchange and the analyst so selected would continue for some limited period (one, two or three years), at the end of which period there would again be a competition for the position of 'designated exchange analyst.' The cost of this subsidy could then be passed on by the exchange to listed companies and broker dealers in the usual annual fees they pay each exchange. Essentially, this idea taxes market participants (both listed companies and broker-dealers) to ensure that there is a minimal level of research available for each listed company. In effect, the market bears the cost of maintaining some minimal level of transparency.

Of course, much in this proposal can be negotiated or adjusted. The actual cost of the analyst might be imposed primarily on the listed company that lacked any analyst (and also on the brokers that principally traded in its stock). This provides a mechanism whereby in substance the issuer does subsidize the analyst, but the linkage between subsidy and control is broken because the selection of the analyst would be made by the exchange, not the issuer. Besides simply being more practical than the voucher proposal, the key advantage of this proposal is that it creates a strong principal to select and monitor the analyst.

Although the cost of this proposal could be fully borne by each issuer, a case exists for imposing some of the cost on the market as a whole. Issuers trading on the same market are, to a degree, interdependent. If scandals break out in the market relating to some companies, others in that same market will most likely suffer. Historically, exchanges specializing in start-up and smaller capitalization companies have collapsed under the weight of repeated scandals, even if most firms on them remained uninvolved.[23] Given this prospect of negative externalities, all issuers on the same market should rationally be willing to share a portion of the costs of ensuring market transparency. Even a small partial subsidy would reduce the cost to the issuer, so that it paid less than if it hired its own analyst.[24] Over the longer run, this cost would also reduce the incentives of exchanges to list every company capable of trading on it, because it would have to subsidize research for such smaller, new listings.

Possibly, this proposal that exchanges select and subsidize analysts may demand more activism from exchanges than they can reasonably be expected to provide voluntarily. Still, from a historical perspective, the major U.S. exchanges have long defined themselves as more than simply trading venues. Decades before the creation of the SEC, the New York Stock Exchange (NYSE) established and enforced mandatory disclosure standards for listed companies, compelling them to distribute annually audited financial statements.[25] Conceptually, little difference exists between the NYSE insisting in the early 20th Century that listed companies bear the cost of an auditor to protect investors and an insistence today that each listed company bear the cost of an objective securities analyst to similarly inform investors. Both follow from the common premise that a securities market has an interest in ensuring transparency.

Although skeptics can still doubt that exchanges will exhibit anything like this level of activism, private ordering has already begun to develop a substitute that copies its essential features. In 2005, the Nasdaq Stock Market and Reuters Group announced a joint venture—known as the Independent Research Network—to find independent analysts to cover 'orphaned' companies without a securities analyst. The issuer would pay the Independent Research Network to screen and hire the analyst, but the issuer would have no say in reviewing or editing the research report.[26] Even earlier, a start-up venture was launched by former senior officers of Nasdaq. Known as the National Research Exchange (NRE), it intends to serve as an independent 'marriage broker' to find objective analysts for under-researched companies without the company itself participating in the selection of the analyst.[27] The NRE will seek its fees from both such 'orphaned' issuers and the 'buy side' investors that want such research. In common, both new ventures are efforts to create an unbiased principal to monitor an important gatekeeper.

Premature as it is at this point to predict the success of either venture, their appearance does show the market perceiving the need for a new intermediary that can stand between the issuer and the analyst and thus provide legitimacy for research that is ultimately issuer-funded. In effect, the appearance of such a 'marriage broker' for analysts represents the birth of a new gatekeeper. To succeed, it must become a credible reputational intermediary that can pledge its reputational capital so that the market trusts the analysts that it sponsors. As always, there are potential conflicts: for example, Nasdaq might quietly pressure analysts for favorable research and 'buy' ratings, because this would increase the trading volume from which it profits. Although the NRE seems less vulnerable on this score, it too could face pressures at the start-up stage to provide early favorable research in order to curry favor with its clients. As they recognize, the test will be whether their 'intermediated research' performs at least as well as 'independent' research. But if these new entities succeed, it would be evidence that the market can fill the void and create a new gatekeeper. Moreover, if 'intermediated research' catches on, it will make securities research a profit center for investment banking firms and end their current indifference to research. Thus, analysts may again acquire a real constituency interested in their services. If these new intermediaries do not succeed, however, then the case becomes stronger for mandating action by the exchanges themselves, funded by listing fees, to subsidize a minimum level of objective research.

Credit-Rating Agencies

Here, subscribers could pay for the services of the rating agency, creating a natural principal–agent relationship. This once was the relationship, but it collapsed, and issuer-paid ratings emerged as its replacement. Back then, the business of credit rating was marginal, and even the largest firms struggled. Today, the business is highly lucrative, but only for those firms able to secure the SEC's NRSRO designation. The rise of structured finance has produced a new ratings-driven form of finance that has enriched the recognized ratings agencies, but produced a closed, oligopolistic market.

What should be done? Opening the door for any rater to provide NRSRO ratings seems risky; similarly, requiring that Moodys and S&P do not charge issuers for ratings (but instead bill subscribers) would be a radical act, likely to produce violent resistance. The best compromise is to encourage expansion of this overly concentrated field by allowing new ratings agencies that are subscriber-funded to win the coveted NRSRO designation based on a fairly modest showing of competence. This is a principal–agent solution, and it involves little risk of a race to the bottom, because subscriber-funded ratings agencies have little incentive to curry favor with issuers. If new firms entered the market (as the result of SEC encouragement), they would also prod Moody's and S & P to provide more current information than they do today.

Disclosure Counsel

In the case of the attorney, one must begin by defining what one wishes to accomplish. Simply attempting to create a stronger principal–agent relationship does not directly address the most visible problems associated with the securities attorney's performance. Those problems include (a) the fragmentation of the attorney's role so that no outside attorney possesses adequate knowledge about the corporate client to be able to assess the accuracy of its overall disclosures; (b) the subordination of the outside securities attorney to in-house general counsel; and (c) the reality that attorneys act only occasionally as gatekeepers, but much more frequently as advocates or transaction engineers—roles that obviously can conflict with a gatekeeper's responsibility.

As noted in the preceding chapter, attorneys are uniquely subject to reputational schizophrenia. A law firm serving a corporation wants, at the same time, to be known as a ferocious defender of the corporation's interests who will oppose litigation opponents and regulatory incursions with unrivaled zeal and also as a wise statesman whose advice and counseling protects investors and ensures transparency. Sooner or later, this desire to play both roles can place the law firm in the hopeless position of a man with one foot on the dock and the other in the rowboat, as the boat begins to drift away. Attempts to straddle this divide are awkward, painful and ultimately doomed.

Yet, what this diagnosis suggests is not that the attorney cannot perform a gatekeeping role but that this role must be separated—indeed, cordoned off—from the attorney's role as advocate or transaction engineer. Separating the two roles is, however, only a first step. The fragmentation problem can best be solved by assigning one independent outside counsel—hereinafter called, the 'disclosure counsel'—the role of monitor of the corporation's overall disclosures to the market and the SEC. Today, multiple attorneys work on the corporation's disclosures, and none may have an integrated perspective. The result may be much like the proverbial seven blind men examining the elephant: each apprehends a portion of reality, but none sees it all. This fragmentation may occur either because it is cheaper to use in-house counsel to perform this recurring task (i.e. a classic 'make versus buy' decision), or because senior management does not want an independent counsel evaluating the adequacy of the corporation's disclosures.

Whichever explanation one prefers, the case for an outside professional to act as a gatekeeper to review the adequacy of the corporation's disclosures seems as strong as that for use of an outside professional (i.e. the auditor) to review the corporation's financial results. Today, the market may rely as much on what the company says in the 'Management Discussion and Analysis' (or MD&A) section of its periodic reports (which contains the company's principal forward-looking disclosures and risk assessments) as on its financial results (which, after all, report only past performance, not future expectations). The auditor certifies only the latter; thus, forward-looking statements may receive no outside review.

To be sure, no other professional—and, in particular, not the attorney—can do what the auditor does: namely, perform an audit. But the attorney can do 'due diligence'. That is historically what the securities attorney did in public offerings. In context, this means that the attorney could regularly confer with senior management and then check their representations against easily ascertainable facts (e.g. contracts, legal filings, internal records) to ensure the factual accuracy of the corporation's disclosures.[28] Until the mid-1980s, securities attorneys conducted due diligence of this sort whenever the corporation made a registered public offering. But with the advent of shelf registration in the 1980s, which brought about a greatly accelerated pace for public offerings, it no longer remained feasible to conduct the traditional level of due diligence. From time to time, the SEC has responded that this problem could be solved if corporations could employ independent outside counsel to conduct 'due diligence' on a continuing basis to assist the eventual underwriters in advance of any specific offering. But few, if any, corporations or underwriters have pursued this option. It was expensive and, in a competitive environment, underwriters could not insist that it be done—for fear that the corporation would simply use other underwriters.

Thus, from a policy perspective, three objectives need to be realized on an integrated basis: (1) an outside and independent attorney should review the accuracy of the corporation's disclosures on an ongoing basis; (2) 'due diligence' should be reintroduced into the disclosure process and extended to cover the corporation's ongoing periodic reports, not simply to public offerings of securities; and (3) the independent attorney should report to a strong principal. All these objectives can, however, be realized simply and in an integrated fashion, as outlined next.

The key step in converting the attorney into a gatekeeper is a certification requirement. The SEC could mandate that all disclosure documents filed with it must be signed by an independent attorney, who would acknowledge his or her responsibility for the preparation or review of the document. Of course, the attorney would not be expected to audit or review financial statements or other technical reports, but disclosures about the company's accounting policies and their impact would be within the attorney's responsibility. The attorney would need to consult with the auditor to ensure proper disclosure of the accounting policies that were being followed. To assure independence, the attorney could not be an employee of the corporation; nor could the attorney's firm receive more than some specified percentage of its revenues from the corporation whose disclosures the attorney was reviewing. Ideally, the SEC could use the same standards as it applies to determine auditor independence, but exact duplication is not necessary.

The phrasing of this certification presents the more controversial issue. The best compromise would be for the attorney signing the disclosure document to certify (a) that the attorney believed the statements made in the document or report to be true and correct in all material respects, and (b) that such attorney was not aware of any additional material information whose disclosure was necessary 'in order to make the statements made, in the light of the circumstances under which they were made, not misleading' (which is the traditional language of Rule 10b–5). This is only a negative certification, and it would not make the attorney an insurer for the accuracy of the statements made (at least unless the attorney knew of, or was 'reckless' with regard to, a material misrepresentation or omission). The real thrust of this negative certification would be to require that some minimal level of 'due diligence' be performed by the attorney before providing this certification. In truth, this is a certification that the attorney commonly gives today in the closely related context of public offerings. Known as a 'Rule 10b–5 letter,' such a certification is typically required by the underwriters of the issuer's counsel at the closing.[29] The SEC could enforce this certification by amending its rules of practice to deem negligence in the preparation of a disclosure document or in the conduct of associated 'due diligence' to amount to unprofessional conduct by the attorney.[30]

At first glance, this proposed certification basically tracks the language of Rule 10b–5. Predictably, however, some in the bar will object that by subjecting the attorney to a requirement that the attorney exercise reasonable care, this requirement will lead to excessive liability. But this overstates. In truth, this proposed certification would only generalize existing practices in the market. Today, in most public underwritten offerings, issuer's counsel already delivers an opinion to the underwriters stating that it is not 'aware' of any material information required to be disclosed that has not been disclosed.[31] But no similar negative certification is required or provided when the issuer files its annual report with the SEC. This is an omission that the SEC should have corrected long ago. SEC rules would therefore simply be requiring for periodic filings under the Securities Exchange Act of 1934 what is already done in the primary market when the corporation makes a public offering. The real difference is that, in the case of periodic filings under the Securities Exchange Act of 1934, there is no analogue to the underwriter to demand such an opinion or certification from the attorney. Thus, the proposed certification would fill this void.

Technical as all this may sound, such a certification requirement would have a profound symbolic and psychological effect on the bar because it would recognize the attorney's obligations as a gatekeeper. Ideally, the SEC should go even further and require the certifying attorney to certify that the attorney believed in the accuracy of all statements made in the filed document 'after making such inquiry that the attorney reasonably believed appropriate under the circumstances.' This would effectively establish a meaningful 'due diligence' obligation. Even absent this certification that the attorney has made reasonable inquiry, law firms would most likely be unwilling to deliver the traditional 'Rule 10b-5 letter' unless they were in a position to maintain a continuing oversight of the firm. A one-time-only certification would be a service that few firms would dare to provide. Thus, this proposal effectively counteracts the current fragmentation of responsibility among attorneys and indirectly requires continuing 'due diligence.'

Legally, such a certification could trigger 'aiding and abetting' liability if the attorney ignored materially false or misleading information of which it was aware, and it might even trigger criminal liability under various federal statutes for a knowing violation. But its primary effect is to recognize that the securities attorney is a gatekeeper for investors. Private civil liability to investors in class actions would not necessarily follow because the plaintiff would still have to establish an intent to defraud, which the merely negligent attorney would not have.

The most controversial aspect of the foregoing proposal is the idea that the SEC could mandate due diligence by the attorney who certifies the SEC filing. Here, the Sarbanes-Oxley Act enhances the SEC's authority significantly, because Section 307 of the Sarbanes-Oxley Act authorizes the SEC to establish 'minimum standards of professional conduct for attorneys appearing and practicing before the Commission…'. This reference to 'professional conduct' arguably empowers the SEC to adopt rules requiring the attorney both to conduct a minimal due diligence review before the attorney files a document or report with the SEC and to certify its good faith belief in the accuracy of the statements made therein. In fact, in its existing Rules of Practice, the SEC already holds auditors to precisely such a standard and asserts the power to suspend or disbar auditors for merely negligent conduct.[32] If auditors can be so disciplined without special statutory authority, then it seems to follow *a fortiori*, after the enactment of Section 307, that the SEC could similarly require attorneys to take reasonable steps to investigate the accuracy of statements made in documents that they prepare.[33]

The bottom line then is that the SEC could adopt rules that could discipline or suspend an attorney for negligence as a form of professional misconduct.[34] No satisfactory reason seems apparent to distinguish attorneys and auditors in regard to their liability to public enforcers. But, under this proposal, because of their smaller size and resources, law firms would be largely spared private liability, as negligence is not actionable under Rule 10b-5. Such a trade-off—that is, public liability, but not private liability for negligence—again seems desirable in that it enhances deterrence without truly threatening insolvency for law firms.

If we assume that the attorney (or at least one attorney performing a specialized role) can be converted into a gatekeeper, the final question is: who should monitor this new agent? As in the case of the auditor, the best answer would seem to be the audit committee. If the audit committee were given the same authority over the certifying attorney performing this special role as it has over the auditor, it would insulate the attorney from retaliation and permit easier dialogue over the company's disclosure policies and practices. This would mean that only the audit committee could retain or fire this attorney. Of course, other attorneys could continue to report to the general counsel (or other persons). As a result, the audit committee would become the terminus for two parallel lines of communication: the auditors would report to it with respect to the corporation's financial disclosures, and the certifying attorney with regard to its non-financial disclosures.

This proposal contemplates that the dialogue between the attorney and the audit committee would be privileged, and no 'whistle-blowing obligation' is here imposed. Although some law firms might come to specialize in this role, a law firm could act as the gatekeeper to one corporation and as an advocate or transaction engineer to others. Indeed, the corporation would have an incentive to hire as its gatekeeper a law firm with existing reputational capital. Most importantly, this proposal does not impose gatekeeping responsibilities on all attorneys. The corporation could still retain its 'hired guns' to fight off the regulators. But it would be required to have at least one attorney independently—and, hopefully, skeptically—reviewing its disclosures.

The Investment Banker

Investment banking firms already act as gatekeepers for investors in certain limited ways. For example, they give 'fairness opinions' in connection with mergers and acquisitions, advising one side or the other that the price is reasonably fair to them. In initial public offerings, investment bankers play an even more important screening role, determining in effect that the new issuer is economically viable. The underwriter's obligation to ensure full disclosure in this context is enforced by Section 11 of the Securities Act of 1933, which makes the underwriter strictly liable for material misstatements or omissions in a prospectus, unless it can establish a 'due diligence' defense (i.e. that it conducted a 'reasonable investigation' and, based thereon, 'had reasonable ground to believe and did believe' in the accuracy of the statements made in the prospectus).[35] As a result, initial public offerings are the one context in which significant 'due diligence' is still conducted.

One could, however, extend the investment banker's gatekeeping obligation by giving it similar liability for the corporation's annual report. This could be achieved by requiring the public corporation to specify a responsible investment banking firm that had reviewed and approved its disclosures. In terms of feasibility, this is probably easier to implement than expanded due diligence for public offerings where the expedited timetable leaves little time for due diligence. In contrast, the filing deadline for the annual report is known well in advance and 'due diligence' could be conducted on a less rushed schedule. To ensure a stronger principal, the investment banker could be required to report to (and be hired by) the corporation's audit committee (just as the auditor is today).

However, while feasible, this proposal is costly. Underwriters would demand a high fee before they would accept such potential liability, and some smaller corporations might be driven from the public market. Yet, as noted earlier in this chapter, a similar obligation has been structured into the AIM market in the United Kingdom, where each listed company must have its own 'Nomad' or 'nominated adviser.' The difference is that the AIM system is private and carries no inherent statutory liability (and the class action is also unknown in the U.K.).

Justifiable as this proposal may be, it is also essentially duplicative of the preceding proposal to make the attorney the gatekeeper for the company's disclosures. Because two such gatekeepers seem redundant, the policy question becomes: which approach is better? Using the attorney as gatekeeper is clearly less costly; indeed, 'Nomads' in the AIM market hire law firms out of their fees from the issuer to perform the actual work of disclosure preparation and review. In all likelihood, use of the investment banking firm as a mandatory gatekeeper would still result in most of the disclosure review being delegated to the investment banking firm's counsel. Potentially, the investment banking firm may also be conflicted by its desire to serve as a lead underwriter or perform other services for its client. Finally, locking the corporation into a long-term relationship with a single underwriter may be anti-competitive. Although this is done under the Nomad system on the AIM market, that market lists only young emerging issuers that might not attract the attention of multiple underwriters. More mature companies may resist such a fixed relationship with a single underwriter.

On the other side of the coin, investment banking firms have two advantages over law firms as gatekeepers. First, they simply have more reputational capital and hence should be more prepared to act as a restraining force on a reckless client. Indeed, because their responsibilities would be more diffused and general in comparison to those of a law firm, they would be motivated to monitor, and seek to influence, overall business policies and strategies (whereas a law firm would be over-extending itself if its advice went beyond disclosure and/or law compliance). Second, an investment banking firm can function in ways that a law firm cannot. For example, it could serve as an intermediary between the corporation and institutional investors (as Nomads in fact do). Whether these additional services justify the much greater costs of an investment banking firm as a gatekeeper can be reasonably debated. Different corporations might well reasonably opt for different gatekeepers.

In any event, the issue of the relative superiority of these two proposed gatekeepers need not be resolved here. Both alternatives could work.

Summary

Across the board, gatekeepers work well only when their performance is subject to effective monitoring, which dispersed shareholders can rarely provide. Yet, outside of concentrated ownership legal regimes, 'true' principals for the gatekeeper are hard to find. The audit committee may thus be the strongest monitor one can find for the auditor, attorney, or investment banker. In the case of the securities analyst, either the exchanges or professional 'marriage brokers' (such as the NRE and the IRE) could develop and over time amass the reputational capital to enable them to play an effective monitoring role. But in their case, the need is not simply for a body to monitor the analyst as gatekeeper, but also to subsidize it in a manner that funds, but does not distort, its research.

In the case of the credit-rating agencies, subscribers could monitor (and support) new ratings agencies and thereby acquire ongoing current credit information. Again, as in the case of the analyst, real reform requires that we find a way to fund the gatekeeper, as well as to maintain its independence.

The final proposal that a corporation be required to appoint an attorney or an investment banking firm as its disclosure counsel will be the most controversial, but may also be the most promising. A functional equivalent to this proposal already exists under the Nomad system currently utilized by the AIM. What that system chiefly lacks is any monitor or real mechanism for enforcement. Here, the proposed gatekeeper would be subject to liability and would report to an independent audit committee.

Getting There From Here

Many of the foregoing proposals may seem unrealistic in terms of their political acceptability. Clearly, the enthusiasm of the U.S. Congress for mandatory regulation crested with the Sarbanes-Oxley Act in 2002 and has since subsided. Changes at the SEC suggest it is entering a more cautious and deregulatory stage of its history and will endorse little new regulation.

Thus, are any of these proposed reforms politically attainable? Here, the short answer is that many of the foregoing reforms can be sensibly packaged not as mandatory new norms, but as 'safe harbor' protections for parties subject to high risks. Today, in the wake of recent judicial decisions, outside directors have an urgent need for protection from civil liability. The threat that most worries them (and should worry them) is Section 11 of the Securities Act of 1933. On its face, this section requires directors to conduct a 'reasonable investigation' of those portions of the registration statement that are not 'expertised' by an expert (such as the auditor). Basically, this means that the directors must investigate anything that another expert does not certify (i.e. basically most everything outside the financial statements). If they do not, directors face virtually strict liability under Section 11.

This has long been the law, but compliance with Section 11's obligations has become procedurally less feasible since the advent of shelf registration in the early 1980s. This tension between the statutory duty and the realistic capabilities of the board has been forcefully brought home by the recent decision in the *WorldCom* litigation.[36] Although that decision dealt only with the liability of the underwriters, it found that they had not established their due diligence defense under Section 11 even though they had retained distinguished counsel and received a 'clean' comfort letter from the accountants, and its logic and holding applies equally to directors. The *WorldCom* Court implied that outside counsel had simply done too little to enable their clients to satisfy the 'due diligence' standard set forth in Section 11 as an affirmative defense.

Although the WorldCom directors were not involved in this decision (because they had already agreed to settle), they are equally subject to liability under Section 11 and must satisfy the same statutory defense which requires a 'reasonable investigation.'[37] Thus, if counsel's investigation was inadequate, they would also be liable as a matter of law. Unlike underwriters, directors make very poor risk bearers. Underwriters can accept or reject a client as a business risk, but directors cannot risk their personal assets in the same way. Finally, the *WorldCom* fact pattern shows that the scale of liability on a corporate insolvency can dwarf all available insurance (WorldCom had issued nearly $17 billion in bonds in 2000 and 2001, and thus the Section 11 claims applicable to these bonds easily exceeded the directors' insurance by tenfold).

The result is a policy dilemma that the SEC has ducked to date: directors cannot conduct adequate due diligence (either on their own or based on their counsel's efforts) to satisfy Section 11 within the abbreviated time periods permitted by shelf registration. As a result, they are at least presumptively liable if there is a material misstatement or omission. And plaintiffs increasingly wish to hold them personally liable (each WorldCom director was required to contribute 20% of his or her assets to the settlement in that case).

The only practical answer to this dilemma is a safe harbor defense for directors with respect to Section 11. The SEC could confer such a safe harbor defense on the condition that (a) the corporation employ a special independent disclosure counsel on a full time basis, (b) who would report to the audit committee, and (c) deliver to the SEC and the board with respect to each filing by the corporation of its Annual Report on Form 10-K the negative certification discussed earlier. Because this counsel would review the firm's disclosures on a full-time basis, the short time periods applicable to shelf registration would not be a constraint. Such counsel would neither have Section 11 nor other private liability (absent scienter on its part), because the attorney would not provide any expertised report in the registration statement. Rather, it would be subject only to SEC sanctions for negligent performance, as earlier discussed, under the SEC's Rules of Practice.

The result is a political compromise that directors should welcome. Their virtual strict liability under Section 11 would be relieved, but overall corporate disclosures would be upgraded and subjected to much closer and more independent professional scrutiny. To be sure, disclosure counsel would be costly, but probably not nearly as much as the increased insurance costs that corporations would face to retain outside directors under the *WorldCom* standard. It is a solution that allows everyone to feel that they have come out better off.

Endnotes

1. For a fuller statement of this fear, see Assaf Hamdani, *Gatekeeper Liability*, 77 S. Calif. L. Rev. 53 (2003).

2. Both I and Professor Frank Partnoy have made and debated this case elsewhere. See John C. Coffee, Jr., *Gatekeeper Failure and Reform: The Challenge of Fashioning Relevant Reforms*, 84 B.U. L. Rev. 301 (2004); Frank Partnoy, *Barbarians at the Gatekeepers?: A Proposal For a Modified Strict Liability Regime*, 79 Wash. U. L. Q. 491 (2001).

3. See Daylian M. Cain, George Loewenstein, and Don A. Moore, *The Dirt on Coming Clean: Perverse Effects of Disclosing Conflicts of Interest*, 34 J. Legal Studies 1 (2005).

4. See John C. Coffee, Jr., *The Unfaithful Champion: The Plaintiff As Monitor in Shareholder Litigation*, 48 Law & Contemp. Probs. 5 (Summer 1985).

5. Indeed, the practice of plaintiffs' attorneys paying undisclosed inducements to the named plaintiff in a class action has recently produced indictments, and the possibility that the federal government may even indict the best known plaintiff's law firm in the U.S. See Timothy O'Brien and Jonathan D. Glater, 'The Government Takes Aim At A Class-Action Powerhouse,' *New York Times*, July 17, 2005, Section BU at 1.

6. See Elliott J. Weiss and John S. Beckerman, *Let the Money Do the Monitoring: How Institutional Investors Can Reduce Agency Costs in Securities Class Actions*, 104 Yale L. J. 2053 (1995).

7. See Stephen J. Choi, Jill E. Fisch, A. C. Pritchard, *Do Institutions Matter? The Impact of the Lead Plaintiff Provision of the Private Securities Litigation Reform Act* (ssrn.com/abstract=706901) (March 2005). These authors do recognize that there may be an alternative explanation: institutional investors may 'cherry pick' the most attractive cases and become lead plaintiffs only in those. The two explanations could both be correct in part.

8. Indeed, a new conflict has appeared: 'pay-to-play.' Because public pension funds alone have been willing to serve as lead plaintiffs and because they are often controlled by an elected state or municipal official (usually a controller or comptroller), plaintiffs' law firms have sought to ingratiate themselves with officials by making substantial political contributions to the elected official. Thus, plaintiffs' law firms in New York or Philadelphia or San Diego can be the largest contributor to a political campaign in a far distant state.

9. For recent assessments of the AIM market, see Heather Timmons, 'A Market Frenzy Raises Worries,' *New York Times*, March 31, 2005 at 12; Edmond Warner, 'The Inside View, Take AIM at a Few Nomads as a Warning to the Others,' *The Guardian* (London), May 28, 2005, p 30; Joseph Morgenstern, 'Beware Manna From Heaven,' Globes [online], July 13, 2005; Paivi Munter, '10 Years of Aim: Nomads Deliver A Link With Reality,' *Financial Times*, June 10, 2005, p 25.

10. See Dominic Elliott, 'Five Investment Banks Take Nomad Registrations on AIM,' *eFinancialNews*, 20 March, 2005 (noting that three major U.S. underwriters registered as Nomads in 2004).

11. Rules 1 and 32 of the AIM Rules for Companies require a listed company to appoint and retain a nominated adviser at all times. The nominated adviser's obligations are spelled out in Rule 37, which requires the Nomad to advise the LSE that the securities are appropriate to be admitted and that it has been available at all times to advise and guide the company as to its compliance obligations. See 'Continuing Obligations of A Company Listed on AIM,' Mondaq Business Briefing, July 18, 2005. An AIM company must prepare a 'half yearly' report within three months of the end of such period. Also, the disclosure requirements of the initial admission application require the company to disclose in it 'all such information as investors would reasonably require, and reasonably expect to find there, for the purposes of making an informed assessment of the assets and liabilities, financial position, profits and losses, and prospects of the issuer of the securities and the rights attaching to those securities.' Ibid. To say the least, this is very general and non-specific, but a well-intentional Nomad could use this instruction to require full disclosure.

12. The Nomad would likely have liability in the U.K. for misrepresentations or omissions in any prospectus used in a stock offering, but absent the class action and the other distinctive features of the American litigation system, this threat is not that formidable. Outside the context of a stock offering, the Nomad would seem to have little liability for misrepresentations or omissions made by the issuer to the secondary market. This is where greater deterrence, either by public or private enforcement, is most needed.

13. See David B. Kahn & Gary S. Lawson, *Who's the Boss? Controlling Auditor Incentives Through Random Selection*, 53 Emory L. J. 391 (2004).

14. The proposal was originally advanced by NYU accounting professor Joshua Ronen. See Joshua Ronen, *Post-Enron Reform: Financial Statement Insurance and GAAP Revisited*, 8 Stan. J. L. Bus. & Fin. 39 (2002). It has been fleshed out in a series of articles by Professor Lawrence Cunningham. See Lawrence Cunningham, *Choosing Gatekeepers: The Financial Statement Insurance Alternative to Auditor Liability*, 52 UCLA L. Rev. 413 (2004).

15. Still another complication is that the insurance company might have a right of subrogation by which it could sue the corporation it insured. But in suing the corporation after the insurer paid claims to shareholders, the insurer would be indirectly suing the shareholders—a circular result.

16. Professor Joseph Grundfest has made precisely this observation in criticizing the financial statement insurance proposal. See Joseph A. Grundfest, *Punctuated Equilibria in the Evolution of United States Securities Regulation*, 8 Stan. J. L. Bus. & Fin. 1, 428 (2002).

17. This is essentially the Delaware law on the director's duty of care, as most recently set forth in *In re Walt Disney Company Derivative*

Litigation, 825 A.2d 275 (Del. Ch. 2003). Any intentional abdication of a director's duty to exercise business judgment and make good faith decisions about law compliance both subjects the director to liability and precludes indemnification or protection through exculpatory provisions in the corporate charter.

18. On April 28, 2003, the SEC, the New York Attorney General, the NASD, and the North American Securities Administrators Association announced that a Global Settlement had been finalized with ten investment banking firms, including Merrill Lynch, Goldman, Sachs & Co., and Morgan Stanley & Co., Inc. The ten firms agreed to pay a total of $875 million in penalties and an additional $432.5 million to fund independent research. See SEC Press Release No. 2003–54 (April 28, 2003).

19. See Josh Friedlander, 'Better to Shine a Light?' Investment Dealers' Digest, April 4, 2005.

20. See Susanne Craig, 'firm to Research Stock Orphans,' *Wall Street Journal*, June 7, 2005 at C-3.

21. See Stephen J. Choi and Jill E. Fisch, *How to Fix Wall Street: A Voucher Financing Proposal for Securities Intermediaries*, 113 Yale L. J. 269 (2003).

22. This is the standard problem with 'buy side' research. It is kept confidential and produces only a modest impact on market price, because the institutional investor wants to buy or sell at the existing price.

23. This was the experience at the Neuer Markt, a German exchange modeled after Nasdaq. After a series of scandals involving some of its listed companies, it was disbanded when the stronger and surviving issuers concluded that they were being stigmatized by their association with a scandal-ridden market. See John C. Coffee, Jr., *Racing to the Top?: The Impact of Cross-Listings and Stock Market Competition on International Corporate Governance*, 102 Colum. L. Rev. 1757, 1804–06 (2002).

24. In addition, economies of scale should also reduce the costs of providing research through this exchange format. Although it might be costly for an issuer to hire a single analyst to review it, the exchange would be seeking analysts to cover many of its companies, and might employ one analyst (or firm of analysts) to cover multiple companies. At this point, the exchange, as the principal, gains economic leverage over the analyst, as agent.

25. See John C. Coffee, Jr., *The Rise of Dispersed Ownership: The Roles of Law and the State in the Separation of Ownership and Control*, 111 Yale L. J. 1, 34–39.

26. See Susanne Craig, n 20 above, at C-3.

27. See David Wells, 'NRE Launches to Provide Equity Research,' *Financial Times*, May 23, 2005, at 22 (Asia edition); Josh Friedlander, 'A New Intermediary in Small-Cap Research, NRE Aims to Resolve—Mostly—the Ethical Taint in Issuer Paid Research,' *Investment Dealers' Digest*,

May 30, 2005. As a matter of full disclosure, this author is a director
of the National Research Exchange. The NRE was founded by David
Wield IV, the former chief operating officer of Nasdaq, and Hardwick
Simmons, Nasdaq's former CEO.

28. This is, as securities lawyers will recognize, the classic standard for 'due
diligence' set forth in *Escott v. BarChris Construction Corp.*, 283 F. Supp.
643 (S.D.N.Y. 1968). *BarChris*, the seminal case in this field, made clear
that the attorney could not simply rely on the client's statements and
representations but had to check the actual documents, at least to the
extent of checking 'matters easily verifiable.' Ibid. at 690.

29. The language of this certification to the effect that the attorney is not
aware of material misstatements or undisclosed material facts is included
in the standard opinion given by counsel for the issuer to the underwriters
in a registered public offering. For a description of this standard opinion in registered public offerings, see Richard Howe, *Rethinking Legal
Opinion Letters: The Duties and Liabilities of Attorneys in Rendering Legal
Opinions*, 1989 Colum. Bus. L. Rev. 283, 287 (1989). The author of this
article, a partner at the New York firm of Sullivan and Cromwell, properly observes that 'such opinions are not really "legal opinions" at all in
that they do not state any legal conclusion but only say that the attorney
believed certain facts to be true.' Ibid. Precisely for this reason, such an
opinion is more a pledge of the law firm's reputational capital, which the
underwriters demand. The counsel giving such opinion does not purport to conclude that all information required to be disclosed has been
disclosed (as an auditor might by analogy), but only that it lacks personal
knowledge or belief as to any such failure. See also Ronald J. Gilson, *Value
Creation by Business Lawyers: Legal Skills and Asset Pricing*, 94 Yale L.
J. 239, 291 (1984) (also describing such opinions); Richard W. Painter,
*Toward A Market for Lawyer Disclosure Services: In Search of Optimal
Whistleblowing Rules*, 63 Geo. Wash. L. Rev. 221, 226–227 and n 19 (1991)
(discussing judicial interpretation of such opinions). The American Bar
Association has characterized this type of opinion as a 'negative assur-
ance' and finds such opinions to be 'unique to securities offerings.' See
ABA Comm. on Legal Opinions, *Third-Party Opinion Report, Including the Legal Opinion Accord of the Section of Business Law, American Bar
Association*, 47 Bus. Law. 167, 228 (1991). Although the ABA considers it
generally inappropriate for attorneys to request such 'negative assurance'
opinions from other attorneys, the special context of securities offerings
is exempted, reflecting the fact that underwriters consider such an assurance to be necessary to them. That the ABA, as the representative of the
bar, 'disfavors' such opinions, because of the demands they place on the
attorney, probably only underscores the value of such a reform.

30. See Rule 102(e)(1)(iv) of the SEC's Rules of Practice, 17 CFR §201.
102(e)(1)(14) (authorizing the SEC to suspend or censure an accountant
for 'a single instance of highly unreasonable conduct ... [or] ... repeated

instances of unreasonable conduct.'). Presumably, conduct that can lead to penalties for an accountant can also justify similar penalties for the attorney if the SEC were to amend its rules to so provide.

31. See discussion at n 28 above.

32. See 17 C.F.R. §201.102(e)(iv) (specifying that two forms of 'negligent conduct'—either 'a single instance of highly unreasonable conduct' or 'repeated instances of unreasonable conduct'—could trigger sanctions under Rule 102(e)).

33. The attorney would, of course, be entitled to rely on the auditor with respect to financial information certified by the auditor, as in the case of the 'reliance on an expert' defense under Section 11(b)(3)(c) of the Securities Act of 1933. See 15 U.S.C. Section 77(k)(b)(3)(c).

34. Historically, the SEC did once hold attorneys liable for professional negligence in 'aiding and abetting' cases. See *SEC v. Spectrum Ltd.*, 489 F.2d 535, 536 (2d Cir. 1973). This is no longer possible after the Supreme Court mandated a scienter standard for Rule 10b-5 actions, but sanctions for professional misconduct could look to a similar standard.

35. See 15 U.S.C. §77k(b)(3).

36. *In re WorldCom, Inc. Sec. Litig.*, 346 F. Supp. 2d 628 (S.D.N.Y. 2004) (holding that underwriters had failed to establish either their reliance under Section 11(b)(3)(c) or that they had 'reasonable ground' to believe in the accuracy of WorldCom's disclosures).

37. See 15 U.S.C. §77(k)(b)(3)(A) (requiring that the director or underwriter have 'after reasonable investigation, reasonable ground to believe and did believe ... that the statements therein [in the registration statement] were true ....').

11

Conclusions: The Future of Gatekeeping

History's Lessons

Law and accounting are very different professions. But the history of each over the last century suggests that professions behave similarly. In common, they protect their autonomy; they resist broad duties to the public; and they invest very little in self-policing.

This pattern is clearest in the case of the accountants. Since the Progressive Era, regulatory attempts to impose uniform accounting standards, or simply to shrink the inventory of generally accepted accounting principles, have united the often divided accounting profession in indignant opposition. Even the suggestion made by the New York Stock Exchange in the early 1930s (in the hopes of forestalling more drastic federal intervention) that accountants should exercise some discretion in reviewing the 'preferability' of the client's choice of accounting principles was rejected out of hand by the profession.[1] Similarly, efforts by the profession's own standard setter—whether the APB or, later, the FASB—to restrict the use of much criticized accounting principles have drawn heated fire and resulted in repeated attempts to curtail the power and/or independence of the standard setter.

Viewed from a distance, this intransigence may seem puzzling. To the extent that reforms limit the client's discretion and preclude potentially misleading accounting conventions, accountants protect themselves by minimizing the prospect of both governmental intervention and future scandals. Strong rules also insulate the profession from accountant-shopping, as clients could not play one firm against another if the rules were clear. However logical these reasons may seem for why the profession should have united to tighten GAAP and prevent its misuse, they were overwhelmed by other forces that induced the profession to acquiesce to the client. Of these, the two most powerful were (i) the individual firm's fear of displeasing the audit client, and (ii) its even greater reluctance to exercise any judgmental discretion that might result in liability. These two related fears need to be distinguished. Understandably, firms do not enjoy saying 'No' to the client—that is, that its proposed accounting treatment is unavailable. Even more, they do not want the client to learn that they supported the profession's decision to close down a particular accounting technique that the client wanted. As a result, the profession almost always chose the side of the client over that of the regulators in any debate on accounting reform—but it thereby lost the opportunity to develop a united front that could resist the aggressive client. A curious cartel, the profession could unite to fight the government, but not to resist the client.

The second and even greater fear was of the consequences of defining the accountant's role so broadly that the accountant possessed discretion over the presentation of the client's financial results. With discretion came a potential duty to constrain the client, and this in turn could lead to liability for the accountant whenever the client's choice of accounting principles proved inappropriate. From the perspective of liability avoidance, it was safer to define the accountant's role narrowly so that the accountant did no more than certify the year-to-year consistency of the accounting principles applied (without ever evaluating their appropriateness). The end result was a self-definition that saw the profession as largely lacking in discretion—in effect a passive agent required to defer to the client's choice of accounting principles, as long as that choice had some colorable basis in GAAP. These same pressures lead U.S. accounting to prefer rules over principles, because the latter are always fuzzy and invite litigation.

If the accounting profession was circumspect in defining its role, it was much more aggressive in defending its autonomy. In its legislative and lobbying battles, the accounting profession proved itself one of the most formidable interest groups on the U.S. national scene. It lobbied the most aggressively for the Private Securities Litigation Reform Act of 1995 (PSLRA) and benefited the most from its adoption.[2] When SEC Chairman Arthur Levitt sought to restrict accountants from providing consulting services to audit clients in 1998–2000, the profession went to Congress and effectively held the SEC's budget hostage, thereby stalemating Levitt. Later, in reaction to Levitt's efforts, the profession lobbied for and secured the appointment of two of its full-time employees as Commissioners to the five-member SEC.[3] Add to this picture the appointment of Harvey Pitt, who had been the accountants' chief lawyer in its confrontation with Levitt, as the new SEC

Chairman under President Bush, and the profession had succeeded in winning the appointment of its agents and employees to a majority of the Commission's seats. No other lobby or interest group has exercised equivalent power (albeit briefly) over its principal regulator.

Nonetheless, these lobbying efforts failed when push eventually came to shove. Possibly because it was the most successful lobbyist in Washington, the accounting profession did not recognize that the scandals of 2001–2002 had produced the proverbial 500-year storm, which no interest group could survive on its own. With the passage of the Sarbanes-Oxley Act, the accounting profession lost much of its autonomy and now faces a powerful and energetic regulator in the Public Company Accounting Oversight Board (PCAOB). But here history also reminds us that the accounting profession lost earlier battles and still seemingly won its war with the regulators. For example, when Congress passed the federal securities laws, it expressly gave the SEC control over both accounting and auditing, but within five years thereafter the SEC had essentially ceded this jurisdiction back to the profession.[4] Conceivably, history could repeat itself. Thus, a major question for the future is whether PCAOB will remain an aggressive regulator of the profession, or, as has happened before, will eventually be 'captured' by those it is regulating. For the short-term, this is unlikely. But, because the PCAOB's commissioners are appointed by the SEC, a more deregulatory SEC (as we now have) may over time imply a more relaxed PCAOB scrutiny of the industry. Also, some in the industry have brought suit, challenging the constitutionality of PCAOB,[5] and this represents another unpredictable wild card for the future.

Much like the accountants, the bar also fought off the attempts of the SEC and banking regulators to impose gatekeeping obligations on it—with relative success for most of the 20th century until the Sarbanes-Oxley Act. Even when the SEC won significant victories (as it did in *National Student Marketing Corp.* and the *Carter & Johnson* cases), it later quietly relented and accepted the primacy of state regulation of attorneys.[6] In contrast, the banking regulators did exact heavier penalties and imposed stronger duties on the legal profession, but their more punitive response followed a greater national crisis (the Savings and Loan industry's implosion in the late 1980s). One implication here may be that only major scandals that visit heavy losses on society can produce a coalition strong enough to modify the behavior of the professions. Thus, FIRREA, the post-S&L crisis legislation,[7] and Sarbanes-Oxley stand as twin monuments to scandals in which passivity by the professions finally provoked Congress to action.

The bar's preferred defense strategy against federal regulation has been to define narrowly those gatekeeping obligations whose imposition it was unable to resist. A good example was the bar's response to Sarbanes-Oxley. A consortium of 25 law firms, including many of the most prestigious firms in the United States, publicly circulated a lengthy memorandum that placed very narrow readings on Sarbanes-Oxley's most expansive provisions.[8] In effect, the bar created its own legislative history. Similarly, the ABA's rule on 'up-the-ladder' reporting, which was adopted contemporaneously with Sarbanes-Oxley's passage, was also considerably weaker and more equivocal than the SEC's corresponding rule.[9] Although the bar ultimately accepted the ethical principle that an attorney may voluntarily warn regulators or a victim of a crime or fraud by the attorney's client where the misbehavior utilized the attorney's services, it still fiercely resists any obligation under which the attorney must so warn, disclose or even make a 'noisy withdrawal.'[10] Even today, the bar remains split over whether attorneys can assume any gatekeeping responsibilities,[11] with the litigators adamantly defending the position that such responsibilities are inconsistent with their hardcore view of the lawyer-as-adversary. Although many individual attorneys do favor reforms, the bar itself—just like the classic cartel—is implacable in its opposition to anything more than the most incremental and modest of changes.

In overview, the SEC's experience with both attorneys and accountants suggests that it is difficult for a regulatory agency to supervise a profession for long. From time to time, the SEC has asserted authority over both professions, but later, it has gradually relaxed its grip. Although the federal banking regulators were tougher than the SEC in their treatment of lawyers, their period of effective oversight was shorter, ending with the close of the Savings and Loans crisis. As scandals subside, a return to 'normalcy' becomes predictable, and professional autonomy is re-established. For these reasons, the PCAOB format seems more promising because it uses professionals to supervise professionals.

Gatekeepers and Conflicts

In principle, the professions should be uniquely sensitive to the dangers surrounding conflicts of interest. Still, the 1990s revealed little, if any, evidence of self-restraint. The accounting profession raced in the 1990s to market consulting services to their audit clients, believing that a metamorphosis of their profession was in progress that would transform them from Dickensian bookkeepers into information services professionals. Although an academic debate continues over whether the provision of consulting services compromised auditing, the rapid expansion into consulting clearly changed the culture of the major accounting firms. Aggressive marketing skills were rewarded, while professional expertise at accounting was downgraded to the status of a lesser virtue. In particular, the marketing of tax shelters placed the professional in the role of a shady salesman, hawking dubious products of questionable legality to its clients. Few activities seemed more inconsistent with the norm of objective detachment that is usually associated with professionalism.

Law firms characteristically changed more slowly than accounting firms, but they largely followed the latter's trajectory throughout the 1990s. Within the ABA, the possibility of 'multi-practice firms' that would practice law along with other disciplines (accounting, consulting, investment management, etc.) was debated throughout the 1990s, and the tide was gradually turning in favor of the multi-practice firm until Enron self-destructed. Probably only this fortuity saved the legal profession from its own worst instincts. The implication here is ominous: professional culture is a weak reed on which to rely when the economic winds are blowing in the opposite direction.

Have the Professions Changed?

Did the corporate scandals of 2001–2002 and Sarbanes-Oxley change how the professions view their roles? Or, are memories already growing hazy? Here, the short-term and long-term answers may diverge. At least for the present, the fear of liability is palpably present within the professions. The major accounting firms have systematically shed their smaller and riskier clients, preferring to focus on major clients with large auditing needs and a lower risk of litigation. Similarly, fear of liability has led most law firms to re-organize themselves as limited liability partnerships or limited liability companies in order to protect the assets of their individual partners. But to the extent that the partners' personal assets have become insulated, the prospect of real behavioral change may diminish.

In the case of securities analysts, liability is less the concern than the survival of the sell-side analyst. Solving the conflicts problem created another problem of nearly equal magnitude, as the sell-side of the profession has shrunk in response to recent reforms, with coverage of the smaller cap market significantly drying up as a result. Because the former principal source of funding for the sell-side—that is, underwriters—is now walled off from almost any contact with analysts, a new business model for securities research seems necessary if the sell-side analyst is to remain a monitoring influence for most public companies.[12]

Beyond these organizational and defensive changes, have the professions' self-images been altered? This question is particularly important in the case of the accountants. Probably, the most important reform imposed by Sarbanes-Oxley was to make the auditors report to the audit committee. Wisely, this reform substituted a risk-averse principal in place of often risk-preferring corporate financial executives. Because the audit committee is composed of independent directors who face the prospect of liability but will typically not profit that much from their corporation's success, the audit committee should resist risk, including accounting policies that might attract public or private litigation. So long as the audit committee remains the true principal for the auditor, the lessons of history here are optimistic: the accountants will respond to what their client wants.

But this does not mean that the accounting profession has moved closer to recognizing an obligation to detect fraud. The profession has long resisted placing any such obligation at center stage, stressing instead the 'expectations gap' between what investors expect and what it can realistically do. Indeed, the profession can today suggest that Sarbanes-Oxley assigns it only the lesser obligation of monitoring the company's internal controls. Section 404 of Sarbanes-Oxley requires the auditor to evaluate and report publicly on the adequacy of the corporation's internal controls. This controversial provision has proven to be an unexpected blessing and major source of new revenue for auditors, but, once again, it provides a new rationale for defining the profession's duties narrowly. Conceptually, the auditor can now argue that its responsibility is primarily to appraise the adequacy of internal controls. If an ongoing fraud is not detected, the auditor can explain that the failure to detect the fraud was attributable either to the client's weak internal controls or to the conduct of a corrupt manager in overriding those controls. Once again, the profession will predictably seek to define its role guardedly: that is, to evaluate the adequacy of the client's controls—not to detect fraud. Only if PCAOB pushes the profession towards assuming a greater responsibility for fraud detection (which it has not yet done), is there much chance that the profession will assume such a responsibility for fraud detection.

Law firms have altered their self-image the least. The prospect of future liability does concern them and may lead them to take a more conciliatory approach in negotiations with regulators. But they remain in their own minds the zealous champions of their clients, not gatekeepers. Even when attorneys inadvertently begin to play a significant gatekeeping role, the profession at its highest levels becomes hesitant.[13]

Costs and Benefits

Overall, by the end of the 1990s, the professions were caught between the proverbial rock and the hard place. Stock option-compensated managers insisted on higher earnings and the use of any accounting device not expressly forbidden. Legal risks that formerly constrained the professions had faded. Even their clients, the stockholders, had suspended their native skepticism and were riding a wave of euphoria fueled by the longest stock market bubble in U.S. history. As a result, fraud erupted on a massive scale.

Has this imbalance between the benefits and costs of acquiescence been corrected? Stock options remain a destabilizing influence on management, but the FASB has at least thrown sand into the gears by requiring their expensing. Predictably, this will occasion some tense confrontations between auditors and managers in the future, as corporate managers are finding novel ways to minimize this expense on their financial statements. But at least the auditor may have an ally in the audit committee. Private litigation remedies have not been enhanced, but the post-Enron skepticism of the professions has left them nervous and willing to settle for record amounts. Even the enthusiasm of corporate managers for creative earnings management may have been chilled by a succession of criminal prosecutions (often ending in Draconian sentences). For the present, the costs to the professional of acquiescing in the client's demands have begun to catch up with the benefits. But for the future, the gap could either widen or narrow.

Reputational Capital

What happened to reputational capital in the 1990s? In principle, this should have been the force that constrained professionals, even when the threat of public and private enforcement weakened. But, it was the force that conspicuously failed. To explain this failure, this book has advanced two principal hypotheses: first, as the gatekeeper came to view the corporate manager as its principal (and not the shareholder), the nature of the reputational capital that the professional wished to possess and market changed. It became more important to be viewed as flexible, problem-solving, and cooperative than as rigorous or principled. The measure of professional skill was not knowledge of the rules, but the ability to manipulate them for management's benefit. Above all, the audience changed; it became less important how investors perceived the gatekeeper than how managers did. To this extent, Chapter 10 has already examined the most logical remedy: to re-align principal–agent relationships so that investors (or their proxy) become the principal who hires and fires the gatekeeper. Professionals are zealous in defense of their clients' interests, but their perceived clients are the persons who retain them, not abstract organizational entities.

Second, this book has argued that the desire to preserve and protect reputation is weaker in concentrated markets. In such markets, one only need not fall significantly behind one's few peers, and a pattern of conscious parallelism can easily develop. If so, it must be recognized that some professions (most notably, the accountants) more closely resemble oligopolies today than they did in the 1990s. Although there are faint hints that these markets could become more competitive, the prospect of continued oligopoly hangs darkly over the future. If so, what policy options remain? To the extent that oligopoly must be recognized as a continuing condition, the future of gatekeeping may hinge on a radical remedy: the break-up of the major accounting firms. If tomorrow, for example, there were ten major accounting firms (instead of only four), the loss of reputational capital would become a significant deterrent, even if litigation remedies were weak. In the increasingly deregulatory climate of the United States, such a radical reform is unlikely (at least absent further scandals or the collapse of a Big Four firm).[14] But in Europe, antitrust enforcement has become relatively more aggressive, and restructuring of the profession is at least thinkable.

Divestiture is, of course, the remedy of last resort. Today, it remains premature to pronounce such a drastic reform to be the only solution. Ultimately, however, competition is the force that makes professionals value their reputations, and competition remains conspicuously absent from some of the principal markets for gatekeeping services. If it is still too soon to call for an immediate breakup, it is well past time to place the issue of divestiture on the policy agenda.

Sticks Versus Carrots

This book would be incomplete if its conclusions stressed only the need for greater deterrence—for two reasons. First, relying on litigation to hold gatekeepers accountable has hidden costs. Already, it has been noted that accountants have defined their role narrowly and mechanically. In large part, this is because of the fear of litigation. To the extent that U.S. GAAP is viewed as more a collection of rules than of principles, this too is a product of the fear of litigation, because rules give the accountant a safe harbor, whereas discretion invites lawsuits. The greater the threat of litigation, the more the pressure for a system of narrow, technical rules that provide certainty and protection. Hence, Europe has less litigation and a more principle-based system of accounting than the U.S.

Although the deterrent threat of litigation is essential to holding gate-keepers accountable, it is not sufficient by itself. The sad irony is that the more we strengthen litigation remedies to make professionals more accountable, the more we will see them respond by seeking narrow, hyper-technical rules that protect them from exercising judgment. Such adap-tive responses are predictable, but not inevitable. A critical responsibility falls on the independent regulatory bodies—most notably, the FASB and PCAOB—to resist these pressures. This much of the future is clear: if left to their own devices and subjected to a significant threat of private litigation, professionals will respond by defining GAAP and auditing standards in their own interest, rather than that of investors.

Second, some gatekeepers—most notably the securities analyst—face inadequate incentives to perform their socially optimal role. Deterrence alone cannot solve this problem; rather, funding must be found to subsi-dize analysts to keep the small to mid-cap market transparent, and such funding must be provided in a way that does not corrupt the objectivity of the research. Carrots, as well as sticks, then must be used.

Today, reform (and, in particular, the Global Settlement) has made the analyst more independent, but it has also left the market less trans-parent. Over the long-run, that would be a Pyrrhic victory. Because securities research has the character of a 'public good' and subsequent users can free ride on the efforts of the original producer of research, a subsidy must be consciously structured into the system—or research will be underprovided. Various ways to provide this subsidy are pos-sible, including requiring exchanges to hire analysts to cover under-researched companies. But the simplest approach may be to encourage the market to develop a new form of gatekeeper: an intermediary who receives payment from the issuer but then selects the analyst for the issuer based on objective criteria. Such an intermediary would have to develop reputational capital before its selections would be credible, but the first auditors also had to surmount this challenge.

The Role of Regulation

At the outset of this book, it was asserted that the principal role of the gatekeeper serving investors was to reduce informational asymmetries, thereby increasing market transparency and lessening the cost of capital. The capacity of markets to raise money from strangers—alone, a remarkable achievement—depends upon their ability to convince investors that they are receiving objective and accurate information. The less reliable such information appears, the higher the cost of capital becomes. In a nutshell, this is the critical role that gatekeepers play in the capital markets (albeit imperfectly), and it is a far more coherent role than the hopelessly broad Brandeisian injunctive to serve the public interest. Indeed, to the extent that gatekeepers can fulfill this function of enhancing market transparency, then by definition they are serving the public interest. But, viewed in these terms, a bottom line assessment of gatekeeper performance must be skeptical. The professions have simply not defined their roles in terms of protecting market transparency or providing accurate, unbiased information. Although few professionals are active opponents of transparency, the only norm that they have truly internalized is that of client service—and the 'client' remains the person or group that hired them, not the organization in the abstract. Even if most professionals are highly law compliant, their unswerving practice has been to define their duties narrowly.

The result is a 'Catch 22' dilemma: absent a litigation threat, professionals acquiesce in dubious and risky practices that their 'client' wants; but once subjected to an adequate litigation threat, professionals insist upon narrow duties, hopelessly specific safe harbors, and a rule-based system that often seems devoid of meaningful principles. In the former environment, they are unaccountable; in the latter, they become useless.

This dilemma in turn defines the role of regulation for the future. Two almost contradictory reforms must be pursued together and in unison. Put simply, gatekeepers need to be subjected to a real threat of litigation that generates adequate deterrence, while also governed by professional standards that require them to exercise discretion and satisfy a 'reasonableness' standard. Specifically, for example, the accountant should be compelled to make professional judgments as to the reasonableness of the client's choice of accounting principles and to accept greater responsibility for fraud detection. The requirement that financial statements 'fairly present' the issuer's financial position has long been present in the law, but the accounting profession has sought to diminish its significance, emphasizing instead that they are certifying only that the issuer has followed 'generally accepted accounting principles.' True regulatory reform must re-introduce an obligation on the gatekeeper's part to monitor the reasonableness of the client's statements, both its financial presentation and its narrative disclosures.

Similarly, the securities attorney should bear a fuller responsibility for the adequacy of the corporation's disclosures. While the attorney cannot, and need not, duplicate the auditor's role, the attorney is better able than the auditor to appraise qualitatively the character of the issuer's disclosures. Do the issuer's 'Management Discussion and Analysis' disclosures, which are contained in each quarterly report to the SEC, truly explain the risks of the business in a cogent fashion? Here, attorneys have the comparative advantage and could do the necessary due diligence through extended interviews with the issuer's management.

So viewed, the challenge for the regulator is not to take discretion out of the system, but to preserve and expand it. But discretion must be accorded to the gatekeeper, not the client (whereas present-day GAAP does the reverse). The gatekeeper must be asked to pass on the reasonableness of the corporate client's behavior and disclosures. Predictably, the more the gatekeeper is threatened by litigation, the more it will resist discretion. To illustrate, because GAAP gives great latitude to the financial manager over the choice of accounting principles, it is essential that the gatekeeper assess not simply whether the inventory of generally accepted accounting principles contains a rule authorizing a given treatment, but whether the company's financial managers have exercised that discretion reasonably.

Easy as this is to say, candor requires the recognition that the professions will need to be dragged, some kicking and screaming, to any new world in which they both enjoy discretion, and face penalties (private or public) that are adequate to deter. Is there any hope that this can happen? At least under some circumstances, one can envision the professions internalizing norms that gave them increased discretion and enhanced their leverage with respect to the client. Such norms would entitle the gatekeepers to demand fuller disclosure, to report misconduct up the ladder, and to search for information the corporation wanted not to disclose. These are the norms that investors, themselves, would impose if they could solve their collective action problems. These are also norms that would make the professions attractive to the young and more satisfying to many members. But they are not norms that are self-enforcing.

What forces could drive the professions in this direction? Litigation can generate the necessary deterrence, but it provides little guidance. The better scenario for reform depends on pressure from three distinct sources: (i) regulators, (ii) investors, and (iii) the young that the profession hopes to recruit. Regulators can define *ex ante* the standard of performance desired, whereas courts and litigation function only *ex post*. Investor pressure can be even more effective, but as a practical matter it can only be brought to bear with the appearance of real competition within the professions. With

competition, the views of investors would matter much more to gatekeepers than they do today. Finally, to the extent that a profession encounters
difficulties in attracting the recruits it wants (as may be the case today in
accounting), then accepting greater responsibility and greater discretion
enhances the profession's image in the eyes of the public (and potential
recruits). For example, although imposing greater discretion on accountants might invite greater liability, it would also transform their image
from that of unappealing 'bean-counters' to that of powerful umpires
exercising real discretion.

Vague and generalized as this prescription may sound, it can be given
some content with specific illustrations of needed policies:

1 To assure an adequate deterrent threat, 'aiding and abetting' liability for the professions should be restored.[15] Although the threat of a
potential catastrophic loss that could render a Big Four firm insolvent is worrisome, the current evidence is that auditors and other
secondary participants are seldom sued in securities class actions.[16]
Thus, the danger of a bankrupting liability justifies at most a 'cap'
on liability, not the conferring of *de facto* immunity upon a gatekeeper who has knowingly or recklessly participated in a fraud.

2 Both the NASD and the NYSE should be instructed by the SEC to
study the problem of diminished market transparency in small and
mid-cap companies and report their preferred solutions. The principle that must be recognized is that companies that trade in public
markets need the professional oversight of securities analysts. How
that oversight is to be subsidized can reasonably be debated, and
private market alternatives may be preferable. But, at least as a last
resort, the market can be ordered to tax itself to pay this cost.

3 The role of disclosure counsel must be formalized with gatekeeping obligations being made explicit. The first step to this
end would be to require the audit committee to retain such a
counsel to investigate and test the corporation's disclosures on an
on-going basis and report to it.

4 The securities analyst needs its own self-regulator, paralleling the role
of the PCAOB, to audit its members' research reports and investigate
their independence. Funding would come from the industry, as in
the case of the PCAOB. Beyond this role, such an agency also needs
to protect the analyst from reprisals and retaliation. Sarbanes-Oxley
addressed only reprisals from within the brokerage firm, but today
the more chilling threats come from the issuer and the buy-side.

These are illustrations, not by any means an integrated policy. But
their common denominator is the recognition that gatekeepers need

continuing scrutiny. Absent such scrutiny, the worst tendencies of cartels resurface, and the professions act in their own interest, not the public's. Ultimately, professional autonomy cannot go unchecked. The government of the professions by the professions tends to produce mainly government for the professions.

Endnotes

1. See text of Ch. 5 at nn 84 to 90.
2. See text of Ch. 5 at nn 235 to 237.
3. Prior to their appointments to the SEC, Commissioner Paul S. Atkins worked as a lawyer at PricewaterhouseCoopers, and Commissioner Cynthia A. Glassman, an economist, was employed by Ernst & Young for five years, working on its regulatory practice. See 'Glassman Fills in as SEC Chairman,' The Accountant, July 31, 2000 at p 9.
4. See text of Ch. 5 at nn 99 to 109.
5. See Stephanie Kirchgaessner and Andrew Parker, 'Sarbanes-Oxley Faces Lawsuit,' Financial Times, February 9, 2006 at p 25.
6. See text of Ch. 6 at n 53 (discussing 1988 opinion of SEC General Counsel that Commission would not use then Rule 2(e) against attorneys unless a state law or ethical rule was also violated).
7. FIRREA is the acronym for the Financial Institutions Reform, Recovery and Enforcement Act of 1989 (codified in part at 12 U.S.C.A. §1464). For an example of its punitive impact on law firms, see *FDIC v. O'Melveny*, 61 F.3d 17 (9th Cir. 1995).
8. Shortly after the passage of the Sarbanes-Oxley Act in 2002, some twenty-four major U.S. law firms (and one Canadian law firm) jointly distributed an interpretive memorandum that read the Act's most restrictive provisions extremely narrowly. For example, Section 402 of Sarbanes-Oxley Act forbids the making of personal loans to executives, or the renewal or 'material modifications' of pre-existing such loans. Nonetheless, this memorandum concluded that a public corporation could forgive or discharge an outstanding loan to a high-level executive because a 'forgiveness constitutes a discharge of the loan obligation or part of it and not a modification.' See 'Interpretive Issues Under the Sarbanes-Oxley Act,' October 15, 2002, at 12. Not only is this a very aggressive interpretation of the deliberately broad legislative language, but the fact that twenty-five major firms signed and distributed it jointly (an unprecedented development among law firms) suggests that it was more an attempt to lobby the courts and the SEC than to advise clients.
9. ABA Model Rule of Professional Conduct 1.13 is triggered only by an attorney's possession of actual knowledge of a material violation of law, and the rule carefully defines the verb 'knows' to mean 'actual knowledge of the facts in question.' See text of Ch. 6 at nn 97 to 100. This is

in sharp contrast to the SEC's standard, which focuses on the receipt of credible evidence that would alert the reasonably competent attorney. Professor Susan Koniak has suggested that on this basis the 'lawyers never know.' See Susan P. Koniak, *When the Hurlyburly's Done: The Bar's Struggle With the SEC,* 103 Colum. L. Rev. 1236, 1271 (2003).

10. In 2000, the litigators even forced the ABA to reject its own draft Model Rules largely because it permitted an attorney to give such a warning. In 1997, the ABA created the Ethics 2000 Commission to update the ABA Model Rules of Professional Conduct. It recommended a revision to ABA Model Rule 1.6 that would have permitted (but not mandated) disclosure of client information to the extent that the lawyer reasonably believed necessary to rectify a crime or fraud that had used the lawyer's services. In 2000, the ABA House of Delegates rejected this change under pressure from its litigators. In 2003, in the different post-Enron environment, it was adopted. See E. Norman Veasey, *Corporate Governance and Ethics In a Post Enron/WorldCom Environment,* 72 U. Cinn. L. Rev. 731 (2003).

11. Even post-Enron, the ABA's Task Force on Corporate Responsibility acknowledged in a nuanced statement that 'lawyers for the corporation ... are not "gatekeepers" of corporate responsibility in the same fashion as public accounting firms.' See Report of the American Bar Association Task Force on Corporate Responsibility. 59 Bus. Law. 145 (2003). In truth, no one has ever suggested that attorneys were the 'same' or even similar to auditors.

12. Some may respond that the decline in the number of sellside analysts is insignificant because they largely migrated to the 'buy-side.' But this ignores that 'buy-side' research remains confidential and hence does not come to the attention of the subject corporation's directors. In this sense, only the 'sell-side' analyst is a 'gatekeeper' who can influence the board of directors.

13. In recent years, public enforcers, both civil and criminal, have conditioned settlements with public corporations on a requirement that they conduct detailed internal studies, staffed by outside law firms, that investigate the corporate wrongdoing and assign responsibility to officers and employees. These reports have often been valuable (as in the case of Enron), but the government also insists that the corporation waive the attorney/client privilege so that the enforcer could then use this information to prosecute responsible corporate employees. Important as this new gatekeeping role has been, the bar has predictably sought to halt its expansion. At its 2005 meeting, the ABA adopted a resolution calling upon governmental agencies to cease demanding such privilege waivers as a condition of deferred prosecution. See ABA Task Force on Attorney–Client Privilege, *Report of the American Bar Association's Task Force on the Attorney–Client Privilege,* Business Lawyer 1029 (May 2005). Why has the bar resisted? Because it arguably chilled the ability of corporate officers to consult with and confide in the corporation's

counsel if there was any risk that the corporation might later waive its own privilege. But if prosecutors do not benefit from deferred prosecution agreements, they will likely begin again to indict public corporations, and investors will suffer. Once again, the litigators seem to be pushing the profession to stonewall the regulators to the disadvantage of investors.

14. The federal antitrust laws do not authorize divestiture as an antitrust remedy simply because competition is lacking in a relevant market. Rather, an antitrust violation must first be shown. No evidence currently exists to this author's knowledge that any of the Big Four have attempted to monopolize their market. On the other hand, Congress could legislate a break-up of the Big Four into smaller, more competitive firms (possibly paying just compensation for any cognizable losses), on grounds unrelated to antitrust violations. Such planning, it is suggested, should at least begin.

15. At present, there is enormous uncertainty in the federal courts as to when a professional who assists in the preparation of a disclosure document or press release that materially misleads the market can be held liable. Compare *Central Bank of Denver, N.A. v. First Interstate Bank of Denver*, 511 U.S. 164 (1994), and *In re Enron Corp. Securities, Derivative & ERISA Litig.*, 235 F. Supp. 2d 549 (S.D. Tex. 2002). A minimum requirement for gatekeepers is that they be subject to fraud-based liability in such a context, and this does require the restoration in some form of 'aiding and abetting' liability.

16. Cornerstone Research has found that in 2004 and 2005, auditors were named as defendants in only eight and five security class actions, respectively. Because 213 securities class actions were filed in 2004 and 176 in 2005, these numbers amount to four percent and three percent, respectively. See Cornerstone Research, '2005: A Year in Review', at 16 (2006). Conceivably, these numbers could understate to the extent that securities class actions are later amended to add auditors as defendants at a later stage, but they suggest that the PSLRA continues to immunize the auditor from any significant threat of litigation.

Index

accountancy profession, growth
    of 108–38, 146–7, 172 n26, 365
accountants 4, 11 n9, 21, 103, 108
    British 109–12
    in United States 114, 172 n26
    CPAs (Certified Public
        Accountants) 149, 150
    and change 366
    and competition 327
    relationship with clients 162–3,
        166–7, 170, 177 nn88, 89,
        363
    and Crash 123–30
    independence of 116, 119
    loss of intellectual rationale
        160–61
    and litigation 152–6, 170
    and professional discipline 156–8,
        188 n246
    and professional societies 114
    and standards 362
    see also auditors; FASB;
        PCAOB;
        'revenue recognition timing'
accounting principles boards *see*
    APB; GAAP
Accounting Research Bulletins 131
actions 60–61
Adecco 87, 97 n35
Adelphia Communications
    scandal 81, 95 n14
agents 1, 2
    monitoring 325–6
Alternative Investment Market *see*
    AIM
American Association of Public
    Accountants *see* AAPA
American Bar Association *see* ABA
American Corporate Counsel
    Association *see* ACCA
American Institute of Accountants
    see AIA
American Institute of Certified
    Public Accountants
    see AICPA

American Society of Certified Public
    Accountants
    see ASCPA
analysts *see* securities analysts
annual reports, corporations 119
antitrust regulation 195–6
    Sherman Anti-Trust Act
        (1890) 174 n54, 199
Arthur Andersen
    and audit partners 163
    and claims 153
    and Enron 4, 5–6, 11 nn11,
        12, 26–30, 47, 158,
        325–6
    *United States v. Arthur
        Andersen* 49 n42
    and Waste Management
        Company 189 n267
    and WorldCom 41–2, 46, 47,
        52nn85, 94, 53 nn98, 104,
        106
    see also Spacek, Leonard
Arthur Young (later Ernst &
    Young) 27
    *United States v. Arthur Young &
        Co.* 4
Association for Investment
    Management and Research
    see AIMR
Atkins, Paul S. 374
attorneys 2, 3, 16, 192
    and certification 231
    and class action litigation 337
    relationship with clients 194–5,
        220, 226
    and competition 318–19, 327
    and conflicts of interest 322
    and discipline 210–12
    and 'due diligence' 192, 203–4,
        205, 206, 231, 236 nn32, 33,
        349, 350, 351
    and Enron 32–4
    as gatekeepers 193, 197, 201–2,
        229, 318–19, 349–50, 351
    monitoring of 352

Brandeisian model 228–9
bribery 65, 144
British Companies Act
    amendments 92, 203, 232
brokerage commission, securities
    analysts 250–51, 255–7
bubbles 77 nn61, 64, 79, 110, 263
Bureau of Corporations 119

CFA Institute *see* AIMR
CFAs (Chartered Financial
    Analysts) 245, 248
CPA *see* AICPA
CPAs (Certified Public
    Accountants) 149, 150, 186
    n214, 188 n245
Carter, Col. A. H. 127
Carter & Johnson, and NTC
    fraud 210–11
cases
    Carter & Johnson 211, 216
    *Central Bank of Denver, N.A.
        v. First Interstate Bank of
        Denver* 60, 188 n238, 215,
        216, 239 n75, 375 n12
    Checkosky v. SEC 238 n55
    Cohen v. Lord, Day & Lord 243
        n121
    *Compuware Corp. v. Moody's
        Investors Servs.* 313 n71
    Demarco v. Lehman Bros. 273 n3
    DiLeo v. Ernst and Young 11 n9
    Dirks v. SEC 258–60, 261
    *Escott v. BarChris Construction
        Co.* 203–4, 360 n28
    *Feit v. Leasco Data Processing
        Equip. Corp.* 235 n28
    Glennie v. Abitibi-Price Corp. 311
        n52
    *Jefferson County Sch. Dist. v.
        Moody's Investor Services,
        Inc.* 313 n71
    *Lampf, Pleva, Lipkind, Prupis &
        Petigrow v. Gilbertson* 60, 72
        n24

    *Lentell v. Merrill Lynch & Co.
        Inc.* 273 n3
    Melder v. Morris 11 n9
    SEC v. Arthur Andersen 73 n38,
        188 n240
    *SEC v. National Student
        Marketing Corp.* 182 n161,
        236 nn35, 36
    SEC v. Spectrum Ltd. 236 n35,
        361 n34
    *Sanders v. John Nuveen & Co.,
        Inc.* 235 n28
    Ultramares Corp. v. Touche 153,
        177 n88, 187 n226
    *United States v. Arthur
        Andersen* 49 n42
    *United States v. Arthur Young &
        Co.* 4
    United States v. Weiner 182 n162
Causey, Richard 29, 33
Cendant 155, 188 n239
Chanos, Jim 35–6, 51 n75
Chartered Financial Analysts *see*
    CFAs
chief executives, and
    compensation 62–3, 75
    n51, 164
    United States and Europe
        compared 84–5
clients, relationship with
    professionals
    accountants 162–3, 166–7, 170
    attorneys 220, 226
    lawyers 194–5, 224, 226,
        227, 230
    see also principal-agent
        relationships
Cohen Commission 140, 182
    nn165
colorable defense 219, 240 n86
commercial paper, investments 290
commission *see* brokerage
    commission, securities
    analysts; fees
Commissions